THE MARCH OF PHILOSOPHY

THE MARCH
OF
PHILOSOPHY

By

HENRY ALPERN

KENNIKAT PRESS, INC./PORT WASHINGTON, N. Y.

B
72
.A4
1968

TO

MY WIFE

THE SOURCE OF INSPIRATION FOR THIS BOOK

Preface

In this volume, I have attempted to show the progress and unity of philosophic thought, from the Ancient Greek period to the present day, as well as the need of a philosophy for our everyday life. To accomplish this purpose, I have, in the first place, tried to give a clear, concise exposition of the doctrines of the leading figures in the history of thought, supplementing it with a discussion of the five important philosophies: Materialism, Idealism, Pragmatism, Intuitionism, and Neo-Realism. Then again, by comment and criticism after each philosophy, I have attempted to show how each succeeding theory was a natural outgrowth of that which preceded it. This also demonstrates how all doctrines are interrelated, and by what logical process the five theories treated in Book III originated. Throughout this treatise, I have presented as far as possible an impersonal view of the cardinal tenets of the history of philosophy, leaving it to the reader to judge for himself whether the conclusions reached are appealing or otherwise. Finally, I have suggested what application each of us may make of any of the principles incorporated in each philosophy to our own conduct. I consider this as one of the chief reasons for a treatise of philosophy, because we so often hear the comment that philosophy is a toy for the amusement of the intellectual, without possessing anything vital to our practical life. Such an attitude does not accord to philosophy the consideration it deserves, and is, besides, most inaccurate. From this angle, I have attempted to treat of philosophic subjects in a manner which may be comprehended not only by the student but also by the layman who may be interested to pursue an inquiry into the subject.

CONTENTS

BOOK II

MODERN PHILOSOPHY

CONTENTS

CONTENTS

BOOK III

FIVE DOCTRINES OF PHILOSOPHY

INTRODUCTION

THE term Philosophy evokes in our minds a picture of something detached from life and purely of academic interest. The moment the study of philosophy is recommended to the average man and even to the student, he at once gets the disagreeable sensation of being obliged to lift himself up from his material environment, to shed his earthly raiment, and gird up his loins, so to speak, to wage battle with a branch of human endeavor which may appear to be useless and senseless to him, but which he nevertheless deems necessary for the acquisition of culture. Not only is this the wrong view of philosophy, but this attitude is also inhibitory. It prevents one from cultivating the proper approach. It is first of all necessary to humanize philosophy, to make it attractive as a study and to show that it is an essential ingredient in everyone's life.

Once one develops a flair for philosophic research, there is no other subject so engrossing and so inspiring. Besides, every one has a philosophy of life, whether he is conscious of it or not. Each person has certain beliefs which guide him, which help him to fashion his life. All of us deal with certain ends, with purposes in view, we tend towards a certain goal. Our opinions and beliefs about things here come to our aid in selecting one plan as against another. This is philosophy in the popular sense of the term. Real philosophy differs from this because it is a critical examination of the grounds of one's beliefs. One does not accept them now as prejudices or as mere superficial likes and dislikes, but because reason shows them to be valid, based on grounds possessing the approbation of universal reality.

To illustrate: Suppose a dyed-in-the-wool native of the State of Maine were asked why he votes the Republican ticket, his reply most likely would be because his father, grandfather, and great-grandfather had done so before him. This is an opinion based either on tradition or on prejudice. On the other hand, if he voted because he felt that the success of the Republican Party would result in placing our nation before the world of nations in the proper light, according to it universal significance; and, besides, if he felt that under its banner the ensuing prosperity would easily satisfy our material wants, thus liberating the soul for the free development of all its potentialities, his opinion would then assume a philosophic tinge.

To go one step further. Life is a process of thinking. Thinking about what? How to measure up to one's significance in the world, to the exalted position the human soul should, and does, occupy in a world which it may probe and understand perfectly, with little effort. That type of thought about things which helps one in subordinating all ends to one supreme goal is philosophy. If it helps one to identify the end of his life, the aim of his existence, the purpose of his striving with that which is fundamentally real in the world, it results not only in a well-ordered life, but also makes one feel more important and more willing to conquer all obstacles for the sake of achieving his heart's desire. Thus philosophy is worth while not only for its own sake, for the enjoyment it furnishes, but also for its pragmatic aspect, for its utility in furnishing the necessary encouragement in this apparent chaos around us.

Then again, it is intimately connected with many other interests in life—Religion and Science, for example.

Are you a scientist? Does that give you a right to scoff at philosophy because it is not practical enough? If you are a biologist, interested in the study of life, do you not need a knowledge of chemistry and physics also? Is it not necessary to understand the relation of your particular science to the other sciences? This is where philosophy fulfills a necessary function. It is general, comprehensive, universal—it is not limited to a particular realm of existence, which is true of particular sciences—but that is exactly what makes it so important. It is the source of the sciences showing their interrelation and connectedness. It has therefore aptly been described as the sum total of all scientific knowledge, or in Aristotle's conception, as the "Science of Universals."

Again, are you a theologian, a member of an organized clergy, or a religious fanatic? Do you then wish to discard philosophy because it conflicts with your religious beliefs? Admittedly, most religious dogmas are based purely on faith. In fact, many such dogmas not only cannot be demonstrated rationally, but are actually in conflict with any ordinary explanation of nature. "Miracles" can under no circumstances (although many exponents of religion have racked their brains to do so) be reconciled with scientific explanation. Philosophy cannot permit such dogmatic statements of belief to be incorporated as a part of its study. It is also evident that religious beliefs have from time immemorial been a product of a collective mind—a sect—a clergy—while philosophy is the result of individual thought. But granting all that, what have you, as a man of religion, to fear in philosophy? Does not life necessitate the existence of both of these compartments of the human make-up? The mere fact that faith is present and fulfills a necessary function shows its utility. The time may come when faith will be entirely supplanted by reason, when it will be rendered useless, like the appendix, but nothing has as yet appeared on the horizon to show that that time is near at hand. Until then, philosophy and religion should be considered as existing side by side, each serving its peculiar mission.

To conclude, a word must be said about the relation of philosophy to common sense. Thomas Hobbes, the English philosopher, said that everyone boasts of possessing as much, if not more, common sense than his fellow man. This feeling of equality is no doubt universally present. Why then do you feel so proud, so smug and self-satisfied, because you are endowed with sense, which is so common, and turn up your nose at a philosopher, who, admittedly, possesses the type of sense which is not quite so common? A president of one of the large banking institutions in one of our large cities referred to a man of a philosophic bent of mind as being too visionary. Needless to say, his application for a loan was unceremoniously rejected. Is this the proper estimate of philosophy? That the answer is in the negative is clearly shown by the fact that so-called common sense already recognizes the problems which philosophy "follows through" to their ultimate solution.

The ordinary man on the street feels that there is a difference between appearance and what lies behind it. This is the foundation of prayer, when we address ourselves to an unseen power. Again, in times of great emotional stress caused by conditions around us, if we let ourselves be swayed by the visible causes, "going to pieces" would be the inevitable result. The saving feature is that subconsciously we glimpse around this confusion a stabilizing force, an anchor, an element that guarantees a final solution fitting and proper for our safety. Thus common sense distinguishes between appearance and reality. Philosophy simply goes further; it wants to know the ultimate reality. This is called the ontological division of metaphysics.[1] Furthermore, all of us, although uninitiated into the mysteries of philosophic research, know that the cause before us is in turn an effect of another cause; the philosopher wants to know, besides, what is the first cause which no longer is an effect of anything. In this manner, the cosmological phase of metaphysics comes to the foreground. We may state further that everyone knows the difference between the means and the end which they serve to effect—also the fact that one end is in turn a means to another end—but the philosopher wants to investigate the final end which writes "Finis" to all means. That is Ethics. It is unnecessary to point out any other examples to convince one with an open mind that philosophy is not far removed from what we term common sense; it includes it, it must have it as its foundation.

[1] This paragraph is based in part on "A Defence of Philosophy," by Ralph Barton Perry, in which the author in a lighter vein, but yet most effectively discusses the relation of philosophy to common sense in the treatment of metaphysics, cosmology, logic and ethics.

INTRODUCTION

How can that which embraces common sense be considered so nonsensical and so remote from life? True enough, the study of philosophy is not intended to engender money-making ability, its purpose is not to yield a profit, it is cultural, meant to train one to have a comprehensive view of the world of nature, of life. This makes us lead more useful lives both physically and spiritually.

But, say you, admitting that all of this is true, how is it possible to acquire a proper philosophy? The first and most obvious method is to study other philosophies, especially those of the leading figures in the history of thought. This history is the subject of the next inquiry.

The history of Philosophy may roughly be divided into three periods: Greek or Ancient, 600 B.C.—525 A.D. Medieval or Scholastic, 150–1600 A.D. Modern, 1450—. Greek philosophy is in turn subdivided into (1) Pre-Socratic Philosophers. (2) Socrates and the Sophists. (3) Plato and Aristotle. (4) Post-Aristotelian Philosophers.

BOOK I

GREEK OR ANCIENT PHILOSOPHY

CHAPTER I

PRE-SOCRATIC PHILOSOPHERS. THE NATURALISTS

1. *The Milesian School. Thales, Anaximander and Anaximenes.*

MANY factors were responsible for the origin of Ancient Philosophy in Greece. We may briefly say that the then prevailing religion, that the scientific spirit of the time, the sayings of the Wise Men, and the insatiable curiosity of the Greek to learn what lies beyond the visible world,—all contributed to some extent to this end. There is also no doubt that the fact that there was no organized clergy, which ordinarily would check the unrestrained study of the world, contributed materially to the free, intellectual development of the Ancient Greeks.

All the philosophers in this period, prior to Socrates and the Sophists, were known as speculative naturalists, because they studied Nature and what lies behind appearances. They dealt particularly with the problems of Substance, Being and Cause.

What is reality? What is the underlying substance out of which all things are made? What is it that forms the world beyond appearances? The Milesian school, composed of Thales, Anaximander and Anaximenes, attempted to solve this puzzle. Thales, the first Greek philosopher, said that all things are made of water. Anaximander, on the other hand, did not find it quite so easy to snatch at a known and popular element for an appropriate answer. He said that the underlying reality is an unnamed, infinite substance. Xenophanes later identified it as earth. Anaximenes said that air has the distinction of being the one element out of which everything is composed.

3

What do these theories indicate as to the mental make-up of the first philosophers? No doubt their attempt to reduce all to the kind of thing present to the senses, which is so essential to life, appears crude and more or less childish to us, surrounded as we are by highly developed scientific theories. It must, however, be admitted that these theories contain a germ of truth in the fact that they are all monistic; they explain the constitution of the world by one substance. This monism exerted great influence upon later philosophy.

2. *The Eleatic School. Parmenides (470 B.C.) and Zeno (490–430 B.C.).*

What is the nature of existence? Is it motion or is it change? Is the world stable, or is it in a state of flux? This problem was tackled first by Parmenides of the Eleatic School. He said that everything is unchangeable, motionless, permanent. Change and motion are deceptions of the senses. "The world or universe is eternal, immutable, immovable, continuous, indivisible, infinite, unique."

His disciple, Zeno, did not have an affirmative, positive philosophy of his own, but attempted to confirm and explain his master's philosophy by showing that if you insist upon the assertion that change and motion are valid phenomena, you become involved in all kinds of logical difficulties, or paradoxes. Two such paradoxes are particularly famous,—the flight of the arrow, and Achilles and the tortoise. There is no doubt that an arrow seems to move from one point to another, but it is also logically true that this line showing the arrow's motion is made up of an infinite number of points of rest. Logically then, asks Zeno, how is it possible for the arrow really to move when it only rests at different points? Therefore, he concludes, the apparent motion of the arrow is only a deception of the senses, because logic shows the contrary to be true.

Likewise, he demonstrates that if the tortoise is permitted to have a start over Achilles at the beginning of the race, Achilles could never overtake it, because at every point

Achilles would have to traverse one-half of the distance remaining between him and the tortoise, ad infinitum. Here again, motion or the fact that Achilles does overtake the tortoise is simply an illusion of the senses and is not the true reality.

3. *Heracleitus. (About 536–470 B.C.)*

Heracleitus, the greatest pre-Socratic philosopher, opposes this theory of Parmenides. He says that the very essence of being is motion and change; rest, sameness, identity is a deception of the senses. It is not possible to descend twice into the same stream; it is not even possible to descend into it once; we are and we are not in it, we make up our minds to plunge into the waves, and behold! they are already far-away from us. This is the theory of the Flux; the world is in an eternal whirl; the nothing constantly changes into something and that is incessantly swallowed up into nothingness. In this way, life and death, origin and decay are identical. To this Flux, Heracleitus finds it quite appropriate to add the conception of Fire as the underlying substance of the world. Fire is well adapted to a theory of transformation. The universe is an ever-living fire, which is periodically kindled and extinguished. It is constantly changed into vapor, water and earth, then it turns to fire again; this process goes on everlastingly.

What is the cause, the reason for the order, and unity of the world? Heracleitus is the first to answer this query. He realizes that the universal change, if unregulated, would result in chaos and confusion. He, therefore, introduces a universal principle of harmony, a principle of proportion— the Logos, which supplies the rhythm and measure for the universal Fire.

Heracleitus is thus shown to offer a solution for the three problems with which the Ancient Greeks were so engrossed: for substance, fire; for cause, the Logos; for being, motion, instability, the Flux. No one can possibly doubt that in view of the immature and undeveloped state of philosophic thought of his time, Heracleitus was very ingenious in his attempted explanation of the world. But this philosophy leaves us dissatisfied. Such absolute impermanence, such insistence on change, only results in pessimism. What is the object in striving, since even just as you achieve the end it is no more. This reminds us of Schopenhauer, whom we shall discuss later. *Pluralists*

4. *Empedocles. (About 490–430 B.C.)*

The next pre-Socratic philosopher, whose doctrines deserve consideration, is Empedocles. Empedocles is an eclectic. He selects the best elements in the philosophies of his predecessors and combines them into a theory of his own. He agrees with Heracleitus that there is change and motion in the world, and he is also in accord with Parmenides that the ultimate realities are eternal and indestructible. He says that the world is composed of four elements, Water, Fire, Air and Earth; thus we see that he selected the substances which had already been advanced as explanations of the world by the Milesians and Heracleitus. He also shows that there are two forces in the world, love and hate. Love combines these elements; hate severs them. Furthermore, he explains that although the elements themselves never undergo change, their combinations are never at a standstill, constantly being torn asunder and re-combined.

5. *The Atomists. Leucippus and Democritus. (About 460–360 B.C.)*

Pluralists

The Atomists, Leucippus and Democritus, call for explanation next. They say the world is composed of an infinite number of indestructible particles or atoms. There are heavier and lighter atoms and they have little hooks attached to them. The heavier atoms move downward faster than the lighter, overtake them, and by means of these hooks, tack on to each other, thus forming the universe—all of this takes place according to mechanical law.

Before proceeding to the next and last pre-Socratic philosopher it is well to point out that the atomists are scientifically incorrect in their theory of the motion of the atoms, because these original particles move in a vacuum, and all bodies, whether heavy or light, possess the same velocity under such conditions. This error was corrected later by Epicurus, who adopted the theory from Democritus. To be sure, once we eliminate the consideration that inequality in the weight of the atoms is the cause of the difference in their motion, the result is disastrous for the atomistic explanation of the world. For how then do the atoms tack on to each other to form the universe?

6. *Anaxagoras.* *(500–429 B.C.)*

Anaxagoras, the next pre-Socratic philosopher, is also an atomist. He, however, differs from the others in two respects. In the first place, he believes that the atoms possess qualities such as color, taste, smell and the like, whereas Leucippus and Democritus asserted that they are devoid of all qualities. In this way they are known as quantitative atomists and Anaxagoras is called a qualitative atomist. Furthermore, the atomists believe that the atoms are regulated by mechanical law. Anaxagoras, on the other hand, stated that there is a World Reason, called Nous, which regulates and orders the world. This of course initiates the problem of Mechanism versus Teleology, which occupies the attention of many of the subsequent philosophers in the history of thought.

In conclusion, we readily see that these pre-Socratic philosophers were interested in the explanation of nature; in the solution of the problem of cause, some offered mechanical reasons, others had an inkling of a World purpose, of a World reason, underlying all appearances. In these theories the germ of many of the later intricate problems were planted; this germ later sprouted into full bloom, resulting among other things in the complex discussions of monism versus pluralism or dualism; mechanism versus teleology; materialism versus idealism. They were not seriously concerned with human relations, with Morality or Ethics. This subject occupied the attention of the next class—the Sophists and Socrates.

CHAPTER II

The Sophists and Socrates

1. *The Sophists.*

The Sophists are known as the Humanists. They did not discuss metaphysics. They did not study nature or the universe in its inanimate elements but their attention was centered on the problem of human conduct. The Sophists were teachers of rhetoric, of argumentation. It was a very important and necessary function in those days. Everyone was supposed to argue his own case before the tribunal at Athens and for that reason it was essential that one have a proper understanding of rhetoric and of the art of persuasion. The Sophists were particularly disliked by the Greeks for these reasons: In the first place, they all taught individualism—or the theory that each man was master of his own destiny, a free agent to determine his own course and conduct in life. Such individualism undermines the foundation of the state, which must be based upon a collective and common understanding, upon common standards. Again, the Greeks had very little respect for them because they taught for hire. The Ancient Greek mind could not tolerate anyone who made a profit out of philosophic teaching. Finally, they were especially censured because they made the "worse appear the better reason." The argument was that since their disciples almost uniformly won their cases, and since they could not possibly be right all the time, they must have succeeded simply because they were able by argument and persuasion to convince the judges that the "worse is the better reason." Certainly, this is not an admirable trait. At this point it is, perhaps, pertinent to

8

point out that Socrates was not a Sophist, because he did not offend in any of these three ways.

The most famous Sophist is Protagoras. He is noted especially for two principles. In the first place, he said that "Man is the measure of all things, determining what does, and what does not, exist." This is essentially an individualistic doctrine. In the second place, he was an agnostic in religion. He said, "As to the gods, I do not know whether they exist or not. Life is too short for such difficult enquiries." The next two Sophists, Prodicus and Hippias, are known as naturalists. Their theory was that in conduct and morality one should follow nature. Although they did not actually say that "Might makes Right," as a result of their teaching that principle becomes clearly evident, for in nature the stronger prevails at all times. Gorgias, the Anti-Naturalist, taught that you must not follow nature in morality. His main philosophy can be summed up in the statement, "My Station and Its Duties." Every one has a certain station in life. That station devolves upon him certain obligations. Life for him, therefore, consists in the fulfillment of such obligations.

2. *Socrates. (469–399 B.C.)*

In conclusion, we must say that the Sophistic individualism resulted in a great deal of discord and disorder in morality and human relations. Everyone was his own master and could do what he pleased. In the midst of this confusion and obviously unsatisfactory state of affairs, Socrates appeared. He wanted to re-introduce order, harmony and uniformity into moral relations between men. His main contention was that "Virtue is Knowledge." This simply means that if one is aware of what he is about, if one understands all the conditions surrounding his acts, all the consequences that might ensue therefrom, he cannot but act virtuously and properly. Socrates impresses us with the fact that "Virtue is Knowledge" is a uniform standard, one that applies to all, one that can be a guide for all.

Method. Besides this doctrine Socrates is also famous for several other things. He is very well known for his use of the dialogue method, which always took the form of question and answer. Socrates would continually question his opponent, and after eliciting admissions, would interrogate him still further; in this way the entire subject was developed to the perfect satisfaction of Socrates. Furthermore, he always insisted upon defining his subject prior to commencing any discussion of it. It is very clear that often participants in a debate on a particular subject may continue arguing for hours on end, only to discover that each had been viewing it from a different angle. This must be avoided. Socrates always defined his subject so clearly, so definitely, that no one could possibly be misled. To guard even more against this very common error of debaters, Socrates also divided his subject into its different branches—a method recommended by Descartes, two thousand years later. Inference, so comprehensively treated by Aristotle, was customarily employed by this remarkable man. He would start from conclusions or premises admitted by all, and then reach the results on controversial points. Socrates is also noted for what is known now as "Socratic Irony." At the beginning of any discussion, he would simulate colossal ignorance of the subject, allowing his opponent to put forth his arguments very pompously and with the convictions of a well-informed person. At the end, however, Socrates would turn the tables, forcing his opponent to the wall, and demonstrating clearly that he thoroughly understood the subject, but that his adversary did not. From all indications it appears that Socrates derived huge enjoyment from this "cat and mouse" game.

Teleology. Socrates is a teleologist; he believes that nature exhibits a purpose in all its branches. To illustrate: we possess legs for the purpose of locomotion, a tongue for tasting, eyes for seeing, and intellect for apprehending. From this we can readily conclude that Socrates was a firm believer in the existence of the gods; only such intelligent beings can account for the presence of design in the universe. Socrates

is also utilitarian in his Ethics.   He believes that the pleasurable is good and the painful is bad.   This finds an echo in
later periods of philosophic thought—beginning with Epicurus and appearing in as recent a moral code as that of John
Stuart Mill.

Surely now we may ask what is the cause of this unparal-
leled popularity which Socrates enjoys?   The doctrines he
taught his followers clearly account to some extent for it.
But the major contribution is the fact that Plato, his disciple,
employs the character of Socrates in order to develop his own
philosophy in his dialogues.   This added materially to the
perpetuation of the reputation of Socrates throughout the
ages.   Reference is here made to the Apology and the Protagoras.

Trial.   The Apology treats of the trial of Socrates.   Socrates has been accused of two charges by his adversaries.   In
the first place, he was charged with corrupting the youth by
teaching them to make "the worse appear the better reason."
Secondly, he was accused of denying the existence of the gods.
Socrates, defending himself, as was the custom in Ancient
Greece, refutes both of these charges.   He shows that he was
not a Sophist; therefore it was not his aim to make "the worse
appear the better reason"; that in fact he always taught his
disciples, in addition to proper behavior, to argue rationally,
truthfully.

The adversaries of Socrates had a very serious grievance
against him—the fact that their children, his disciples, made
them appear foolish in argument.   Just imagine a parent, a
contemporary of Socrates, an Athenian, who pompously and
vainly displayed his superiority on all occasions.   Just imagine
this proud man sitting at the dinner table surrounded by his
family partaking of a very appetizing meal.   Finally, as is
customary at all dinners, the father begins a discussion of a
popular subject, politics, for example, addressing his remarks to the oldest child, who happens to be a Socratic
adherent.   The parent makes sweeping statements about vot-
ing for a Republican Senator, and the young offspring inno-

cently asks why; the parent explains that the Republican votes on all public questions properly and wisely. The child still does not see why the Democrat, simply by virtue of being a Democrat, must be condemned without a trial. In this way the argument is continued until the father is wholly confused and feels keenly his impotency in convincing his own son, who formerly would have accepted his statement without a murmur. Such a sensation was extremely unpleasant, and the parent felt it showed disrespect for him. For this he blamed Socrates. This only shows that the young man employed "Socratic Irony" in reducing his parent to such a sorry plight.

Socrates clearly refuted this first indictment by pointing out that not only did he abstain from teaching his disciples to use Sophistic arguments but that he himself tried to serve as a model of good behavior for them to copy. True enough, he says, some of them turned out to be bad examples of propriety and honor, but that cannot be traced home to his teaching. He himself always practiced temperance, never engaged in anything other than the honorable and the just—all of this he impressed upon his followers. How then, he asks, do his prosecutors charge him with teaching lack of respect for parents, and with other such unfounded accusations?

The second charge, that he "denied the existence of the gods," Socrates refuted very simply by pointing out that whenever he undertook any serious task, he consulted the oracle at Delphi to learn the wish of these Divine Beings. At this time, it is perhaps well to point out that this oracle always gave equivocal answers to any questions, which made it impossible to trap her. Socrates also directed attention to his teleological teaching to prove that he believed in the gods, because they are responsible for nature exhibiting a purpose in all directions, especially with reference to the human body. Socrates very often referred to a divine voice which directed him what to do in a particular case—this no doubt represents what we call conscience. Notwithstanding all of these arguments, both charges were sustained, although not by the overwhelming majority that might have been expected under the circumstances.

After Socrates was found guilty but prior to passing sentence, the judges offered him the opportunity to impose a penalty upon himself. Socrates suggested thirty minnæ, or a matter of perhaps six cents in our currency. Now it appears extremely foolish for Socrates to have treated the matter so lightly—a matter involving such serious consequences. Perhaps he did not dream that a man of his fame would be severely punished, or he in fact was too proud to admit that he was wrong. His behavior irritated his judges, and Socrates was sentenced to death. He elected to die by drinking hemlock. The manner in which the final curtain descends on his life is beautifully described in the Phaedo. As the jailer brings in the cup of poison Socrates says:

You, my good friend, who are experienced in these matters, shall give me directions how I am to proceed. The man answers: You have only to walk about until your legs are heavy, and then to lie down, and the poison will act. At the same time he handed the cup to Socrates, who in the easiest and gentlest manner, without the least fear or change of color or feature, looking at the man with all his eyes . . . took the cup and said: What do you say about making a libation out of this cup to any god? May I or not? The man answered: We only prepare, Socrates, just so much as we deem enough. I understand, he said. . . . Then holding the cup to his lips, quite readily and cheerfully he drank off the poison . . . and at the moment, Apollodorus, . . . broke out into a loud cry. . . . Socrates alone retained his calmness: What is this strange outcry? he said. . . . Be quiet then, and have patience . . . and he walked about until, as he said, his legs began to fail and then he lay on his back, . . . and the man who gave him the poison now and then looked at his feet and legs; and after a while he pressed his foot hard and asked him if he could feel; and he said No; and then his leg, and so upwards and upwards, and showed us that he was cold and stiff. . . . He was beginning to grow cold about the groin, when he uncovered his face . . . and said (they were his last words)—he said: Crito, I owe a cock to Asclepius; will you remember to pay the debt? . . . but in a minute or two a movement was heard and the attendants uncovered him; his eyes were set, and Crito closed his eyes and mouth.

Morality. The dialogue by which Plato develops the Socratic moral theory most exhaustively, is the Protagoras, named after the Sophist. It presents several Sophists, Socrates and some of his disciples in a discussion of virtue. Socrates in his usual manner attempts to force Protagoras into certain admissions. Protagoras says that virtue can be taught because, otherwise, how do the Athenians punish the non-virtuous and reward the virtuous? What is this virtue? asks Socrates. Protagoras, goaded on by the Socratic darts, very pompously goes on a verbal rampage. He says that it consists of wisdom, courage, temperance, justice and holiness. These five parts are entirely distinct from each other. Socrates, at first appearing to be ignorant of the subject, finally, by very skillful manipulations, extracts from Protagoras the fact that at least four of these parts of virtue, excluding that of courage, really are similar to each other. In fact, Protagoras admits that these four have the same opposite or contrast, namely folly or ignorance. In other words, the man who possesses wisdom necessarily is opposed to him who is ignorant; the temperate individual is contrasted with him, who, because of ignorance, foolishly does things to excess; the just knows what he is about, as distinct from him who is swayed by folly to commit injustice. Thus Protagoras is led step by step to make concessions to the Socratic demands, until in desperation he holds to one fort, that courage cannot be identified with the other four parts. But, asks Socrates, what is courage? Is not the courageous man one who knows how to behave in moments of danger, who evaluates properly the particular situation? Protagoras must of course admit, though unwillingly, that ignorance is also the cause of cowardice. Consequently, since the five parts of virtue have the same opposite, by the familiar axiom that all things equal to the same thing are equal to each other, they must really be identical, or virtue is one.

Also this opposite of virtue has been shown to be ignorance.; virtue, therefore, must consist of knowledge.   The original Socratic doctrine "Virtue is Knowledge" is thus brought forcefully to the attention of philosophy.   This analysis of the Protagoras may appear very technical, but Socrates has another card up his sleeve by which to prove his point.   All agree that the pleasurable is good and the painful bad.   How then will you select pleasure as against pain?   How, again, will you choose the more, as against the less, pleasurable?   Knowledge is the only possible, valid power which can help us here.   It is the instrument by which we may acquire the good and avoid evil or pain.   Therefore, knowledge has again been shown to be identified with virtue.   This doctrine exerted the greatest influence upon Plato, which we shall discuss under the Platonic theory of Ideas.

Character.   The character of Socrates is best depicted by another Platonic dialogue, the Crito.   It pictures Socrates in his cell just prior to his death.   At that time a great many of his friends urge him to escape.   They assure him that every possible provision has been made to insure success; they offer him, besides, the means to live leisurely in another country. Very few could resist a temptation of this sort, especially when on the brink of death.   Socrates, however, refused the offer. He adduced several reasons for his course.   In the first place, his children in Athens will never be able to live down the shame of having a father, an escaped felon.   This attitude is very difficult for us to understand, for is it not humiliating enough to have as one's father a convicted felon, who has been executed?   Perhaps Socrates refers to the shame of children for a father who was too cowardly to face his just punishment—just from the standpoint of the laws of the country which imposed the death penalty.   In the second place, what would he at his age do in a strange country? How could he get along?   What friends could he make? In fact, he feels that he would be a traitor to his government and to his old friends to escape the punishment meted out to him by the state.   Lastly, he points out that all his life he taught his disciples to obey the laws of their country.   If he were not to practice what he preached, his entire life's work would be rendered futile.   Certainly this is not the course that his own friends would recommend to him to pursue.

To sum up, then, Socrates was a humanist.   He concerned himself particularly with human relations, conduct, ethics. He was not much interested in the cold-blooded facts of metaphysics.   He was not a naturalist; he did not speculate about nature or the underlying reality, which occupied the exclusive attention of his predecessors.   Socrates, however, is much more important in the history of philosophy because of his influence upon Plato, Aristotle and subsequent philosophers, than for the doctrines which he himself had taught.   The next subject of study, therefore, is the philosophy of Plato.

CHAPTER III

PLATO (427–347 B.C.)

1. *Life.*

PLATO was born in Athens in 427 B.C., of a distinguished family. He became a disciple of Socrates at the age of twenty, when he decided to devote his life to philosophy. He studied with Socrates for a period of eight years, and after the death of his master, he traveled in Egypt, Italy and Sicily. In Sicily, he was invited into the Court of Dionysius I, where he became so obnoxious that he was kidnapped and put to sale in the slave-market. A friend ransomed him and sent him to Athens about 388 B.C. There he established his school of philosophy in a garden near a gymnasium, called the Academy. Here he spent the last forty years of his life, numbering among his pupils his great rival, Aristotle. Plato was consulted in reference to the re-organization of the government at Syracuse, but his scheme failed, due to the violent opposition that developed to his measures. He died in 347 B.C., at the age of eighty-one.

Plato was born an aristocrat. This, no doubt, had a great deal of influence upon his philosophy. His desire for an ideal aristocracy or republic, his argument for the education of the upper classes, his insistence on the fair treatment of women in the state, offering them the opportunity to become rulers and soldiers on an equal footing with men, and a great many of his other doctrines can most certainly be traced to his noble birth.

2. *Influence of the Pre-Socratic Philosophers upon Plato.*

Plato, as may be expected under the circumstances, was very much influenced by his predecessors. In the Timaeus, in which he discusses the creation of the world of nature, he shows that nature consists of four elements, water, fire, air and earth.   Empedocles had already mentioned these elements and showed that they compose this world of sense; he in turn had adopted them from the Milesians and Heracleitus.   In his conception of the world of Ideas, the influence of Parmenides is readily traceable—this world of Ideas never changes, its constancy and identity constitute its most essential characteristics.   His Idea of the Good is more or less similar to the Logos of Heracleitus and the Nous of Anaxagoras—all of these emphasize that the world is controlled by a universal intelligence, impersonal and teleological in character.   Thus Plato is an eclectic to a large extent; this is by no means to be taken as a reflection on his line of thought, for the wonder of it is that although he started with such meager material, he was able to lift himself to such supreme heights.

3. *Influence of Socrates upon Plato.*

But the greatest source of inspiration for Plato was the philosophy of Socrates.   At this point we may recall that Socrates was very much put out by the moral teaching of the Sophists, who urged each one to follow his individualistic tendencies; he attempted to remedy this by furnishing us with a single rule of conduct which everybody may follow. This rule "Virtue is Knowledge" is the same criterion for all; it is applicable to all situations and to all problems; it has a most general application; in short, it is a "universal" standard. This theory of a "universal" inspired Plato's conception of a world of universals, or a world of Ideas.   What is this Platonic Idea?   At the very outset it may be defined as neither mental nor physical.   It is not the ordinary idea in the mind which can be eliminated at will, nor is it a physical object, which may be divided or destroyed.   It is, says Plato, a really existing thing; but where is it to be found?   Not in the mental world with which we are familiar nor in the physical world of nature—it has its real existence in an intelligible world of its own.   Furthermore it serves as the universal model for a great many of the particular objects in this world which express its nature and essence. To illustrate: take a statue expressing beauty, a beautiful woman, an exquisite piece of architecture—all typify beauty, yet they are so widely different. How, asks Plato, can so many divergent subjects be united in this exhibition of the beautiful unless there is a universal standard of beauty which they all follow—an Idea of Beauty? The same is true of any other universal represented by things in nature, chair, table, man, goodness and the like. Thus we conclude that the Idea has universal application similar to the Socratic universal. Socrates, however, limits his theory only to morality, while Plato's world of Ideas is all-inclusive.

The second important influence of Socrates upon Plato is in the use of the dialogue method. Plato, like his master and teacher, employs this method to promote his philosophic thought. In fact, Plato's writings are known as his Dialogues. While these are the tangible effects of Socrates upon Plato, we can entertain no doubt that the spiritual, intangible influences on Plato due to his close association for many years with his preceptor are immeasurable in their results.

Plato exerted a tremendous influence upon subsequent thought. He is essentially a dualist. He draws a line of demarcation between the spirit and the flesh, between body and mind, the Idea and the particular object. Such dualism lends itself easily to the popular mind. The lay understanding, too, conceives of body and mind as distinct—in philosophy this doctrine was particularly emphasized by Descartes, although modern theories discard dualism in favor of monism. Plato's conception of the Idea of the Good, which is teleological in character, recalls to mind the later problem of *mechanism* versus *teleology*. Theology was especially affected by Plato's division between spirit and flesh; it was a ready-made doctrine for the Scholastic purpose of emphasizing the spiritual phase of life at the expense of the corporeal. Then, too, the mathematical method emphasized by Plato greatly influenced subsequent scientific thought. Descartes used it, and Spinoza employed it exclusively in the "Ethics."

Plato's philosophy may be divided into two main branches: Metaphysics and Ethics.

4. *Metaphysics. World of Ideas.*

Plato conceives of two worlds—the world of sense, the world of particular objects, a world which is presented to us in our daily life, a world in which we move and strive to achieve our ends; on the other hand, a world of Ideas, a world of permanence, a world of universals.   ~~We have already seen what this world of Ideas signifies; we found that~~ Plato considers it far more real and indestructible than this world of nature, the objects of which are in a constant Flux, ~~in the Heracleitan sense.~~   But he goes even further to show his utter contempt for these things in the world which assume such significance to us in our daily struggle.   He says the world of sense is a copy or an imitation of the world of Ideas.   Therefore, just as in the world of sense there is an hierarchy of objects ranging from the lowest to the highest in importance, in the same way in the world of Ideas, which serves as its model, there must be an hierarchy of Ideas, ranging from the Idea represented and expressed by the lowest class of objects in experience, to the universal typified by the most significant natural objects.   At the pinnacle of the world of sense we have the sun—it sheds light on all objects of nature and is indispensable to our complete understanding of all that it contains; at the peak of the world of Ideas stands the Idea of the Good.   It is the sun so-called, of the world of Ideas; it shows the purpose, the good of everything in the universe, including both realms of existence.

This analogy between the Idea of the Good and our sun Plato develops in the Republic,[1] by the parable of the cave. Socrates says to Glaucon:

Imagine a number of men living in an underground cavernous chamber, with an entrance open to the light, extending along the entire

[1] Book VII.

length of the cavern, in which they have been confined, from their childhood, with their legs and necks so shackled, that they are obliged to sit still and look straight forwards, because their chains render it impossible for them to turn their heads round: and imagine a bright fire burning some way off, above and behind them, and an elevated roadway passing between the fire and the prisoners, with a low wall built along it, like the screens which conjurors put up in front of their audience, and above which they exhibit their wonders.

I have it, he replied.

Also figure to yourself a number of persons walking behind this wall, and carrying with them statues of men, and images of other animals, wrought in wood and stone and all kinds of materials, together with various other articles, which overtop the wall. . . .

. . . For let me ask you, in the first place, whether persons so confined could have seen anything of themselves or of each other, beyond the shadows thrown by the fire upon the part of the cavern facing them?

Certainly not, if you suppose them to have been compelled all their lifetime to keep their heads unmoved.

And is not their knowledge of the things carried past them equally limited?

Unquestionably it is. . . .

Then surely such persons would hold the shadows of those manufactured articles to be the only realities. . . .

Let us suppose that one of them has been released, and compelled suddenly to stand up, and turn his neck round and walk with open eyes toward the light. . . .

And if he were further compelled to gaze at the light itself, would not his eyes, think you, be distressed, and would he not shrink and turn away to the things which he could see distinctly, and consider them to be really clearer than the things pointed out to him? . . .

Hence, I suppose, habit will be necessary to enable him to perceive objects in that upper world. . . .

Last of all, I imagine, he will be able to observe and contemplate the nature of the sun, not as it appears in water or on alien ground, but as it is in itself in its own territory. . . .

His next step will be to draw the conclusion, that the sun is the author of the seasons and the years, and the guardian of all things in the visible world, and in a manner the cause of all those things which he and his companions used to see. . . .

And now consider what would happen if such a man were to descend again and seat himself on his old seat? . . .

And if he were forced to deliver his opinion again, touching the shadows aforesaid, and to enter the lists against those who had always been prisoners . . . would he not be made a laughingstock?

In the same way, Plato points out that this world before us only furnishes us with the shadows, with the reflections of the world of Ideas, that it is only an imitation, and not a very good imitation at that. What then is the remedy? The philosopher must be so trained and so educated that he will intuitively behold the world of Ideas and especially the Idea of the Good; that the sun of the world of universals will be revealed to him in its true glory. Then he will be in a position to teach us, poor mortals, what the difference is between the temporary, ephemeral objects and the true essences, their models.

It must be clear to us by this time that the Idea of the Good supports Plato's entire metaphysical system. Consequently, he is anxious to elucidate it further. He says that Idea may be apprehended also as Beauty or as Truth. Thus the triumvirate of the Ideas of the Good, Beauty and Truth really represent the climax of the permanent world. Then again, they relate to three of the most essential compartments of human life: ethics, love and knowledge. Ethics we shall discuss under the second division of Plato's philosophy. Let us, therefore, now turn to his theory of knowledge and beauty.

Knowledge. What is scientific or real knowledge? The ordinary man using common sense, might say that if our idea of a table corresponds to the actual table outside of our consciousness, then it is a true idea. This is entirely too simple and too defective a theory of truth to suit Plato. He asserts emphatically that the particular table has no relation to the truth of the Idea of table. The soul, according to him, has in a previous existence perceived the Idea of table, and the particular object in this world simply recalls to the mind what is already innate as a result of its previous vision. In short, knowledge in the Platonic sense is intuitive, the object of sense is not even a good copy of the Idea; it is simply an approximation of it; it causes the memory of the Idea which is latent in the mind to be revived. This, in the Platonic sense, is the only legitimate purpose which the world of sense serves.

How does one attain to the knowledge of the Idea of Beauty, is our next query. If Plato were consistent he would naturally conclude that art which represents the beauty of earthly objects is of great help to remind the soul of its previous vision of the Idea of Beauty. This would be analogous to his conception of the objects of sense in relation to truth. But, strange as it may seem, that is not Plato's thought on the subject at all. He derides art; he calls it an imitation of an imitation; the Idea of beauty is the original, the object of nature representing it is an imitation of the Idea, the picture of the object is therefore an imitation of that which already imitates. For example, the Idea of table is the model; the particular table is its imitation, the picture of the table is the imitation of the imitation. This type of approach to beauty Plato uncompromisingly discards. What then is the proper way to behold beauty in its true essence?

Love. The answer is love; love is the motive force by which one can proceed to perceive goodness under the guise of beauty. Love is the desire of the soul for the beautiful; it is not of the flesh, it is not of individual persons. It is an attraction to the universal. Love proceeds by the following steps in order to attain to the vision of the Idea: first, there is love of bodies, then of persons, then of theories, then of institutions, then of ideals, finally of beauty itself. In this conception of love, sex attraction plays a minor role. It can readily be seen that Plato differs essentially from Freud. Plato admits that love makes the soul yearn not only for a vision of the good and the beautiful, but to possess it and to possess it everlastingly. This creates, in turn, a desire in the soul for immortality. This desire, in the ordinary individual, necessarily means procreation. This is the only place where the actual sex element enters in Platonic love.

That person who possesses talent of some kind can immortalize himself in some other way; the poet perpetuates his name by writing a masterpiece; the architect, by the creation of an exquisite monument. Thus we can see that as love recedes from its lowly origins, and ascends to the heights whence it can view the Idea, sex attraction loses its force and the pure, sexless, spiritual elements assume complete control. To Freud, on the other hand, sex is the underlying principle, not only for procreation but for all other ideals that one can possibly imagine—religion, art and similar aspirations of the human.

This powerful influence in human life, this weapon of love, is discussed by Plato in the Phaedrus and Symposium, two beautiful dialogues and very artistically developed. There is a great deal of nonsense in both of these dialogues which might have been used by Plato to enliven the conversation. Such nonsense about love is an especially fitting topic of discussion when the participants have eaten heartily and are somewhat under the influence of liquor; this is especially true in the Symposium in which all the characters are banqueting at the house of Agathon. Aristophanes, one of the revelers, who has been cured of the hiccough, says that the sexes were originally three, men, women, and the union of the two; Zeus severed the last, and ever since, the two halves have gone about looking for one another. Marriage is supposed to put an end to this nerve-racking search, and enable the sexes to go their way to the business of life. No one can possibly suppose that this picture is meant to be taken seriously. On the other hand, the statement by Eryximachus, the physician, that there are two kinds of love, the good and the evil, the noble and the coarse, in all things in the universe, and that medicine must attempt to produce harmony between them, does not advance the argument very far. It is a pure trusim. We must admit, however, that these speeches prepare the way for a real analysis of love, which Plato brings to us through the mouth of Socrates, in both of these dialogues.

This love is intimately connected with the peculiar constitution of the soul. The soul, Plato represents by the figure of a charioteer who is driving two steeds, the one a noble animal who accedes to the driver's every wish, the other an ill-looking villain who will not yield even to blows. The charioteer typifies reason, the highest element in the soul. The unruly steed represents the appetites and the desires which must be checked, moderated and controlled at all times. The other steed is will, which is guided by reason. This idea of the soul Plato employs in the Republic to explain what constitutes the ethical, the good and the just life.

Now we are ready to talk about love. It is a form of madness of the soul, referring particularly to the rational element. There are four kinds of madness, he points out. One is the art of prophecy, the other the madness involved in initiation and purification ceremonies which prevailed among the Greeks during Plato's life. Next we have the madness involving poetry, when the poet is inspired by the Muses, and finally, there is the madness which actuates the soul to get away from its earthly existence, to break off the shackles that chain it down to the world of sense, and ascend to the heavens, whence it can behold the vision of the Ideas, especially the Ideas of Goodness, Beauty and Truth in their nakedness. Every time the soul observes an object of beauty in nature it is reminded of real beauty in the home of the gods; it becomes more eager than ever to shed its earthly garments and return to its pure spiritual form. Such is the influence which love exerts upon the soul.

God. Surely the next question about Plato's metaphysics must be what is his conception of God? If you feel that he identifies God with the Idea of the Good you may conclude that God is impersonal, that God is the principle of goodness, that God is the purpose and underlying meaning of the entire universe. On the other hand, we may consider that the Timaeus portrays Plato's true conception of God. There Plato conceives of God as an artist who fashions a world out of matter; He is a personal Being, a Creator, an Artificer. At the same time, God is also pictured as fighting matter; He is not the all-powerful force in the ordinary religious sense of the word, but He must fight the principle of evil. He overcomes it in the end, then forms nature out of matter composed of the four elements, water, air, fire and earth, but that is not the end of His task. He must supply a soul to this material world. This soul is a combination of irregularity and order, of confusion and harmony, hence the world of sense possesses all such elements. It is governed by universal laws, yet its temporary character, its motion and change, focuses attention upon its contrast with the world of Ideas. Plato especially emphasizes the fact that this soul of the world exists prior to the matter in it; in the same way the human soul, which is fashioned out of the same substance as the world soul, also antedates the body. This explains how the human soul gets a glimpse of the Idea, in a prior existence.

World of Sense. The outstanding difficulty in Plato's metaphysics is: Why the need of a world of sense? It will be remembered that the world of Ideas is the permanent world, the only world of reality, the world of essentials, the world of universals. That world is the model which is imitated by the world of sense. Plato, as a matter of fact, does not concern himself in any way with this world of nature; it is simply hanging on, so to speak; it is an imitation and may very well be discarded. The question necessarily comes to one's mind: Why then have two worlds, why is not the world of universals quite sufficient? Plato gives a very fantastic answer to this. He says, God is good: goodness likes to express itself. Goodness must by its very nature be disseminated. Therefore, this goodness of God wants a world of sense in order to express its character. The same thing may be said of love. God is love. The Idea of the Good is apprehended as beauty which can be approached best through love. That too likes to express itself, therefore, nature simply functions as an expression of the world of Ideas.

5. Ethics and Politics.

Ethics. / The next major division of Plato's philosophy is ethics. / Here, as in the case of Aristotle, politics and ethics are so closely interwoven and so closely allied to each other that it is impossible actually to draw any real line of demarcation between them. Man is a social animal and cannot possibly develop outside of the state. It is, therefore, essential to talk of the ethical development of an individual only in relation to his life with his fellow beings in a social community or a state.

/ What is the goal of human life? is the first query in Platonic moral philosophy. It is not to be identified with pleasure, with honor, with wealth, with social position, because these are either too undignified for the human's final aim in life or they serve only as a means to an end. What then is a worthy pursuit that is appropriate for this rational animal, man? Justice, says Plato. / This justice is further defined as a life of reason, a life in which one's rational nature sits in the saddle and enlists the will to aid it to suppress the appetites and moderate their demands/ Just as the scientist studying the amœba first examines it under a microscope to enlarge it, in order to see all of the minute characteristics which would otherwise escape the naked eye, so Plato diagnoses the composite elements of justice by magnifying it on a very large scale, by examining it in the state. Then, he expects to find it relatively easy to apply his conclusions to the individual. To this treatment of justice, he devotes the entire Republic. There Socrates discusses justice with a number of characters. Let us designate those who argue against Socrates and interpose objections to his pronouncements as his opponents.

Justice is first of all defined by the opponents of Socrates as giving every man his due, or rewarding your friends and punishing your enemies. The natural objection leveled against this type of definition by Socrates is that if one mistakes an enemy for a friend and vice versa he will then punish his friend and reward his enemy. The argument then shifts, and justice is defined as doing good to those whom you know to be honest and virtuous men; harm to those whom you know to be the opposite.   Here again, Socrates objects that it is not of the nature of justice to punish a man, which is tantamount to making him less virtuous than he was previously.   The opponents finally say that justice means serving the interest of the stronger.   It is just to obey the laws; the laws are made by the legislators for their benefit; the legislators are the stronger, in so far as the political community is concerned; therefore to obey the laws in reality means to serve the interest of the stronger.   The answer to this is known as the famous Socratic doctrine of the "art of wages."   Socrates points out that in every art, the artist practices his art not for his own sake but for the benefit of some one other than himself.   For example, a physician practices the art of medicine, not for the sake of curing himself, but for the purpose of helping his patients.   In the same way the legislator practices the art of legislation not for the purpose of benefiting himself, but for the sake of the governed, the subjects.   By the previous definition these are the weaker in the political community; therefore to obey the laws really turns out to mean serving the interest of the weaker.   This preliminary skirmish causes the Socratic opponents to beat a hasty retreat; but the question is still open, what is justice?   The suggestions made by Socrates that they should have recourse to the state in order to get to the bottom of the nature of the subject is quickly adopted.   We turn now to an inquiry concerning the evolution and development of the political community.

Politics.   In the good old days, says Socrates, the state was a very small affair, there were few interests occupying the attention of its constitutents, there was no cogent need for a comprehensive division of labor.   As time went on, however, population increased, wants expanded, a variety of needs arose, and with this complex progress, there developed a crying need for a division of labor, an indispensable necessity for larger territory; in fact, all our present political, perplexing questions demanded a solution.   How should an ideal state behave

under these circumstances? How should an ideal political
unit arrange its respective elements in order to promote the
greatest happiness, harmony and well-being among its members? This is where the Aristocracy, so dear to Plato, takes
root.

The Aristocracy is the most ideal embodiment of political
justice. It consists of philosophers at the helm, soldiers, the
willing serfs of these governors, and an artisan or producing
class consciously directing their efforts to support the higher
two classes. By thus satisfying their need for material wants,
the philosophers and the military men are able to devote
themselves wholly to the administration of affairs of state.
But how, you may properly ask, does this even remotely bear
the slightest relation to justice? Let us, at this point, refer
to the Greek conception of virtue. The Ancient Greeks conceived of four cardinal virtues—wisdom, courage, temperance
and justice. Surely, says Socrates, in this Aristocracy we shall
find all four represented. The philosophers must govern,
this personifies wisdom in the state; the soldiers will perform
their tasks under the control of the philosophers, this typifies
real courage. The populace, or the class of artisans, not
boasting of the rational nature possessed by the philosophers,
will very often attempt to get out of bounds. It is, therefore, necessary to control and temper them. This is done by
the philosophers, who avail themselves of the aid of the
soldiers in order to determine the limits within which the
class of artisans may act and move in the state. This group
of producers, if properly controlled by the military, personifies temperance. In this way, wisdom, courage and
temperance are already present in the ideal state. What else
is lacking here, that needs to be supplied by justice? True
enough, says Socrates, the first requirement is for each class to
do its own peculiar work well, to perform its appropriate
function admirably; but we must go one step further. There
must be harmony between them. Each must do its own work
in relation to the others; the philosophers must govern well;
they are obliged to call upon the soldiers to help them suppress

the working classes, to guide the populace not to overstep their boundaries.   This ideal harmony, with the wise men at the helm, constitutes justice.   In this state, the artisans willingly serve to maintain the upper two "parasitic" strata of society, because they feel that it is for the best interests of all concerned, that this condition be maintained.

Before proceeding to strike an analogy between justice in this ideal aristocracy and justice in the life of the individual, it is necessary to point out a few more salient elements in the Republic of Plato.   The philosophers and the soldiers will be educated by the state.   They will be first of all trained by proper music to develop an harmonious temperament.   Then again, gymnastics will be a very essential part of their training; this will help not only their bodies but their minds as well. Lastly, the philosophers must possess no property of any kind; they must also not be burdened with private families.   Lest it be considered that this type of community life, known in Platonic philosophy as "community of women and children," was meant to permit loose and licentious practices, we must consider that Plato expected it to be under the proper guidance of magistrates; being sanctioned by political and religious authority.   The one thing that we must guard against in our rulers is not to furnish them with motives that might induce them to act selfishly.   What interest has a philosopher to rule other than for the common welfare, since he can neither enrich himself by inequitable laws, nor apply the maxim, "to the victor belong the spoils," because he has no children or other relatives to whom to give sinecures, and his election does not depend upon the good will of the voters, in our sense of the word.   Furthermore, in order to become philosophers, they must show the characteristics of the true philosophic disposition.   These are an eager desire for the knowledge of all real existence, a hatred of falsehood, the contempt for the pleasures of the body, the indifference to money.   They must be high-minded, they must possess gentleness, they must have a musical, regular, harmonious disposition.   Then again, the philosophers must go through a certain set training, being taught arithmetic, geometry, astronomy, and dialetic, or the science of real existence. Dialetic will enable them to get a true conception of the World of Ideas; especially of the Idea of the Good, showing the significance of all existence. If the philosopher is a genuinely learned man he will always attempt to teach his subjects that the world in which they put so much stock is a sham, and always to lift their eyes to the world of Ideas. Plato, however, realizes the practical difficulty of finding such a genuine philosopher; he points out that philosophers as a class are held in contempt, because of those who only simulate wisdom. This artificiality renders them vain and pompous to an intelligent audience.

To sum up then, the ideal Platonic state or the Aristocracy consists of the philosophers as governors who are aided by the fighting class to temper those willing serfs, the workers. The harmony existing in such a state is justice. To the objection that such an ideal state is unattainable, Socrates asks: What of it? Are we claiming for it actual realization? Is the practicable aspect of the scheme even necessary to be considered? Needless to say this state is pictured as an ideal, which by its very definition can never be achieved. It is to serve as a model for all extant political units to copy and thus attempt to improve their actual constitutions.

Now, we are ready to devote our attention to justice in the individual. Here again, the soul which has already been represented as a charioteer driving two steeds, is now considered from a different angle. The soul is divided into three parts: reason, will and the appetites. If reason is so developed that it can rule, then it is wisdom; will obeying reason is courage; the appetites, being moderated and tempered by the will under the guidance of reason is temperance. Therefore, justice in the individual life is the harmony among these three different parts of the soul in which reason will govern, and aided by will, the gentle, tractable steed, will control the appetites, the desires, the passions. In short, a life of justice is simply a life of reason. In such a life, Plato rules out practically all pleasure; only the most necessary may be considered as an element of the just life, all others must be discarded.

To go further, Plato points out that there is a devolution of the state; the state deteriorates under certain conditions, descending to a lower level at each stage. The highest and most ideal is the Aristocracy, which has just been fully described. Then there is the Timocracy, in which the military class governs. Next is the Oligarchy, which means government by the wealthy, the propertied classes. Then comes the Democracy, which is a government by the masses of the people, and finally, the Tyranny, governed by a single tyrant.

How does this devolution take place? We start with the Aristocracy. Then the state becomes embroiled in war. At that time the leader or leaders who were responsible for winning the conflict are extolled in the public eye. They return from the battlefield and are borne on the shoulders of their admirers. The public in its enthusiasm elects them to the highest offices as the governors of the state. This has been true even in the history of the United States on several occasions—in the case of General Grant, for example. (The general public is still enamored of uniforms especially if worn by those who achieved victory.) These military leaders, who have not developed as rational a nature as the philosophers, enter on an orgy of spending. They finally become heavily indebted to the wealthy classes of the state. As is usual in the case of any indigent debtor, the creditor not only holds him in the hollow of his hand, but also loses all respect for him. So here, the wealthy creditors usurp the power of the military classes and become the governors of the state. This is the Oligarchy.

The propertied classes are much less rational than their predecessors in office; their interest is centered solely upon personal profit; all their legislation is directed to increase their possessions. They enact many laws for the taxation of the poor to fill their own coffers. Thus the state ultimately is divided into two classes: on the one hand, a few extremely wealthy; on the other, the overwhelming majority, poverty-stricken. The poor finally rise up, revolt and usurp the power of the public parasites. This is the Democracy, which occupies a very low position in the scale of states.

Democracy is short-lived, however; it hardly comes into actual being. The leader of the revolt tells his followers that since he led them out of their servile condition, he should have their confidence in leading and governing them. He then elects himself king or governor of the state; thus a Tyranny comes into existence. Tyranny is the most unjust state of all, due to the fact that it contains no harmony of any kind, and the tyrant rules purely for his selfish interest.

By analogy there are also five different types of individuals. The Aristocrat, or Philosopher, is the highest and most ideal. Next is the Timocrat, the military man. Next is the Oligarch, the propertied, the wealthy man. Next comes the Democrat, who is simply a member of the masses of the people, and finally there is the Tyrant, whose nature has already been described. Here, too, a devolution takes place in accordance with very logical principles. The philosopher is the starting point. His son beholds the glory and power heaped upon the soldier. His impressionable nature is so affected that he is led to consider how futile it is for him to follow in the footsteps of his revered father, possessing no property and enjoying none of the other good things in life; always grappling with knotty philosophic principles. Even if he succeeds in solving the most intricate problems, no one will shower glory upon him. (This is psychologically true, for in our day, a popular baseball player is far more acclaimed than a famous scientist, as far as the masses are concerned.) Therefore, he adopts a military career. His son may find that his father's life is constantly in danger; that is especially brought home to him if his father returns from the battlefield, maimed, minus a leg or an arm. Not for him such an end. He prefers to lead a placid life; he engages in a life of commerce; he is the oligarchical man. His son, who spends more money than is good for him, which makes him impatient at any obstacles or opposition, becomes what Plato conceives as the Democrat, a man living without rhyme or reason, a man who is guided by no rational principle, a man who is simply controlled by passion and desire. Lastly, the son of the Democrat brooks even less opposition than his father, and wants no obstacles at all in his way. This is essentially characteristic of the tyrannical nature.

Thus far, Plato has answered the primary questions of the Republic. He has defined both political and individual justice. But the opponents of Socrates, at the very beginning of the discussion, asserted that the unjust man is happier than the just; that he enjoys honor, glory, social position and all the other desirable things in life. They also emphasized the fact that justice is only a cloak to cover one's iniquities. Without hedging, Socrates faces this problem squarely. Who is happier, the just or the unjust individual? Here too, let us first consider the state, then the individual.

The Aristocracy, being the most just state, is contrasted with the Tyranny, the most unjust state. In the first, liberty and the happiness of its subjects are preserved. There is harmony and an equitable division of labor; it runs like a well-oiled machine. Clearly that is a happy condition for its constituents. In the Tyranny, by contrast, there are conflicts, there is no adequate division of labor, danger to life and limb is a constant threat. The tyrant proceeds on his way and leaves havoc and desolation in his wake. Happiness is an impossibility. This state is therefore the most unhappy of all.

By analogy, Plato considers the individual. On the one hand there is the Aristocrat, the Philosopher; as his counterpart we have the Tyrant. True enough, the Philosopher, the most just man, possesses nothing; no private property, not even a family. We should expect him to be a most unhappy person, but as a matter of fact he considers his lot happily and calmly. He worries about nothing; he goes placidly on his way doing the work set out before him, fulfilling his proper functions in life. That clearly, says Plato, is a most happy condition of existence. On the other hand, consider the Tyrant. He apparently has everything the world offers. He possesses property, honor, wealth, a host of friends. Everywhere he goes he is showered with honors and from all appearances is enjoying every bit of happiness that life can furnish. Yet when you look beneath the surface what do you discover? You conclude that the Tyrant is afraid to walk on the streets unescorted, that the Tyrant even fears that his food is poisoned. The Tyrant, having gained his power by deception, fears the loss of that power. He has no genuine friends except those for whose friendship he pays. He must always have a bodyguard and does not trust the citizens of his own state to serve as his protectors. He must import soldiers from another country for that purpose. To secure enough funds with which to pay them, he must rob his subjects; he must murder, he must go on murdering and robbing in order to cover up his previous robberies and murders. In this way he is not only threatened from without, but his conscience is constantly harassing him from within. He may aptly be described as an individual over whose head "the sword of Damocles hangs." Need any more be said about the wretched existence this Tyrant leads?

(To recapitulate: Plato's conception of Ethics is justice, or a just life. Such a life consists of the four cardinal virtues, wisdom, courage, temperance and justice. In short, it simply means a life of reason. All other things are subordinated to reason./ It is a very rigorous life that Plato advocates, it is a life in which pleasure has very little place, a life in which the lower elements are always subordinated to the higher; it is almost Stoical in character. Since the life of the individual is very closely interwoven with the life of the state, since life in the state is in fact the primary requisite for the development of the individual, what is true in the case of the individual in relation to justice is equally true in the case of the state. It has already been shown that the state, too, if just, will contain the four cardinal virtues that are so vital in our lives.

Fine Arts. There are one or two other matters which should be mentioned in Plato's philosophy—in the first place, Plato's conception of the fine arts. We have already seen that Plato considered art as the imitation of an imitation, and therefore it is to be treated with contempt. Plato also strenuously objects to the type of music which rouses the emotions. He would certainly take great exception to "jazz," which has been so popular for the past several years. He further objects to the type of play which deeply excites the passions. In his opinion what is most desirable and necessary is to develop an individual with an even temperament and a calm mind, placidly treading his way through life. In this he differs radically from his pupil and successor, Aristotle.

6. Doctrine of Immortality.

It is also worth while to mention Plato's conception of the immortality of the soul as it is treated in the Phaedo. There again Plato has a very fine dramatic setting in preparation for the discussion of this all-important subject. He represents Socrates sitting in his cell, calmly awaiting his death, and having a chat with a few of his friends. The obvious topic on the eve of his death is, What happens to the soul after the body is gone? Why do men consider suicide wrong, is the first query. Socrates answers, because everyone is a possession of the gods and it is their privilege to call us from this life when they so desire. Then again, Socrates points out that the philosopher is never unhappy in leaving this life. He craves to have his soul unfettered from its bodily chains in order that it may ascend to the heavens and observe beauty, truth and goodness in their nakedness. The question then is, How does one know that the soul will survive the body and will have the opportunity so to behold the Ideas? Is there immortality?

To support the argument for the immortality of the soul Plato adduces a number of reasons—in the first place, the principle of opposition. Opposites are always generated from each other, light from darkness, darkness from light, heat from cold, cold from heat, for instance. In the same way, death is generated from life, and it is impossible to write "Finis" at death, but we must say that life is generated from death again.

To confirm this argument, Plato introduces a second principle, the "doctrine of reminiscence." By this doctrine,
Plato shows that the soul remembers things it has seen in a
previous existence, otherwise, how account for the fact that
uninitiated and uneducated people answer correctly certain
questions, especially mathematical questions, which are put to
them? Since then the soul has had a previous existence, it is
not very difficult to conceive of it surviving long after our
bodies turn to clay. Furthermore, Plato says the soul is a
simple substance, indestructible, indivisible, therefore it is
not subject to the laws of matter and must be immortal.
Then again, the soul is the harmony of the body, the body may
die but the harmony remains. The soul, too, is the very
principle of life itself. How can the very principle of life
contain, or be subject to, death? Finally, the doctrine of
retribution gives support to the hypothesis that the soul cannot be mortal, for it must survive in order to be punished or
rewarded in after-life for the type of existence it has led in
this world. The doctrine of retribution as conceived by
Plato is extremely crude: the virtuous soul will ascend to
heaven, while the eternally damned will rot in hell forever.
Between these extremes, some sinners will be given an opportunity to ask their victims for forgiveness; if successful,
their purgatory period will end, otherwise, they will be
obliged to return for further punishment.

To this discussion of the immortality of the soul a great
many objections may be raised. In the first place, the idea
that the soul is a simple substance is untenable in fact; the
soul has been defined as a "plurality of psychical experiences
comprehended into a unity not further definable." Descartes
later adopted the Platonic conception of the soul and located
it in the brain. The soul does not appear, nor has it ever been
shown to be, a simple substance residing in a particular locus
in the body, or in the brain. Then again, the fact of retribution
seems to be entirely foreign to a man of Plato's character.
Retribution is the type of belief which may appropriately be
invoked by superstitious and crude religions, similar to the

conception of "happy hunting grounds" in heaven, so prevalent among primitive Indians, but it certainly ought not to
be incorporated in any argument used by Plato. He should
insist in accordance with his idealistic temperament that the
life of goodness be lived purely for its own sake, not because
of reward; a life of evil is bad in and for itself, not because
of the dread and fear of punishment in the hereafter.

Let us now say a parting word about Plato's theory of
knowledge. We have already seen that empirical knowledge
or knowledge acquired from the world of experience Plato
rejects as insignificant in our desire to learn about the Idea
of truth. This is pure rationalism, which means that there
is a non-empirical element in knowledge, whereas empiricism,
developed by the English philosophers, signifies that experience, and experience alone, furnishes all the materials
for knowledge. To prove that the soul has had a previous
experience of things, Plato depicts a scene in the Meno in
which a slave boy with no training faced by questions of philosophers and mathematicians is able to display a knowledge
of arithmetic and geometry. Plato teaches that experience
invokes what is already latent, that the world of experience
never proves the Idea but rather approximates it. Plato
goes one step further. He divides the knowledge of this
world and of the world of Ideas into two parts. The knowledge of this world is first guesswork, illusion, which is the
lowest type of knowledge imaginable. Then beyond that
there is belief, or opinion, which is a result of normal sense
perception. In the other and higher kind of knowledge,
Plato shows that there is first understanding, which needs
science and mathematics and demonstration in order to reach
and attain its goal. On the other hand, we have the dialetic
in which the mind grasps the Ideas independently of all
symbols. This is philosophy and it is the business of the mind
here to analyze all the notions of science and mathematics and
test their validity.

To return for a moment to Plato's metaphysics. We cannot emphasize too strongly the complete dissociation of the

Idea from the object of sense. The Idea does not divide itself up, imparting a particle of itself to each sense object that represents it; it is too lofty even to have the particular thing furnish an example of it. The most that can be said for the thing present before our eyes is that it is an approximation of the Idea. Plato, however, felt that nature exists and some explanation must be offered for it. This raises the question of creation, for a discussion of which we must study the Timaeus.

We have previously seen that God is represented there as an artificer who fashions the world out of matter. This matter is composed of the four elements, water, fire, air and earth, and the elements in turn are composed of number, not in the sense that we add all the objects of the universe to find how many things it embraces, but it is the substance of reality similar to the Heracleitan fire. The soul of the world Plato fantastically represents as being composed of two principles —the principle of regularity, of order, of harmony, which he calls the principle of *the same;* then the principle of irregularity, of discord, of disorder and confusion, which he calls the principle of *the other.* The combination of the two he calls *the essence.* That truly represents the world-soul, which antedates the world of matter. This essence God injects into the matter of the universe and in that way our world of nature is formed. Of this essence which formed the world-soul, Plato conceives God as fashioning the soul of the individual. Here again, Plato shows the relation, the close contact, between the soul of the individual and that of the world. The soul exists prior to the body, the ideal exists prior to the actual, the intelligible and unseen exists prior to the visible and corporeal.

In the Timaeus as in the Phaedrus, Plato develops the doctrine of the transmigration of the soul. The soul in a prior existence beholds visions of truth and goodness in their nakedness. But if the soul sins, it loses its wings and falls to the earth; it then takes the form of man. That soul which has seen most of the truth passes into a philosopher or lover, that which has seen truth in the second degree, into a warrior, the third into a householder or moneymaker, the fourth

into a gymnast, the fifth into a prophet, the sixth into a poet
or imitator, the seventh into a craftsman, the eighth into a
Sophist, and the ninth into a tyrant.   So man may also descend
into a beast and then return again into the form of man, but
the form of man can only be acquired at all by those who had
once beheld truth.   The soul of man alone apprehends the
universal, and this is the recollection of that knowledge which
the soul attained when she was in the company of the gods.
At the end of every thousand years, the soul has another
choice and may go upwards or downwards.   Only the soul of
the philosopher or lover who has three times in succession
chosen the better life, may receive wings and go her way after
three thousand years.   In the case of all other souls, ten
thousand years must elapse before the soul can wing her way
back where she once beheld divine visions of beauty, truth and
goodness.

Thus everything in the whole universe, everything that one
considers as an important thing in his experience, in life,
acquires such importance and such significance purely because
the world of Ideas is thereby aided in recollection.

In conclusion we may consider the chronological development of Plato's philosophy.   In his early days he dealt with
light ethical subjects, which interested his master, Socrates,
most.   We refer especially to the Protagoras in which the
doctrine "Virtue is Knowledge" is so exhaustively cultivated.
During his mature years, or in the middle period of his life,
he dealt with subjects of metaphysics, with his world of Ideas.
Reference is here made to the Republic and to the Phaedo.
In the Phaedo he points out that the soul is the only instrument
by which the human being can perceive the Ideas, because the
senses are suited only for empirical experiences, but cannot
possibly sense the essences, or the universal realities.   This
is another argument for the immortality of the soul, the point
being that only like can assimilate like, and since the Ideas
are eternal, indestructible, the soul which beholds them must
likewise be eternal or immortal.   Finally, in his last days,
he acted as any other elderly man would.   He turned his

attention to nature, to the gods, and to other matters per-
taining to this life.   The Timaeus is a product of this period.

7. *Conclusion.*

In accordance with the purpose of this inquiry the critical
and important question now arises: What, if anything, is there
in Plato's teaching which may contribute to the formulating
of a philosophy of our own?   Plato is an idealist, a rationalist,
a defender of the teleological character of the universe.   The
line of demarcation which he draws between the world of
Ideas and the world of sense seems to be entirely out of place
in the ordinary philosophy of one's daily life.   Furthermore,
his utter disregard for the world of sense in which every individual appears to find his life's ambition is again beyond
the comprehension of the common man.   The fact that
Plato denudes his life of justice of all pleasures, is another
consideration which makes it impracticable for the humdrum
existence most of us must of necessity lead.   In short, Plato's
philosophy is too lofty, too high up in the clouds, to warrant
its being adopted *in toto* by the ordinary individual.   Plato
offends in many other respects as far as practical philosophy
is concerned.   His insistence on the ideal, his utter disregard
for the facts of experience, his lack of sympathy for all those
who are below the class of philosophers—all of these elements
put his philosophy in a great many respects beyond our reach.
On the other hand, there are many elements in his doctrine
which are commendable.   His psychological insight into
human nature which prompts him to deny ownership of
property and even family ties to the philosopher so that he may
unselfishly govern the community deserves respect.   His
treatment of women is entitled to consideration, especially in
view of the fact that his contemporaries treated women, if not
with contempt, certainly with very little regard.   He insists
that women should have equal rights with men, they should
have the opportunity to become philosopher-queens, they
should also have the opportunity to serve in the military class.
He insists that the difference between men and women is one

of degree and not of kind.   His doctrine of common ownership of property found an echo later in all kinds of utopian
schemes of communism.   In short, many of his beliefs are
very refreshing and almost modern in character.   True
enough, his doctrine of creation, his theory of retribution, introduce a foreign note into his philosophy.   His conception
of God, almost like a human artist, even if crude, does offer an
explanation of the world of experience.   It shows the contrast
between God and matter, it also shows the reason for the existence of the world of sense in relation to the world of Ideas.
There is always the possibility, too, that all theories which
seem incongruous with the rest of his philosophy are not to be
taken too seriously, they may only represent Plato's sincere
desire to impress them in an effective manner upon his contemporaries.

In the final analysis one must concede that a life of justice
is preferable to one of injustice, that a life of reason is to be
preferred to that of emotion, that a life in which pleasure
does not predominate is to be preferred to one in which
pleasure appears to occupy the chief and central position.
True enough, Platonic philosophy is too idealistic for everyday, practical purposes but here one can use Plato's own
thoughts as an answer.   Plato refutes the objection that his
Aristocracy is too idealistic to achieve by stating that it is not
meant to be attained in practical life, it is only designed to
serve as a model for existing states to try to copy.   In the
same way, while Platonic philosophy is very idealistic and
apparently beyond the reach of anyone engaged in practical
affairs, it is a beautiful conception of a philosophic life which
everyone ought to attempt to imitate as perfectly as possible.

Plato's philosophy leaves us with a feeling that there are
certain incongruities inherent in it.   It leaves us with a sense of
dissatisfaction for many reasons, chiefly because of the light
manner with which Plato regards the world of empirical experience.   All of this Plato's successor, Aristotle, attempted to
cure; his philosophy, therefore, forms the subject of our next
inquiry.

CHAPTER IV

ARISTOTLE (385–322 B.C.)

1. *Life.*

ARISTOTLE was born in 385 B.C. at Stagirus, a little city of
the Chalcidic peninsula, called by its ancient name Chalcis,
and died at the age of 62 in Euboea. His pupil, Alexander
the Great, later overthrew the Persian Empire and carried
Greek civilization to the banks of the Jumna. In studying
the constitutional theories of Aristotle it is necessary to bear
these facts in mind. They explain the limitations of his
outlook, which might otherwise appear strange in so learned
a man. His life throws a great deal of light on his conviction of the natural inferiority of the barbarian both in
intellect and in character. "His apparent satisfaction with an
ideal of a small, self-contained city-state with a decently
oligarchical government, a good system of public education
and no social problems, but devoid alike of great traditions,
far-reaching ambitions," may also be traced to the fact that
he was born in such a tiny community without a past and
without a future. His father was the court physician and a
member of a family which claimed descent from Asclepius and
in which the practice of medicine was hereditary. It is not
unlikely that as a boy he helped his father in dissecting, and
it seems certain that he himself practiced dissection in later
life. This early connection with medicine and with the court
explains largely both the predominantly biological cast of
Aristotle's philosophical thought and the intense dislike of
princes and courts to which he more than once gives expression. Aristotle was a great biologist. He was much
more successful in his biology than in physics, chemistry and

astronomy, though not because he thought different methods were appropriate in biology from those applicable in the other sciences.   In both alike he meant to study the phenomena as carefully as possible and to put forward only such theories as he was able to prove.   But in the physical sciences much more than in biology, he was influenced by the existing beliefs, which it did not occur to him to doubt any more than it did to any of his contemporaries.   Aristotle loved to define, he loved to classify.   "He made the mistake of supposing that the main work of science lies in deducing conclusions from definitions, whereas the truth is that it is often only after a long study of the terms that we are able to make their meanings precise and clear, and even then we can deduce little or nothing from our definitions."   All of these influences can readily be traced through his entire philosophy.   Although one may not think very much of his success in solving all problems, few people have ever either described so many, or seen so clearly which are the most important.

2. *Classification of the Sciences.*

Philosophy may be defined in the Aristotelian sense as the organized whole of disinterested knowledge, knowledge which is carried on purely for the satisfaction that it brings in studying it and not as a mere means to useful or practical ends. True philosophy must be distinguished from sophistry in the fact that sophistry is the profession of argumentation for the purpose of making a living.   Philosophy also differs from sophistry in the fact that sophistry uses general wisdom for profit, whereas philosophy or science is the disinterested employment of the understanding in the discovery of truth for its own sake.   Logic in Aristotelian philosophy is not a separate science, it is only an instrument employed by all the sciences. Science or philosophy is classified into two branches: On the one hand, the theoretical sciences.   Under this class we have what Aristotle calls first philosophy or metaphysics, mathematics and physics.   On the practical side, he includes ethics, politics, economics.

Metaphysics deals with being *qua* being, the nature of existence. It is separated from matter and devoid of motion. We have already touched upon the problem of being in the philosophies of Heracleitus and Parmenides. Physics deals with objects which possess both matter and motion, while mathematics deals with objects which have matter but no motion.

3. *Logic.*

In Aristotelian logic one is particularly interested in the syllogism or inference, which he discusses very exhaustively. Inference had been employed constantly by Socrates in his famous arguments. Aristotle defines the syllogism thus: "Syllogism is a discussion wherein certain things, namely the premises, being admitted, something else different from what has been admitted follows of necessity, because the admissions are what they are." A more concrete illustration of the syllogism he gives in the following manner:

Major Premise: All men are animals.
Minor Premise: Socrates is a man.
Conclusion: Therefore, Socrates is an animal.

The syllogistic method, as will be shown later in the discussion of his theory of knowledge, is not always scientific, because the conclusion is by no means certain from the premises given. Consider this syllogism:

Major Premise: All animals that have no gall are long-
lived.
Minor Premise: X, Y, and Z have no gall.
Conclusion: Therefore, X, Y, and Z are long-lived
animals.

We cannot show why no gall gives long life.

Induction, another term discussed by Aristotle in his philosophy, is defined as "The way of proceeding from particular facts to universals." Aristotle insists that the conclusion, the universal law, is proved only if all the particulars have been examined and found to be true. A single contrary instance, for example, a single instance of an animal which has no gall, yet is not long-lived, would upset the entire conclusion, as exemplified in the last illustration. Aristotle does not regard induction as scientific proof at all, because it is actually impossible to test all the particular instances. This brief discussion demonstrates that logic is not a specific science, but only an instrument employed by the sciences in the search for truth. The particularly interesting point about Aristotelian logic, however, is his "theory of knowledge."

Aristotle starts his theory of knowledge by scoffing at Plato's conception of Ideas. To him the Ideas explain nothing, they are useless. He calls them poetic fancies. Plato, as we no doubt remember from our earlier discussion, considers science or knowledge exact, like mathematics, and no sense data enter into it. Sense objects only remind us of the Idea by giving, not examples, but approximations. The Ideas are conceptual and not mere conclusions of sense experience. Due to the fact that Aristotle rejects this Platonic conception of knowledge, we would expect that he will formulate a theory in which sense data will play a very significant rôle. But that is not the case. Aristotle says that scientific knowledge consists of (1) the simplest truths not possible to demonstrate in any form, axiomatic, which can be observed only by the intelligence. (3) the more comprehensive truths, the more general conclusions. The most important part of scientific knowledge, however, is (2) the middle term. The middle term is the real object of science to show the why of things, and is the connecting link between the axiomatic truths and the rest of knowledge, or between (1) and (3). Thus, Aristotle also concludes that sense data do not enter into the simple truths of science, because they cannot possibly be observed by sense experience; such experience, according to him, only reminds us of these simple truths. Therefore, he differs in no material way from his teacher, Plato. Both conclude that scientific knowledge ultimately contains a non-empirical element, contributed by the mind. Plato, however, is more courageous in stating at the outset that scientific truth is above sense experience. In the light of this discussion, one can readily see why the previous example of a syllogism in which we concluded that "all animals that have no gall are long-lived" does not yield scientific knowledge, because science must inquire why or how no gall gives long life.

Suppose, asks Aristotle, one questions the simplest or so-called axiomatic truths which are so important an element in scientific knowledge, suppose one denies these simple truths or is skeptical of their validity, what then? How can we silence such an objector, since an axiomatic premise by its very definition cannot be demonstrated to be valid? All that can be done under the circumstances is to allow him to adopt his premise, to follow it through to the ultimate conclusions and thus become convinced of his error. This is where dialetic serves its proper function. Its chief use is to show to him who does not adopt the simplest truths of science, the result, if you adopt his principles. It is not possible to prove that 2 and 2 make four, but you can show the absurd conclusion reached if you call it five.

4. *Metaphysics.*

Matter and Form. Let us now turn to Aristotle's metaphysics or first philosophy. Here again, Aristotle starts by rejecting the notion of Plato as to the metaphysical constitution of the universe. We remember that Plato divided the world into two separate realms, one the world of Ideas, of essences, of realities, and the other the world of sense. The Idea was entirely separated from the particular object of sense which represented it or modeled after it. The Idea was considered form, the particular object matter, by Plato. Hence Plato's conclusion was that matter and form are absolutely distinct and separated from each other. Aristotle, rejecting this conception, formulates one as follows: he says that matter and form are never separated from each other, that there can be no pure form without matter, nor matter without form. In short, the form is always embedded in the matter of the particular object which represents it. This table consists of its matter, wood, and the form of table, which it expresses. We must not consider at this point that Aristotle denies the actual, valid existence of form. The only difference between him and Plato is that whereas Plato separates the Idea entirely from matter, or form from the particular object, Aristotle believes that although the form furnishes the essence to the matter, at the same time it cannot exist without it. Thus Aristotle rejects the Platonic idea of two worlds and insists that there is only one realm of existence, the world of empirical experience, this world of nature. True enough, this world embodies the Platonic world of Ideas, but there is no other distinct idealistic region of reality.

Aristotle is not satisfied, however, with the initial statement that matter and form co-exist in every object in the universe. He goes further. He says that every object has two forms, one the potential form, the other the actual form. The potential form always strives to be actualized. The moment it reaches the actualized form, it again acquires a potential form for something that may become even more actual in the future. In this way the entire universe is in a process of development in which each potential form attempts to realize itself, and the goal of it all is God, who is the only exception to this scheme of things, because God alone is pure form. To illustrate, the child possesses two forms, one is the actual form of child, already realized in its life, and the other is the potential form of the adult, which the child strives to realize in the future. The reason why all this evolutionary striving goes on is because all natural things want to become purified and approach as closely as possible their ideal, God, pure form.

Four Causes. Aristotle finally proceeds to explain his notion of the four causes. He says that every object in the world is a result of four contributing elements. In the first place, there is the matter out of which the object is fashioned. This is known as the material cause. Then again, the matter must be fashioned after a certain form. That is the formal cause. Thirdly, there must be motion or energy of some kind employed in order to produce the object.   That is known as the efficient cause.   Fourthly and lastly, there must be a purpose or an end in view which the particular object is meant to serve.   That furnishes the final cause.   The efficient cause in turn may be a result of human intelligence, consciously applying energy to produce the object; it may be a result of a force of nature, or it may be a matter of chance.   The Aristotelian conception of a final cause permeating the world gives his entire philosophy an extremely teleological character. In this he is entirely in accord with Plato.

God.   It will be recalled at this point that the Aristotelian notion of potential and actual form explained the progressive development of the entire universe and its striving to actualize and realize its potentialities.   Whither is the universe striving?   What is its goal?   What is the final purpose of the entire evolutionary process?   Before answering these questions we must understand that all the development, all the realization of actual forms, is supplied by the efficient cause, or, in the last analysis, by motion.   Therefore these queries may be answered by identifying the source of the motion of the universe.   Who, then, supplies this energy? The answer given by Aristotle is God.   God is pure form, God is the ideal towards which the whole world is moving, God actuates the universe to strive for fulfillment and realization.   Thus it can be seen that the notion of God occupies a very important position in Aristotelian metaphysics.   What is the nature of this God?   What is the conception which one can form of this Aristotelian theory of a divine being who draws the whole world to himself?   He is a God who is distinct and separated from the world of nature.   He is called the "Unmoved Mover" by Aristotle.   While God himself does not move, while he leads a life of contemplation, a life of leisure, the whole world nevertheless is set in motion by him. A concrete illustration of this conception of God is that of a magnet; the magnet attracts other objects to it while it itself is stationary.   The idea of God as the "Unmoved Mover" but nevertheless causing the entire world to be stirred up to activity, directs our attention to a study of that Aristotelian science which is exclusively occupied with matter and motion —Aristotelian physics.

5. *Physics.*

Here it is not very important to dwell upon his distinction between perfect and imperfect motion. He believes that circular motion is perfect because it is the type of energy imparted to those heavenly spheres which are nearest to God, and linear motion is imperfect because it is farther away from God's direct influence. Furthermore, his discussion of the heart as being the common sense, namely the sense to which all the emotions, all the sensations from the various sensory nerves, are directed, as a result of which we find a unity of perception in the midst of the apparent diversity, may also be passed by without further consideration. The chief emphasis that one should place upon Aristotelian physics, however, is upon his conception of the composition of the soul. The soul, he says, consists of three parts: reason, sensation and vegetation. Reason occupies the same eminent position as in Platonic philosophy. Sensation is that element of the soul which senses, which feels, which has emotions. Finally, vegetation is similar to what Plato calls the appetites, the lowest element in the soul, which requires the greatest attention for moderation and limitation. This psychological conception of the soul is very necessary for us to digest in order to understand thoroughly the essence of Aristotelian ethics.

6. *Ethics.*

In Aristotle, as in Plato, politics is an integral part of ethics and the two must be treated together. Man, being a social animal, cannot possibly develop except in a state. Aristotelian ethics differs from Plato's in the fact that it is much more practical and much more applicable to one's daily life. What is the goal of human life? asks Aristotle. The short answer is happiness. What then is happiness? Here Aristotle especially emphasizes the fact that happiness is not to be

identified with honor, pleasure, social position, wealth, because happiness must be an end in itself and not a means to
an end, whereas all of these are simply a means to an end.
The question of happiness resolves itself into the question,
What is the end or goal of life?

As we have seen in the discussion of Aristotle's metaphysics,
every object has a final cause, a purpose which it must serve.
Its value is then judged in relation to the manner in which it
serves this purpose. For example, if a knife is used for
cutting, if it fulfills the purpose well, if it cuts well, it is a
good knife; otherwise, it is an imperfect instrument. In
the same way, in order to discover what is the true end of
human life one must find what is the peculiar purpose which
human life must fulfill in the world of nature. In order to
understand this, one must again have recourse to an analysis
of the composition of the human soul. In Aristotle's physics
we have seen that the soul consists of three parts. Aristotle
here attempts to show that there is only one part of the soul,
which is peculiarly human, and that is the rational element.
He says, as far as vegetation is concerned, plants and other
animals possess it in common with us. Therefore it cannot
possibly be a characteristic of human nature as such. On the
other hand, sensation, too, humans and other lower animals
possess alike. This cannot then possibly be the chief distinction between human and other animals. But the rational
element of the soul, we can boast as our exclusive property.
Hence, that element is the real distinguishing feature which
marks the line of demarcation between the human organism
and lower forms of life. Such being the case, the first
solution of the problem of happiness is to lead a life of reason,
for such a life fulfills the peculiar function of human striving;
it is the end or purpose of human desire.

Thus far it appears that Aristotle's ethics is similar to
the moral theory of Plato. But as we examine it further we
find that there is a vast difference between these two philosophies of life. Aristotle realizes that merely to advocate a
life of reason is too abstract, resulting in very little good to the

ordinary human being. To help us achieve this goal, he analyzes this life into goodness of intellect and goodness of character.

Goodness of intellect, in turn, is divided into theoretical wisdom and practical wisdom. Theoretical wisdom apprehends the eternal laws of the universe. There is no direct relation in this knowledge to human conduct. Practical wisdom, on the other hand, is identical with the science of human life; it supplies the right rules of conduct. Goodness of character is the application of these moral principles to one's daily life. It is clearly seen that goodness of intellect is acquired by study, while goodness of character can be developed only by discipline.

But how can one as a practical matter acquire a good character? It is relatively easy to study and learn moral precepts, but the crux of ethics is their application to life. Aristotle faces this problem squarely. He says character, either good or bad, is produced by habituation. It is a result of the repeated performing of acts which have a similar or common quality. This process is naturally one of assimilation, largely imitation by the child of the acts of the adults around him. The result is the development of habits in the individual. But these habitual acts do not acquire moral significance until such time as the agent voluntarily and of his own free choice performs them, until he can act rationally.

Doctrine of the Mean. How are we to know what is an act of reason? After all, life is very complex and it is impossible when confronted with many situations, to waste too much time solving this problem of rationality in each case. This would render us slow and ineffective in life. For this purpose, Aristotle supplies us with a very forceful weapon, the "Doctrine of the mean." As a general rule, he says, the right act is the one which conforms to reason. As a practical matter one knows that he is acting in accordance with reason, when he acts in accordance with the mean. Whatever situation confronts us, there are two extremes, which we must avoid, else we shall be acting irrationally. On the other hand, if we select the middle course, then we are surely on the right track. This doctrine of the mean is illustrated in many ways: consider courage. In a situation of danger one extreme is to run away from it unthinkingly. That is cowardice. On the other hand, one may rush boldly into it, disregarding all the vital circumstances. That is foolhardiness. But a rational man, a man who acts in accordance with virtue, a man who acts in accordance with reason, or the mean, is one who stops and considers the consequences that may follow either in avoiding the danger or in facing it boldly. That is true courage. The same reasoning may be applied in the case of the expenditure of money. The extremes here are prodigality and stinginess; the latter invariably applies to those who are over-careful about wealth, while the former relates to those who uncontrollably spend for the gratification of their passions. The mean here, however, is liberality; the liberal man knows "right giving"; he gives from a motive of honor, in accordance with rational principles. Aristotle particularly stresses the characteristics of the Great-minded man, who stands between the Small-minded and the vain man. It has often been remarked that in describing him, Aristotle really is referring to himself. What then, are his outstanding qualities? "Well then, he is thought to be Great-minded who values himself highly and at the same time justly. . . . The Great-minded man is then, as far as greatness is concerned, at the summit, but in respect of propriety he is in the mean, because he estimates himself at his real value. . . . So the Great-minded man bears himself as he ought in respect of honor and dishonor. . . . It seems too that pieces of good fortune contribute to form this character of Great-mindedness; I mean, the nobly born, or men of influence, or the wealthy, are considered to be entitled to honor . . . He is not a man to incur little risks, nor does he court danger, because there are but few things he has a value for; but he will incur great dangers, and when he does venture he is prodigal of his life as knowing that there are terms on which it is not worth his while to live. He is the sort of man

to do kindnesses, but he is ashamed to receive them. . . .
Neither is his admiration easily excited, because nothing is
great in his eyes; . . . nor does he talk of other men. . . .
Also slow motion, deep-toned voice, and deliberate style of
speech, are thought to be characteristic of the Great-minded
man." [1]

Aristotle concludes that every mean is a virtue because it
is an act of reason; hence, suitable to the nature of the human
being.   Such "means" are states of mind of the agent, not
passions or emotions.   It follows that the agent or actor is
responsible for all voluntary acts in his daily life; only two
factors may possibly do away with moral blame, coercion and
ignorance of relevant circumstances, which render the act
involuntary and exempt the doer from responsibility.

To return then to the original question: What is happiness?
Happiness consists in living a life of reason, in acting in accordance with the mean; in short, it is an activity involving
the most excellent part of human nature.   This type of
happiness can be attained by everybody.   It does not depend
upon any external circumstances.   It is not based on wealth,
leisure or on any other factor which is not within the reach of
all humans.   But Aristotle reserves the highest part of happiness for only a select few.   That type of happiness consists
of a life of contemplation, a life of contemplation similar to
that led by God.   This life in which the subject is absorbed
in theoretical study, not for practical gain, necessarily involves a great deal of leisure.   For that, external possessions
become vital and only the few who are so favored by fortune
can enjoy it.

To achieve both or either of these kinds of happiness,
Aristotle points out that life in a state is the primary requisite.
This leads him to evolve a theory of politics.

7. *Politics.*

Aristotle points out three stages in the development of the
state.   First comes the family, then the village community,

---

[1] "The Nicomachean Ethics of Aristotle," Book IV. (Translation by D.
P. Chase).

then the state. He shows that "out of the relation between men and women . . . the first thing to arise is the family." The family is an association established by nature for the supply of man's everyday wants, and the members of it are called "companions of the cupboard" or "companions of the manger." But when several families are united and the association aims at something more than the supply of daily needs the next type to be formed is the village. When several villages are united into a complete community, large enough to be nearly quite self-sufficing, the state comes into existence and continues for the sake of a good life.

The state is a creation of nature, and man is by nature a political animal. The state is prior to the family and to the individual, as the whole is prior to the parts. Aristotle adduces as proof of this contention the fact that the individual, when isolated, is not self-sufficing. Therefore, he is like a part in relation to the whole. Aristotle differs from Plato in regard to communism. Plato advocated the common ownership of property; Aristotle is firmly against it. He says the beginning of reform is not so much to equalize property as to train the nobler soul not to desire more, to prevent the lower soul from getting more. He must be kept down but not ill treated. He also differs from Plato in reference to slavery. Plato eliminated all forms of slavery in his ideal state, while Aristotle believes that slavery is a natural condition in a state, and especially in one which supplies the wherewithal for leading a leisurely life, which cultivates a class who want to lead a life of contemplation. We must in all fairness to Aristotle state that the slavery he advocates is not the barbarous type which was prevalent in parts of the South, but very humane and considerate; the slaves were really to occupy the position of menial servants.

To return then to the relation between the state and the ethical development of the individual. The best form of state must be one which not only provides for the existence of a leisure class, but it must also make possible all the conditions necessary for leading a good, just and noble life for all its citizens. The conclusion, therefore, is evident.

Those governments which have regard for these common interests function in accordance with strict principles of justice and represent true forms, but those which regard only the interests of the rulers are defective, they are despotic. The genuine state is a "community of freemen."

The most ideal state is the monarchy; next is the aristocracy, and then comes the constitutional government. The counterpart of each of these in the perverted forms of government are: of monarchy, tyranny; of aristocracy, oligarchy; of constitutional government, democracy. That form of government in which one rules is known as a kingship, royalty, or monarchy.   That in which more than one, but not many, rule, aristocracy, so called because the rulers have at heart the best interests of the state and of the citizens.   When the citizens at large administer the state for the common interest, it is called then a constitutional government.   As a practical man, Aristotle realizes that it is very difficult to find one man who so excels all his fellow citizens in justice and virtue to whom we may with impunity entrust the reins of power; he also realizes that it is equally rare to find several such individuals of excellent character.   He therefore suggests as a compromise that the best kind of state for practical purposes, is the constitutional government, in which the majority of the people control.   In this, again, Aristotle simply selects the mean between two extremes.   In every state there are three elements to be considered.   One class is very wealthy, another very poor and a third is a mean between the two.   The mean is represented by the constitutional government.   In such a state the middle class, which is the governing class, is least likely to shrink from rule or to be over-ambitious for it, both of which are injurious to the state.   The majority also are less likely to commit fatal blunders.

Since the state is a community of families for the purpose of a self-sufficing life, it can only be established among those who live in the same place and intermarry, continues Aristotle. This is the principal reason why he advocates a so-called city-state, having approximately a population of 100,000. All education in the state must be under public control, it must be universal and compulsory. That is necessary in order that the community may instruct future citizens in a way which will make them most loyal to the end the state is designed to further. To be sure, it is necessary that some useful subjects be taught, reading and writing for example, but he emphasizes especially the fact that the state must aim to provide a liberal education, because so-called mechanical subjects make one a slave in body and soul, and not a "free man." Those who insist that a university education ought not to include specialization in purely professional subjects are really in accord with this theory of Aristotle.

8. Fine Arts.

Aristotle agrees with Plato that music is one of the ways in which character is moulded, that all art has a direct influence upon character. There is a vast difference, however, between the two theories. Plato, in the Republic, proposed to exclude unduly exciting forms of music from life altogether because they had a tendency to foster a morbid character in those who enjoyed them. Plato for a similar reason wanted to suppress certain types of drama which may have a like influence on character. Aristotle, on the other hand, feels that exciting or sensational art may be very useful as an outlet for one's pent-up energies. He believes that even the most sensational and the most exciting of arts, tragedy, for example, has a purgative value. "We assume," he says, "that, for the finest form of Tragedy, the Plot must be not simple but complex; and further, that it must imitate actions arousing fear and pity, since that is the distinctive function of this kind of imitation. It follows, therefore, that there are three forms of Plot to be avoided. (1) A good man must not be seen passing from happiness to misery, or (2) a bad man from misery to happiness. The first situation is not fear-inspiring or piteous, but simply odious to us. The second is the most untragic that can be; it has no one of the requisites of Tragedy; it does not appeal either to the human feeling in us, or to our pity, or to our fears. Nor, on the other hand, should (3) an extremely bad man be seen falling from happiness into misery. Such a story may arouse the human feeling in us, but it will not move us to either pity or fear; pity is occasioned by undeserved misfortune, and fear by that of one like ourselves; so that there will be nothing either piteous or fear-inspiring in the situation.   There remains, then, the intermediate kind of personage, a man not preëminently virtuous and just, whose misfortune, however, is brought upon him not by vice and depravity but by some error of judgment."   We can thus see that the type of plot which appealed to him most was one in which melodramatic horror predominated.

Whatever one may think of Aristotle's treatment of the fine arts, there is absolutely no doubt that his treatment of this subject is by no means as profound as that of the theoretical sciences, especially metaphysics and physics.

9. *Conclusion.*

To sum up then: Aristotle's state is an organic necessity for the development of the ethical individual; just as the bee cannot exist but in a social environment, so the human must express his social instinct in gregarious life. This is the biological theory of the origin of the state as contrasted with the contract conception of Spinoza, Locke, Hobbes and Rousseau. From this standpoint, the purpose of the Aristotelian state becomes very clear indeed.   It is the condition for the development of the "best life" of its members—such a life must of necessity give happiness.   True enough, the average citizen can only enjoy the lesser happiness—a life of rational behavior. The extremely happy life is reserved for a select few, who are blessed with the material goods of fortune.   The ideal state will necessarily provide for both of these requirements.   In short, Aristotle clearly conceives of the social organization as one which furnishes the opportunity for every worthy member to lead a well-ordered existence.   For example, a good citizen must be one who, if he undertakes to serve the government, will not be subject to bribery; he will not be deterred by promises of reward from sponsoring the right kind of legislation. Aristotle would not condemn such a person if he misbehaves in some other respect; if, for instance, he is somewhat intemperate, as long as he fulfills the main purpose of his existence well. That is a life of reason. Although it is not to be identified with pleasure, yet, the mere fact that one does subordinate his less admirable traits to the rational part of his make-up, which differentiates him from the beast, will in the long run yield the greatest enjoyment. In this respect, pleasure becomes a very necessary element in the "good life."

Comparison with Plato. No account of Aristotelian philosophy can be complete unless it is supplemented by some comparison with that of Plato. Both deal with a variety of subjects, materialism, ethics, politics, logic, psychology, God, nature. Both are rationalistic, admitting of a non-empirical element in knowledge; both are idealistic, both are teleological, believing as an integral part of their constructive systems of philosophy that the world exhibits a purpose. Both introduce a new note into the Greek conception of religion, politics, ethics and art, as will be seen later. There are vast differences, however, in their philosophies.

Metaphysics. Plato's conception of two worlds distinct and separate is very difficult to digest. Why should one renounce that realm of existence in which all his interests are centered, in which all that is worth while may be developed and cultivated, in favor of a world of ideals? True enough, ideals are very essential, they introduce a certain zest in practical life, a life spent moulding one's daily existence in accordance with the demands of one's ideals, but once such contrast between ideal and actual is admittedly removed by discarding the world of nature, the ideal becomes meaningless. The practical difficulty also remains. Why the need for such a world of experience since its existence simply confuses and blinds one to the essential reality behind it? Plato's attempted explanation that love wants to express itself is not convincing. Could not love find a better means of self-realization than such a distorted world of nature? Is it not

more practical and more in accordance with the facts to believe with Aristotle that there is only this world before us?
Is it not a more fitting and proper task for the human being
with his intellect and his general superiority over other creatures of existence to face boldly the facts before him, in spite
of their apparent confusion, than to run away from them in
the Platonic sense?   Of course it is more agreeable to turn
away from unpleasantness than to be obliged to introduce some
harmony in the confusion all around us.   But certainly, who-
ever succeeds in this task, and in addition derives pleasure out
of doing it, deserves our heartiest commendation.   There is
no doubt, therefore, that Aristotle's metaphysics is more
practical, more in accordance with the needs of ordinary
humans, than that of Plato.   Plato's other-worldliness may
be proper for mystics, but it is not conducive to the bringing
forth of heroes, reformers and others who make the world
progress.

God.   What is Plato's genuine belief about God?   Some
feel that the Idea of the Good is what Plato means by God—
an impersonal principle permeating the world, explaining
the purpose, the good and the significance it embodies.   If
this is Plato's real belief, for practical or religious purposes
it has little significance.   Even if the personal God represented in the Timaeus is the true Platonic conception, again
it is not a very imposing doctrine.   God is too crude, too helpless, too much at war with matter, too much the artificer, to
be a great influence in the ordinary man's thoughts and acts.
It is true that William James has a somewhat similar theory
of God, but then James' other statements concerning God in
particular and religious and ethical doctrines in general are
open to some question, refreshing as they may be to read.
Aristotle, on the other hand, furnishes the kind of God more
in accordance with our needs.   Admittedly, he does not
clothe his Lord of the world with religious habiliments, yet
He is a personal Being distinct from the world, He leads a life
of contemplation, He sets the whole world in motion. He is
the acme of perfection, pure form.   Needless to state,

Aristotle's God is not the last word as to what He should really represent, but it is a step in the right direction.

Soul. Both have a similar conception as to the constitution of the human soul—to both it consists of three parts, with reason uppermost. They differ in the belief of immortality. To Plato, immortality is the *sine qua non*—the indispensable condition for his world of Ideas, for only through the Soul can we behold the Idea; that requires that it be constituted of the same eternal stuff as the universals. Aristotle, on the other hand, divides the rational part of the soul into passive and active intelligence; the passive is a recipient of experiences in the world, it shares the same fate as the other and lower elements of the soul; only the active intelligence is eternal. That is the element of the mind which leads the life of contemplation, similar to that of God. The soul as a whole is the form of the body, and since matter and form must always exist together, once the body or its matter is gone the soul also perishes.

Logic. Although Aristotle initiates his theory of knowledge by scoffing at Plato's conception, yet, as we have already seen, both really assert that the world of experience cannot, and does not, contribute materially to the real theory of knowledge. Plato says sensation merely reminds us of that which the soul has experienced in a previous existence; Aristotle, that it does not enter into the simplest truths of scientific knowledge, which are axiomatic in character. Of course Plato's theory of preëxistence seems fantastic, but it serves to explain the basic principles of science by calling them innate or latent, as well as if you call them axioms, in the Aristotelian sense.

Ethics. Both cannot emphasize too strongly the rational life as the best and happy life. Both do not identify this with pleasure, with honor, with wealth, with social position and the like, because it would be entirely too undignified and inappropriate to human existence. On the other hand, Plato eliminates almost all pleasures, except such as satisfy the essential requirements of the body, from his life of reason;

Aristotle, having regard for the practical life of the individual, allows for the inclusion of a great many pleasures with which one can ordinarily dispense.   Plato admits that the life of the philosopher is the happiest of all; Aristotle also proposes a life of contemplation as the highest ideal.   Here again, Plato's philosopher needs no external goods, no property, no family, in fact such a sacrifice of all earthly possessions is the very essence of his happy life; Aristotle, the practical philosopher, clearly demonstrates that you cannot lead a life of contemplation, a life devoted not to gain but to theoretical study, unless you already have the wherewithal for the maintenance of the body.   This is by far the more practical philosophy.   Aristotle's conception that such a life, or as he terms it, such an activity in accordance with the most excellent part of the human soul, yields the greatest of pleasures is psychologically true, since what can be more satisfying than to carry on in a way which appeals to us most?   Finally, there are similarities and differences in their politics.

Politics.   Both urge the need for social life as the indispensable condition for the ethical development of the individual.   Both, therefore, base the formation of the state on biological grounds; or on the fact that the social instinct in the individual is the groundwork of the social organization so essential for its development.   Plato's ideal is the Aristocracy, a government of philosophers, unselfishly devoting themselves to the public good; no slavery, equality of women, community of women and children and other utopian schemes are included.   Then of course there are other states in the course of the devolution of the political unit.   Plato is not very much interested in the practical achievement of this state.   It simply is to serve as a model for practical political units to imitate.   Thus we see that even in politics, which is the acme of practical considerations, Plato discards the actual for the ideal, all in conformity with his temperament.   Aristotle here especially has his feet firmly planted on the ground.   To be sure, he demands that the state serve the common interest and not that of the individual.   Then again, he believes that the ideal state is a Monarchy,—one good king governing unselfishly—similar to the world of nature which is governed by a God. He also realizes that half a loaf is better than none, hence if there are several good men who can serve the state, or an Aristocracy, it would also be ideal, but this Aristocracy is far different from that of Plato; it must exist for the purpose of enabling a few to lead a life of contemplation; it excludes communism of property, equality of women, and the like, because it must conform to a pattern which may become a practical accomplishment. But Aristotle goes even one step further. Realizing that it is very difficult to find a few good rulers, he says that the constitutional government, a government by the middle class, is best under ordinary circumstances, because there is "safety in numbers." Of course Plato's theory encounters fewer practical difficulties, because it is remote from life, it is high up in the clouds—you are not obliged to solve many knotty problems of legislation which confront the legislators, and which confound the citizen by their variety and complexity. Plato points out that his philosophers would be obliged to pass only on the most important issues, which are few in number, but in the Aristotelian state, we encounter many of the questions of the modern political unit, How much taxation, how far shall we allow inequality to be carried, to whom shall we give the right to vote, who are to be citizens, and many other such difficulties. But is this a fatal objection? Far better to try to solve these problems than to avoid them. It is certainly more in conformity with our rational natures, and with the adventurous spirit which moves every red-blooded man, to encounter obstacles and overcome them. All in all, Aristotelian philosophy is more practical for the needs of the individual in his daily life, from every angle—metaphysics, ethics, logic, psychology, politics and God.

CHAPTER V

RELATION OF PLATO AND ARISTOTLE TO CONTEMPORARY GREEK THOUGHT

1. *Religion.*

BEFORE proceeding to the last part of Ancient philosophy, the Post-Aristotelians, it will be well to explain the reference made previously to the fact that Plato and Aristotle, especially Plato, introduced a new note into Greek thought. What were the Greek conceptions of religion, the state, the individual and art? What, if any, changes were suggested by the last two famous philosophers?

To get a picture of the background of Greek religion let us turn to the analysis which the historian, Henry Thomas Buckle, makes of the influences of the physical environment on religious faith. Contrasting the types of religions which prevailed in India and in Greece he says:

The works of nature, which in India are of startling magnitude, are in Greece far smaller, feebler, and in every way less threatening to man. In the great centre of Asiatic civilization, the energies of the human race are confined, and as it were intimidated, by the surrounding phenomena. Besides the dangers incidental to tropical climates, there are those noble mountains which seem to touch the sky, and from whose sides are discharged mighty rivers which no art can divert from their course, and which no bridge has ever been able to span. There, too, are impassable forests, whole countries lined with interminable jungle, and beyond them, again, dreary and boundless deserts,—all teaching Man his own feebleness, and his inability to cope with natural forces. . . .

But in Greece, the Aspects of Nature are so entirely different, that the very conditions of existence are changed. . . . While in the Asiatic country everything is great and terrible, in the European country everything is small and feeble. . . . Dangers of all kinds were far less numerous than in the tropical civilizations. The climate was more healthy; earthquakes were less frequent; hurricanes were less disastrous; wild beasts and noxious animals less abundant. . . . The highest mountains in Greece are less than one-third of the Himalaya, so that nowhere do they reach the limit of perpetual snow. . . .

. . . The tendency of the surrounding phenomena was, in India, to inspire fear; in Greece to give confidence. In India Man was intimidated; in Greece he was encouraged. In India obstacles of every sort were so numerous, so alarming, and apparently so inexplicable, that the difficulties of life could only be solved by constantly appealing to the direct agency of supernatural causes. . . . In Greece opposite circumstances were followed by opposite results. In Greece Nature was less dangerous, less intrusive, and less mysterious than in India. In Greece, therefore, the human mind was less appalled, and less superstitious; natural causes began to be studied; physical science first became possible. . . .

. . . The mythology of India, . . . is based upon terror. . . .

. . . In Greece, the causes of fear being less abundant, the expression of terror was less common. . . . The tendency of Asiatic civilization was to widen the distance between men and their deities; the tendency of Greek civilization was to diminish it. . . . The gods of Greece were always represented in forms entirely human. In that country, no artist would have gained attention, if he had presumed to portray them in any other shape. He might make them stronger than men, he might make them more beautiful; but still they must be men. . . .

. . . The Greek gods had not only human forms, but also human attributes, human pursuits, and human tastes. . . . The Greeks generalized their observations upon the human mind, and then applied them to the gods. The coldness of women was figured in Diana; their beauty and sensuality in Venus; their pride in Juno; their accomplishments in Minerva. . . . Neptune was a sailor; Vulcan was a smith; Apollo was sometimes a fiddler, sometimes a poet, sometimes a keeper of oxen. . . .

. . . In Greece we for the first time meet with hero worship, that is, the deification of mortals. . . .

. . . It is thus, that in Greece everything tended to exalt the dignity of man, while in India everything tended to depress it.[1]

[1] "History of Civilization in England," by Henry Thomas Buckle, Chapter II.

This quotation shows that the Greeks felt very much at home in the world of nature. Because they felt so little dread of the natural forces they established friendly relations with the gods by personifying them. They entertained no doubts that sacrifices and atonements would placate them and evoke their coöperation. As a result of the same influence, they attributed human emotions to the gods. The gods waged battle, they loved and hated, they were jealous; in fact, they were pictured as being actuated by all the admirable as well as undesirable motives of the human. Furthermore, the gods and descendants of the gods were the founders of the state, which shows the close relation between the political and the religious.

What does this discussion of religion show? It proves that the lofty, idealistic character of religion, in our sense of the word, is absent from that of the Greeks; it shows further that once you humanize and personify God, once you attribute to Him that which you yourself possess, although on a magnified scale, once you do not dissociate God from yourself so that you may look up to Him, with the desire to purify your own life, what is the need of conceiving of a God altogether? To justify the lust of war, for example, because Mars sanctions it, is far from expressing adequately the proper function of religion. Religion should be the embodiment of the permanent ideals of life, a criterion by which we should measure what we ought to retain and what we ought to reform. Certainly that need is by no means satisfied by Greek religion. Then again, this religion undermined morality. How can one be condemned for any base passion, since the gods command him to exercise it? Immortality, too, was not especially emphasized. They did believe in some kind of afterlife,—shadowy forms ruled over by Pluto, but religion demands a more substantial soul, so that it may serve as a basis for the doctrine of retribution. Real immortality is also a prerequisite for the theory of redemption. How then did Plato attempt to change this? First of all Plato wanted monotheism—one God who dictates for all the world—a permanent ideal working only to realize the good in the world. No longer did He desire, love, hate, have jealousy and possess all other kinds of human qualities, for that derogates from His dignity. This God is far away from the human—the purpose of the world is to display and cultivate only the good He represents. Plato reconstructed religion also in relation to morality. The permanent ideal or the Idea of the Good no longer depends upon the whims of gods; it is the very structure of the world and of humans. Also immortality is especially stressed by Plato in the Phaedo to supply the element of permanence in spiritual life, which was so necessary to the Greeks of his time. The same contention may be made for Aristotle's philosophy. He, too, was monotheistic, emphasized immortality, and attempted to make life of permanent value and significance.

2. *The State.*

Here again, the Greeks had two types of states before them, neither of which was a success—Sparta and Athens: Sparta an oligarchy, a government by the rich, in which the individual was greatly suppressed; Athens a democracy, a government by the masses of the people, in which each one had unrestrained liberty. Both fell: Sparta, because of too much inequality; Athens, because of too much equality. The institution of private property caused all the difficulties. Also, the Greeks based the state on a foundation of law, which is too impermanent to withstand the ravages of time. Plato, however, wanted to idealize the state, to remedy all the existing defects, particularly to eliminate private possessions. Plato wanted the state to be a permanent organization, based on that which is grounded in human nature and not on changing law, hence the biological theory of the state. He also wanted it to represent the moral ideals—that is what his Aristocracy meant to portray. Aristotle did reflect in his political views more of the existing state of affairs than Plato; he was more practical, he wanted slavery, private ownership and the like, but even here we find a new note. Aristotle also adopts the biological theory, guaranteeing permanence; he also proposes an ideal state to help the citizens cultivate the best life.

3. *The Individual.*

Here Plato and Aristotle concurred largely with the prevalent opinions. The artisan was not held in high esteem. Athletics and music were considered essential to the development of a proper body and a proper mind. To understand the exalted position the Greeks accorded to athletics, we must realize that the goddesses and graces were sponsors for them; all athletic meets were therefore held in the temples. Our philosophers agree with all this; also with the fact that early training should be directed to the development of an harmonious temperament. But the Greeks held women in very low regard; it was the function of the housewife to cook, stay at home, rear children, but to associate with men in their councils was an unheard-of idea. Even courtesans were more respected. In the Republic, Plato advocates equality of women; a woman, he says, may be a philosopher or a soldier, for the difference between the male and female is one of degree and not of kind. He also differed as to the conception of pleasure. Naturally the Greeks were pleasure-loving people; Aristotle practically follows the prevalent opinion and permits the inclusion of all pleasure that is not harmful in his code of an ethical life. Plato, however, allows only necessary pleasures, such as drinking to quench your thirst, eating and other similar functions to keep the body healthy—but he will not dream of going any further. All unnecessary pleasure is dogmatically ruled out.

4. *Art.*

Greek art was especially interested in the subject matter and not so much in the treatment. Modern art, on the contrary, is the opposite, the form of expression is much more important than the subject. In Greek life, art like music, was to control emotions, develop harmony. Painting, sculpture and poetry represented the Gods and heroes.   The statue of Zeno at Olympia is an example of this.   Not only does this art attempt to express character rather than form, but idealized character, such as only gods and heroes possessed.   The modern artist is interested primarily in arrangement of color and form, his interest in the subject is secondary.   His art is purely subjective, what the artist's moods may be for the moment, those he expresses.   Certainly to limit himself to subjects of national life and national religion would appear absurd and extremely unorthodox to the present day "impressionist."   There is no doubt that both Plato and Aristotle agreed with these conceptions of art which made it indispensable for the development of character, of harmony; of treating the subject most national in character.   But while Aristotle concurs almost entirely with the prevailing view, Plato feels that the type of poetry, music, drama which stir your emotions, are to be rejected.   He heartily disapproves of Homer's representation of the gods with their human infirmities as well as virtues.   Plato's rejection of art in general is based, as we have already seen, on his metaphysical conception of the Idea, which shows art to be an imitation of an imitation.

This brief resumé [2] of the relation of Plato and Aristotle to contemporary Greek thought shows more than ever how outstanding they were in their philosophical doctrines.   To be sure, Aristotle incorporates after a fashion most of the current beliefs, but Plato certainly is far ahead of his times. Even judging his philosophy from our present-day outlook, it is a finished piece of work, but when you evaluate it from the point of view of the immature thought of his day, his undertaking is really colossal.   True enough, it contains many defects and a number of elements too remote from life and too idealistic for practical purposes, but in the abstract and as a thing of beauty no other philosopher has as yet equaled Plato.   Had philosophy, however, been inter-

[2] This discussion is based in part on "The Greek View of Life," by G. Lowes Dickinson.

ested only in idealistic, impractical theories, the censure often directed towards it as being unnecessary and visionary would be justified indeed. The redeeming feature is that the history of thought shows that philosophy always returns to the solution of real problems confronting us in life, to the explanation of the very essential and indispensable conditions that surround us. It attempts to supply us with a haven, with a port of refuge in this turbulent sea, in which we are tossed about like the most insignificant and fragile bits of driftwood. From this angle we now turn to the last division of Ancient philosophy, the Post-Aristotelians, the Stoics and Epicureans.

CHAPTER VI

THE STOICS AND EPICUREANS

1. *Stoics.*

SOCRATES, as we remember, said that "Virtue is Knowledge." This has been interpreted in a twofold manner—the Stoics, virtue for virtue's sake; the Epicureans, virtue as a means to pleasure. The predecessors of the Stoics in the same line of thought were the Cynics, founded by Antisthenes. They said that the only life worth while is one of pure reason, no element of pleasure must enter into it; pain and suffering are the badge of human existence. They did not concern themselves with the development of a comprehensive philosophy to support their doctrine. The Stoics, on the other hand, propounded a real, positive system of thought of which the central theme is to live according to reason.

Ethics. Briefly, their philosophy is this: God penetrates the whole of nature, interesting himself very seriously with our affairs. Nature is composed of a living fire like that of which Heracleitus speaks, and it serves as the body of God. Nature is teleological, for God must act according to a plan or purpose. Starting with this theory, the Stoics find it comparatively easy to cultivate a system of ethics. Since God is identified with nature, the first principle of life is to follow nature; obey the law of nature and you obey God. To be more specific, God has given each of us a part of his divine reason by which to guide our conduct; therefore to follow the dictates of reason is really tantamount to following nature. But what does this following reason actually mean in our daily affairs? Epictetus, one of the later Stoics, gives us a hint of the significance of this principle. We must make the right

use of appearances of things, he says.   In nature we have:
1. Things which are beyond our power to control, such as
death, disease, earthquakes and the like.   Reason dictates
that we must resign ourselves to them, not making ourselves
miserable by attempting to deflect the course of nature.   Such
resignation to our fate is the essential characteristic of that
philosophy which is summed up by the maxim, "Be Stoical."
2. Then again, there are some things in nature, some appearances of things, which are within our power to control.   Here
reason bids us to select only those which help its development and reject others which hinder its course.   Nothing in
the world, says Epictetus, can make one surrender his soul,
his will, to the demands of another.   Even if the emperor
should torture you, he can only have your body, but you
must not even then enslave your soul to him, he cannot rob
you of your freedom of thought.   Again, you must not subject your free mental development, the rational exercise of
your will, to the emotions; appetites and desires must be controlled in a way suggested by the Platonic exhortation.   3. Finally, there are still other appearances of things which are
within your power, but which have no bearing on the cultivation of reason.   Then it is unnecessary to concern yourself
with them; be indifferent to them.

This is a brief summary of the Stoic doctrine.   It offers a
life of contentment, there is no need of ruffling one's com-
posure under any circumstances.   It urges you to be resigned, to put your faith in God, to cultivate the highest
element of the soul, reason, so that you may be able to follow
the governing principles of nature, in short, to follow God.
Epictetus delves more specifically into the duties which the
Stoics recommend as a part of their moral code.   1. To self:
take care of your body, be athletic, be chaste, be temperate.
The Stoic here, unlike Plato and Aristotle, does not deride
common labor, he considers it sufficiently dignified even for the
sage.   2. To God: respect Him, have the right convictions
about Him, follow His dictates.   3. To one's neighbor:
this includes the duties of social life, more specifically with

regard to the performance of civic duties, to the development of patriotism, to pity, to punishment—in short, the Stoic recommends all such acts and obligations which may improve and better community life.

Zeno (340–265 B.C.), the founder of the Stoics, committed suicide at the age of seventy-five. He felt that since life is to be lived only for the purpose of following, of using reason in conduct, once you feel that your usefulness is over, you may take leave of the world, or as he put it—"the door is always open." This is a very dangerous doctrine, for where will you draw the line between the useful and the useless? It has never been quite clear whether this teaching is general with all Stoics; the preponderance of the evidence is to the contrary. From the foregoing it is clear that the Stoic did not find any romance in the world or in life. He recommended a course of rigorous conduct, righteous living, elimination of as much pleasure as possible, in fact, almost an unnatural life. Lest it be understood that this type of behavior is good because you will be rewarded in a subsequent existence, we must at once state that the Stoic did not believe in immortality of the soul. The most that he said on this matter is that the soul of the sage survives after the death of the body, but even here it perishes ultimately. Aside from any consideration of the validity of this doctrine, there is no doubt that to live rightly as the Stoics propose, without any sanction of a doctrine of retribution, is far more ideal than the theory of Plato, which urges reward and punishment in after-life as the reason for a life of morality.

Evil. To sum up then, the Stoic religion is really pantheistic, God and nature are identified. That alone differentiates it from our theistic religion, which separates God from the world. But there is even a vaster difference between them. The ordinary theistic religion conceives of God as one of love, of sympathy, while the Stoic God is one of duty. The only consideration here is to act because duty demands it. There is one very important problem which the Stoics, because of their conception of God, must solve; we refer to the problem of evil.   If God is in nature, and God is perfect, how can we explain imperfection or evil in the world?   They attempt to answer it in this manner: evil is necessary to contrast with the good, we need the sour to emphasize the sweet, we need the imperfect to bring out the perfect, just as the artist must have a shadowy background to emphasize the picture in the foreground.   Again, they say, only that is evil which we choose to regard as such, in other words, evil is in our thoughts and is not really objective.   This appears ridiculous, for why could not the perfect God furnish us with only perfect or pleasant thoughts?   Why, in short, could not God give us pleasant dreams instead of nightmares?   The Stoics go one step further; they say that what may appear as evil for the individual may really be good when viewed from the standpoint of the universe as a whole.   The example of the artist applies equally well here.   If you look only at the shadowy background, it means nothing, it is useless, but taken as a whole, the picture represents the proper proportion, the proper contrast, the perfect whole.   Lastly, we need evil to fight it, to overcome it, so that we may develop our characters. It really appears that with the exception of the final solution, which deserves some consideration, especially from the pragmatic point of view, all the other attempts to explain evil are evasive and a waste of effort.   It is far better to admit its existence and fight it rather than to run away from it, an objection which seems to be similarly directed against Plato's *otherworldliness* and which may be considered almost fatal.

Conclusion.   This Stoic philosophy is consistent in its emphasis on a particular type of life, it conceives of the human being as a machine able to conform to one principle without deviation.   It urges you to stifle your instincts, to suppress your desires, to subjugate your emotions, to cease living, as we understand the word.   To show that they considered conformity to one type of conduct as the most essential characteristic in life, we may simply state that to the Stoic, there are no degrees of virtue; you cannot be virtuous in one respect and offend in others, you are either wholly right or wholly wrong.

They do not allow you to digress from the righteous path, even in the smallest degree.   A little intemperance, a little unholiness, a little letting down of the bars, will not do at all.

One of the most important outgrowths of the Stoic teaching is the idea that we are all citizens of the world.   This of course is clear.   Since God gives each of us a part of his divine reason, and since this element must not be subjected to the will of any mortal, even of an emperor, we all surely belong to the world, we are the children of the one God.   Epictetus illustrates the relation between God, man and the world by a very beautiful example.   He says: "As on a voyage when the vessel has reached a port, if you go out to get water, it is an amusement by the way to pick up a shell-fish or some bulb, but your thoughts ought to be directed to the ship, and you ought to be constantly watching if the captain should call, and then you must throw away all those things, that you may not be bound and pitched into the ship like sheep; so in life also, if there be given to you instead of a little bulb and a shell a wife and child, there will be nothing to prevent (you from taking them).   But if the captain should call, run to the ship, and leave all those things without regard to them. But if you are old, do not even go far from the ship, lest when you are called you make default." [1]

2. *Epicureans.*

One rarely discusses Stoicism without at the same time contrasting it with Epicureanism, to which we turn our attention next.   The Epicureans, as has already been mentioned, said that we need knowledge or virtue not for its own sake, but to use as a means, as an instrument to pleasure.   Their predecessors, who advocated pleasure as the aim of life, were the Cyrenaics, founded by Aristippus.   They did not distinguish between pleasures of the moment and lasting pleasures, while Epicurus preferred the latter, although he did not condemn the former.   Furthermore, Epicurus (341–270 B.C.) developed a complete and all-inclusive phi-

[1] "The Discourses of Epictetus" (The Encheiridion, Section VII).

losophy to support his doctrine of pleasure as the end and goal of human life. When we examine the Epicurean doctrine we find that every branch of its philosophy is concentrated on one issue, namely, to eliminate all fear of punishment in this existence or in a subsequent life, and as a result, therefore, to enjoy ourselves to the utmost. From this angle let us examine Epicurean metaphysics, its conception of God, of the soul, and its ethics.

Metaphysics. Epicurus and his successor, Lucretius, the Roman poet, adopt bodily the entire atomistic theory of Democritus. They introduce two distinctions, however: 1. They argue in accord with scientific theory that all bodies heavy and light, possess the same velocity in a vacuum. But these indestructible particles or atoms move in straight lines and not only downward; once in a while they swerve from the straight path, connect with the others by means of hooks and thus form the universe. 2. The second change is by far the more important for the purpose of ethics, for which the Epicureans are famous—they claim that chance and not mechanical law is responsible for the motion of the atoms. This explains free will and moral responsibility in the world.

God. The Epicureans do not affirm absolutely the existence of the gods, but they argue that even if they do exist, they have nothing to do with us or with our world of nature. They are happy beings living in a home of their own; why should they worry over our puny and insignificant troubles? Furthermore, the atoms are infinite in number and space is unlimited; therefore, there may be an infinite number of worlds like ours—how can the gods take care of so many worlds? If you say they cannot, why do you single out only this world for their exclusive concern? Lastly, we come to the most fatal argument of all. The gods are perfect, the world is full of imperfections, how could the gods have created such a world? This is the familiar question of evil, to which the Stoics gave evasive answers, but which the Epicureans admit and do not attempt to explain, because they realize the futility of such an effort. The conclusion reached as a result of this view of God is to relegate all the beliefs about the gods punishing us with thunderbolts, with plagues and the like to superstition.   All such occurrences are natural phenomena.

Soul.   The soul is mortal because it has a parallel development with the body; when the body is young the mind, too, is immature; in old age, both body and mind are feeble; then again, a blow on the head stuns the mind, thus showing that both are similar in texture.   What shows, finally ask the Epicureans, that the soul survives the body?   Is there any evidence that the soul escapes from the body at death?   Since the soul is mortal, they conclude that there is no fear of punishment after death.   In this way, a very fine background is prepared for the final doctrine of Epicurean philosophy—*their ethics.*   Why not enjoy a life of pleasure, why not yield to your instincts, desires and emotions?   But, say you, how can we enjoy such a life when at every moment the gods may frown upon us, hurl one of their thunderbolts and crush us?   Or perhaps, you may argue, continue the Epicureans, even if we escape the wrath of the gods in the world, they have our souls under their control everlastingly in a subsequent existence.   You imagine all kinds of tortures in hell; the fear of retribution grips your heart and even while you enjoy the pleasures, you tremble for fear of the consequences.   Epicurus scoffs at this frame of mind.   The gods are not concerned with us here, hence, there is no fear of punishment while we are alive.   There is also nothing to worry about after death, because once we are dead we stay dead.   What fly is there in the ointment under such conditions?   Have a good time while you may.   Of course, Epicurus realizes that there is always a morning after, following the night before.   That type of physical pleasure which is temporary, fleeting, very often is accompanied with pain.   It is therefore preferable to select, if possible, the mental, permanent pleasures which are pure and entail no disagreeable consequences.   This theory of ethics, to derive as much enjoyment as you can out of life, was adopted by Horace, Stevenson, Herbert Spencer, Walt Whitman and John Stuart Mill. The last, however, is an Epicurean heretic, for he emphasizes the pleasures of others in preference to your own; such a doctrine could not possibly be accepted by the ordinary Epicurean.   By way of passing, it is perhaps well to mention that Epicurus and his followers actually practiced what they preached.   They formed a colony where men and women lived promiscuously, whose sole ambition in life was to enjoy everything to the utmost.   They did not select only lasting and mental pleasures, in fact, the physical predominated.

3. *Comparison of Stoicism and Epicureanism.*

What does a comparison between these last two philosophies contribute to a philosophy of the ordinary individual? Metaphysically both Stoic pantheism and Epicurean atomism may be of special significance in our daily life, if interpreted correctly.   No one doubts that the atoms play a great rôle in nature; science, experience, vouch for that.   On the other hand, who does not prefer to feel that God watches over, and is concerned with, him?   Of course Epicurean insistence on chance, conflicts with the mechanical theory of atoms, and Stoic emphasis on necessity to act in accordance with nature, contradicts the theory of moral responsibility so essential in their ethics, but who urges us to adopt both of these theories in every particular?   Then again, the Epicurean emphasis on the indifference of the gods to human affairs leaves us out in the cold; there cannot be real comfort in human life, if in moments of great trouble we cannot turn to God with the conviction that he will help us.   But the Stoic God is really no better.   True enough, he permeates the world and is supposed to take care of us, but does he possess any love or sympathy?   Not at all, he is just a metaphysical God necessary to support their metaphysics and their ethics.   Concerning the constitution of the soul there is very little difference between them.   The real contrast appears in the ethics of each of these schools of thought.   On the one hand, we have the Stoic doctrine of a life of reason and no pleasure; on the other hand, we have the Epicurean insistence on a life of pleasure and very little reason. Each is defective, not taking cognizance of the complexities of human life. How can the ordinary man be expected to eliminate all instincts, emotions and desires and cold-bloodedly devote himself exclusively to a life of virtue for virtue's sake? This Stoic doctrine does not recognize that the human being is not an automaton, he is not a machine. On the face of it, the Stoic paradox that there are no degrees of virtue, that you are either wholly virtuous or wholly vicious, is absurd. The entire scheme of life is based on compromises, on the evaluating of certain obligations, on the selection of certain modes of conduct as against others. Very often a little vice may sweeten virtue; why then condemn the person? But that does not justify us in adopting the Epicurean system of morality. The more pleasure we enjoy, the more we desire; if we become satiated and our appetites are jaded, what else is left in such a life? Each of us possesses appetites and desires, the desires are short-lived, which can always be satisfied. Our appetites, however, are of long duration and can never be satisfied. This results in a despairing of ever achieving a really happy, pleasurable life. In short, each of these theories is by itself not suited to life; the Stoic is too fundamentally rigid, the Epicurean is too shallow. Under the latter, the men will not work, will not pay their obligations, will be a useless and wasteful lot; the women will be no better, flitting about without centering their attention on anything serious in life. The best solution, therefore, is perhaps to have a life in which there will be some rational principles to point the way and also some pleasure to make it less burdensome, offering encouragement in moments of despair. This type of philosophy was most closely approached by Aristotle.

4. *Relation of Stoicism to Brahmanism, Buddhism and Christianity.*

In spite of its unsuitability for practical life, however, Stoicism is entitled to serious consideration, especially be-

cause of its similarity to other great systems of thought, and
particularly its relation to Brahmanism, Buddhism and Christianity.   Since the dawn of civilization, men have felt that it
was unjust to punish or reward anyone simply because chance
of circumstances made him act in a certain way.   For example,
at the very beginning of the development of human society,
if a man killed another most accidentally, the tribe exacted his
life on the theory that "blood calls for blood"; later, however,
the ancient Hebrews provided a place of refuge for such innocent victims of fortune.   Ever since, this idea progressed
until it became a settled doctrine that reward and punishment
must be administered only according to desert.   But then
human society faced a very knotty problem.   What sanction
is to be found in nature for such a course?   Is it not true that
in nature the innocent suffers often?   Is it not also a fact
that the guilty, the aggressor, usually prevails in the natural
realm and escapes all punishment?   In short, these different
human aggregations were confronted with the same problem; how explain the fact that nature does not follow the
theory of justice developed by us humans?   The two great
Indian philosophies, Brahmanism and Buddhism, attempted
to solve it in an almost identical manner, with but slight
modifications.

Brahmanism.   In accord with the opinions that prevailed
among the pre-Socratic philosophers, Brahmanism conceived
of the universe as composed of an underlying substance, which
they called "Brahma"; the individual, too, was made up of
this substance stuff called "Atman."   The only reason why
the individual is separated from the "Brahma" is because he
is surrounded by desires, emotions, pleasures, pains, in fact
by all that constitutes his phenomenal existence.   Every
individual has a certain personality, a certain character, known
as "karma."   Now we get the answer to our original question.   Why does nature permit the innocent to suffer?   Why
does nature exhibit such moral indifference?   Because, say
the Brahmans, this "Karma" transmigrates, passes through
successive existences, modified and influenced by the manner

in which you live in each of your phenomenal existences. Therefore, even if the individual suffers in his present existence, although he may be innocent now, he pays the penalty for having sinned in a previous existence.   In any event, the innocent actually does not suffer, which is in accord with the human belief in justice.   But how can the individual stop this constant round of transmigration?   By renouncing the will to live, by suppressing his desires, by eradicating his very instincts, by asceticism; he must not only yield up all pleasure, but must actually undergo all kinds of pain in order to cure his "Karma."   The moment he does this, the phenomenal barrier between the "Atman" and the "Brahma" disappears and the individual is swallowed up in the world of cosmic substance.   That ends his suffering for all time.

Buddhism.   Buddhism is another famous Indian philosophy, founded by Gautama.   He denies the existence of any substance, either in the cosmos or in the individual.   All we have are sensations, phenomena; everything is "such stuff as dreams are made of."   "Karma," however, remains, and is transmitted from one existence to another, similar to the Brahman doctrine.   What then is the Buddhistic answer to our puzzling question?   Here again, the individual suffers, because the defects in his "Karma" brought about in some other existence, have not yet been cured.   The remedy Gautama offers is not self-imposed suffering, not asceticism, for that is crude, useless and often harmful.   He suggests controlling your appetites, your passions, your desires, by critically examining their foundation, by cultivating such habits as will oppose them effectively; in short, return good for evil, be humble, renounce the will to self-assertion.   Once you accomplish that, you reach complete happiness, because it is complete cessation of the desire to live, complete rest, the end of all dreaming—this goal is "Nirvana."

To return to the Stoics: They too, say "follow nature," but that is the very crux of our problem.   If we follow the dictates of nature, how can we justify the type of moral conduct we advocate—humility, justice, benevolence and all other similar virtues which have absolutely no foundation in the world of experience? This is the age-old problem of evil. We have seen what evasive replies the Stoics give to this most insoluble puzzle. The Stoics finally in despair must reach practically the same conclusion as the two great systems of Indian philosophy, to resign ourselves to our fate, not to fight that which is beyond our power to control, to believe with blind faith that God knows what he is about; in a word, to cease living.

It may be well to comment at this point that these philosophies may possess great merit because of their imaginativeness, because of their realization of the difficulties in nature which appear almost insurmountable, because of the pleasant, lethargic feeling they desire to instill in their adherents by the renunciation of the will to live; but is this the type of life we crave? We have already pointed out in Plato that to run away from this world, because of its apparent confusion and utter incomprehensibility, is cowardly. Why not enjoy this unequal struggle, why not derive zest out of the very attempt to conquer as much of your natural environment as is necessary for your development? We must realize that ultimately the cosmic process, the world order, will overcome our feeble struggles, but is that sufficient reason for "lying down on the job?" William James pointed out that when two men play chess, one a novice, the other an expert, the expert will ultimately win, but even he does not know all the moves his opponent will make. We say that the novice, while he makes the moves, can derive much enjoyment out of the game, although he knows that he will lose in the end. To be sure, it is not a foregone conclusion that nature will inevitably vanquish us, for the idealistic metaphysics holds out promise for our final victory. This we shall discuss later.

Christianity. What comparison may finally be drawn between Stoicism and Christianity? Briefly we may say that both conceive of God as spirit in nature, both agree that God is not the aloof Being in the Aristotelian sense, nor the indifferent personality in the Epicurean belief. He is very intimately concerned with our affairs. Then again, both emphasize duty and consider it a demand of man's own inner life, based really on conscience. Self-denial or asceticism, contempt for the ephemeral, unimportant things of this world, is evident in these great systems of thought. But this identity is not to be carried too far. The God of the Stoics is an impersonal reason who looks upon nature as a whole, and if the individual's lot is contrary to the whole, he alone suffers. He is not a God of love, of sympathy, to whom you can turn in moments of distress. He is not a God to whom you may pray for forgiveness. This cold-bloodedness, which is an essential characteristic of the Stoic God of duty, is carried to the moral relations between men. Help your neighbor because it is your duty, not because he rouses your sympathy; help him because reason impels you to do so, not because you desire to do so; in short, Stoicism demands that all emotions, all feelings that mellow life be suppressed, and the human become a cold, calculating, logical machine. They caution you not to express sorrow at death, not to console anyone in his bereavement; this may be perfectly proper as a matter of reason, for such happenings are inevitable, but how much does it ease our burden of life? How much more bearable does it make life? We have seen in the Phaedo, as Socrates is about to die, after drinking the hemlock, there is an outcry among his disciples, but he coldly frowns upon it and further shows his imperturbability by asking Crito to pay a trivial debt he owes. This is a Stoic procedure, but no amount of argument could persuade us to imitate such behavior under similar circumstances. Christianity naturally does not countenance such principles. God is love; he concerns himself with the individual, each man's fate is within His control. He is the power to whom we appeal in prayer, a personal God who will not always judge too harshly our transgressions, a God who will let duty be replaced by forgiveness, if we repent. It is also true that Christianity regards sympathy and love as great virtues, even in the relations between humans. It recognizes grief and sorrow at the loss of a loved one; it offers consolation and hope in times of trouble.   The Stoics did not require immortality of the soul in a philosophy which was not interested in engendering hope in the human breast for redemption in spite of all past sin, but Christianity is based upon the fact that every soul can be redeemed and it is given an everlasting opportunity to be taken back into the spiritual fold; hence, immortality is essential.   Stoicism and Christianity attempted to solve the problem of evil almost in the same way, and both are open to the same objections.   This final word, however, may be said, that Stoicism is really an ethics, and Christianity a religion.   A religion must appeal to the masses, must offer a practical guide for life, whereas the Stoic ethics offers ideals that are extremely illuminating but not sufficiently satisfying for the ordinary man.

5. Conclusion.

In conclusion, we find thus far five great philosophies of life represented by Plato, Aristotle, the Stoics, the Epicureans and Christianity.   We may graphically illustrate the interrelation of these systems of thought by adopting a Platonic setting for a discussion between the characters promulgating them.   Let us suppose a banquet scene; at the head of the speaker's table sits Socrates, calm, imperturbable, rather homely, but radiating peace and intelligence.   On his right, sits Plato, the Aristocrat; beyond him, Zeno, the Stoic, a look of resignation on his pain-lined countenance; on the left of Socrates, is Aristotle, the scientific observer, displaying perhaps the courtly manner which he acquired while in the service of Alexander the Great; beyond him, reclines Epicurus, the pleasure-loving individual, already marked with the signs of the care-free man who is not concerned with the serious matters of life.   They have all eaten heartily and perhaps have drunk some, for surprising as it may seem, Plato, apparently does not practice what he preaches, as far as his banquet scenes are concerned; Plato always advocates temperance; whereas his characters are often portrayed as drinking

somewhat to excess.   A discussion then ensues between these
five about life.   Socrates, in his customary manner, does not
wish to debate on life in its general meaning, for that would
lead all of them astray.   He therefore pictures a particular
individual.   This man is described as a citizen of a large
country, a parent of two children, a good husband in the
ordinary meaning of the term; he enjoys some of the pleasures
of life, attends moving pictures, reads some detective fiction;
at the same time he is also a member of a church, enjoys philosophy and is a very sympathetic friend in time of need;
in short, he is a man of average intelligence and leads the
ordinary existence.   Shall he be admitted into the inner
shrine of the select few?   Is he the proper person to be accepted by any one of them as exemplifying the life each
advocates?   The older members courteously yield the floor
to the younger, to Zeno and Epicurus.   Zeno rejects him
without further question; he is not ascetic enough, he does not
lead a life of pure reason, he attends to the world of experience
in too large a degree.   Epicurus does not want him, because
he is a fool to endure the hardships and pain involved in the
duties of parenthood, society, religion.   Being a member of
a church, he believes in God and in His intervention in
human affairs; that surely eliminates him from the Epicurean circle.   Now Plato speaks up; he says this person is
not wholly bad, as a member of the artisan or the producing
class; but as a member of the select circle, he cannot hear of
it.   His life includes unnecessary pleasures, he does not subordinate his finite existence to the infinite, the Idea.   He prefers to be a husband, a father, to interest himself in the daily
life of experience, and removes himself from the life of pure
philosophic contemplation.   How can he, asks Plato, admit
to his society, a man who combines philosophy with detective
fiction?   Aristotle frowns a great deal at all of these answers.
In his eagerness not to be accused of such thoughts as the
others have expressed, he interrupts Plato's speech.   He says
that as long as he lives a well-ordered life, as long as he fulfills the plan or purpose that he sets out before him, what does

it matter if some of the other elements in his life are not quite up to the standard? He emphasizes the need of a plan, of a goal, in everyone's life. But Aristotle, too, finds a fatal objection to this particular individual. He has been raised in too large a social group, he should have developed in a city-state. Also, Aristotle feels that since this individual has no external possessions, he cannot lead a life of contemplation; he therefore is not entitled to the highest consideration. If he is a worker or a producer, Aristotle cannot possibly associate with him, in spite of the fact that he leads a properly guided and rationally directed existence, acting always moderately, or according to the mean. Just when it seems that this individual under discussion is to be wholly barred, in walks a patriarch, with an extremely benevolent air. He overheard the last part of the conversation, and he offers to admit him to his inner group. He says no other test applies to anyone except the guide offered by love. Love bridges all gaps, overlooks many defects, takes to its bosom all individuals, artisans, slaves, members of small and large communities. Love renders pleasure more pleasurable, it makes a life of reason more mellow and it offers encouragement to continue with it; love does not sacrifice the finite to the infinite, it does not sacrifice the husbands and wives in this world to some conception of an ideal in a previous existence. To be sure, he continues, Christianity, based on love, does emphasize the suppression to some extent of the lower elements in the soul to the higher, it recommends a life of self-denial, yet it countenances many other desirable things that may be included in it, such things as are found in the average man's life. This patriarch then explains that he agrees with the last speaker that one needs to formulate a plan for one's life, that then some small transgressions may be overlooked. He protests vigorously, however, against excluding members of large states, for all men of the world are children of God; he does not bar those without external goods, although he admits that you can do more for your fellow men if you have the means.

The others are at first shocked by the patriarch's words, but gradually their manner changes and soon there is a general hand-shaking around the table and hearty approbation of his pronouncements.   Thus the banquet ends.

BOOK II

MODERN PHILOSOPHY

CHAPTER I

Scholasticism. The Intervening Period between Ancient and Modern Philosophy

SCHOLASTICISM is the philosophy of the Middle or Dark Ages; it was meant to support the doctrines and canons of the Church. The Scholastics were extremely dogmatic, basing all their beliefs, criticisms and principles on faith and revelation. They felt, however, that if this could be bolstered up with reason, no matter how specious it might be, their position would be unassailable. This resulted in the type of philosophy which has retarded real, enlightened progressive thought many centuries. When the illuminating rays of truth finally penetrated this medieval darkness there was such a reaction, beginning with the Renaissance, that we are still thinking and acting under its influences.

Is it not paradoxical to formulate a philosophy to serve as the handmaid to faith, when by its very definition philosophy is the product of rational, independent thinking? What was the cause for this change in emphasis placed on the human's endowments—from reason to faith? In the Greek period, reason was extolled, it was the pivot around which all other interests centered. Now it has been deposed and its position usurped by blind faith, answerable to no one, except perhaps to God, who, by very definition is the Unknown, and, therefore, in the Baconian conception, not the subject matter of philosophy. Needless to say, this change was not abrupt. Other things being equal, evolutionary progress is gradual and continuous. Saltatory evolution, even if it does contribute substantially to the progress of the world, is the exception rather than the rule. The human, subject to this law of development, should not be considered as undergoing abrupt transformations from one type to another. The same reasoning must apply to the human mind. In fact, this consideration led Comte to develop the conception of the three stages—the theological, metaphysical and positive—through which the mind passes in order to reach the level of complex thinking that is such a vital factor in modern scientific and social activity.

What then was the system of thought linking the Greek enthusiastic acceptance of reason as the ultimate arbiter with the Scholastic notion of the supremacy of faith? The key is supplied by the religious, mystical philosophy of Neo-Platonism represented by Plotinus (204–269 A.D.).

1. *Neo-Platonism.*

We have seen the distinct line of demarcation Plato draws between the Ideal and the actual, between the spirit and the flesh, between God and the world. This type of philosophy lends itself readily to a religious interpretation. Such dualism supplies the very breath so vital to dogmatic faith. Plotinus, no doubt discouraged by the bleak picture of life, of nature, if it is viewed from the intellectual aspect alone, desired to infuse some warmth, some emotional satisfaction into the world. He adopted the Platonic doctrine in a general way, but gave it a slightly different twist. More specifically he conceived of God as the One, ineffable principle in the world. You cannot define him, you cannot know him intellectually. You cannot reach him by dialectic. There is only one successful ladder by which to ascend to him— by a direct union with Him intuitively. We must prepare ourselves in different ways for this immediate experience— by certain abstinences, by purification ceremonies, by running away from the world, by prayer, by self-denial. The mystical experience in which we unite with the One is most enjoyable, and it furnishes us with a potent antidote to despair and to discouragement.

This, however, is only part of the picture Plotinus presents of the world. He furnishes us with the theory of creation as emanation. The universe emanates from the One or God, as light emanates from the sun. Intelligence is the first direct emanation; it is therefore the highest form of existence. The soul emanates from the Intelligence and is thus removed one step further from the Divine. Finally we have the body as the final emergence. Beyond body there is matter, or what he calls non-being. Matter has infinite potentialities on which God can exercise His creative productivity.

This brief survey of Neo-Platonism serves to show how reason as an instrument of life has been greatly weakened. It does not enable us to unite with God, or approach God; in fact, this highest goal is to be achieved by an ineffable experience. The One, too, is indescribable and must be postulated as the *raison-d'être* of the Universe. Does not this shift the emphasis from reason to faith? Such extolling of faith makes it relatively easy to understand why the Church of the Scholastic type could entrench itself in a position of power from which it has not completely been displaced even to this day.

2. *Problems of Scholasticism. Faith and Reason.*

Scholasticism began by extolling faith. While reason could not be denied entirely, its function was simply to confirm dogma. The moment there was a conflict, faith emerged triumphant. St. Augustine, although not strictly a Scholastic, nevertheless as early as the fifth century showed the trend of this belief, in his famous statement *Credo ut intelligam*—"I believe in order that I may understand"—or faith is superior to reason. This conception marks Scholastic development at its peak. But such a situation could not last long. Later we find the doctrine of the twofold truth; according to this, reason and faith occupy positions of equality. When you engage in theological thought, faith necessarily is the guiding principle; on the other hand, in all scientific and secular activities, reason is the only principle to follow. The artificiality of such a theory shows its weakness. As a result, in the final stages of Scholasticism, reason was considered as superior to faith.   That surely sounded the death-knell of this type of thought.

Barren as Scholasticism may appear to the casual student, it nevertheless embraces a great many doctrines worth mentioning, especially because of their connection with modern philosophic reasoning.   It deals with certain problems which are of interest to students of philosophy—the problems of Nominalism and Realism, Freedom of the Will, and Evil.

Nominalism and Realism.   Plato's conception of the Idea as a really existing thing, even more permanently and essentially existing than the particular, influenced the Scholastics to be Realists.   As such they were able to present the doctrine of the Universal Mother Church as actually existing—thus validating the foundation of religion.   It is clear that if the Universal in theology is more permanent, and possesses greater essence than the secular or particular factors in life, a philosophy supporting such belief assumes great dignity and is to be placed on a high pedestal.   Conversely, if the Universal, the Ideal, is only a name, a term by which to describe the innumerable details and complexities of the world, then the very props are forced out from under religion.   It is perfectly proper for loving couples to desire to be married in the "Little Church Around the Corner" but unless such church is an expression of some unchangeable eternal institution, behind appearances, what is left for Scholasticism to defend?   Such considerations led practically all Scholasticis to be Realists.   The moment nominalism made its appearance Scholasticism was doomed.   One of the last Scholastics, William of Occam, taught such nominalism.

Freedom.   Are we free, may we choose between alternatives voluntarily, or are our actions predetermined by a Divine Being?   What does it matter, you ask?   Upon the solution of this question depends our theory of moral responsibility.   How can one be punished for his sins, if he has no choice in his conduct?   Strict determinism is frank about this matter.   It holds that we humans are tossed about in the universe like atoms subject to laws of mechanism. Materialism, however, need not furnish any answer to the query why a Divine, merciful father should punish us, when no blame ought to attach to our actions.   It holds simply that we suffer, because the world is governed by universal laws which apply to us, the same as to other objects.   Religion, however, cannot adopt this attitude.   It must allow for moral responsibility based on freedom of choice.

It follows, therefore, that the Scholastics predicated free will.   But do they consider the will as acting capriciously, or is it subject to some other part of our make-up?   The answer to this furnished the bone of contention between Duns Scotus and Thomas Aquinas.   Scotus said that God created the world by caprice, that is the very essence of free will.   We, His creatures, also possess such unrestrained freedom.   Aquinas does not concede such capricious activity even to God.   To him God's Will is subject to his intellect, which does not deny freedom, but simply modifies it.   Since God is controlled by his own intellect, he is not constrained to do anything, he is not compelled to act from without, but by his own nature.   The same holds true for us.

Evil.   This problem is the Waterloo of all religions. The Epicurean argument applies with as much force now as in the days of Epicurus.   If God, a perfect being, created the world, how explain the imperfections, the suffering in the universe?   The Stoics answered the question in various ways, all of which were evasive and made no impression upon the intelligent mind.   The Scholastics, likewise, struggle futilely with this unanswerable question and reach equally barren results.   Would it not be better to face the facts squarely, admit the existence of evil, and devote all our efforts to its amelioration, rather than waste our energy in explaining away something which obviously cannot be so treated?   Even if we are religious fanatics, such a procedure is not tainted with heresy.   For who are we, mere humans, to attempt to understand all the ways of God?

3. *Famous Scholastics.*

St. Anselm. (1033–1109.)   Among the Scholastics there are some figures who deserve special mention.   St. Anselm is the originator of the famous ontological argument for the existence of God, which was later adopted by Descartes. The argument is very simple.   Each of us has an idea of a supremely perfect being, or of a God.   Perfection implies existence, for a being with the added element of existence is more perfect than one who is only an idea.   Therefore God exists.   But we object, just as Aquinas does, that such an idea of God cannot prove his actual existence, because the idea does not show that there is an objective reality corresponding to it.

Abelard. (1079–1142.)   Abelard, another Scholastic, is particularly noted for his theory of conceptualism.   We have shown before what a vital factor to this philosophy of the Middle Ages was the belief either in Realism or in Nominalism.   Abelard takes the middle course.   He says universals are neither existing realities nor are they mere names—they are concepts by which particulars are designated and classified. This is similar to the commonly accepted opinion as to the nature of abstract ideas at the present time.

Thomas Aquinas. (1225–1274.)   The most outstanding character in this period, however, is Thomas Aquinas.   In him may be directly traced all the influences of Aristotle.   He adopted the theory of the Aristotelian four causes, potential and actual forms, classification of the sciences, and the dualism between God and the world, although at this point we must note that Aquinas clothes God with religious habiliments as contrasted with the aloof, intellectual Aristotelian God—the Unmoved Mover.   We referred to the rejection by Aquinas of Anselm's ontological proof for the existence of God.   But he supplied two other arguments, which he considered very cogent, but which in our opinion are also subject to severe criticism, culminating in their complete annihilation by Immanual Kant, in his Critique of Pure Reason—we refer to

the Cosmological Argument and the argument from contingency. The first begins by accepting the obvious fact
that there is a cause for everything in the world. We
cannot go on *ad infinitum* seeking for preceding causes—
hence we must stop at a first cause, itself uncaused. This
first cause is God. Without delving into all the difficulties
raised by this argument, suffice it to ask, How does Aquinas
make the transition for causality prevailing in the world of
nature to a Being, who, admittedly, is outside the world? As
to the proof from contingency, he says that everything in this
world depends upon something else; one physical object,
for example, must depend upon another—a house must rest
on the ground. Here, too, we must direct attention from
the contingent non-necessary existing thing to a necessary independent Being upon whom the whole universe rests. This
necessary being is God. The objection leveled against the
preceding argument applies with equal force to this proof.

4. *Influence of Plato and Aristotle.*

This résumé of Scholasticism is sufficient to indicate some
of its main characteristics. It was influenced by Plato and
by Aristotle. The latter influence was felt in a great many
respects, aside from its effect upon Aquinas. Aristotle's conception of a God, outside of the world, causing all motion in
nature, supplying the efficient cause for the universe, was
just suited for a philosophy whose primary purpose was to
find confirmation for the Church. The fact that Aristotle's
God was devoid of all qualities so essential for a religious
Divine Creator offered small difficulty to the theologians,
whose minds were very quick to find reasons and explanations
even for things most mysterious. Certainly Aristotle was
not concerned with attributing mercy, love, sympathy and
similar qualities to God, who, he considered, was leading a
life of contemplation and supplied purely the metaphysical
need for explaining the efficient cause and the goal for universal progress. The Scholastics described God in the most
glowing terms. Whether such description was in the nega-

tive or in the affirmative, He was conceived as possessing all that the human mind can imagine, and more. To borrow from Aquinas in this connection: "The highest knowledge which we can have of God in this life, is to know that He is above all that we can think concerning Him." We know God by analogy in attributing to Him all perfections; by negation, in excluding from these perfections all elements of imperfection—he is the transcendent Being, without limitation, he is infinite, pure existence. Aquinas discusses God's simplicity, goodness, immutability, unity, justice and similar attributes. Aquinas concludes, nevertheless, that we must demonstrate the existence of God; the truth of God's being is not immediately evident to us. In connection with this description of God's qualities we should contrast this Scholastic with Herbert Spencer. The latter says that the individual, who considers God so far above his comprehension as to designate Him the Unknown, is by far more religious than the Theist who feels so confident of his ability to describe the Divine, even negatively. Is this not a just criticism of the vanity of the theologian to permit himself even in the slightest degree to be an adequate vehicle through which to express God?

5. Conclusion.

Common Characteristics. In conclusion, we may say that the Scholastics have many characteristics in common. They are dogmatic, desiring to have their doctrines taken at their face value; if reason does not support them, they have recourse to faith. Does not the Spinozistic statement "an asylum of ignorance" characterize this attitude? They are also extremely orthodox. Most naturally, those who weave the webs of religious dogmas must themselves be thoroughly convinced of the validity of their beliefs.

The Scholastics all advocate moderation. The union of soul and body places man midway between the purely spiritual and the purely material. In their ethics, intellectual happiness does not exclude the reasonable satisfaction of the body

—in this way duty and pleasure may go hand in hand. The individual well-being is harmonized with the good of the state. They advocate a sense of proportion in all things—this is a result of Greek influences.

They also supply us with a doctrine of coherence. In the first place, they emphasize the value of personality. The individual is extolled; his happiness, his immortality, his equality with his fellow men are especially emphasized. Then again, God is at the head of the Universe. Man finds Him the sole object worthy of his love and reverence. All interests in life, whether they be social or individual in character, are to be directed towards God as the goal.

All Scholastics are dualistic; God and the world are distinct. The world was created out of nothing, and owes its continued existence to the will of God. A theistic religion must support such a dualistic conception, otherwise, pantheism would be the result. That is so fatal to the Church, that merely entertaining such a thought branded one a heretic and made him a subject for punishment. Bruno, as we shall see shortly, exemplifies this attitude on the part of the medieval church. Then, too, they were all optimistic. God is the author of this world, hence it must embody all possible good. Lastly, Scholasticism considered *being* as static. The world is not undergoing constant change, but is right here and now a complete and perfect creation of a perfect God.

Metaphysics. Is there any element in Scholasticism that we may utilize in a philosophy particularly suited for our individual needs? Its metaphysics contains very little to recommend it. At this point, we may perhaps answer the unspoken question of many, who are curious to learn what is the need of a metaphysics for life? Obviously, metaphysics by the very definition that it is a study of reality, of that which does not appear to our senses, of truth in the absolute sense, cannot be connected with practical life very readily. It is the groundwork, however, of any theory concerning all phases of human behavior. David Hume, whom no one can charge with shutting his eyes to experience

as we understand it, said that metaphysics is necessary for art, morality, religion, economics, sociology; for the abstract sciences, as well as for every branch of human endeavor, considered from the practical angle. It is the foundation upon which one builds his career, consciously or unconsciously; it is the guide, the anchor of the human's interests; upon its truth or falsity depends what type of man you may develop into.

To return then to Scholastic metaphysics. It borrows almost wholly from Aristotle, but with this exception. Aristotle "followed it through" from the rational point of view, examining everything cold-bloodedly and logically, stopping up gaps, which required cementing, from a metaphysical standpoint. Scholasticism, however, could not proceed similarly. Its purpose was different, it was obliged to adopt a new orientation, stressing the religious, at the expense of the philosophic element. Aquinas did indeed accept the Aristotelian teaching of the four causes, including an efficient cause, which was supplied by God. But how different a conception of God! In examining the Aristotelian philosophy one feels a certain detachment, a sincere desire on the part of the author to work out a system which should satisfy our intellectual curiosity. In Aquinas, we recognize a personal element, the wish to have this God a creator, not in the sense of supplying a need for the explanation of the world, but a Being who did it all for us, humans,—a Being whose love, mercy or their opposites can be invoked by our efforts or by our actions. His philosophy becomes a vehicle for human aspirations, for the individual's desire, inferentially and indirectly, to have his needs and wishes considered exclusively. We do not mean to criticize adversely this attempt on the part of Scholastics to infuse a religious note into their philosophy, we simply wish to distinguish between metaphysics proper and religion. Our conclusion is that while both attempt to treat of the unseen, of the ultimate, they proceed along different angles, one on faith, the other on reason, and they must not be confused.

Then again, the attempt to demonstrate the existence of God by theoretical arguments was bound to result in failure, for the subject matter of religion cannot ordinarily be given the cogency of a logical foundation. True, God may be postulated in the Kantian sense, or we may will to believe in His existence in accordance with the theory of William James, but the objection is directed against their attempt to prove rationally His existence. Descartes also made use of similar arguments for a like purpose, but then, Descartes, too, was very much under the influence of the Church.

Once you disregard the Scholastic metaphysics, what remains that may vitally affect us? Needless to say, as a religion we cannot discuss it, for that is not the purpose of this treatise. There is no doubt that the Church supported by the complex, intricate and specious reasoning of its adherents exerted great influence in moulding the religious thoughts, not only of its contemporaries, but also of many individuals since. That, however, as has already been mentioned, is beside the point. Its ethics, based on a sense of moderation, influenced by Plato and Aristotle, would indeed be worth while but for the fact that here, too, it was interwoven with foreign elements, which are not quite so appealing. To act properly because of reward or punishment by the Creator, cannot possibly be considered as ideal a doctrine as the insistence on the application of a sense of proportion to one's life, because reason dictates it to be the wisest course. Is it not more effective to address ourselves as moral theorists, to a man's own sense of what is right and wrong, than to hold a club over his head in the form of God's punishment, if he were to transgress? Moses, leading the Jews through the wilderness, was obliged to instill fear of the wrath of Jehovah for any sins, because he was dealing with a wild, untutored tribe. We trust that we have outgrown such a need and we are vain enough to feel that more refined methods may be even more effective in keeping us within the limits of moderation and propriety.

CHAPTER II

Transition to Modern Philosophy

Scholasticism occupied the stage for several centuries, but it was bound to become supplanted by something more congenial to the human mental make-up. Faith is perfectly proper in its place, but it must not dominate to the exclusion of everything else. A great reaction set in against this blind dogmatism, this conception that all is well with the world, because the Lord of the Universe willed it. The reaction was all-comprehensive; it embraced all phases of human life. In the world of letters it was known as the Renaissance; all literature was influenced by a renewed interest in the classics; it breathed an air of freedom and emancipation. The whole post-Scholastic period, marking the transition between the philosophy of Middle Ages and Modern Philosophy, was ruled by the determination to cast off the shackles of the Church. It emphasized the dignity of the individual; it replaced reason on its high pedestal; it gave expression to the soaring spirits of man. The Fall of Constantinople, in 1453, when it was captured by the Turks, caused scholars gathered there to scatter all over Europe; the new methods of commercial intercourse were responsible for the exchange of ideas; in these and similar ways the new development took place.

These influences permeated everywhere. Art, politics, morality, science and philosophy were actuated by them and new methods were devised for their study and growth. In science, Galileo, Kepler, Newton, Copernicus and many others may be mentioned as illustrating what heights the mind was capable of attaining, once it was permitted to have full, independent sway. The Church, to be sure, fought valiantly against the ascendency of these tendencies. No better example can be adduced to show this than the burning of Giordano Bruno at the stake, because the religious body which was still very powerful felt that his thinking was tainted with heresy. He adopted the Copernican astronomical system. This held that the planets revolve around the sun—as a result heaven at one time may be under the earth; what then becomes of the consideration of heaven as God's dwelling, situated way above us? Bruno also taught that the universe is infinite, all-inclusive; since there can be only one such infinite, God, who certainly must be so designated, is then identified with the Universe. This is sheer heresy, for it spells pantheism, and religion must be based on the dualism between God and the world. Bruno attempted to distinguish between them by hairsplitting differences, but the Church fathers were astute enough to realize the evasiveness of these doctrines, hence they suppressed his philosophy and caused him to be burned at the stake, a delightful and purifying way of extinguishing human life, very much in vogue at that time. Fear of the wrath of the Church even influenced the philosophy of Descartes, as we shall point out in our study of his doctrines, to which we next turn our attention.

CHAPTER III

RENÉ DESCARTES (1596–1650)

1. *Life.*

René Descartes was born March 31, 1596, at La Haye, in Touraine, of good French stock. He was a very delicate child, yet he undertook a military career. The years between 1618 and 1628, he spent in wandering as a volunteer in the army of the Prince of Orange in the Netherlands, then in the Bavarian Army, and again in the military service in Hungary. He enjoyed a great deal of leisure while in winter quarters, which gave him much time for thought. In 1629, he went into seclusion in Holland, and there he began to set down his philosophy on paper, beginning with the Discourse on Method, and his entire doctrine was brought to the foreground between the years 1629 and 1649.

From the age of eight to sixteen he spent at the Jesuit College at La Flèche, then he made a grand tour of the world, which, as he describes in the Discourse ended in disillusionment. He was very much influenced by Father Mersenne, who perceived his genius. He was afraid to publish a revolutionary book on Physics because of the Church; he took excessive precautions in everything he did for the same reason. A fragment of this scientific work was published only after his death.

In September, 1649, Descartes accepted an invitation from Queen Christina of Sweden. There he was obliged to arise before sun-up, at 5 A.M., in order to teach the Queen how "to live happily in the sight of God." He had been accustomed previously to stay in bed to a very late hour, and this change caused his death. In 1667 his body was brought to Paris and

placed in the Church of Saint-Geneviève, later it was trans-
ported to the Church of Saint-Germain des Près, where it now
rests.   A storm of protest broke out against his doctrines long
after his death, but it was too late to suppress them then.   We
have seen that the reaction that set in against Scholasticism
influenced philosophy, which now attempted to discard faith
and replace reason to its proper position.   This is shown in
the philosophy of René Descartes, the originator of modern
thought.

In his extensive travels over Europe, Descartes discovered
that there existed no single issue on which there was not a great
divergence of opinion.   In his wide studies of the sciences,
he found that flaws could be detected in all, with the exception
of mathematics, which was sound throughout.   Descartes
was very much discouraged; he wanted to build a philosophy
on a sound foundation.   What better way to do this than to
furnish it with a mathematical basis?   This suited him perfectly, for he was the author of analytical geometry, and was
considered, besides, a mathematical genius.

2. *Method and Philosophy.*

Descartes, therefore, set out to wipe the slate clean, to discard all the prevalent ideas and theories which actuated
Scholasticism.   Let us, he says, procure a new method for our
philosophic thinking.   In the first place, accept as true only
that which is self-evident, about which there can be no possible dispute.   Then proceed from the simple to the complex; in that way, the mind is not obliged to bridge over gaps,
but can grasp the subject naturally.   You must, moreover,
divide the subject into as many parts as possible; this helps
to perceive all the ramifications of the topic under discussion.
Finally, it is necessary to make the most complete examination
of your conclusions; this guards you against omitting anything vital, and makes your procedure most comprehensive.

Cogito ergo sum.   Once this method is adopted, you are
ready to proceed to the study of philosophy.   How do you
know that anything exists in the world? asks Descartes.

Perhaps there is some evil demon who deceives you into believing in such existences. It is even doubtful whether your own body is an actual fact. In our dreams we seem to be vividly aware of many things, although on awakening we know that they were merely dreams. Why may it not be true that we are daydreaming even when we seem to be awake? Such considerations lead Descartes to the belief that the only self-evident truth we possess is that we doubt everything, but that is the very element furnishing the basis of his philosophy. The more we doubt the more we think, therefore it is obvious that we exist at least as doubting, or as thinking, beings—or *cogito ergo sum*—"I think, therefore, I exist," at least as a thinking being.

God exists. Having furnished this simple proposition, Descartes finds it easy sailing to proceed with the rest of his philosophy. As a thinking being, I have ideas, among them is the idea of a supremely perfect being, or a God. From this follows the ontological argument for the existence of God which we met in St. Anselm's philosophy. Descartes also adduces the cosmological argument for God, which has already been expounded by Aquinas. He proves it in this manner. The human being continues to exist from moment to moment. What is the cause of this continuity? If you say his parents are the reason for it, the inquiry then is about the cause for their continued existence. In this manner you proceed from cause to cause until you come to a first cause, itself uncaused, or God. Hence *God exists.* Although our ideas, continues Descartes, may be due to our imagination, or they may be adventitious, that is, derived from the outside world, or they may be inborn in us, the idea of God can be only innate, for there is no possible way by which we can conceive of such a perfect being as a product of the imagination, or as given by objects in the world, apparent to our senses. This existence of God is just as demonstratively true as the proposition that the angles of a triangle are equal to two right angles. The natural light, as he calls it, vouches for it.

Corporeal World Exists. God has thus been shown to be

the cause of everything in the world, including all of our ideas.   Since God is a perfect being, how can he deceive us into believing that we have ideas of corporeal objects in the world, unless such a world actually exists?   Previously, we felt that perhaps a demon deceived us, but now this so-called evil genius has been replaced by a perfect God who cannot by his very nature mislead us.   Therefore, He vouches for the fact that a world of objects is responsible for our ideas of it, or that such a corporeal world exists.   Thus we see the method used by Descartes to demonstrate the three vital principles of his philosophy—*cogito ergo sum*—God exists, the corporeal world exists.

Error.   In view of the fact that God, a perfect being, is responsible for our actions and thoughts, how can you explain error?   How can a non-deceiver cause us to be deceived? Descartes has an ingenious explanation for this.   He says, we possess an intellect and a will.   The intellect is limited in its scope, the will is an unlimited faculty.   If the will always waited docilely for the intellect to check, before it grasped, everything, we would never commit error; it is only the fact that the will outdistances the intellect and decides on matters prior to their being scrutinized by the mind, which causes deception.   All that we can expect from God is the fact that he gave us both faculties, then it is up to them to work out their own salvation.   The same type of explanation applies to other things which seem difficult to understand, in the light of a perfect creator.   Why does a dropsical body desire drink, although it is harmed by it?   Because, says Descartes, in case of thirst, God in order to preserve us, endowed the body with the faculty of telegraphing the mind for drink.   Therefore, it is better to allow the body always so to make known its wish, even though sometimes, as in the case of dropsy, it may be injurious, than to permit the body itself to discriminate between the different situations.   We are better protected for the purpose of preservation in the one way than in the other. The brief criticism to all this is, why could not an all-powerful God so have worked everything that our wills would not out-

run our intellects, or that dropsical individuals should not desire drink?   Once you allow any limitation in the work of
God, you derogate from his powers.   If you answer that God
felt a better way of making us develop was by having conflicts,
then you are injecting your personal views into the matter.
You are looking at the world through your eyes, and that
philosophically is untenable.   Either you discuss God from
the standpoint of a Being omnipotent, omniscient, full of
mercy, who should act differently from us, or he becomes anthropomorphic.   In the latter case, philosophy becomes subject to the just criticism that such a God is really no God at
all, but an idol fashioned according to your own fancy.

Mind and Body.   To return for a moment to Descartes'
discussion of mind as distinct from body.   He illustrates by
a piece of wax how superior the intellect is to sense perception.
If you melt the wax, all the qualities perceived by the senses
disappear; therefore, it would seem that there is no longer
any object called wax, but still the intellect knows it is wax,
to whatever form it may be reduced.   This, too, shows another distinction between mind and body.   The intellect is
one, unchangeable, while body can undergo many transformations.

From this we catch a glimpse of the Cartesian line of demarcation between mind and body.   Mind is inextended,
does not occupy space; its essential attribute is thought.
Body, on the other hand, is extended, does occupy space; this
space-occupying quality is its essential attribute.   How then
do they act upon each other?   There can be no denial that the
body is useless without its ability to invoke the mind's aid,
and vice versa.   To explain this, Descartes adduces the most
fantastic conception, the idea of a pineal gland.   This gland
is situated in the brain, and through it mind and body interact.
It is unnecessary to go to great length to expose the fallacy
of such a theory.   It is absurd on its face, but apart from that,
how about its scientific unsoundness?   Scientifically, the law
of conservation of energy demands that the amount and the
direction of energy always remain the same.   If the mind can

deflect bodily energy, then one part of the law is at once violated.   Furthermore, if Descartes will also permit physical and mental energy to be converted into each other, through interaction, the other part of the law is invalidated, that the amount always be conserved.

God and the World.   We have seen that Descartes by his training in the Jesuit order was influenced by the Medieval Church; also that the fear of the Church was always upon him, since he was not particularly desirous of making a "fiery" exit from this world.   This no doubt is responsible for his explanation of the relation between God and the world.   God, he says, created matter and motion, then stepped out of the picture and let them work out their own salvation.   He supposes the existence of matter and three laws of motion: 1. That a body always remains in the same state if undisturbed.   2. That if it comes into contact with another body it will either add motion to it, or detract motion from it.   3. Finally, the particles of matter, although they move in a circular manner, nevertheless tend to scatter in all directions.   If all of this had been created by God, Descartes concludes that the resultant world would resemble our realm, including the planets, their forms, sizes, organization, the laws of gravity, the nature of light, and all the other elements with which we are familiar. Why then, cannot this supposition actually be considered as a fact, leading us to the conclusion that God did create matter and such motion subject to the laws just enumerated?

With reference to the proofs for the existence of God, which Descartes adduces, the ontological argument requires no further criticism than that which has been shown in the case of St. Anselm.   As to the cosmological proof, aside from the fact that it is impossible logically to make the transition from the finite world to the infinite Being, the further questions remain, What need is there for such a first cause altogether?   In the first place, why cannot the universe as a whole be its own self-sufficient cause?   What need to go outside of it? This is just as deadly a weapon against the Thomistic proof from contingency as against that from causality, for why not

consider the world in its entirety as the independently existing entity vouching for itself?   Then again, if we consider
the universe analogous to a circle, which is composed of an
infinite number of points and is yet grasped by the mind in its
entirety, without any need to look for a beginning or end, we
readily see that the world may be just that type of entity.
This dispenses with the requirement to search for first causes.
Such a need is only due to the fact that we consider causation
from a linear point of view, and not in the manner just
described.   Lastly, the fact that there is a first cause does not
necessarily identify him with God; that robs the Cartesian
argument of its religious setting, unless you identify the
first cause with God by the ontological argument, which is
absurd on its face.   Thus the entire structure for the existence
of God erected on a logical foundation falls to the ground.

3. *Criticism.*

What estimate may we make of Descartes' philosophy?
No more cogent criticisms can be leveled against Cartesianism
than those set out by P. Gassendi, theologican and Epicurean
disciple, who was considered an excellent philosopher as well
as a man of letters.   Why, he asks, does Descartes go to such
absurd lengths to deny the existence of everything, when as
a matter of fact he could have established his premise by
casting suspicion only upon those things which really appear
doubtful?   That would be adequate to show that in doubting,
we are thinking beings.   The sweeping denial of the certainty
of existence of all things, which Descartes is at such pains to
make, smacks of artificiality and insincerity.   Then again,
why not choose some other activity, as walking, to demonstrate that we exist?   Of course, at this point we can justify
the Cartesian position that behind all other activities, there
is thought; why then not start with the source?   But even
assuming that our existence is dependent purely on thought,
there is this serious objection, do we cease to exist in our sleep,
since we do not think then?

The most fatal criticisms, however, are directed against

the conception of God.   We pointed out the untenable reasoning behind the logical proofs for God.   But Gassendi wishes to know by virtue of what line of argument does Descartes claim that everyone possesses the innate idea of a supremely perfect being.   In fact, a great many never had such an idea. Furthermore, we learn about God purely from the teaching of our elders.   That does not argue for the existence of a Being who imprinted the stamp of His essence upon us.   The Cartesian insistence upon the fact that the existence of God gives rise to mathematical certainty, and therefore the natural light which validates mathematics must equally prove God, is subject to the severe criticism that no mathematician would permit his scientific reasoning to depend upon any element external to what the exigencies of the situation itself demand. There is nothing in Descartes' argument that if such mathematicians knew God as he does they would argue in a similar vein, for if the natural light is such an axiomatic proof of the validity of anything it supports, why is it not of universal influence?   How can anyone doubt God or the very things which depend on Him for their certainty?   That would seem to corroborate the original contention that not all humans possess the idea of a perfect God.

But we may go still further.   How does a perfect God allow us to err?   To be sure, Descartes explained it by the dualism between the intellect and will, but is such a theory sound?   In the first place, why allow such an artificial line of demarcation in the human make-up?   Then again, even if such were the case, as has already been pointed out, the question still remains why should God have created things in a manner which would seem to argue for a Being subject to limitations.   The same line of reasoning applies to his explanation of evil.   Here, too, Descartes claims, if we considered it from the standpoint of the universe as a whole, it would cease to be evil.   The question still is why should a powerful Being create a world in which evil is even an appearance?   Why be subject even to evil dreams?

Now we come to body and mind.   It has already been

pointed out that the scientific law of the conservation of energy is violated, if we assume interaction between body and mind. But judging from the ordinary, logical standpoint, the objections are just as valid.   How can mind connect with body at any point unless it is extended, or how can body connect with mind unless it is inextended?   How can mind suffer pain, which Descartes admits, unless it partakes of the nature of body, that is, unless it is extended?   To answer that the nature of the union between mind and body cannot be scrutinized in the ordinary way by the imagination, because the mind by its very nature is not a subject for the imagination, is evasive and meaningless.   This mind-body difficulty is one which has troubled human thought ever since, and almost all efforts to find a solution have failed.   Two disciples of Descartes, Geulincx and Malebranche, hit upon an ingenious plan. They say that every time the body wants the mind to respond, God intervenes to make the contact; on every occasion that the mind desires some action on the part of the body, God again helps by establishing a link of communication.   This is known as the Doctrine of Occasionalism.   What an absurd idea!   God certainly is not a space-occupying being in the sense of possessing bodily extension.   Therefore, if logic finds it impossible to show the connection between the human body and the human mind, because mind is inextended, how much more reason is there to assert that you must not derogate from God by supposing that he can make contact with body, whose essential attribute is extension?

4. *Conclusion.*

This brief survey clearly indicates that a great many elements in the philosophy of Descartes are untenable, some appearing irrational, even almost senseless, in their import, especially when scrutinized by the intelligent thinker.   Nevertheless, this philosophy greatly influenced subsequent thought. Descartes is the originator of modern philosophy, he marks the transition from Scholasticism to modern thought.   In his doctrines, the medieval influences merge with the tend-

encies in subsequent philosophic development.   His dualism between body and mind, no different from the distinction
Plato makes between spirit and flesh, is certainly a result of
his Jesuit training.   His insistence upon the dualism between
God and the world, conceiving of God as a personal Being in
the religious sense of the term, is almost identical with that
of Thomas Aquinas.   Even his arguments for God are in
accord with those of St. Anselm and of Aquinas.   Furthermore, the separation of intellect from will, although at first
glance it would appear to have no connection with any religious
element, yet seems to explain error, free will and the existence
of evil, which prove such stumbling-blocks to all creeds.   His
religious training influenced his theory of creation of the
world, dependent upon God as the artificer, as crude a conception as any religious theory ever devised.   It is impossible
to differentiate between what his sincere opinions were in
those matters and what elements he was compelled to include
as a concession to the Church, but in judging his philosophy
we must consider only what we find and not what he was
obliged either to suppress or to express.   Doubtless, the age
in which he lived, when freedom of thought was by no means
allowed full sway, his early training, which left an indelible
imprint on him, his delicate physical constitution, which ordinarily is not conducive to engendering the type of courage
necessary to endure bodily torture such as the Church meted
out to those who were not "in the fold"—all concentrated in
influencing him to formulate the type of philosophy he actually produced.   For the same reason, his theories are full
of flaws, are not congruous with each other, do not possess
the soundness and the cogency of pure metaphysics, for you
cannot serve two masters at the same time and serve them well.
You must either proceed along the lines of reason, the basic
factor of philosophy, or you must dogmatically assume on
faith, the foundation of religion, many factors which are emo-
tionally satisfying, but rationally offensive and unconvincing.
    In spite of these comments, Descartes exerted great influence
upon subsequent philosophies.   Generally speaking, the em-

ployment of the mathematical method by later philosophers, especially by Spinoza, is directly traceable to Descartes.   This deductive method, the complete development of an entire philosophy from the original simple premise of *cogito ergo sum*, without resorting to sensible experience, influenced Spinoza, Kant and German Idealism.   More specifically, however, this insistence on the supremacy of mind was the starting point of idealism, both subjective, as illustrated by Berkeley, and objective, typified in the doctrines of Hegel, Schopenhauer and of many others.   Then again, he held that we know intuitively the existence of the ego; this led numerous philosophers either to adopt the same kind of knowledge of the self, or to state that there is no such self at all, as did Hume and James.   These did not take intuitive knowledge seriously, hence they reasoned that since all experience shows that the so-called ego is composed of a succession of mental images and ideas, *that* comprises the essential constitution of the soul.   On the other hand, the fact that body, too, is significant, sounded the battle cry which all materialists answered.   These simply felt that matter and motion are the only existing realities, mind is of little or of no account.   His dualism in relation to mind and body had a negative influence, in the sense that philosophers rejected it in favor of monism: the materialists in favor of one substance, matter; the idealists, in favor of mind alone.   Spinoza, however, was an agnostic monist, he identified the universe with one substance, but it was neither mental nor physical in character. Needless to repeat, the dualism of Descartes was clearly a product of Church influences, because Scholasticism was the sworn enemy of monism.   We may also add that so-called common sense leads us to believe firmly in the existence of body and mind, distinct from each other; that seems to be the type of thought which appeals to the layman, since it is the obvious and requires little effort to understand.   This consideration is certainly no excuse for a man of the philosophic temperament of Descartes to have adopted dualism.

The sole question now remaining is, What does this phi-

losophy contribute to our own needs?   We may say at the
very outset to anyone who is sincerely interested in philosophic
research, that no purpose is served by simply scoffing at a
man's thought, or by rejecting it without a hearing.   No
doubt the philosophy of Descartes as a whole is not attractive
intellectually; a good case may be made out against the too
many inconsistencies embodied in it.   At the same time we
must keep our minds open, attempting to discover any kernel
of truth it embraces, which may bring us nearer to a clear
understanding of what life and the world signify.   This is
particularly true in the study of the doctrines of a great man,
and Descartes most assuredly is that, from a philosophic point
of view.   It is so surprising to find how many people boast of
their acquaintance with some comparatively insignificant exponent of a theory unrelated to our experiences, and yet are
perfectly content to be ignorant of the philosophy of an Aristotle or of a Descartes.

   To return then to a consideration of Descartes.   In estimat-
ing his philosophy it becomes increasingly difficult, in fact
almost impossible, to show that it does, or even that it can,
make a universal appeal.   He discusses so many things in
such diverse ways, he raises so many questions by his treatment and by his subject matter, that we may be pardoned for
pointing out how it affects people of different temper.   The
scientist finds some elements very comforting.   The fact
that this world of experience, which is the subject matter of
science, is governed by mechanical laws, subjecting matter and
motion to their control, is indeed all that he should demand.
The further element that mathematical certainty is to be
applied in philosophic study certainly detracts nothing from
the scientific angle.   Of course, the scientist must disregard
the insistence upon a God, as the author of this nature.   He
must also close his eyes to the presence of final causes in the
world, which Descartes embodies in his thought, once he
assumes that a Divine Being is responsible for the world.
The deductive method, which admits of knowledge from the
mind, without reference to experience, is one of the obstacles

which he may not be able to hurdle. But what of it? Descartes intends to offer a philosophy, not a science in the strict sense of the word; Descartes proposes to develop a metaphysics, which admittedly goes behind experience.

Those who are of a practical bent of mind may find his dualism quite refreshing. Why discuss at great length the difficulties of idealism or of materialism? Why waste effort in finding solutions for these complex questions, when as a matter of fact we may simply consider things as they are? This attitude is by no means recommended, for after some thought the dualistic conception raises more troublesome issues than either of the monistic theories. There is, however, a more significant objection to his philosophy, from the practical point of view. It has often been remarked that pragmatism is the philosophy of men of affairs. Americans have constantly been referred to as pragmatists because of their methods in business, because of their attitude that only that which works is worth while. Cartesianism is a far cry from that. William James pointed out that besides being a theory of truth, pragmatism also employed a different method from that prevailing at the time. It turned away from searching for first causes, for the origin of things; it directed its attention away from explanations for the past to the desire to understand the future, to the understanding of the consequences of your beliefs, theories. From this angle, Descartes is not a pragmatist. His main motive is to find the first cause, he attempts to prove a God in order to show the origin of the universe; he seeks adequate explanations for the past, convinced that the future will take care of itself. This type of theory might appear fatal to the practical man, yet, as we have already pointed out, a metaphysic is essential to life. Certainly it is a mistake on the part of Descartes to devote himself exclusively to metaphysical speculations about the origin of things, but that objection may be directed against any other metaphysic. While this answer may not be sufficient to justify his philosophy, yet it brings forcefully to the mind the fact that all metaphysical explanations are not useless; they serve a very real purpose indeed, but they tell only half of the story.   It is necessary to have a clear understanding of what has gone before, delving into regions which may appear mysterious and barely possible of logical explanation, at the same time it is also essential to look at the future, to weigh the consequences that may ensue depending upon the adoption of one theory or another.   James is just as surely to be censured for neglecting the study of the background, and riveting his attention only upon the later consequences, as any metaphysician, including Descartes, is to be criticized for adopting the opposite view.   Both are necessary for a complete picture of one's environment, enabling him to develop his personality to the highest degree.   Incidental to this discussion it may be well to point out that Descartes is indeed to be censured for the exclusive use of the deductive method as against the method of induction, which starts from experience and gradually builds up a universal law.   But so is Bacon to be criticized for delegating to the inductive method exclusive importance in the search for truth.   Here, as in the previous discussion, our conclusion must be that both are necessary to understand exhaustively any subject.

The Cartesian emphasis on free will is bound to exert influence on the practical behavior of anyone who agrees with the doctrine.   The materialist, the strict determinist, who insists that mechanical law controls all of our actions, even though he may found his argument on very solid grounds, robs life of a great deal of its significance.   Without invoking the aid of William James, at this point, who brilliantly showed with what dilemma determinism is confronted, we can readily show that mechanism, by the denial of free will, results in fatalism, pessimism.   This in no way is meant to support any religious dogmas which require free will to explain reward and punishment, for a sinful or a virtuous life.   All we claim is that the human, who is convinced that his own volition counts for naught, that his own faculties do not control his destiny, but that like any physical object he is tossed about by the elements, loses all vigor of living.   Such an individual cannot "live hard," cannot shape his destiny in the way he really desires, in short, he must despair of any amelioration of existing conditions.   The most potent argument against such a theory is the fact that even the determinist really acts and moves as if he possessed free will and could do what he pleased.   It must be quite apparent that it is far better to advocate free will at the outset, permitting the individual full sway in his own small world, entitling him to control such elements as may help or hinder his development. Furthermore, the arguments for mechanism are no more cogent than those for freedom, hence, why not adopt the latter, since it helps us to live so much more effectively?

In conclusion, we must say that Descartes has focussed attention upon many problems of philosophy.   The Idealists, the Materialists, the Agnostics, the Pragmatists, the Subjectivists, the Intuitionists, the Free-willists, the Determinists, the Mathematicians, the Scientists, the Common-Sense Advocates, all find some source of inspiration in his philosophy. Even if Descartes accomplished no more than to furnish so many points for controversy, so much subject matter for serious thinking, he deserves commendation.   But as we have shown, he has effected a great deal.   He directed attention to the dignity of the human as a thinking being, he endowed him with free will, he attempted to show the difference between imagination and reason, he showed that the human body as such is like any other machine, but what gives it distinction is the soul; he emphasized the difference between brutes and humans, showing the superiority of the human in his use of language, which is a result of ideas, the psychological conception that "ideas are motor," they must be expressed.   To be sure, his theory bristles with difficulties, it embodies many weaknesses and incongruities, but that is the fate of every philosopher.   We should be thankful for this, because thought progresses as every successive thinker attempts to solve the questions left unanswered by his predecessor.   That in fact is true in the case of Spinoza, who sincerely desired to improve upon Descartes' doctrines, and thus solve the puzzling issues with which we were confronted in Descartes. This, therefore, leads us to a study of the Spinozistic philosophy.

CHAPTER IV

Spinoza (1632–1677)

1. *Life.*

Baruch de Spinoza was born in Amsterdam on November 24, 1632. The intolerance of the Inquisition forced his parents to flee to Holland, which offered freedom to the Jews. They were permitted to conduct religious services in synagogues, but they were obliged to bar anything that might be offensive politically. Their intellectual life was very much limited, the most they could do was to cling to the past rather than to strike out boldly into new investigations. Socially, they were in no better condition. They led a narrow, timorous life, clinging to their own fold. Such was the environment in which Spinoza was reared. He received a fine education, and many expected great things of him, in view of the genius which he exhibited as a young man.

Spinoza did not live up to the hopes and expectations of the Rabbis. He desired to get away from religious dogma; he sought the wisdom of secular philosophy. He studied Latin for that purpose under Francis van den Ende, who, besides, taught Spinoza the fundamentals of philosophy and physics, and who introduced him to the philosophy of Bruno and Descartes. This teacher influenced Spinoza to think freely and independently not only in the abstract sciences but also on social and political questions. We can readily imagine how shocking and fear-inspiring Spinoza's freedom of thought and outspoken opinions regarding certain questions, such as immortality of the soul, God, angels, was to the Jews, who were not very firmly entrenched in the political community. He was therefore excommunicated, cut off from all intercourse with his fellow Jews, the most extreme penalty that could be imposed.   No amount of persuasion either by argument or in the form of monetary compensation could induce the erring soul to abandon what in their eyes constituted the path to perdition.   From the moment excommunication was pronounced, Spinoza renounced his allegiance to his Jewish ancestry.

He occupied himself with polishing lenses for a livelihood. This type of work aggravated his inherited tuberculosis and considerably hastened his death.   Intellectually, he devoted himself to philosophy, his works consisting of a "Short Treatise on God, Man and His Well-Being," "Tractatus Theologico-Politicus," "The Improvement of the Understanding," "Principles of Descartes' Philosophy, Geometrically Demonstrated" and the "Ethics."   The last work was published about a year after his death, and is his most important contribution.   To maintain his independence of thought, he refused the chair of philosophy at Heidelberg; he did not accept the financial help his friends offered; he declined to permit one of his admirers to bequeath to him all his fortune; this he did in spite of the fact that his own means were extremely limited.

He lived most of his life in seclusion; he cultivated many friends, but his devotion to the development of his philosophy kept him from carrying on an active social life.   He was very gentle, he possessed great nobility of character; he was never either unduly gay or unduly sad.   When he became tired of working, he would smoke a pipe, chatting with his landlady and landlord about the simple affairs that concerned them. On Sunday, February 21, 1677, he died, with Dr. Ludwig Meyer, his friend and physician, by his bedside.   Since his death, Spinoza has been hailed by Jews and Gentiles as the most exalted of philosophers, in spite of the fact that he was despised and feared by both during his lifetime.

To resume then with the doctrines of Spinoza.   Ordinarily in philosophies which treat of several phases of human thought, a clear line of demarcation may be drawn between what is usually thought of as metaphysics, ethics, God, immortality and similar lines of study.   In Spinoza, however, his entire philosophy, as portrayed especially in the "Ethics," is such a unit, that it is only with great difficulty, in fact only artificially, that we shall attempt to develop it from its two most important aspects, Metaphysics and Ethics.   Even these two branches of thought are so interwoven and merge so necessarily with one another, that in retrospect we marvel that such a philosophy could be the product of a comparatively young mind; the wonder is even greater that it was all developed by the strictly mathematical method.

2. *Metaphysics.*

To return to Spinoza's Metaphysics: Here the keynote is the identity of God with nature.   Once you agree that nature is all, that it is the Divine Principle, that there is no dualism between God and the world in the relation of creator and created, that we need not go beyond the immediate present experience to seek for a Being outside of it—once you admit all that, all the consequences of Spinoza's philosophy must necessarily follow.   In a discussion of Descartes' conception of God, we pointed out that his arguments for the existence of such a Being are untenable.   Certainly, we have the right to doubt that the idea of a Perfect Being, even if all possessed such an idea, which is extremely questionable, yields his necessary existence.   Similarly, we cannot logically proceed from the presence of causation in this world to an external first cause, even if we could identify such a first cause with the religious God.   How different a picture of God we see portrayed by Spinoza!   Neither ontological nor cosmological arguments are needed to prove God.   All you must believe is the existence of nature; that proves God.   Clearly, no one seriously doubts the validity of this realm in which he moves and lives; it is only necessary to admit that the whole of it, the universe in its entirety, is the very God you are seeking, and then your troubles in that respect are at an end.

This God or nature is its own cause, is self-sufficient, depends on nothing else for its existence, is infinite in the sense of being all-inclusive, the only infinite, because it is and must of necessity be all-comprehensive; in short, once we have nature we have everything that we require to satisfy both our intellectual curiosity as well as our practical wants. Taking this as a premise, the proofs of the existence of God need no longer be based on questionable grounds. In the first place, the whole of reality, the whole of nature, undoubtedly exists, but that means God exists. Secondly, if God does not exist, what is the reason for it? It cannot be found outside of God because he is all-inclusive. It cannot lie in God, since, as we have seen, his very essence is existence. Of course if you are ready to state that nothing at all exists, then by denying all being to nature or to things in nature, you must reject these proofs. Spinoza, however, proceeds further. We know, in accordance with Descartes, that the ego, or the finite self exists; if, then, the finite exists, God, in the sense of the whole of things, the infinite reality, must exist, because existence betokens power and the infinite is more powerful than the finite. In this way, we find nothing mysterious, nothing logically contradictory in asserting definitely that God or nature exists. We can further positively affirm that this nature necessarily exists without beginning or end. That is purely a scientific thought, and is also borne out by the logical reasoning that once the whole of reality exists, it does so by virtue of itself, for there is no other basis on which you can found it, there is also no external cause which is responsible for its origin, hence no cause for its termination. This is what Spinoza means by God being eternal, outside of the category of time. The temporal consideration cannot apply to God, because while he includes the time element in the sequence of cause and effect, He Himself, viewing nature in its entirety, is not subject to such laws of time.

Spinoza's God is one, indivisible. He is the all-inclusive reality, the totality of things, hence there can be no other being outside of Him. Nor can He be divided, for if you answer in the affirmative, then if He is divided into infinite

parts, there will result two or more infinites, which is a contradiction in terms, since infinite means all-inclusive. If, on
the other hand, He can be divided into finite parts, then He can
be destroyed, for the finite by definition is subject to dissolu-
tion, and a God who may be resolved into such elements, loses
all the characters of eternity; He thus becomes subject to
that which can readily vanish into nothingness.

Thus far, what are the distinguishing marks by which
Spinoza may be said to improve on the conception of God of
his predecessor, Descartes?   Once you adopt the premise of
an impersonal God, then you discard all considerations of
design in nature, a God who loves, hates, and who possesses
all other attributes anthropomorphic in character.   Nature,
subject to mechanical laws, cannot possibly develop or evolve
things because of some purpose in view.   Events occur because they are forced to take place, of necessity.   The reason
why we attribute design and purpose to things in nature, is
because we view them from our own standpoint.   We, no
doubt, plan, build and fashion our lives because of certain
ends, because of certain goals in prospect, which we are desirous of achieving, but how does that apply to Nature as a
whole?   We prefer to attribute to reality those motives
which sway us, when as a matter of fact the totality of existence
is far above us, and is indifferent to our desires and aspirations.
God, in the Spinozistic conception, cannot love or hate, because
he is acting in accordance with natural law, which by no stretch
of the imagination can be conceived as possessing such or
similar emotions.   From the practical point of view, continues Spinoza, God cannot act for the purpose of achieving
some end in the future, for that would indicate that God lacks
something now, which in turn must mean that He is by that
much imperfect.   This conception of God goes even further.
We saw on previous occasions what difficulties the question of
evil presented.   Here, however, we have little difficulty.
What is evil?   Something that exists in nature, otherwise,
we would be ignorant of it.   But if it exists in nature, it cannot be evil, for matter and motion, working by mechanical

laws produced it, therefore it is just as necessarily existing as
all other things, which admittedly are not considered evil.
Thus, as far as the unlimited possibilities of natural development are responsible for all things in the totality of reality,
they must all be treated with the same regard.   The only
reason we call some elements, evil, and others, good, is due
to our own inclinations.   Such things as please us, we denominate good, those which displease us, evil.   This is subject
to the same criticism as the injection of purpose and design
into the natural realm.   Calm deliberation, however, will
convince the thinking mind that nature majestically proceeds on its way, guided by scientific, mechanical principles.
All explanations based on design and on similar considerations
constitute an "asylum of ignorance," a means by which to refer
such things as we are unable to understand, to God or to some
other source, the nature of which, we adopt as a premise, is
itself inexplicable.

Such is the general description of the Spinozistic God.   He
furnishes us, however, with a more concrete delineation.
God is the infinite substance, all-inclusive, self-caused, independently existing, but he possesses essential characteristics.
These are so vitally descriptive of the substance in which they
inhere that through them we can thoroughly understand their
source, their basis.   Since God is infinite, logically his essential characteristics, or his attributes, must likewise be infinite
in number, otherwise it would mean that God is limited,
therefore finite.   But of these infinite number of attributes,
two are known, body and mind.   These, we possess in a finite
way, and thus they point out to us the validity of our premise,
that God must possess them.   Body is extended, occupies
space; mind is inextended, has no space-occupying quality;
in other words, body is essentially extension, mind is essentially thought.   This description is in accord with the picture
presented by Descartes.   From this follows the theory of
psycho-physical parallelism: for every mind there is a corresponding body and vice versa.   According to this doctrine,
God or nature may be studied from the viewpoint of mind

alone, explaining all things, inextended or mental in character, purely through the laws of association controlling
thought.   On the other hand, the physical or material aspect
of nature must be explained exclusively through the mechanical laws governing body.   The two never meet, there is
neither causation between them, nor interaction.   We also
have modes or modifications of this God, of this Substance.
The Infinite Modes are Motion, Intellect and Will.   The
first applies to body, the last two to mind.   Our bodies, minds,
intellects, wills and motions represent the finite modes.   The
law of psycho-physical parallelism applies to us, as well as
to Nature as a whole.   Then again, in man's make-up, all
that concerns his mental life must be explained causally only
through mental laws, proceeding step by step from the finite
intellect and will to the infinite and thus to God, who is the
substratum behind it all; that which is connected with the
physical phase of his life must likewise be carried causally from
his finite existence to the infinite until we reach God, who is
the final stopping point.   This briefly shows the manner in
which Spinoza refers everything to God or to nature.

The body serves the very useful function of supplying the
mind with ideas.   The greater its association with other
bodies, the more wealth of ideas does it offer.   Also, the
more things in common it possesses with other bodies, the
more clear and distinct are the ideas which its mind possesses.
The mind is dependent for its knowledge upon the kinds
of ideas it entertains.   This results in three kinds of knowledge: 1. Opinion or imagination.   The mind may form
ideas from individual things represented by the senses to us
in a mutilated and confused manner, or from what the imagination offers.   This results in the first or the least satisfactory
knowledge.   2. Reason.   When the mind possesses adequate ideas, or ideas which refer to things in relation to their
proper setting in nature as a whole, we derive knowledge of
the second kind, or rational knowledge.   3. Intuitive science.   By this knowledge, we derive the highest kind of
validity of our ideas.   Spinoza continues by stating that the

first kind of knowledge is the cause of falsity, but all things perceived by the last two kinds must necessarily be true, since they refer adequately to God. To explain further. Suppose we behold the sun as a round ball of fire. That is the first type of knowledge derived from images. In so far as the image is concerned, it is true that the sun is simply a ball of fire, for that is the actual manner in which it is presented to the senses. To be sure, reason shows that the sun in reality is something quite different. Its size, its distance from us, its relation to the other planets, in fact, all its essential characteristics do not, nor can they, appear to our senses. Reason, therefore, alone furnishes the adequate, the true conception of the sun. It places it in its proper setting, in relation to nature or to God. But Spinoza admits that even knowledge of the first kind is necessary, otherwise, it would not exist, for nature, due to its infinite capacity for producing things, must develop everything we perceive. He merely cautions us not to substitute the image of the sun for the reasoned-out conception of its true nature. Error, therefore, consists in confusing the first kind of knowledge with either of the other two, and in the attempt to substitute one for the other, but not in the mere fact that each offers different kinds of ideas, which necessarily must be so. This surely is a great improvement over the Cartesian explanation of truth and error. Descartes said it was due to the separation of the intellect from the will, a most fantastic theory. Spinoza denies categorically any such distinction. He identifies the two faculties, he denies the unlimited capacity of the will as against the so-called limited power of the intellect. He denies the capricious, unrestrained quality which Descartes asserts of will. He denies that we have the power of suspending judgment. This objection is made to the Spinozistic conception that there is no free will. Suppose a man were placed in a state of equilibrium and food and drink were equidistant from him, he would then perish from hunger and thirst, being unable to exercise any will power to do what he likes. Spinoza grants that such would really be the case, if the premise of the objectors were assumed. In this manner, Spinoza flatly denies any freedom of the will in the Cartesian sense, or that there is a line of demarcation to be drawn between will and understanding.

Such in brief is the general outline of the metaphysical basis Spinoza lays for his ethics. To be sure, it is full of flaws, although it is consistent throughout in resolving all to the one thought that God and nature are identical, that reason or intuition are the only proper kinds of knowledge by which we may grasp this identity. Theoretically, we may raise the following objection: if an attribute means the essence of the substance, then to ascribe both thought and extension, or mind and body, to the same God is a self-contradiction. For how can the same substance be essentially throughout that which occupies space and also that which has none of the qualities of matter? Spinoza attempted to solve the difficulties encountered by Descartes, in the latter's attempts to explain the relation of matter and spirit, by portraying them not as separate substances, but as two attributes of one and the same substance. It seems, however, that this solution results in such a logical contradiction that it cannot adequately satisfy our intellectual doubts. Then again, these attributes are infinite, each must be exclusive of the other, in order to have any meaning attach to them; each also must describe the essential make-up of God, you therefore really get two infinites, which is illogical.

To go one step further. Spinoza emphasizes throughout his philosophy the importance of man as a finite being, by referring all his thoughts, actions and motion to the Infinite God. But this is exactly the crux of the matter. How does he make the transition from the finite intellect, will and body to the infinite? Merely to state that such must be the case does not shed greater illumination than the dogmatic statements of the Scholastics. If you argue for allowing the bridging of this gap to remain a mystery, the whole philosophy receives a fatal jolt. Everything in it possesses cogency simply because God is at the bottom of all things; that is the reason for the elimination of the religious insistence on the

Divine qualities as a part of God, for the denial of free will, for the explanation of evil, for the presence of falsity and error. The moment such contact with Nature or God is broken, the whole edifice must topple down.

We must also question the psycho-physical parallelism in our own lives. Strictly speaking, this means that for every body there is a mind, for every thought there is a physical re-action, but has Spinoza proved this? We must admit that a great many thought processes do not show the accompaniment of physical or of reflex acts; Spinoza himself seems to emphasize thought as the superior element in life. On that he bases, as we have seen, the three kinds of knowledge, which, in turn, lead us farther and farther away from the immediate experience to establish the connecting link with the eternal element in the universe; that, we shall also observe, yields blessedness and the intellectual love of God. How then can we accept the parallelistic theory without demur? We may argue that, while under our present state of knowledge such perfect correlation between the mental and the physical is not shown to exist, as science progresses it will be cleared up. That, however, is not in Spinoza's mind. He furnishes us with a philosophy which is all-inclusive, which is considered as adequately explaining all occurrences, which, as it now exists, offers a sufficiently satisfying theory to the intellect, and which is not subject to fluctuation, to change, because of some progress that may occur in the future. Once the parallelistic theory is not a complete analysis of life, in its physical and mental phases, why should we adopt it altogether? As a metaphysical explanation, Spinoza's doctrines stand or fall on the completeness with which they can clear up and adequately satisfy our search for the facts of nature and of life. To be sure, we always refer to Spinoza's philosophy as agnostic monism, but if agnosticism as to the constitution of God and his relation to us were to be taken literally, what remains of his thought to guide us?

Be that as it may, however, Spinoza portrays for us a picture in which God is the comprehensive Being, in Whom all things find play, in whom there is such an infinite capacity for production that all occurrences necessarily follow from His being.   This God is not an unmoved mover in the Aristotelian sense, not an artificer in the Platonic conception, nor a creator in the religious meaning of the term.   These all represent him as outside the world of nature, either actively participating in guiding the world, or being a disinterested observer who cannot help but influence the world to move towards him as the goal.   Spinoza's God is the immanent cause of the world; just as in milk the whiteness cannot be separated from the milk, in the world, God bears the same relation.   When we understand this God, and act accordingly, continues Spinoza, we become truly human beings, with all the resultant consequences that make for a rational, peaceful life.

To complete the story of Spinoza's philosophy, to show its unity, a brief preliminary survey of his Ethics will be very helpful at this point.

3. *Ethics.*

What is the goal of human life?   What is virtue?   These questions are asked by Spinoza in a vein similar to that of Plato and of Aristotle.   His answer, however, follows mathematically from what has already preceded.   The human being, like other creatures of nature, endeavors to persevere in his being; he is essentially interested in self-preservation.   Of course, some external cause may destroy him, but Spinoza stresses the fact that the life principle must exclude death.   This instinct of self-preservation is called desire, it applies to the preservation of both body and mind. We have already seen that because of the parallelism existing between them, if the body's power of action increases, the same is true of the mind.   From this follows the consideration that anything which helps to enlarge the power of body and mind yields joy or pleasure, for that is conducive to self-preservation; anything to the contrary, which diminishes such power, results in sorrow or pain.   Granting these three factors, desire, pleasure and pain, Spinoza points out that we possess the bases for all emotions, for all passions, by which we are affected.   What relation then have the emotions to our ethical life?   Here Spinoza argues that since we are human beings we should be guided by reason, which is our birthright.   The moment we are subject to our passions, anger, hate, love, and all of the other emotions included in the passion category, we are not acting like humans, we then behave like lower brutes.   The only time we are considered as truly living, and as properly personifying the human qualities, is when we eliminate as far as we can the influence of the passions, subjecting ourselves only to the guidance of reason. Virtue, then, may as a preliminary step, be defined as acting according to reason, an echo of the theories advocated by Plato and by Aristotle.   This is easier said than done, however. How will you dispense with emotional influences?   We must emphasize again that the emotions are just as validly existing as reason, therefore we cannot advocate that they be entirely eliminated.   The most that can be done is to control them, to minimize their effects.   This in turn depends upon the power of mind, aided and abetted by the body.   We referred before to the fact that the mind derives many of its ideas from the association of its own body with other bodies, and by noting the properties it possesses in common with other bodies.   Such ideas may be either true and adequate or confused and false, depending upon whether they are a result of reason or of the imagination.   The imagination causes us to consider ourselves as the center of all things, the criterion by which to judge óccurrences, the pivot around which all things concentrate. Naturally then, we passionately react to all events from this angle.   If something pleases us, we favor it, we like it, and if the source of such an experience is a human, we love him. The opposite is equally true; we hate, are angry at, hold in contempt, the sources of things which are displeasing or harmful to us.   This imagination thus starts a whole train of passions and emotions.   We act accordingly, and while the person swayed by anger, for example, appears to possess great activity, actually he is no better than any other animal which would react similarly under like conditions.   The result is that we are passive, not characteristically human.   But if we develop our reason by adequate ideas, by referring all things to their relation to God or to Nature, then we discover the futility of acting under the influence of the passions.   Suppose someone hurts us, the imagination guided by confused ideas will stir us to punish, to hate this someone; reason, however, will point out that this individual is subject to the mechanical laws of nature, that he had no choice in the matter, that we must not censure him any more than the brick, which, subject to the law of gravity, in its descent to the ground, strikes us, if we happen to be in its path.   Such a view of things shows that we are not the center of things, that we are not the criterion by which to judge, in short that we are all a part of nature, governed by the inexorable laws of the universe.

The essence of virtue then is to control the emotions. Spinoza shows that reason can counteract one emotion by another, more powerful, or by groups of passions.   An emotion referring to something in the present or to a necessary object can readily conquer one which relates to an object or event in the future or to something contingent.   Besides counteracting passions by passions, the most important force is to develop reason, which will master them by forming clear and distinct ideas of them.   Therefore, all that contributes to this cultivation of a better understanding must be considered good; anything that hinders the improvement of the mind is bad.

This by no means completes the story.   Spinoza offers us even a greater perspective if we turn away from knowledge based on imagination to rational knowledge, which brings us closer to intuitive science.   When the human continually develops his reason, when he constantly, by means of adequate ideas, refers all things to nature as a whole, he is bound to end with the kind of blessedness resulting in immortality. The mind, advancing step by step in its observation of nature in relation to any particular event, finally by intuitive insight catches a glimpse of God or of the universe in its entirety, working by mechanical laws, impartial, necessary and subject to no external influences.   At that moment, the mind beholds the fact that all occurrences which form the proper objects of mental conception, because they inhere in nature, are eternal, since God has been shown to be eternal.   Therefore, the mind by identifying itself with things outside of the temporal element, conceives itself as imperishable, hence immortal.   This is the meaning of Spinoza's immortality, which is achieved right here and now, without being obliged to wait for another, supernatural world, in the religious sense. This final step yields blessedness, it results in a life of calm deliberation, unmoved by passions, possessing the essential characteristics of immortality.   It liberates us from the bondage resulting from passions, it sets us free.   This, too, is known as the "intellectual love of God," which, paraphrased, means the disinterested, scientific contemplation of nature. Certainly no one who understands Spinoza's meaning of God can doubt that the mind by intuitive insight, beholding a world in all its splendor regulated by mechanical laws, perceives that such a Being must not be described as possessing mercy, love, hate, and all the other anthropomorphic qualities.   In the words of Spinoza, everything follows necessarily from His nature.

To complete this preliminary ethical study, we must briefly discuss Spinoza's political philosophy.   True enough, reason is the most essential element requisite for leading an active life, in accordance with what is truly human.   What better, or more effective, method can be devised for such an improvement of the understanding than a life with your fellow men in a social organization, in a State?   No doubt, your reason sharpened by clashing with other reasons will emerge as a far more powerful instrument for guiding your own life, than if it were isolated, dwelling only upon occurrences within your own province.   Also reason is common to all, therefore, a life in the State is very helpful to curb anti-social passions.   Because of this, Spinoza develops the contract theory of the State similar to that of Thomas Hobbes.   Before proceeding to comment on Spinoza's political theory, it may be well for us to make a brief survey of this kind of philosophy propounded by the English philosopher, Thomas Hobbes.

THOMAS HOBBES (1588–1679)

Although Hobbes in metaphysics was a materialist, reducing everything, including thought, more or less unsuccessfully, to matter and motion, he is best known for his political philosophy, which influenced Spinoza, Locke, Rousseau, and others.   Originally, he says, in the natural state of man, there was *bellum omnium contra omnes,* "the war of all against all". Man in his natural state is selfish, aggressive, grasping, subject to no ethical principles; then, might makes right.   But such a condition cannot last.   No single man is powerful enough to protect his life and property against others.   To put an end to this conflict, to obtain security, to preserve peace, all men got together and formed a State for their common protection.   To this Sovereign they all transferred their individual rights and powers.   Thus all covenanted to respect one another's rights and agreed to submit to the single will of the Sovereign.   From this follows that whatever the State commands is right, what it prohibits is bad.   There is no superior power to judge the State's actions.   The only conclusion we reach is that the permanence of the Sovereign depends upon his power to furnish this common protection for which all the subjects gave up their individual rights, which they possessed in a state of nature.   The government is thus an artificial creature brought to life by the voluntary association of the governed.   We have seen that Spinoza also advocated life in a State for the purpose of leading a rational life. At first glance, it appears that both philosophical doctrines are identical, but close scrutiny will show the difference.   To Hobbes, man's nature does not require a State; in fact, his make-up as judged by his life in a state of nature demands rights won through might; if unrestrained, it would wrest all that is possible from the others; the State really is imposed by the subjects upon themselves, not demanded by their own natures.   In Spinoza, however, the situation is quite different.   Man's reason requires, for more adequate expression of himself, such a State.   It enables him to fulfill himself more perfectly.   This theory must not be confused with the biological conception discussed by Plato and Aristotle. They asserted that the social instinct is responsible for the State, hence the political unit is prior in time to the individual. Spinoza was certainly influenced sufficiently by Hobbes to agree that the individual is prior to the State in point of time, but he denies its artificial character so firmly insisted upon by Hobbes.   Spinoza gives it a more fundamental, more permanent basis; so long as each man's reason remains there will be need for the Sovereign to develop it further, to suppress the passions which are anti-social in character.   This theory that the State is an expression of our inner constitution, that it is an objectification of our deeper selves, resembles, although it is far from being identical with, the idealistic conception that it is the expression of the will to power of each member, so ably expounded by William Ernest Hocking.

To form a proper estimate of Spinoza's philosophy, with special reference to his system of Ethics, we must dwell further on the bewildering array of the theories and facts which he presents.

At the outset we may briefly point out that Spinoza actually practiced what he preached.   Being a Jew, he was naturally given a rather severe training in theology, but owing to his independent way of thinking, he was excommunicated. Spinoza, however, persisted in his resolution to think freely, and thus he was left a man without any affiliations.   This did not hinder him apparently, for he later wrote his philosophical treatises, which are classical masterpieces.   This perseverance, this independence of thought, this self-preservation, which he insisted upon by not permitting his reason and clear understanding to be impaired by any theological considerations, he has vigorously expressed throughout his ethics.   The will which he identified with the understanding in his philosophy, this doctrine he adhered to in his own conduct. There was no wavering on his part; he saw clearly that his duty was to think for himself, and that, his will obeyed. Again, he was secluded and given to meditation; his remarkable doctrine of the intellectual love of God is a natural outcome. What could be more enjoyable or more pleasant to a man who is removed from all worldly affairs by virtue of his desire to meditate freely, than this self-same meditation for which he has suffered? Consequently, Spinoza took delight in meditation, reflection, thought, not with any end in view, but for its own sake, and this conduct on his own part he recommends in the Ethics for other people to follow. Furthermore, since this meditation was his greatest enjoyment, he called it the intellectual love of God, meaning by God, the highest and most comprehensive matter for thought, or nature. Thus we can correlate Spinoza's personal behavior and his philosophical doctrines in several instances.

When one begins to read the Ethics, he is at first taken aback by Spinoza's peculiar treatment of his subject. He may even go so far as to admit that with regard to God and the theory of knowledge, the geometrical method is perhaps as good as any other; but when he sees that even the passions of man are thus dealt with, he is at first astonished, then dismayed, and finally regards it with derision. How can my anger, says he, which I myself cannot explain on account of its variability, be treated by geometrical principles, which are fixed and always true? But the eager student of philosophy will continue with the work, and find in the end that Spinoza has succeeded in treating the passions as "planes and triangles." Moreover, if he will grant the axioms and definitions, he will see that the unity of the world is very clearly demonstrated; that the necessity in nature, as well as in the conduct of human beings, naturally follows from the premises, and that the only logical way of obtaining happiness is to understand this necessity, and to resign oneself to the processes of nature. Such resignation, however, must be accompanied by a clear understanding of man's relation to the universe.

Having established his theory of metaphysics, which we have discussed previously, Spinoza proceeds to found his system of Ethics, properly so-called, upon it.   His main object in Ethics is to analyze the facts, define the possibilities, and exhibit the ideal of human character.   By identifying will with the understanding he transfers will to the intellectual realm, subjecting it to the laws of assent only.   According to him, there is no distinction between natural and moral history.   He urges the peace of mind arising from dependence upon God; the equanimity with which allotments of fortune should be received, for they follow necessarily from God's nature.   With these few preliminary remarks, let us now examine more closely his ethical doctrine.

The key to his whole system is found in Prop. 6, Book 3: "Everything in so far as it is in itself endeavors to persist in its own being."   In other words, self-preservation for the mind consists in active scientific thinking; but its self-denial means suffering of things in sensation and feeling.   Consequently, the former is good, because it is conducive to self-preservation, and the latter is bad, because it has the opposite effect.   The question now confronts us: How free ourselves from our passions which hinder our self-preservation?   In order to answer this Spinoza logically proceeds to define the passions, all of which he deduces from three primary ones— Desire, Pain and Pleasure.   He shows their psychological bases, and demonstrates clearly that their baneful influence is due solely to the imagination, which supplies us with confused and mutilated ideas.   Such emotions, when they refer to the states of the body, are experienced when we are passive, and for that reason they must be dispensed with.   All actions, however, which follow from the emotions that have reference to the mind in so far as it is active, he refers to fortitude, which consists of courage and nobility.   The former means the desire by which each one endeavors to preserve what is his own according to the dictates of reason alone.   The latter signifies the desire by which each endeavors to help and join to himself in friendship all other men. This is worthy of note, for we readily see that this desire for self-preservation includes not only the selfish motives but pays some regard also to the social instincts. We shall, however, say more about this matter later in our discussion.

At the end of the third book of the Ethics, we are still confronted with this persistent question: If the passions designate that we are passive, which is against the principle of self-preservation, whereby we are required to be active, how shall we get rid of them? The next two books furnish the answer, but before proceeding to this, Spinoza shows the relative strength of the emotions, and to what extent man is subservient to them. Finally, he proclaims the doctrine which we expected at the very beginning, namely, that reason or the understanding can prevail over the emotions. He touches upon this when he says: "To act absolutely according to virtue is nothing else than to act under guidance of reason, to live so, and to preserve one's being on the basis of seeking what is useful to oneself." From that we clearly see that to preserve one's being, or in other words, to be active, it is necessary to be guided by reason, which really is tantamount to saying that reason will discard the baneful effects of the passions, thus rendering us capable of preserving ourselves. Now that which is useful to oneself is nothing else than that which is conducive to the understanding; such a thing is good, and in so far as anything agrees with our nature, thus far it is necessarily good, for it will aid the development of our understanding. Consequently, since men agree in nature only when they are guided by reason; then, and then only, are they useful to each other; for, in so far as they are subject to passions, they are different in nature. From this we derive another advantage by banishing the passions; for, in a society where all follow reason, "man is a god to man"; he is his best aid to attain virtue. Thus we see that the good, a man who is virtuous, desires for himself, he also desires for other people; hence, we cannot censure Spinoza for advocating selfishness, for that so-called selfishness is so closely interwoven with altruism as to be almost indistinguishable from it.

Thus we have our previous question partially answered. To get rid of the "bad" influence of the passions, follow reason, that is, be virtuous; but since other people help you to be virtuous, therefore, a society is one of the mainstays of morality.   But Spinoza goes still further.   In this society, you must not yield to the passions at any time, but repay hatred, rage, contempt, by love, which will aid you to follow reason in all your actions.   Again, emotions of partiality, pity, anger, fear, envy, repentance, are bad because they do not arise from reason; hence discard them.   But does that mean that you should not help your neighbor at all?   No; help him, but follow reason in doing so.   By thus establishing the régime of reason, men will cease to struggle against the vicissitudes of fortune, for they will understand that everything follows from the necessity of God's nature.   Moreover, they will be tolerant in their judgment of men; for they will understand that their conduct is the result of their nature; to understand that means to forgive.   Thus reason aids the self-preservation of the individual, the maintenance of an ideal state, in short, it aims at the perfection of life.

We have already said that the passions are the correlatives of the imagination, which yields confused ideas.   Consequently, to get rid of such emotions we need but form clear and distinct ideas of them.   This idea Spinoza brings out by saying: "An emotion which is a passion ceases to be a passion as soon as we form a clear and distinct idea of it."   Now since there is no bodily modification of which we cannot form some clear and distinct conception, and, since the mind can bring it to pass that all bodily modifications should have reference to God, which fact in itself would make them distinct, then we can form clear ideas of all of our passions, which spells our salvation, or freedom from bondage and from subservience to the imagination with its accompanying passions.

Thus far we have considered knowledge as a means to free

us from bondage, as a means to enable us to preserve ourselves by understanding all our bodily modifications; but knowledge is also an end in itself. Here the characteristically individualistic doctrine of the "intellectual love of God" finds its proper place. This love of God is an absolutely disinterested feeling, for God is free from passions, and we therefore cannot expect any reward for our love of him. We cannot hate God, who is conceived of as the necessary order of things, as the eternal and involuntary cause of everything that exists. The thinking man cannot help loving God, he feels contented and resigned in contemplating him. This absolute devotion to the natural law, to necessity in the realm of the universe, is blessedness. "This love which we bear towards God is the same as the one which God bears towards himself"; thus the border line between the finite and the infinite becomes obliterated and the consciousness that the substance of our personality is imperishable is what constitutes immortality and blessedness. This blessedness is not the reward for virtue but virtue itself.

Thus we conclude that the Supreme Standard of ethical value is Right Knowing. That is virtue. Its aids are: (1) A highly complex organism, supplying a great variety of bodily relations to other bodies. By securing for us a large number of properties in common with other bodies, such an organism contributes to right knowing, for it yields clear and adequate ideas. (2) Pleasure; because it enhances bodily and mental power. Hence it is commendable to make some provision for the gratification of the senses, for a life brightened by amusements and adorned with art. (3) Social or concurrent life. Our fellow men have more in common with us than any other living thing, therefore, they are serviceable to us to a high degree. Society is a help to rational life, and rational life is indispensable to an ideal society. Feelings stirred up by external objects make us slaves; but living under the guidance of reason, we all move toward the same goal; hence, we are very useful to each other. Without freedom from the passive emotions, we cannot lead a rational life;

such freedom is to be won by fortitude.   From this we see that the inner necessity controls the outer, for the passive emotions are subdued as soon as they are known.   In training oneself for such self-analysis which results in self-mastery, Spinoza recommends an habitual reflection during tranquil hours on maxims of rational life and examples that enforce them, such as, hatred should be conquered by love.   Such an association of ideas will aid us at the time when we really need to restrain or to control our passions.   To all of these considerations, which show how knowledge may be used as a means, Spinoza also adds the doctrine of the intellectual love of God, which pictures knowledge as an end in itself.

Now before we consider Spinoza's ethical doctrine from our own standpoint, it would be well to review briefly the outstanding problems involved in his philosophy, which have a direct bearing upon morality:

PROBLEM OF FREEDOM

This problem has been one of the most perplexing in the history of philosophy.   St. Augustine tried to solve it, then in the Middle Ages, the Scholastics carried on speculations regarding it for years, until Descartes declared that we have free will.   But Spinoza, his successor, categorically denies that. The popular notion of freedom, that one can do what he pleases, he ridiculed, and declared that the notion is due to the fact that people are conscious of their actions, but not of the causes of their actions.   This popular notion of freedom cannot apply even to God, for His liberty, although it does not signify constraint, is yet synonymous with necessity; that implies that God cannot act as He pleases.   He acts necessarily from His essence, and He could no more change the physical order than you or we.   With regard to man, even the thought of freedom cannot be entertained.   Man is determined by an external cause in every one of his actions; his will, which is identical with the understanding, merely affirms what is true, and denies the opposite.   When a man commits any deed, he does it because of the law of necessity which prevails in nature.

That is determinism pure and simple, but still Spinoza is not a fatalist. Just because man must or is constrained to act as he does, he will have freedom only when he understands that such is the case. This clear comprehension of the all-embracing law of necessity, which reigns in the natural realm, is what makes a man resign himself to the physical order, wherein his peace of mind, his happiness, consists. Thus we see that Spinoza's determinism instead of leading us to a pessimistic view of life, actually raises us to the highest optimism.

At first glance it seems that Spinoza's denial of freedom of the will is directly contrary to Kant's insistence that an ethical system can be based only upon such freedom; but when we examine it a little more closely, we find that the difference is one of degree only. Kant, too, admits that in the corporeal world, man is subjected to the law of nature, but freedom predominates in the rational world, where the law of reason holds sway. Spinoza also advocates that reason only be obeyed; but whereas Kant would perhaps claim that the law of reason is superior to that of nature, Spinoza insists that both laws are one and the same thing; this conception must follow from his established premises. Besides this consideration, however, there is a much graver thought that confronts us; if everything is determined and man must be swayed by external forces, why should he be guilty of sin? Also, if nature or God is responsible for everything, how can there be evil in the world? This leads us to a consideration of the *Problem of Evil.*

This problem, too, is nothing new, but had been discussed long before Spinoza's time. Even Plato had great difficulty in explaining it, which he finally did by attributing it to matter, or to non-being. Spinoza gives practically this same answer. Evil, says he, is a mere negation. Sin is non-being and non-being requires no cause; hence, let us not bother with it. Whatever exists, considered in itself, is perfect; for, says he, you have no more right to ask why a blind man is blind, than why a stone lacks sight. He has even the courage to apply this principle to Nero's matricide. In its positive elements—

the external act and the intention to kill his mother—there was no wickedness; the evil elements are mere negations.

Spinoza maintains that God's power is revealed in the bad passions and actions of man, and yet God is not the cause of their baseness. He holds these views, because he denies that evil is anything positive, for if it were positive, God must be its cause; and if so, how can it be evil? But the fact remains, if evil is non-being, why call it evil at all? Why should it trouble us so much, if it is simply a mirage? Why should morality and religion press it so hard and give it no rest, if it is from God's point of view an illusion? If bad actions and passions vanish as soon as they are adequately known, why do we need ethics, politics and religion altogether? But these questions Spinoza answers quite readily.

He points out that all actions, bad or good, are divine energies. A bad act is not as an activity any less real than a good one. But the fact that the activity has taken a bad form does not justify us to call it bad or false, for it expresses divine power. Thus a bad action is not as an activity a mere negation. The distinction between good and bad falls entirely within human life. No power that man has from God is in itself bad; nor can it ever become so. Good and evil are distinctions within the individual's nature. They are only modes of thinking. A bad act is due to a defect of knowledge concerning what is good for our own welfare. If we knew what is our good we would do it; but if we do not do it, it is because we do not know. If any man had been so made that he could know a course of action to be the best for him, and yet not follow it, then evil would indeed be a mystery. In such a case, evil would be incurable; but the bad will is curable just because it can be traced to a definite cause. A man's conduct is his theory of the good. All are seeking a perfect happiness, and a bad act is such, because it belies its own promise to bring us to our happiness. Yet it is not wholly bad, for its positive quality is good. You have no right to blame anyone for being bad; educate him, punish him, if that will teach him the right manner of acting. All men can be made good, because God has written "the idea of himself" so deeply in their hearts that they never get away from this. "For this reason, moral and social regeneration is possible because God is already working in men's hearts through all their folly, wretchedness and their sin."

At this point, the question naturally arises: If all evil is due to a defect of knowledge, why did God not create all to be guided by reason? This Spinoza answers by saying: "because material was not wanting to him for the creating of all things from the highest grade to the lowest. . . ." Here, in passing, we may also note the resemblance of this doctrine that a man would act rightly if he adequately knew the consequences of his actions, to the Socratic teaching that Virtue is Knowledge. Both, Spinoza and Socrates, claim that a man acts in a bad way, because he does not know any better; that the only remedy for that is to teach him or to punish him. From all of these discussions we conclude that to be guided by reason spells virtue, that such virtue is an end in itself, regardless of any rewards here, or in the world to come. This leads us to the consideration of the final problem involved in Spinoza's ethics—

THE PROBLEM OF IMMORTALITY

Here, we believe, Spinoza is far in advance of his successor, Kant. The latter proves the existence of immortality by the consideration that to develop spontaneity of right-acting we need an indefinite time, thus immortality is the only consequence. But it appears that if an indefinite time is needed to reach a certain goal, then the desired goal will always keep just ahead of us in point of time, and we shall never reach it, hence, what promise does such a doctrine hold out for us? But Spinoza says that immortality consists of your contemplating God; in other words, you render yourself immortal by simply understanding, and meditating on, the working of natural laws, disinterestedly. Every moment of your earthly life, you can become eternal by doing just what he advocates; you need not dream of a future world for your salvation, but act now, here in this world.   This is of deep significance, for it is rather dangerous to found an ethical system upon the consideration of immortality, because the basis is too hazy and too weak.   Again, by advocating such a doctrine, every moment of our present life is diminished in importance, for it is supposed to be merely a means to attain a certain desired end sometime in a future world, of which we know nothing. Consequently, when Spinoza says that your salvation is near at hand, that the good and the virtuous may be incarnated in every act which is guided by reason, he not only enhances the importance of right acting, he not only holds out immediate blessedness as contrasted with an uncertain future, but he, moreover, furnishes a much more solid foundation for this ethical system.   No matter in what station of life you are, provided you learn to follow reason, you may share in the immortality he holds out for you, the intellectual love of God. Indeed, such a view of life is preferable to that which considers life merely as a stepping stone to a future world.   Just as I cannot help but be overwhelmed by the melodious sweetness of a certain musical composition, regardless of how long it may last, so the quality of every moment of my life must be considered, not the quantity of time.   "Life is a melody, a tone full of soul and mind"; the tone itself may be long or short, but does this affect its quality?

4. Conclusion.

Let us now return for a brief consideration of some of the outstanding features in Spinoza's system of ethics.   Spinoza certainly fulfills the basic requirements of an ethical system. Ethics, says Paulsen, should (1) point out the end of life, or the highest good, and (2) show the means for realizing it. Both of these points have been brought out in the system under consideration.   Spinoza has demonstrated that the highest good is, in the first place, self-preservation, around which everything centers; the means for realizing it is reason which can turn passions into actions by forming clear and adequate ideas of them.   But he goes still a step further and says that the employment of reason brings also with it the highest happiness or greatest blessedness; this, other systems promise by holding out the somewhat illusive hopes of a future world. The intellectual love of God will render one happy, immortal, and practically yield him the pleasures that heaven itself is supposed to furnish.

Thus far then, Spinoza's system has carried out all the essential requirements of a system of conduct; now, what else may be said about it?   At the outset, we may designate Spinoza as individualistic, rigoristic, deterministic, intellectualistic and naturalistic.   We have already pointed out wherein he agrees with, or differs from, Plato, Socrates, Descartes and Kant.   How can we also consider him with reference to the Stoics and Mill?   He agrees with the Stoics in the fact that the attainment of happiness is realized by man through his intimate union with the whole nature of things; that there is a distinction beween things in our power and things not in our power; that all disturbing passions should be avoided and social duties be performed from the rational desire for the common good.   He disagrees with them, however, in declaring that vice is not unnatural or contrary to the order of things, and also that the mind has not complete power over the passions, which are the effects of external causes.

Moreover, Spinoza, may from one point of view, be called a Utilitarian in that he designates that good which is useful for self-preservation; but he differs materially from Mill. Spinoza employs "utility" in the general sense of human welfare, and he does not admit that this is synonymous with its pleasure-giving value.   The principle that each man should seek his own advantage appeals to him, because it is the foundation of both religion and morals.   Religion to him means power gained through the knowledge and love of God. True religion, according to Spinoza, is the maximizing of human life, the liberation of man's energies, the enlargement of his visions.   Nothing that is for a man's advantage can be at variance with morality.   The conatus of the moral law is simply the effort to make the most of one's nature, under the conditions which that nature necessarily involves. Because the wise man knows what is right, he naturally is more virtuous, and therefore lives more happily than the ignorant man who follows blindly. This is the gist of Spinoza's utilitarianism.

But what shall we say now about some of the concrete problems connected with ethics, in the light of Spinoza's system? In the first place, we can readily admit that duty and happiness may go hand in hand. Your duty is to follow reason, but this gives you control over your passions, which means a transition to "greater perfection," which again spells pleasure. Thus the objection leveled against Kant's theory of being too extreme in separating duty from inclination may be excluded from this doctrine. Moreover, Spinoza's entire system of duties refers to self-preservation, which also involves the preservation of others, as we have already shown; hence, the principle of "value life" approaches it rather closely. Furthermore, in a case of homicide, Spinoza would say that so far as the positive elements are concerned, the action cannot be bad, for it is a divine energy; but the elements of evil are merely negations. The State he would say, we believe, is allowed to exercise capital punishment, provided it is done under the guidance of reason; for society being necessary for the practice of virtue, any hindrance to its preservation must be ruled out of the way, if reason clearly and adequately shows such to be a real obstacle. We also think he would favor universal military training if reason would show it to be necessary for the preservation of society.

With reference to suicide, he would not consider it a problem, because if the essence of a thing necessarily means its self-preservation, how can it possibly destroy itself? He says that no one from the necessity of his nature can commit suicide or turn away from food with the intention of starving himself to death. Such actions are justified, however, when forced to be done by external causes. In regard to veracity, he gives us his judgment in the most clear-cut manner imaginable. He says: "A free man [meaning, one guided by reason] never acts by fraud, but always with good faith." When he was asked whether a man could liberate himself from a present danger of death by deception, he answered, "that if reason persuaded him to do that, it would persuade it to all men, and therefore, reason would persuade men not to unite their forces and have laws in common save in deception one to the other; that is, not to have common laws, which is absurd." This is almost identical with Kant's solution of the problem of veracity. Again, he says that marriage based on reason is more lasting and eventually happier than if based on mere love. Furthermore, in dealing with concrete problems of conduct, as we have already mentioned, Spinoza goes so far as to advocate the kinds of indulgences which would be conducive to the welfare of the body, and thus to that of the understanding.

Yet in spite of all these concessions, Spinoza's system lacks something, something which we cannot exactly analyze, but still something against which we rebel. His geometrical treatment of the deepest and most fundamental problems of human life lends a certain cold-blooded, inhuman, aloof, and foreign aspect to his system. There are fallacies in his moral structure. His artificially constructed concepts are insufficient; they are not congruent with reality. He seems to have fallen into the same error as Rousseau, who judged all men by himself. Arguing from himself, from his own pure and overwhelming desire for knowledge, to mankind in general, he makes reason the essence of the soul, thought the essence of reason, and holds that the direction of the impulse of self-preservation to the perfection of knowledge is most natural.

We know that all men endeavor after continuance of existence, why not all after virtue, since virtue consists in that very self-preserving pursuit? If all do endeavor after it, why do so few reach the goal? Whence come the sadly large number of the irrational, the selfish, the vicious? Whence the evil in the world? For his theory of evil does not by any means explain it away. Vice is, according to him, as truly a product of nature as virtue.   Vice is weakness, virtue is power; vice is ignorance, virtue is knowledge.   Whence the powerless natures?   Whence imperfection in general?   If you answer that everything is comprehended in the infinite intellect of God, and that we shall become happy by recognizing that fact, the question simply becomes: How can the finite rise to be united with the infinite?   We must say that a world-theory without agents and without ends cannot pay its way, but goes into liquidation when it has to be worked by the self-directing essences of things.

In this brief discussion we have given in a nutshell the main objections to Spinoza's theory of ethics.   His determinism offends us.   He makes man a mere "spiritual automaton." Nothing can be demanded of him except that which from moment to moment he will unfailingly produce.   The automaton, if it be out of order, may be mended, provided the neighboring automata are so constructed and wound up as to get hold of it and carry the proper tools for opening its inside, and oiling it; but it cannot mend itself.   We want a higher station than that, and in our conduct we want to show that we are on a higher plane than that of a mere mechanical device so wound up as to ring at certain consecutive moments. That is one of the reasons why so many philosophers have preferred to attribute to man free will and independence over his surroundings.

Moreover, Spinoza claims that reason would teach us to be lenient with the wicked, because their acts follow from their natures.   If that is the case, what is the good of punishment altogether?   Now if punishment were inflicted only upon those who are ignorant of the bad qualities of their deeds, then we should be justified in teaching them, through certain penalties, to know better, but when punishment is inflicted upon those who do not know the effects of their actions, but do them apparently from the necessity of their natures, then we are absolutely inhumane in maltreating them.   To say that all criminals and all violators of the law act in an evil way because they do not know any better is far-fetched indeed.

Again, if all things follow necessarily from the nature of God, then evil fortune also belongs to this class. Now if it follows necessarily from God's essence that a man should suffer poverty, what right have we, even if guided by reason, to thwart the working of the physical order by improving this man's condition? In fact, the very reason that we are to act under the guidance of the understanding in this matter ought really to keep us from helping him, for reason points out that his evil fortune is just as necessary as the sinking of a ship, and he must suffer it with equanimity in the same way as we would endure the vicissitudes of fortune, which are not within our power to control.

In spite of the many contradictions in Spinoza's ethics, however, he unquestionably contributed valuable ideas to philosophy. He has shown the unity of the universe; he has elevated reason above the imagination; he has demonstrated the baneful influences of the passions and has attempted to give a remedy for them. He has, moreover, succeeded fairly well in probing, in his geometrical way, the innermost feelings of the human heart. He has established good, workable, moral maxims for different occasions; his system comprehends the care of the body, as well as of the mind, for he has recognized the truth of the maxim, a sound mind in a sound body. The selfish and altruistic instincts are so interwoven as to furnish the foundation for the State. This reminds us of Plato, who also says that the individual's morality can be developed only in an ideal State. To be sure, Spinoza has overreached himself in certain ways, like all others who attempt to treat of all-inclusive subjects by apparently all-inclusive theories, which, however, are found, in the end, to have disregarded various considerations. But "to err is human," and Spinoza was no exception to the rule. There is no question that he was sincere in his doctrines. He lived up to them; he regarded fame, honor, and riches, not only as worthless, but even as evils.

No doubt, Spinoza's name will be handed down to future generations as one of the great philosophers. He will live not merely as a dreamer, as a mystic, but also as a man who was most earnest in his preaching; a man who renounced life for the sake of having freedom of thought and freedom of expression.   He was a man who suffered because of his philosophical doctrines, and therefore, we should respect his theories, although, we may partially, or wholly, disagree with him.   In no small measure does his life remind us of that of Socrates, who also denied himself pleasure, and even died, for the pursuit of an ideal, of freedom of thought and of liberty of expression.

To conclude: Constant reference has been made to the fact that thought progresses because of the differences in opinion prevailing among successive philosophers.   This was very true in the case of Descartes and Spinoza.   Both used the mathematical method in the development of their doctrines. Spinoza actually employed propositions, axioms, corollaries, and all of the other symbols used by geometry.   Both advocated the cultivation of reason; Spinoza considered it, besides, as conducive to a proper social life, in which no hate, anger, will play any part.   He also felt that a State founded on reason makes us free citizens instead of beings in bondage, subjected to, and enslaved by, the passions.   By means of this doctrine Spinoza showed that life is good, that this existence is to be emphasized rather than the hereafter. Both recommended for the good life the adage "to conquer yourself rather than fortune"; to submit to the natural occurrences, since it is impossible to change them.   Descartes, by the theory of free will, certainly could give more play to man's own influence over his environment than Spinoza, whose insistence on the individual's being subject to mechanical law was bound to result in fatalism, no matter how disguised it may be.   Both believed that the ideal life is one in accordance with the will of God, but how different a conception each had of this God.   Although both were influenced by theology and other religious factors, Descartes, either out of fear for the wrath of the Church or because of his sincere beliefs, pictured God as a creator, possessing all the religious qualities, acting by caprice in all his undertakings; Spinoza, having been hurt and deeply wounded by the religious elements of his day, turned to secular philosophy for comfort; his God is nature, subject to the laws of necessity. If, as we assume, Descartes was not sincere in his portrayal of God, but simply acceded to the demands of the Church, Spinoza certainly is the more to be admired of the two, on that score. At this point we may mention that Spinoza, unlike Descartes, based religion on knowledge, not on ignorance, on natural law, not on superstition. To him science and religion harmonize, the only conflict is between science and superstition. Both, furthermore, furnish a source of inspiration to the materialists, Spinoza, the more so, in view of his out and out emphasis on nature and natural law. Spinoza, too, like Descartes, gives mind a very important position in life, which may very well be seized upon by idealists. Descartes was a dualist, Spinoza, a monist; of the two, Spinoza is the more influential, in view of the modern advocacy of monism both by materialists and idealists, although Hume, James and the Neo-Realists are pluralists, perfectly content to let experience in its manifold aspect vouch for its own constituent elements.

The most conspicuous problem, however, which caused philosophy to move forward a step is the attempt to solve the union between body and mind. Descartes left the question open; he designated body and mind as two separate substances dependent on God for their existence, but in view of their essential characteristics, diametrically opposed to each other; hence, no logical connecting link is possible. Spinoza attempted by monism to show that these are but two attributes of one and the same substance, namely God, therefore no explanation for their interaction appears necessary. We have seen, however, that this by no means is a proper solution; the result is that Spinoza attempts to offer a self-contradictory substance, which is both extended and inextended. To solve this problem, a new satellite appeared on the philosophic horizon—Gottfried Wilhelm Leibniz.

CHAPTER V

GOTTFRIED WILHELM LEIBNIZ (1646–1716)

1. *Life.*

LEIBNIZ was born June 21, 1646, at Leipzig. His father was a Professor of Philosophy at the University of Leipzig. He was a very precocious child and at the age of 14 was considered a prodigy of learning. He studied the classics— Cicero, Pliny, Xenophon, Plato, the historians of the Roman Empire and the Fathers of the Church. He entered the University of Leipzig at the age of fifteen, at which time he made his acquaintance with the philosophy of Bacon and Descartes. In 1666, the University of Leipzig refused to confer upon him the degree of Doctor of Laws, presumably on account of his youth, and this ended his connection with that institution.

In 1672 he went to Paris, where he remained for four years, studying higher mathematics and the Cartesian philosophy. At the conclusion of his stay in Paris, about 1676, he discovered the Differential Calculus; this, Newton no doubt had discovered as early as 1665. Although some have attempted to show that Leibniz must have learned it from Newton, a consideration of the facts leads one to the conclusion that each developed it independently. Leibniz published his method in 1684, Newton in 1693.

In November, 1676, Leibniz obtained an interview with Spinoza at the Hague, where he spent some time. To Leibniz, Spinoza showed the MS. of the Ethics. Apparently, even then he objected to the naturalism of Spinoza, and that hostility showed itself in his philosophic system. Leibniz also became acquainted with Locke's Essay after 1690; he then wrote his new Essay on the Human Understanding criticizing

Locke, but because Locke had died prior to its publication, Leibniz did not publish it, being unwilling to cast reflections on the dead. It was, therefore, first published in 1765, fifty years after the author's death.

Leibniz' intellectual activity found expression among other things in establishing an Academy at Berlin, in 1700, and he became its first President. He attempted unsuccessfully to induce the King of Poland, the Czar, and the Emperor to found similar academies at Dresden, St. Petersburg and Vienna. But Europe was torn by conflict and by rumors of war, and the peaceful plans of Leibniz were set aside. The Berlin Academy, too, had a struggling existence, and no other was founded until long after its creator's death.

While these attempts were made by Leibniz, he had his residence at Hanover, where he was librarian to the Duke of Brunswick. When the Duke died in 1698, Leibniz lost favor with the Duke's son, who later became George I, and who succeeded to the English Crown in 1714. Leibniz wanted to abandon his Hanover residence, but illness prevented that, and he died November 14, 1716, during an attack of gout.

Leibniz knew only the bright side of life throughout his career. Endowed with all the gifts of fortune and nature, he led a brilliant career as a jurist, diplomat, and universal thinker. He was a man of the world, taking a large part in the political events of his day. He was a great mediator, as shown by his drawing up a compromise to heal the differences between Protestants and Catholics. He attempted to effect an alliance between the Czar and the Emperor. He enjoyed intercourse with all kinds of men, believing that he could learn even from the most ignorant. He spoke well of everyone and made the best of everything. He proposed marriage at the age of fifty, but as the lady took time to deliberate, that gave him an opportunity to consider also, and the marriage was not consummated. He was gifted with two qualities, an eager desire for discovery and for method. He was just as eager for titles and honors as he was for truth and knowledge.

At his death, he was Librarian and Court Counsellor to the Duke of Hanover, Privy Counsellor, Imperial Baron, and he had a number of other titles to his name.

This survey of Leibniz' life gives some idea of the reason for many of the salient features of philosophy. His practical experiences evidence the fact that he was desirous of effecting compromises, hence his attempts to bring together opposing and conflicting philosophies. The fact of leading a career which furnished him with the brighter pictures of life, necessarily led to his doctrine that this is the "best of all possible worlds." Although the attempt to convert him to the Catholic faith failed, in spite of offers of posts at the Vatican, with great advantages, nevertheless, his contact with many religious controversies no doubt influenced his doctrine of God as the highest Monad. His intimate acquaintance with the philosophies of Descartes and Spinoza, to which may be added the fact of his personal acquaintance with the latter, immediately influenced the development of the system of thought for which he is famous, and because of which he is known as the "father of German philosophy."

2. *Theory of Monads.*

Descartes was an avowed dualist. Spinoza was a vigorous monist; Leibniz' philosophy shows traces of both. Gassendi's objection to Descartes' *cogito ergo sum* is reiterated by Leibniz in a different form. If thought, he asks, means only conscious perception, how about the unconscious states, such as exist in the cases of deep slumber, swoons, fainting spells and similar experiences? As a matter of fact, he says, we know that the subconscious as well as unconscious states are included in the wider category of the thought concept, hence we must revise our theory to embrace these as well as the conscious thought processes. Then again, Descartes calls matter extension. But such a description of the physical represents it as static, inactive, inert, when experience and reason picture the realm of body quite differently. Everywhere, there is action, motion, appetition, desire, resistance;

in fact, behind extension there is a force that extends itself, that appears in the characteristic of occupying space. From this it is easy to conclude that the external manifestations are simply the appearances of the force within. This force must therefore be inextended, or as he defines it, it is perception or appetition and desire. If this is the case, we no longer need worry about the union of body and mind. True enough, Spinoza attempted to show that thought and extension are characteristics of the same substance, nature, or God; or as it is sometimes put, thought is nature looked at from within, and body, if viewed from the outside; but then Spinoza logically furnished us with a self-contradictory substance, which is untenable. According to Leibniz, however, the whole universe is force; this in turn, in the sense of resistance, exhibits itself as extended matter, but at the same time, it also has the mental aspect of perception, beginning with the vaguest kind of such perception in the lowest realm of inanimate body, and ascending to the highest sphere of conscious reasoning.

Thus far, Leibniz really is monistic in that he reduces the whole universe to force. By thus picturing the essential element of the world in a concrete manner, Leibniz improves on Spinoza's substance, because Spinoza is agnostic as to its nature. Leibniz, however, does not stop at this point. He introduces into the world the theory of monads. According to this, nature consists of as many centers of force as there are things in the world. A monad simply means an original force; he calls them formal atoms, substantial forms; each constitutes an individual, independent of all other monads, depending only on itself for form, character, mode of life; no external cause can modify it; it is endowed with spontaneous activity. It eternally remains what it is, only a miracle can destroy it. "It has no windows by which anything can enter or pass out." Each monad is a mirror of the universe, reflecting within itself all that nature contains; there is no outside source whence it may derive knowledge. The lowest monad, too, contains such mirrored knowledge, but its perceptions are the most

minute and vague.   As you ascend in the scale of importance
of the monads, the higher they are the more clear and intelligent do their perceptions become; when you reach so-
called soul-monads, you find the most conscious, clear, comprehensive reflections of the world.   Finally the "spirit"
monads, besides knowledge of nature, also have an understanding of God, the Monad of Monads; hence they constitute
the City of God, in which the King Monad of the world
presides.   Besides, God serves other purposes.   He supplies
the reason for the existence of the Universe of Monads.   We
may, says Leibniz, have two kinds of truth, necessary, such as
mathematical certainties, and contingent, or things which by
their very nature depend upon other things for their existence.
True enough, each monad is independently existing, but the
whole of nature is contingent and needs explanation.   Why
this world and no other?   The independent cause for the existence of this world must be relegated to something outside of
the realm of the contingent.   This cause is God.   Thus
Leibniz shows that the principle of Sufficient Reason, the
explanation for the reason of the existence of the world, leads
us to the highest Monad, God, who is outside of the world.
God, who is endowed with all the religious anthropomorphic
qualities with which we are already familiar, who is also conceived of as able to work miracles in this natural realm, is
governed by the laws of Intelligence—this does not mean
that God is determined from the outside but from the laws
of His own nature—which must lead us to the conclusion
that of all possible worlds He might have brought into being,
due to His omnipotence, He selected this one before us, because it is the "best of all possible worlds," offering the finest
opportunities for life and for development.   Therefore, so-
called evil is bad when we judge it by itself, but once the
universe as a whole is viewed, it ceases to be evil, either because it furnishes a necessary contrast to the good, or because
its existence is actually required to furnish obstacles to overcome for proper development.   Since this is the most perfect
world, it must show no gaps in the progressive evolution of

all that it contains. Thus the principle of continuity comes to the foreground. According to this, Leibniz shows that there is a gradually ascending scale in development from the lowest monad with its *petites perceptions* to the spirit monads. By this we bridge the chasm supposed to exist between the mineral and vegetable kingdoms, and between the vegetable and animal kingdoms. No gap appears between brute and man. Plants are imperfect animals, animals imperfect men. Leibniz expressed his belief that souls of men have preëxisted not as reasonable souls but as merely sensitive souls. This states clearly that man preëxisted in the animal, although it would appear from an examination of his theory of monads that no such transformation can possibly take place, since each monad eternally remains what it is from the very start. This principle of continuity goes even further. Owing to it, nature never makes leaps, there are insensible transitions everywhere. Strictly speaking, there is neither birth nor death; the monad, being eternal, is not created *ex nihilo*, nor is death destruction; death is but a turning point, a stage in the monad's development. Rational souls will pass to a grander stage of life at the end of this existence.

Law of Preëstablished Harmony. Thus far we have had easy sailing. By establishing force as the ultimate element, the Cartesian opposition between thought and extension is eliminated. It is all an unextended substance appearing as matter or as mind in its different manifestations. This, too, is meant to remove the self-contradictory substance of Spinoza's creation, for at bottom it is all perception, vague or clear, as the case may be. But now into this veritable Garden of Eden, the best of all possible worlds, the serpent enters. Let us apply this theory, for example, to man. In the human being, says Leibniz, we find a body and a rational soul. The body consists of a group of monads of the lower kind. The soul or central monad is of the higher category, hence it is the ruling faculty. Every such soul is always surrounded with a group of inferior monads, which phenomenally appear as its body. We are now confronted with this query:

If the monads are self-contained, with no windows through which anything "can pass or enter" how does the so-called soul-monad communicate with the body-monads? Here Leibniz offers the most ingenious explanation, "The law of Preëstablished Harmony." From the very beginning, God has established a law whereby the body and soul act in harmony with each other. The soul follows its own laws, the body likewise follows its principles, but they always agree with each other, in view of this law of preëstablished harmony. To give a concrete illustration: Suppose two clocks keep time together. One reason may be that one mechanically causes the other to harmonize with it, that is the ordinary theory of interaction between body and mind. Another explanation may be that the clockmaker who has charge of them sees constantly to it. This is the doctrine of occasionalism. But the third explanation, or the one Leibniz offers, is to construct the two clocks from the beginning in such a way that they will keep time together forever. This is the task of the Divine Creator.

God. Relevant to this discussion we may also ask what is the relation between God and us? If you say God is a monad, how can He have influence over us, since no such communication is logically possible between monads? If on the other hand, God is different from us in His characteristic make-up, then He is not a Monad, which throws a monkey-wrench into several phases of this philosophy, the Principle of Sufficient Reason, City of God, and the like. To the ordinary man, such objections might have proved fatal, but to one with the fertile brain of a Leibniz, instead of hampering his thought, this really enhances it. He says the very fact that we cannot understand this God shows His superiority, in the same way as the plant cannot conceive of the mind of the animal, and the animal, that of man. The conclusion of all this is, that the monads really have no freedom in the Cartesian sense, since from the very beginning they must act in a certain way; their conduct is determined by an outside cause, introduced into the world by God, the Law of Preëstablished

Harmony. God, on the other hand, cannot act from caprice, but is subject to His intellect; nevertheless He does not act from constraint. Leibniz is thus shown not to agree with Duns Scotus or with Descartes in ascribing unlimited free will to Him.

Does this philosophy of Leibniz answer successfully the question it originally set out to solve? Unequivocally, no. In fact it renders it even more difficult and more mysterious. The monads are worlds in themselves, no link of communication can logically be established between them. There is clearly no apparent union between the ruling monad, the soul, and the other monads constituting the phenomenal body. How then do they influence each other? The law of Pre-established Harmony supplies the answer. But is it satisfactory? Perhaps as a dogmatic statement it may satisfy the lukewarm curiosity of one who by faith desires to attribute more and more power to the Divine Being, but certainly it is not intellectually or rationally satisfactory. Incidentally, we may mention in this respect that in the union between body and mind there are two gaps we must bridge; one is the connection between the monads in the body itself, and then between them and the central or king monad, the mind. The explanation offered by Leibniz is a most perfect example of the Spinozistic "asylum of ignorance." Then again, what about the action of one human upon others—what, in short, of social experience? Is not this doctrine subject to the criticism of solipsism so effectively directed against Berkeley? Each man is his own isolated world, and it is only by the Grace of God that we know each other. That is an extremely laudatory exhortation to address to the "fold," but how about its appeal to the independent thinker? But the most extreme absurdity in this system is the explanation offered by Leibniz for God's intervention in our affairs. If God is a Monad in a world of Monads He is not able to influence us, He also cannot be the cause of this world; but to hedge at this point and assert that this very mysterious working of the Lord shows His excellence, is not only the statement befitting an ignorant man, but logically it sheds no light on the subject. For is not that equivalent to no explanation at all? Moreover, if He is mysterious, how does Leibniz describe Him in such detail? Once we eliminate the law of Preëstablished Harmony, and cogent reasoning obliges us to do so, the fallacies in the system become insurmountable. If we carry them to their logical extreme, we may well ask how does Leibniz as a Monad or as a composite of a group of Monads except us, as alien Monads, to make contact with him? How does he expect to communicate his philosophy to us? Surely he wants us to learn from him, which logically is rendered impossible by his own system.

3. *Relation to the History of Thought.*

Once we abandon the religious aspect of his philosophy, and we have already shown in many instances that it has no place in our exposition of the progress of rational thought, it would seem that Leibniz offers very little for our purpose. But before dwelling on this phase in somewhat more detail, let us first observe the influences that converged in the formulation of his doctrine, and also what effect it exerted upon successive thinkers. Leibniz was very well acquainted with the classical philosophy of Plato and of Aristotle. That no doubt accounts for the presence of purpose in his theory. He conclusively demonstrates to his own satisfaction that this world exists for some goal, for some end, by insisting that God could have fashioned many worlds but selected this particular realm because it offered the greatest opportunities. This certainly is analogous to Plato's Idea of the Good expressing itself in this world of nature. That excludes the unrestrained working of mechanical laws so strongly emphasized by Spinoza. The Aristotelian God as the efficient cause of the world is echoed by his Principle of Sufficient Reason. The Scholastic influences are also directly traceable here in all the religious coloring with which this entire system is bedecked. The anthropomorphism of God, the emphasis on the mysterious working of the Lord, Immortality, the City of God, in fact, every phase of his doctrine is permeated with such orthodox, dogmatic assertions as might have been contributed by Thomas Aquinas himself. The most direct influences came from Descartes. Needless to repeat, Leibniz was dissatisfied with the dualism of Descartes and with the kind of agnostic monism offered by Spinoza; hence he devised a scheme intended to rectify these defects, with results even more disastrous. To return to God, however, Descartes' theory of God, based on the ontological and cosmological arguments, which was intended to furnish the reason for this world of nature, finds response in the Leibnizian doctrine that the King Monad rules all the other monads. Whether you employ the proofs of Descartes or the Principle of Sufficient Reason, the result is the same; we get a God who is responsible for it all. Of course Descartes allowed this nature to be governed mechanically. Leibniz, in a sense, did not, but that is by no means comparable in importance to the more significant fact, which both assert, that it is a religious, personal God who fashioned the universe. Spinoza leaves no room in his world for final ends, he decries the human fallacy of ascribing its own way of doing things to a mechanical, deterministic world, but he, too, makes the finite assume a place of importance only because of his relation to the infinite. Is not this really analogous to what Leibniz means in describing the human as composed of monads following the law of Pre-established Harmony, introduced by God to govern the universe as a whole? Does not this too ascribe dignity to the finite only by assigning him a place in the whole of things?

What about the influence of Leibniz upon succeeding philosophers? Reference has been made previously to the fact that he was known as the "Father of German Philosophy," and it is on the later German philosophers that his effect was felt. Wolff restated his philosophy, and Immanuel Kant was at first a follower of Wolff, later, however, becoming hostile to him. To be sure it is relatively easy to trace the connection between the Kantian emphasis on Will as the all-important thing and the idea of force in the sense of appetition and desire in Leibniz. Here, too, we may mention this similarity between Leibniz and Schopenhauer, who conceived of Will as the essential Universal reality, but with this difference—Schopenhauer ruled reason out almost entirely, while our philosopher most assuredly did not. Kant also considered this world as not sufficient in itself, requiring something that is beyond experience. This external power he identified with God, who was only a regulative ideal sought by the logical understanding, but whose existence could not be proved. Why is this any different in a practical way from the Leibnizian God based on the Principle of Sufficient Reason? Leibniz proves his God by theoretical principles, whereas Kant postulates Him as the requisite for morality, but in the end we arrive at the identical thought that an external God gives meaning to our lives here. This is especially shown by the City of God of Leibniz and by Kant's Kingdom of Ends. It is needless to carry the analogies of their system much further at this point, but in conclusion let us mention a point of similarity with Fichte. Leibniz considers the monad as self-sufficient, reflecting within itself the universe, carrying within itself its own principle of development. How does this differ from the doctrine of Fichte, which eliminates the thing-in-itself of Kant, reduces all to the self-consciousness of the ego, concluding that it creates a non-ego, something alien to itself, in order to overcome it and thus develop itself morally? Fichte, too, confines all to the ego, emphasizing that it contains its own principle of progressive evolution.

Aside from these influences, however, Leibniz does not contribute materially to a philosophy necessary to meet our own requirements. True enough, he offers great encouragement to one with a religious bent of mind. No doubt, a God who is the creator, who, even if logically incomprehensible, can be a monad and at the same time have intercourse with the other monads, fulfills all the wants of the religious zealot, who is perfectly content with achieving his main objective, an omnipotent, omniscient God, regardless of any other consequences. Moreover, such a fanatic surely finds an ally in

Leibniz, who argues from the logical incomprehensibility of such a Being to His supremacy over us. Even miracles, our philosopher allows as a possibility in his system. All this, however, is a religious matter, hence not a material part of our discussion.

From the philosophical angle, his metaphysics may be a source of influence for materialists and idealists. His conception of force as the substance behind all external phenomena surely is analogous to our modern conception of force as the element to which all things may be reduced. Spencer also emphasized force as the ultimate element of the constitution of the universe. His emphasis on monads as centers of force is analogous to the scientific conception of atoms, with this exception, that Leibniz believes God by a miracle may destroy them, an untenable proposition, scientifically. The idealists, too, may discover in his system a source of inspiration. His reduction of force to appetition, desire, perception, is an indication of his leaning towards a world composed of mental stuff. In fact, Leibniz in that way proposed to show that there is no problem of body-mind connection, because at bottom it is really all mental. His desire principle, as we have already seen, was the starting point of will for Fichte and for Schopenhauer. We may even go so far as to say that the pragmatist, like William James, emphasizing the supremacy of will in the solution of certain problems, which the mind cannot tackle, shows an analogy to the Leibnizian conception of will as the important element.

Leibniz is in effect a dualist, setting off God against this finite world, a common-sense conception. He also is a pluralist in that he reduces the world to innumerable monads. His conception of force as the only underlying reality, if carried to its logical extreme, may be interpreted monistically. To be sure, we cannot argue that Leibniz embodied all of these theories, which are opposed to one another, but we merely indicate how the roots of these are already planted in his philosophy, although the philosopher himself insisted on developing exhaustively only one of them.

4. *Conclusion.*

In spite of these comments we may conclude that the philosophy of Leibniz lacks logical consistency. It also wants rational persuasion. No one can seriously accept at its face value the law of Preëstablished Harmony. No one is really persuaded that God must be the most supremely perfect being, incomprehensible to us, because we cannot analyze His working in the realm of nature. His treatment of the union between body and mind is beset with even more insuperable difficulties than appeared in the case of his predecessors, Descartes and Spinoza. His description in clear detail of the characteristics of this Supreme God, who by his premise is incomprehensible, is the kind one might expect of an ignorant man, but is inexcusable on the part of a philosopher who posed as a genius. We must, therefore, conclude that while his philosophy may offer more or less interesting reading, there is only one concept he furnishes which is of real value, but which his disciple, Wolff, entirely overlooked in his re-statement of the master's system of thought, and which, therefore, did not exert the influence of which it was capable; we refer to the conception of force.

This concludes the philosophies of the so-called rationalistic school, consisting of Descartes, Spinoza and Leibniz. There are many points of similarity between them. They all permit a non-empirical element in knowledge, an element derived from the mind itself, independent of experience. That specifically gives the name rationalism to this school of thought. They are deductive, eliciting all types of particular doctrines from the general conclusions premised on the basis of certain self-evident truths laid down by our mental processes. Descartes' *cogito ergo sum*, the basis for his entire philosophy, even for the existence of this corporeal world, is analogous to the geometric foundation laid down by Spinoza that substance or God is the infinite, self-caused, independently existing Being on whom all depend, and from whom, all existences, even the finite human beings, are shown to derive their validity. Both of these in turn bear a close resemblance to the conception of the monad as a center of force, from which everything in the world flows. These premises have been woven out of the mental fabric, untrammeled by the obstacles ordinarily confronting us in the multitudinous experiences which surround us. These theories, based on premises which exclude the difficulties of experience, may proceed along logical lines, unhampered by the many problems concrete life presents; but that is a cogent objection against them. They do not explain life, and that is, or should be, the problem of a philosophy worthy of its name. A pure fiction writer no doubt presents a more interesting picture of an occurrence, because it is uncommon and therefore entertains us, but clearly that cannot be taken as a substitute for a typical event in one's daily life. To illustrate more concretely, at the risk of some repetition: In Descartes the existence of God is derived from *cogito ergo sum* but, as we have seen, the arguments are untenable. Then again, the corporeal world depends upon this God being a supremely perfect being, but once you undermine this conception, what becomes of the whole theory? We are then left only with doubting, but such cynicism is not very constructive as a system of thought; it makes no positive contribution. In Spinoza, too, all depends on our acceptance of his premise of substance. But this substance turns out to be self-contradictory, embracing within itself both mind and body as characteristic elements. That alone is sufficient to force the props from under the whole system, but even if we allow that fatal error to remain, still how explain the transition from the finite to the infinite, so essential to explain the world and our own existence? In Leibniz, we need go no further than to show that the conception of Monad as an isolated world by itself cannot explain, except with the most absurdly inconsistent, illogical and unpersuasive arguments, what actually exists, namely social life. It results in solipsism, which, in and of itself, condemns any philosophy. Thus we see that all of these systems are too one-sided. Their insistence on clearness and unity offends against the multiplicity and complexity which is the true picture presented to us. No doubt deduction is a useful method to pursue, but why at the expense of induction? Do we not have both reason and sensation? Should we not attribute some importance to the second phase of our make-up? Should not experience play a real part in our knowledge? True enough, it often plays havoc with a comprehensive, unified, and clean-cut theory woven by the mind, in its theoretical setting, but if such is the case, why not revise the theory a bit to include these contradictions, which experience clamors should be solved. If a theory cannot possibly yield satisfactory answers to such concrete problems, it would present a more healthy argument, if it admitted doubt as to its ability to offer a solution, rather than attempt to be all-inclusive.

Before concluding with this school, it may be well to point out some of the influences the lives of these philosophers exerted upon their respective doctrines. A philosopher usually wants to have it appear that his theory is an impersonal matter, similar to a scientific experiment, but as Professor William James pointed out, every philosophy is a product of the author's temperament, say what you will. Descartes was a sickly child, this naturally eliminated a great deal of the physical interests to which a youth usually directs his attention; this in turn diverted his attention to study, contemplation. Also, his military career was not very strenuous, the numerous rest periods in winter quarters were actually responsible for his "meditations," the embodiment of his philosophy. Finally, his physical weakness was the cause of his premature death. This, besides being a regrettable occurrence in any event, in Descartes' case was especially so, for he might have developed his philosophy more thoroughly and perhaps modified it to be more consistent, if he had had more opportunity for thought. Needless to dwell further on the Jesuit influence on his system. Positively, it caused him to include certain religious considerations; negatively, it restrained him from giving full play to his faculties.

Spinoza led a wretched life, judging from the ordinary point of view. The product of a persecuted people, with the type of mind which made him supersensitive to his position, it is no wonder that he did not seek consolation in a world beyond, the usual haven promised by all religions to the downtrodden, but felt that he ought to improve his lot right here and now. That no doubt directed his attention to a consideration of the wonderful things this world of nature holds; even immortality can be achieved here. "Excommunication" did not help matters, it caused him more than ever to turn away from dogma to that which can naturally be explained. Even religion he founded on reason, on scientific, mathematical principles, instead of on dogma, fanaticism. Tuberculous by inheritance and too proud to accept help to lead a life of leisure, he developed a fatalistic outlook on life, although it was tempered with the only type of optimism that naturalism can offer, the fact that whatever you do, it is due to your own nature, not to an external, determining cause.

In Leibniz, however, we find an entirely different situation. A life of leisure, a normal constitution, a man sought after by the leading figures of the day, a king, an emperor, the Kaiser, the Vatican, appreciation of his ability as shown by the conferring of titles on him, why should not such a man feel that the "world is his oyster"? Why should he not be thankful to God who made it all possible for him? Is it any wonder that he considered this "the best of all possible worlds?" Is it surprising that out of the depth of his heart, he should be so thankful to the Supreme Being, that nothing could interfere with the belief in His greatness, in His Supremacy, even at the expense of logic?

We must at this point state that Descartes left open the problem of the union of body and mind; Spinoza did not satisfactorily solve it; he complicated it still further by presenting us with a self-contradictory substance; Leibniz also failed in his attempt. Although preëstablished harmony does offer a solution, nevertheless it is no improvement on the Cartesian occasionalism which has been previously discarded.

We must therefore wait for the treatment of this problem presented by idealism.

⌐In the meantime, let us turn once more to another school of thought, which sprang up as a result of the philosophical reform, resulting from a rejection of Scholastic dogmatism— the philosophy of the English Empiricists. These philosophers distrusted not only the subtleties of the medieval thinkers who trusted to faith primarily for the verification of their theories, but they had no greater confidence in theories spun out by the mind, independently of the facts presented by the senses. They emphasized another factor, one which has thus far been outrageously neglected, the factor of experience. It is fitting and proper that thought should take this turn in England. The Anglo-Saxon mind is sober, matter of fact, practical, with a great deal of common sense, all of which are the very qualities essential for the observer and for the experimenter. This leads us to the study of the philosophy of one who was responsible for diverting attention from the rationalistic, deductive course of study to the empirical, inductive method—the philosophy of Francis Bacon.⌐

CHAPTER V·I

FRANCIS BACON (1561–1626)

1. *Life.*

FRANCIS BACON was born in London on January 22, 1561. He entered Trinity College, Cambridge, at the age of twelve, and in 1576 he interrupted the study of law to go to France with the English Ambassador, Sir Amyas Paulet. At his father's death, which occurred three years later, he resumed the study of law, and became a barrister in 1582. Two years later, he entered the House of Commons. He was a candidate for several offices of state during Elizabeth's reign, but gained no substantial promotion. He was always hard-pressed for money. The Earl of Essex extended great aid to him, but in spite of that, Bacon later prosecuted him for treason.

After the accession of James I, Bacon was knighted. The following year he became Solicitor General, and in 1618, he was appointed Lord Chancellor. During the same year, he was raised to the peerage, and in 1621 he became Viscount St. Albans. Within four months, thereafter, he was convicted of bribery, and sentenced by the House of Lords to imprisonment and to pay a large fine. He died in retirement April 9, 1626.

He wrote on natural philosophy and on many other subjects. The first, he treats in "The Advancement of Learning" and in "Novum Organum." Besides, he wrote "History of Henry VII," "The New Atlantis," an account of an ideal state, "The Wisdom of the Ancients," and legal "Maxims." The most popular work, however, is his "Essays," published during his lifetime. These deal with conduct, moral behavior, human nature, the author's opinions on affairs of State, on men, and on kindred subjects.

Although Bacon emphasizes experiment and observation as great aids to philosophic research, his own experiments are of slight scientific value. He was even ignorant of many of the important discoveries of his own day, yet the principles he expounds form the foundation of the modern scientific method.

2. *Philosophy and Method.*

Descartes is known as the originator of modern philosophy; Bacon as the father of modern positivistic philosophy. To him, science and true philosophy have common interests, in both the method of induction is the only proper instrument to employ for the discovery of truth. Metaphysics, as the word has thus far been used, is futile. Religious subjects, such as God and immortality, are proper objects of study for theology, which must be distinguished from philosophy; theology is founded on faith, philosophy, on reason. This absolute line of demarcation which he draws between religion and science, revelation and reason, classifies him as being a naturalist in science and a supernaturalist in theology. Like Descartes, he is impressed with the hopeless confusion, with the imperfections, with the lack of coherence, with the uncertainty, with the total lack of persuasiveness, embodied in all the preceding philosophic theories. Then again, like Descartes, Bacon wants to clean the slate to build anew in order to furnish a type of study that in his opinion is bound to convince us of its certainty and of its truth. Descartes, as a result of his skepticism, was driven to take refuge in the mind for a so-called axiomatic groundwork of a new system of thought, which is to manifest mathematical certainty; Bacon turned to nature for the source of his philosophy, recommending painstaking, laborious work of exhaustive observation and experiment which might yield such certainty as would persuade us of its cogency. At this point we must remember that Bacon is not the originator of this inductive, experimental method he so highly recommends, but we must concede him the honor of being the one who pointed out that it should be applied to philosophy, besides science.   On account of his reputation as a statesman, being possessed besides of gifts of great learning, his pleas in this direction were given great weight and exerted great influences upon his successors.   In all great ventures, we must have not only those who execute, in a practical sense, the orders necessary for success, but also the leader who outlines the whole purpose and whose function it is to persuade his subordinates willingly to exert their efforts to the utmost to that end.   This function Bacon performed.   He was obliged, at a time when people's thoughts were concentrated in one direction, to divert them, to impress upon them the need of a new method, the necessity to overthrow the old in favor of the new; he was obliged to generate new hope, to eliminate despair and the sense of hopelessness that are usually attendant upon any attempt to haul down a structure that has been erected for centuries, to convince them that the new edifice will be even more solid, more resplendent and much more satisfying than the old.   All of this Bacon actually attempted to do; while he continually promises more than he is able to perform, while as a thinker he did not achieve anything deserving of extreme admiration, while as a philosopher he is not the author of any positive philosophic doctrine, while even his method is not accepted nowadays as adequate scientific procedure, while his personal character is not of the highest, as attested to by his checkered career, which resulted in his removal from the Lord Chancellorship—in spite of all this, he did succeed in elaborating the new method and in showing its relation to human life as a whole.

Idols.   But to succeed in introducing the new method into philosophy we must first rid ourselves of all the prejudices, whims, prepossessions, which influence us.   These are Idols, consisting of four kinds—Idols of the Cave, Idols of the Tribe, Idols of the Market Place, Idols of the Theater.   The first are due to one's individual nature, which discolors the light of nature, because of his peculiar mental and physical constitution, education and habits.·   The second are prejudices due to human nature itself and to the tribe or race of men. These cause us to distort nature, because the human understanding is prone to suppose that there is more order and regularity in the world than it finds; it also attempts to draw upon all things to support an opinion it once forms, regardless of the actual state of affairs; it is restless and always, in its striving, conceives that there is no limit in the world, but of necessity there is something always beyond; it is hampered also by the dullness, incompetency and deceptions of the senses; finally it resolves nature into abstractions, whereas it is more to our purpose to dissect her into parts, as did Democritus, who studied nature much more thoroughly than the other philosophers.   The Idols of the Market Place are due to the intercourse and association of men with each other; they communicate by discourse, and the ill and unfit choice of words wonderfully obstructs the understanding.   Words plainly overrule the understanding, throw all into confusion and lead men astray into numberless, empty controversies and idle fancies.   Due to such words, the mind devises such notions as Prime Mover, Planetary Orbits, Element of Fire and like fictions.   Lastly, the Idols of the Theater are impressed upon the understanding from the playbooks of philosophical systems and from the perverted rules of demonstration.

It is perfectly natural for Bacon to devote a great deal of attention to the discussion of these Idols of the Theater, because they touch upon the very purpose of our philosopher to show the weakness of the philosophies then extant. He points out that the parent stock of error, the false philosophy, is of three kinds: the Sophistical, the Empirical, and the Superstitious. Aristotle exemplifies the first, for he corrupted natural philosophy by logic, fashioning a world out of categories.   The Empirical School is even more to be condemned than the theories of Aristotle; it bases its conclusions on only a few experiments; such conclusions seem incredible and vain to all who really seek after truth.   The alchemists exemplify this trend of thought.   But philosophy is corrupted more by superstition and an admixture of theology than by the others; this type of philosophy, being fanciful and half-poetical, misleads the understanding by flattery.   Pythagoras and Plato are fine instances of this.   Bacon pleads that we be sober-minded, and give to faith that only which is faith's. He urges us to renounce all of these Idols, thoroughly to free and cleanse the understanding and to enter into the kingdom of man, founded on the sciences, which is analogous to the kingdom of heaven.

The question still remains, however, why during all the centuries intervening between Thales and Bacon did philosophy flounder, unable to establish itself on a sound foundation, such as Bacon recommends?   Why, in short, was the progress of science hindered?   Bacon briefly enumerates the causes for this.   In the first place, out of the twenty-five centuries referred to above, we can pick out hardly six that were fertile in the sciences.   In the second place, even during these periods, the least attention was paid to natural philosophy.   Moreover, this philosophy, the mother of sciences, has been degraded to the offices of a servant, useful only to attend on the business of medicine or mathematics.   A third, very powerful, cause for the meager progress of science is the fact that men have misplaced the goal.   The real aim is to endow human life with new discoveries, new instruments, but men have embarked upon learning either out of natural curiosity, or out of vanity, or for ornament and reputation, and most often for "lucre and profession."   Again, men have failed to make progress because of a mistaken reverence for antiquity, for the authority of so-called great philosophers. Besides, there has been too much respect for what has already been accomplished, too much specialization, too great a confidence in man's own abilities apart from the contemplation of nature, too much contentment with the progress already made —all of these explain further the reason for the little advancement which had been made.   Finally, Bacon mentions the fact that very little has been attempted by people in the sciences; this, together with the influences of superstitious bigotry and the lack of encouragement, accounts partially for the want of development in natural philosophy.   To eliminate these causes, Bacon urges reform, a true understanding of the purpose of philosophy, a fresh start.

Lest we become skeptical of the possibility of any new progress, in which doubt we may be encouraged by the "distrust" that anything might be now discovered which the world should have missed and passed over so long a time, Bacon adduces certain reasons for hope of such advancement in learning in the future.   God must be the author of this, our understanding, because the end philosophy is to serve is so worthy and noble.   Besides, the errors of the past which have been instrumental in confusing us as to the true nature of the sciences, can readily be corrected or eliminated, resulting in great improvement in the future.   At this point, Bacon introduces a partial statement of the relation of his method to those previously used.

"Those who have handled sciences have been either men of experiment or men of dogmas.   The men of experiment are like the ant; they only collect and use; the reasoners resemble spiders, who make cobwebs out of their own substance.   But the bee takes a middle course; it gathers its material from the flowers of the garden and of the field, but transforms and digests it by a power of its own.   Not unlike this is the true business of philosophy; for it neither relies solely or chiefly on the powers of the mind, nor does it take the matter which it gathers from natural history and mechanical experiments and lay it up in the memory whole, as it finds it; but lays it up in the understanding altered and digested.   Therefore from a closer and purer league between these two faculties, the experimental and the rational (such as has never yet been made), much may be hoped." [1]

In addition, great hope is engendered from the fact that if without any correct method, but accidentally, notable discoveries have been made, how much more reason for expect-

[1] "Novum Organum," Book I, Aphorism XCV.

ing real progress by the use of the proper instruments of
reasoning?   Many discoveries would have been thought of
as impossible prior to their coming to light, yet they were made
and appeared simple then, such as "gunpowder, silk, mariner's
compass"; therefore, we can rest assured that in the future,
things also unrelated to what is known will be developed.
To be sure, the new course that we are to pursue requires a
great deal of observation, experimentation, but what of it?
Look at me, says Bacon; I am a man busied in the affairs of
State, weak in health and yet I have advanced somewhat in my
attempt, how much more reason is there to expect people of
more leisure to contribute?   Bacon, therefore, concludes that
we must turn our faces away from the declining past to the
budding future, with courage and hope in our hearts that our
venture, though difficult, will meet with success.   The one
way that points to the accomplishment of this aim is to use
the new method, to which we turn our attention next.

Induction.   We have already mentioned that Bacon is the
originator of the School of Empiricism, as opposed to the
rationalistic, *a priori* reasoning used by the Scholastics.   More
specifically, by this method we come to nature with an open
mind; having abandoned all the Idols, we observe at great
length, aided by experiments, whenever possible; then, after
gathering exhaustively all kinds of particulars, we arrive at
generalities by a gradual process.   We must not be too hasty
to reach conclusions, we must note all opposing instances.
The true method does not confine itself to a few objects, an
error the old Empiricists fell into, but it must be universal in
scope; it must exhaustively investigate its object, unaffected
by consideration of utility or of personal predilection.   By
such procedure we are bound to conquer nature, which will
improve man's lot in this world.

To go one step further: Bacon more definitely develops the
theory by his conception of Tables.   The purpose is to discover the law or "form" which the essential quality of every
object follows.   To do this it is necessary to compile and
present all known instances which agree in the same "form,"

though apparently most dissimilar.   For example, if our aim is to discover the form or nature of heat, we present all instances in which heat is present; such as the sun's rays, fiery meteors, burning thunderbolts, all flame, ignited solids, natural warm baths, boiling or heated liquids, heat vapors and fumes, air confined in caverns, all bodies held near a fire, roses packed in baskets, hot herbs in their impressions on the tongue, intense cold and other instances.   Such a classification of things in which heat is present, he calls the Table of Essence and Presence.   Next, we must present all instances in which such heat is totally absent.   This is the Table of Deviation, or of Absence in Proximity.   In compiling both of these we must recognize that the senses may be deceptive, imperfect, that they must therefore be aided by experiment and by similar processes.   Once these two Tables are completed, by a process of comparison and exclusion we find that heat is really motion, for it is always present when heat is present and vice versa. This method also shows that heat cannot be weight, for heavy bodies are found in both lists; for the same reason heat is also shown not to consist of any other quality except that of motion.   But Bacon wants to check the result still further. We must, he adds, present a list of instances in which this heat is found in different degrees, more or less.   This is the Table of Degrees or Table of Comparison.   This Table will prove whether our former conclusion is correct, for if heat is motion, the more motion, the more heat, the less heat, the less motion.   This method can be applied to the discovery of any other law or essential quality that requires investigation.

To conclude: Bacon's chief object was to distinguish between deduction, which he called Anticipation of Nature, and induction, or Interpretation of Nature.   To substitute the latter for the former is the main function of the philosopher. Bacon admitted that he did not wish to found a new sect in philosophy, after the manner of the ancient Greeks, nor did he desire to carry on fruitless speculations concerning the origin and the first causes of things.   All he aimed at was to furnish people with a new perspective, a different objective, a practical goal. But did he succeed? Probably not. He was not scientist enough to be able to enter into it whole-heartedly, his method is incomplete, it is mechanical, it left little to scientific imagination, which is very necessary for the development of any complicated theory. William James aptly remarked that when a scientist embarks on the investigation of a novel theory he must have faith in the success of his venture, otherwise he would abandon it prematurely. This element of faith cannot be grounded on mere induction, it must leave a lot to the fertility of the scientist's brain, to his imaginative faculties. Bacon utterly overlooked the function served by the deductive method. We have commented many times that both methods play an important rôle in study and in thought. His philosophy is barren, it exerted little influence, aside from the fact of emphasizing the use of the experimental method in philosophy. Viewing it from this angle, the English school of Empiricism, whose chief exponents are Locke and Hume, takes its lead from Bacon. Let us therefore next consider the philosophy of John Locke.

CHAPTER VII

John Locke (1632–1704)

1. *Life.*

Locke was born at Wrington in Somersetshire, on the 29th day of August, 1632. He began his studies in Westminister School, and in 1651 entered Christ-Church College, Oxford, of which he was elected a Fellow, a position he held for many years. He was considered the most ingenious man in the College. He was dissatisfied with the method of study that prevailed there, however, since it was dominated by the Scholastic spirit. Then he studied medicine, and though he never practiced very much, because of ill health, nevertheless, he was held in great esteem by the most able physicians of his time. In 1664, he left England for Germany in the capacity of Secretary to Sir William Swan, Envoy of the English King to the Elector of Brandenburg. A year later, he returned to Oxford, where he applied himself to the study of Natural Philosophy.

In 1666, while at Oxford, he met Lord Ashley, who afterward became Earl of Shaftsbury and Lord High Chancellor of England, under the following circumstances. The Lord became ill and commissioned Dr. Thomas, a physician at Oxford, to send for some mineral waters for him. Dr. Thomas left this commission in charge of Locke, who was obliged to make his excuses to Lord Ashley for the waters not being ready, due to the neglect of the person in charge. This meeting initiated a lasting friendship between the two men; bringing Locke, besides, into contact with public life. Upon the fall of his patron, when the king sent him to the Tower, Locke was obliged to take refuge in Holland in 1682, until the accession to the throne of William of Orange opened a way to his return to his native country.   He came back to London in February, 1689.   The air of London grew more and more troublesome to him, since he was afflicted with asthma.   He, therefore, spent most of his time at Oates, about 20 miles from London, at the home of his friend, Sir Francis Masham, where he was permitted full freedom to apply himself to his studies as far as his health would allow.   There he died on the 28th day of October, 1704, about three in the afternoon, while Lady Masham was reading aloud to him from the Psalms.

This brief résumé of Locke's life indicates that together with Lord Ashley, he was a victim of political tyranny, which in turn is always based on intolerance and perhaps ignorance. It may, therefore, be more easily understood why all of his writings center about the doctrines of tolerance, freedom, clear understanding.   His treatises on Government emphasize that the relation between the Government and the subjects is based on expediency.   With Hobbes he agrees that the State is founded on contract, but the Government can be permitted to remain only so long as it serves the interests of the governed.   Once this purpose cannot be fulfilled, a revolution to overthrow the Government is a most justifiable weapon.   In his Letters of Tolerance he emphasizes religious freedom, not an intolerant, dogmatic suppression requiring all to submit to the same religious authority.   Lastly, in his "Essay Concerning Human Understanding," his aim is to show the capacity of the mind, to mark its limits, to show what the origin, the extent, and the certainty of our knowledge may be—by means of all of these he simply wants to supply light, reason, as guides, instead of ignorance, blind faith and irrationality.   He knows full well that once conduct is based on a proper, clear understanding, the result is bound to be tolerance and liberty, no matter in whatever branch of human life it may be, politics, religion, philosophy.

2. *Origin of Knowledge.*

In accordance with these aims, Locke turns his attention primarily to the epistemological problem, the problem of knowledge.   As an empiricist, his purpose is to base all knowing in the first instance upon experience, upon the study and observation of nature.   We shall see shortly that the mind, too, is not neglected, but what we must particularly emphasize, however, is that Locke denies the possibility of knowledge prior to any experience whatsoever.   In short, he denies the existence of innate ideas.   The Rationalists were compelled to assume such ideas to be inborn, to be a result of an agency, other than experience, presumably God; otherwise the webs they wove could not hold, but Locke furnishes the other side of the picture.   It has been argued, he says, that certain principles must be innate, as shown by the universal assent of mankind to them; for example, the proposition that "whatever is, is."   But upon close examination we must conclude that children, idiots, and a great part of illiterate men have no knowledge of it.   To say that they possess knowledge of such innate axioms, but they are unconscious of them, resolves itself into the contradiction that a "thing is and is not in the understanding" at the same time.   Do so-called innate moral principles fare any better?   No, for here, too, there is no universal consent, since moral precepts vary from nation to nation. Again, conscience cannot be adduced to prove that they are innate, because different consciences prompt their possessors to act differently on similar occasions.   Even such a presumably universal idea as the existence of God cannot be innate, for many either do not possess it or deny His existence, such as atheists; others have different notions of such a Being, ranging from the savage spirits to the refined conceptions of modern times, and still others acquire such a belief from their contacts with other people.   Therefore, he concludes, the soul is an empty tablet, and only experience can impress upon it the original sources of knowledge.

More specifically, Locke shows, that although there can be no thought without sensation, yet once such sensations are furnished, the Mind, too, begins to operate.   Thus our knowledge originates from sensation and reflection.   This knowledge consists of simple ideas and complex ideas.   The simple may come into our minds by one sense, such as solidity through touch; they may come through more senses than one, such as motion, rest, figure, in the experience of which both vision and touch coöperate; still others may be had from reflection only, such as the idea of perception, or of willing; finally we may receive them through both reflection and sensation, these may be exemplified by pleasure and pain, also succession.   At this point, it may be well to point out the division Locke makes between primary and secondary qualities.   He says that whatever the mind perceives in itself is an "idea," and the power to produce such an idea is the "quality" of the object in which that power resides.   The primary are the original qualities of body which produce in us the simple ideas of solidity, extension, figure, motion or rest and number.   "The secondary qualities are in truth nothing in the objects themselves but powers to produce various sensations in us by their primary qualities, *i.e.* by the bulk, figure, texture, and motion of their insensible parts, as colours, sounds, tastes, etc." [1]   It cannot be too strongly emphasized that to Locke the primary qualities exist independently of the mind; they remain, no matter what alteration the object undergoes.   For example, "Take a grain of wheat, divide it into two parts, each part has still solidity, extension, figure and motion; divide it again, and it still retains the same qualities; and so divide it on till the parts become insensible; they must retain still each of them all these qualities." [2]   The secondary qualities, on the other hand, have absolutely no independent existence; they are nothing but sensations produced in us by the primary qualities; these sensations do not resemble the qualities existing in the objects.   "Let not the eyes see light or colours, nor the ears hear sounds; let the palate not taste, nor the nose smell; and all colours, tastes, odours, and sounds . . . vanish and cease, and are reduced to their causes, *i.e.* bulk, figure,

---

[1] "Essay Concerning Human Understanding," Book II, Chapter VIII, Section 10.
[2] *Ibid.*, Section 9.

and motion of parts." [3]   But as we have seen, the primary
qualities never disappear, even if you divide the object into
the most insensible parts.

Besides these simple ideas, Locke points out there are complex ideas, in the framing of which the mind acts in the following manner: (1) Combining several simple ideas into one
compound; thus all complex ideas are made; (2) Bringing
two ideas, whether simple or complex, together and setting
them by one another, so as to take a view of them at once, without uniting them into one; by which way it gets all its ideas of
relations; (3) Separating them from all other ideas that accompany them in their real existence; this is called "abstrac-
tion," thus all its general ideas are made.   "Among these
complex ideas we find those of substances, which simply mean
such combinations of simple ideas as are taken to represent
distinct particular things subsisting by themselves."   Examples of this are man, table, chair.   A collection of such
individual things would be a complex substance, as an army
of men or a flock of sheep.

To recapitulate: Locke starts with the simple proposition
that experience is the source of knowledge.   Sensations supply the materials on which the mind operates and forms ideas.
The mind may passively receive them, as in the case of many
simple ideas, or it may actively coöperate to formulate them,
as is evident in the complex.   Many of these simple ideas resemble the qualities which induce them in the mind, these are
the primary as contrasted with the secondary qualities, which
have no external existence; hence there can be no resemblance
between the latter and their resultant ideas.   To make this distinction more clear, let us consider color or sound or any
other of the sensations due to these secondary qualities.   How
can color inhere in the object, if to a color-blind person, it
will appear differently than to one with normal vision?   The
same thing is true of sound.   A deaf individual hears nothing, although a particular noise may actually deafen the

[3] *Ibid.*, Section 17.

average man.   You may go through the entire list of such
sensations and become convinced that since they vary with
different individuals, they can have no independent existence,
but must be a modification of our own nervous system and the
sensory organs.   The primary qualities, Locke contends, are
of a different caliber.   They do not change with different
individuals, hence they must exist externally to us.   But is
this distinction tenable?   No, for with Berkeley, we can
point out that the same arguments Locke adduces for showing
the non-existence of secondary qualities, apply with equal
force to the primary.   Does not the size of an object vary
with different individuals?   To a very tall man, an object
will appear smaller than to a dwarf; distance, too, will make
a difference.   The same is true of any of the other sensations
produced by the primary qualities.   Therefore, we are justified in concluding either that all the qualities, primary and
secondary, do exist independently or that they do not.
Locke's arguments are not convincing and rationally not persuasive.   We may further note another fact at this point.
Locke uses substances in a manner distinct from the rationalistic school; to him they designate what we ordinarily call
things, objects in the world, not in the sense of an underlying
substratum in the universe, in which all things inhere.

Thus far, then, Locke shows us the materials for knowledge, consisting of ideas, based in the first instance on sensation.   From this his definition of the nature of knowledge
readily follows: "Knowledge," he says, "seems to me to be
nothing but the perception of the connection and agreement,
or disagreement and repugnancy, of any of our ideas." [4]
This definition indicates the extent, the boundaries, the limits,
of knowledge.   Since it works with ideas, it cannot certainly go
beyond them.   But it is impossible to know all that is implied
even in our ideas.   We cannot know all the connections, the
combinations, the contrasts, between our ideas.   We cannot
know, for instance, whether matter thinks or whether the soul
is material; what connection there is between secondary and

---

[4] *Ibid.,* Book IV, Chapter I, Section 2.

primary qualities; or whether the ideas correspond to the things that produce them.

3. *Certainty of Knowledge.*

What then, does this doctrine of knowledge offer? Is there any certainty in our knowing, or is it all illusory? To that, Locke has a ready answer. Knowledge can be certain and real, only if the idea conforms to what it represents. From this angle, simple ideas yield certain knowledge, because the mind cannot make these by itself, they must necessarily be the product of things operating on the mind in a natural way, they cannot be the product of fancy, nor can they be fictions. Then again, all complex ideas except those of substance, must be included in this category of certain knowledge, for they are archetypes of the mind's own making, not intended to be the copies of anything, therefore the mind is its own criterion for their truth. This shows that mathematical knowledge is real, for it is not intended to conform to anything external of the mind.

The same consideration, Locke applies to moral ideas, which are archetypes themselves, hence they need no external criterion by which to judge their validity. Here we note that, like Spinoza, Locke believes that morality can have mathematical certainty. Ideas of substances, however, admittedly have their archetypes without us, hence they are only real and true if they conform to them. This is the crux of the whole matter; this concerns knowledge of real existence, and is of great practical importance. How certain then is such knowing? We have *intuitive* knowledge of our own existence; this is so axiomatic that it is incapable of further proof. This method of establishing the existence of the Ego is analogous to that of Descartes, whose *cogito ergo sum* claims to be the most unassailable of self-evident truths. We also can demonstrate the existence of God, continues Locke. Here he employs the cosmological argument; he says, once we establish our own existence, we must continue to search for the cause until we stop at God, a first cause. Since nothing cannot produce a being, therefore something eternal, most powerful, most knowing, or God, is responsible.

Finally, we have sensitive knowledge of other things in the world. Although it does not possess the certainty of the other two kinds, for the existence of an idea does not necessarily show its correspondence to the object without, it is probable knowledge and proves the existence of such external things. Such existence may also be attested to by these considerations: It is plain that these perceptions must be produced by exterior causes affecting our senses, because those that lack a certain sense cannot have these perceptions belonging to that sense. (Note the previous discussion of the certainty of simple ideas.) Then again, an idea from actual sensation and one from memory are entirely different, and the pleasure or pain which accompanies an actual sensation is absent, when it is only reviewed in memory. Witness the pain when you actually burn your finger, and its absence when you recall it later. This bears witness to the fact that the actual experiences must be induced by things existing without us. To add to this probability, we have the testimony of more than one sense on many occasions. He that *sees* a fire, if he imagines that it might be only a product of his fancy, may also *feel* it, this doubtlessly will convince him of the reality of its existence.

Thus, Locke concludes that in knowledge of real existence, we have intuitive knowledge of our own existence, demonstrative knowledge of the existence of God, and sensitive knowledge of things in the world. The last is only probable. Yet upon consideration of all the factors involved, it offers sufficiently convincing proof of the existence of things without us, to be more than adequate for our purposes in our daily lives. We can now readily see that in the main, Locke established his aims in dealing with the epistemological problem; the origin of knowledge he establishes on what to him is a most firm footing, on sensation and experience; he further sets limits to the understanding by pointing out that knowledge not only cannot extend beyond the ideas in the mind, but must be narrower than these, since we cannot know all the implications involved in these ideas; lastly, knowledge is certain in all complex ideas, in which it is its own criterion, but as to ideas of substances, there are archetypes without, to which they must conform; certainty can therefore be present only if this conformity is evident.   This is a difficult task to perform. Locke, therefore, furnishes us here with three kinds of knowledge, intuitive, demonstrative and sensitive.   A parting word on this theory of knowledge may be said here.   In conformity with the empirical doctrine, Locke denies any reality to genera, species, universals; they are mere words.   Platonic and Scholastic realism he rejects.   Experience does not vouch for their existence.

4. *The Will and Liberty.*

In the course of his treatment of the problem of epistemology Locke was of necessity obliged to describe in more or less detail that phase of the self which is so often troublesome to philosophers—the will.   "The Will," he defines, "as the power which the mind has to order to consideration of any idea or the forbearing to consider it, or to prefer the motion of any part of body to its rest and vice versa." [5]   Liberty is the power of the agent to do or forbear any particular action, or idea, according to the determination of the mind.   When such forbearance or performance of an action are not equally in a man's power, not depending upon the determination of his thought, we have necessity.   To illustrate: A man falling into water, accidentally, is not a free agent.   For though he has volition, though he prefers his not falling to falling, yet the forbearance of it, the stopping of that motion of falling does not follow upon his volition, he is therefore not free. The same distinction holds in our thoughts as in our physical motions.   A waking man is not at liberty to think or not think, because he necessarily must have ideas constantly in his mind, but he is at liberty to remove his contemplation from one idea to another.   Sometimes even that is impossible, a man on the

---

[5] *Ibid.,* Chapter XXI, Section 5.

rack is not at liberty to lay aside for the time being the idea of pain.   From this discussion we find that will is a power of the self and liberty is another power of this self, therefore, you cannot speak of free will, for that is tantamount to saying that one power has another power, which is absurd, like speaking of swift sleep or of square virtue.   Liberty is not an attribute of the will.   The voluntary is opposed to the involuntary, not to necessity.   A paralytic may prefer to sit still instead of moving; in so far, it is voluntary, but because he cannot move even if he should desire to do so, there is want of freedom in his case. The conclusion is clear that a man is not at liberty to will or not to will anything to which he once directs his mind, for then he must prefer one or the other line of action or thought. "A man that is walking, to whom it is proposed to give off walking, is not at liberty whether he will determine himself to walk or give off walking, or not, he must necessarily prefer one or the other of them, walking or not walking." [6]   The will, therefore, is determined by the mind, which in turn is swayed by uneasiness or desire.   The most pressing desire is the desire for happiness.   Such happiness in the fullest sense of the word is the utmost pleasure we are capable of.   Misery is the utmost pain.   Good and evil are nothing but pleasure and pain; moral good and moral evil consist of the conformity or disagreement of our actions to the moral law of God, who rewards and punishes us according to our deserts.

5. *Politics.*

This gives us a brief glimpse into Locke's theory of ethics, which he did not develop comprehensively.   Now to follow this up with a brief discussion of his politics.   Reference has already been made to the fact that Locke founded the State on the theory of contract, first initiated by Hobbes, but there are radical differences between them.   To Hobbes, man in his natural state possesses no rights, no justice, these sprung into being only with the formation of the State.   The political organization, therefore, is the supreme power, never subject

[6] *Ibid.,* Section 24.

to attack or criticism by its subjects.   In Locke's view, man
in his natural state already has implanted in him rights and
justice.   The State simply serves to guard them, to stabilize
justice.   Therefore, it may remain only as long as it serves
this purpose, as long as it is useful to the governed, otherwise it has no *raison d'être*, and may be overthrown by revolution.   To illustrate concretely Locke's conception of rights
as appurtenant to man's own nature, let us consider the right
of property.   Originally, he says, God gave the earth and
all of its contents to mankind in common.   Man by his labor
made some part of the earth useful; that gave him property
rights to that portion against all others.   At first, no one
quarreled with any of his fellow men in reference to property, for each appropriated only as much as he could use,
only so many apples as he could consume.   But trouble
began when gold came into use.   Then there was no limit
to what man wanted, for even if he could not consume all he
appropriated, he could sell and acquire gold, which was durable.   Laws or the State then became necessary to put limits
to, and to offer protection for, such property rights.   The
ultimate conclusion, however, is that the right to property
has its roots in man himself, his labor.

6. *Conclusion.*

The Self.   This philosophy of Locke, as may be expected,
is an integral part in the development of thought.   With
reference to the three concepts, Self, God and the World,
which are of special interest to us, he both agrees with, and
differs from, his predecessors and contemporaries.   He also
exerts some influence upon succeeding thinkers.   He agrees
with the three advocates of the rationalistic school, in insisting upon the unity of the ego, upon the existence of that
indefinable something called the Self.   We have intuitive
knowledge of this spirit, he argues.   That is similar to the
Cartesian theory, but even Spinoza and Leibniz must have
similar thoughts on this subject, for they advance no other
factors to prove its existence except to assert that we have a

mind or a king monad. David Hume denies such intuitive knowledge, and since he is a thoroughgoing empiricist, he admits that there is no identical self, but mind consists of a train of mental associations, ideas, experiences. Kant on the other hand contends that the self is a reality, it accompanies all of our perceptions. We may add that to Berkeley the reality of the ego is the most certain, since he is the exponent of spiritual substance as the sole, underlying reality.

God. Locke's God is similar to that of Descartes and of Leibniz. He is personal, endowed with all the religious characteristics, responsible for the world and all it contains. This conception is radically different from the Spinozistic doctrine of the identity of God and Nature. Locke is so far in agreement with Descartes on this score, that he employs the same argument to demonstrate God's existence, the cosmological. Surely, this is against Bacon's exhortation to eliminate such subjects of theology from the philosophic category. Hume clearly is against demonstrative knowledge of God, while Kant postulates such a personal Supreme Being, as the basis for a moral life. This last is analogous to Locke's emphasis on God's being the author of the moral law. Berkeley considers God, the Highest Spirit, the keystone for this whole system of nature. It may be noticed here that even Locke, as well as those who agree with him in the need for the existence of God, does not contend that God's existence is as certain as that of the Self. The latter is known intuitively, the former must be demonstrated.

Locke's empiricism, we should expect, should cause him to deny or at least to doubt the existence of anything that is not borne out by experience. But is this the case? Most assuredly not. He divides objects into primary and secondary qualities, the former exist independently, the latter, not. But does experience show that? Then again, is a discussion of God appropriate to a man who began by being an empiricist and who really influenced the positivistic school of philosophy, especially in England? It seems that Locke cannot be a thoroughgoing empiricist, for he discusses too many subjects unrelated to experience, God, the Ego, reward and punishment. His successor, Hume, certainly demonstrated how far experience can take us; his theory shows that we must eliminate many of the concepts found in Locke's system of thought. To be sure, Locke agrees with Spinoza and Leibniz that there is no liberty of indifference, that we cannot even talk of free will. This is a proper attitude for the empiricists, since nature, as far as we can sense it, exhibits necessity. But even here Locke's discussion of the mind's directing the will towards one line of action as against another goes beyond what experience can teach us.

In spite of these comments, Locke makes a vital contribution to our needs. By marking the limits of the human understanding, by pointing out that experience is the starting point for all knowledge, and therefore we ought to stick to it, by insisting upon clearness of thought, he encourages a positive, scientific way of thinking. Once you eliminate confusion, once you base your conclusions upon the proper foundation—dogma, superstition and tyrannical submission to principles and doctrines, unsupported by anything else but tradition and authority, vanish and are supplanted by a liberal policy in religion, politics, morality, and in many other phases of life. In politics, he is the advocate of revolution, but while we may prefer the overthrowing of government by more peaceful means, we must agree that psychologically Locke is correct in his statement that in human nature all rights inhere, and the State should offer the opportunities of stabilization, where all can realize to the fullest extent their potentialities. To the religiously inclined individual, Locke's conception of God calls for nothing better, even reward and punishment God metes out to the just and to the unjust. To the common-sense person, a world in which sensible experience plays a leading part is certainly most refreshing. Although the division between primary and secondary qualities may be too abstract, still he admits the existence of objects without us, which are the cause of our sensations. Mind and body also are taken for granted; no question is raised as to their union, nor is any explanation offered for it. The philosopher should give a great deal of thought to Locke's denial of innate ideas, to his discussion of free will, to his theory of politics, to the explanation of God as the cause of all things, a God who is not the Aristotelian metaphysical Being, but a loving, all-powerful Spirit, and finally to his epistemological theory in general.

In conclusion we must say that no solution for the union of mind and body has been offered by Locke. Also, that the chief exponent of valid empiricism is David Hume, not Locke; but before proceeding to study Hume, we may interpolate at this point the philosophy of another thinker, who turned his attention in a particular direction because of this doctrine —we refer to George Berkeley.

CHAPTER VIII

George Berkeley (1685–1753)

1. *Life.*

George Berkeley was born near Thomastown, in County Kilkenny, Ireland, on March 12, 1685. At fifteen, he entered Trinity College, Dublin, where he was elected a Fellow in 1707. The years 1713–1721 he spent in England or abroad. In 1724 he was made Dean of Derry. Later he persuaded Walpole to promise a government grant of £20,000 for the purpose of establishing a great missionary college in Bermuda, from which he could exert a religious influence on the United States. In 1728 he sailed for Rhode Island to interest New Englanders in this project, but during his absence, the English government lost its enthusiasm for the promised grant, and Berkeley was obliged to return home, a disappointed man. In 1734, he was made Bishop of Cloyne; he left there for Oxford in 1752. He died the next year The main propositions of his philosophy are contained in the "Treatise Concerning the Principles of Human Understanding," the "Dialogues between Hylas and Philonous," "Essay towards a New Theory of Vision," all of which were published before he was thirty years of age. Apparently he shot his bolt then, for his philosophy developed very little in his later life. He was greatly influenced by Newton's scientific discoveries, by his theological training and especially by Locke's "Essay," which was most directly responsible for the main thesis of his philosophic thought—*esse est percipi*—"to exist means to be perceived as an idea."

2. *Theory of Existence.*

Berkeley directs his polemic against Locke's illogical division between primary and secondary qualities. Locke, too, admits that secondary qualities, such as color, sound, taste, smell and the like have no independent existence; they are a result of our own senses. Thus far Berkeley is in thorough accord; this resolves itself into the theory that such experiences are ideas, perceptions by us as perceiving subjects. But now comes the wide split between them. Locke insists that primary qualities do exist independently of us, they are not a result of our senses; in fact, Locke means to entertain the thought that our simple ideas of these qualities may actually resemble these archetypes without. Berkeley cannot accept that. To enforce his idea that such a distinction is inconceivable he "turns the tables" on Locke by employing the latter's own arguments. Locke says that the secondary qualities differ with different people, color to the color-blind, sound to the deaf, means something other than to the normal individual; on the other hand, size, figure, extension, motion and solidity, the primary qualities, never differ, hence they cannot depend upon our senses, whereas the former must. Berkeley logically shows that even the primary qualities differ with different individuals, therefore by Locke's own contention, they, too, must be merely our sensations, our perceptions, our ideas only. Consider figure and extension, for example. A mite must be supposed to see his own foot, for that is necessary to its self-preservation; yet to you it appears scarcely discernible, or, at least a mere visible point; to a creature smaller than a mite, it will appear much larger. The same is true of solidity. What appears hard to one animal may appear soft to another. This shows conclusively that the primary are just as relative as the secondary qualities; hence nothing exists independently of us; or we return to his *esse est percipi;* all such existences are merely our perceptions, or our ideas. To go one step further. How can you separate the qualities? Locke himself admitted that our knowledge cannot furnish valid information as to the connection between any of the secondary qualities and the primary. Add to this the consideration that the intense sensation of color, sound, taste or smell yields either pleasure or pain, which clearly cannot exist but in a sentient being, which in turn argues for the fact that these secondary qualities, the inseparable causes of this pleasure or pain, exist only in us as perceiving or sensing subjects, and what have you?   Again the result, that since the primary and secondary qualities cannot be separated, and since obviously the secondary are only a product of our own experiences, the primary must likewise be reduced to that which is perceived by the mind.

We now conclude that the central theme of Berkeley's thought is that all existence may be resolved to sense data. But this creates further trouble.   How about matter?   Is it a chimera?   What shall we say of reality?   Is there no such existence?   Is everything to be reduced to ideas in our minds without any external criterion?   It would seem that such conclusions may be difficult for anyone to digest.   Nothing daunted, Berkeley proceeds to attack these problems.   Material substance, he argues, not only does not exist but is actually inconceivable.   If matter exists and it can be known or perceived, then it is similar to any other thing which we may sense, therefore it is only an idea.   If it exists and cannot be known, then in the first place of what use is it?   Such a mysterious existence is so futile for our purposes that we ought not to give it a second thought.   But if you argue that although matter itself cannot be proved, it serves as the basis, as the substratum, for things which are perceived, is not that a contradiction in terms?   How can that which cannot be reduced to idea contain things which are ideas?   Moreover, to say that God wants matter to exist, although we do not know its constituent elements, is begging the question. Of what use is it to God, once we premise that it is a mysterious something?   Then again, Berkeley admits that "reality" is as valid in his theory as in any other; he defines it as *standard* experience—it is stronger, more orderly, more coherent, than the creations of our own minds, yet it is still composed of ideas in the most powerful spirit of all, in God. This brings us to the consideration of another phase of Berkeley's system, his proof for the existence of God.

3. *God and Nature.*

Once we adopt the premise that even the most tangible existences point to the inevitable conclusion that they are nothing but ideas in a perceiving subject, we may question its cogency and validity in the application to nature. If nature is to be reduced to our ideas, why can we not eliminate an unpleasant natural occurrence, in the same way as we can discard some of our other ideas? Suppose we are unpleasantly affected by the idea of performing a disagreeable task, we may give it up altogether, or we may suspend it, but why do we lack the ability to act similarly with relation to rain, to lightning, a tree, a mountain, and the like? That, says Berkeley, is the most pressing proof for the existence of the most powerful spirit, God, who is the cause of such ideas and who has the omnipotence to impress them upon us against our will. Because all such ideas appear differently from those of our own making we give them the collective name, *nature.* The same considerations apply to natural law. We find a more orderly, coherent sequence in so-called nature than in our ideas, we therefore call it natural law. All of which shows that there can be no more valid proof for God's existence than this: the very existence of that realm of ideas, nature, with which we are confronted every moment of our lives.

Thus far, then, Berkeley has divided existence into mind or spirit and ideas. It is clear that the mind creates the ideas, the latter are passive, therefore all we need to assert is the existence of spirit, and the rest will logically follow. Thus Berkeley's philosophy ends with the existence of spiritual substance as a substitute for material substance so ably advocated by most of his predecessors.

4. *A Society of Spirits.*

The universe is composed of a plurality of souls or spirits. Each individual spirit has the impression or picture of the world through his own ideas only, for no other existence is possible except that which is perceived by the mind of the

observer.   Each, therefore, possesses a little world of his
own, and God, although the highest and most powerful
Spirit, is still only one of the many.   This conception is similar to that of the Leibnizian monads and encounters similar
difficulties, solipsism being the most fatal.   It will be remembered that Leibniz could not explain common social experience, except through the law of Preëstablished Harmony;
our philosopher does not have even the help of such a theory,
absurd on its face as it is, for explaining how one spirit can
possibly know another, since each must experience the world
in his individual, isolated manner.   Berkeley says we infer
from the behavior of others that they exist, but that is not
knowing them.   How again, do we know God under this
theory?   Logically it is impossible; if that is so, the whole
system falls, for God is essential even for supplying nature,
reality.   We are the cause of our own behavior, so is God.
What is the connection between us and God?   In this and
similar ways, we encounter such difficulties, that at the very
outset it does not augur well for the Berkeleyan philosophy.
He actually admits that we can have no idea even of our own
spirit; we cannot form a passive idea of an active spirit, which
is the cause of the idea; all we have is a notion of it.   The
mental act is transparent, it cannot be observed.   All we
know is that it is different from our ideas, which are inert.

5. Conclusion.

This is a résumé of the philosophy of Berkeley.   What
may we say about it?   Berkeley's predecessors furnished
either material substance as the underlying foundation of the
world or a combination of material and spiritual.   He alone
definitely resolved all into spiritual substance.   There is no
doubt that he most ably annihilated matter.   No matter how
forcefully you may argue, the fact still remains that all we
know consists of our own ideas.   No one can reach beyond
his own impressions, perceptions, thoughts.   Schopenhauer
saw the truth of that in that phase of his philosophy dealing
with the "World as My Idea."   Negatively, therefore,

Berkeley is to be highly commended. But his positive contribution bristles with numerous difficulties, which prove fatal to its adoption as a metaphysical explanation of the world.

Consider his primary doctrine; *Esse est percipi*. To this we direct the "Neo-Realistic" criticism of the "egocentric predicament" and the "fallacy of definition by initial predication." Berkeley makes existence depend upon its being perceived by the Ego, by the perceiving subject, but the mere fact that they are always connected does not prove that they are identical. Is it not possible that we may have existence without the Ego's perception? In the second place, Berkeley commits the fallacy of defining an object by calling it an idea. What right has he to consider, as a premise, that being perceived is an essential element of existence? There may be numerous types of existence, which are not perceived at all. In short, according to both of these objections, Berkeley reasons in a circle; by limiting all existence to perception, to its being known, he must necessarily conclude that there is no existence which cannot be perceived. As a philosopher he should not eliminate all the possibilities because he desires to conform to a conclusion reached by him in advance. It is needless to repeat the objections of solipsism, so fatally directed against his theory that the world consists of a "society of spirits." Nor do we need to go into the fact that this solipsism not only distorts the true picture of the social life that is so apparent in nature, but it also forces the props from under his conception of God as the metaphysical support for this world of spirit.

These illogical elements, however, must not blind us to the fact that Berkeley's philosophy is another step in the unity and the development of philosophic thought. The rationalists, especially Leibniz, emphasizing the importance of mind, innate ideas, gave impetus to the theory that mind is superior to matter. It does not require much effort, once spirit is extolled, to gather sufficiently cogent arguments to deny the existence of matter altogether. Locke supplied added material to support Berkeley's conclusions by furnishing the grounds for the denial of the material existence of secondary qualities, which an agile mind, like our thinker's, could readily turn to advantage in denying similar existence to the primary qualities. To the objection, at this point, that according to this theory we eat and drink only ideas, Berkeley answers that we certainly eat and drink nothing else except such things as we perceive, or as we experience. To the further contention that if only things which are perceived exist, we must deny existence to such things as planets, deserts and other known existences, because no human mind is present to perceive them, he replies they are ideas in the minds of angels, and certainly in that of God, who vouches for everything. To be sure, we must frown upon such reference, for it is an "asylum of ignorance," it takes refuge only in words, and removes the mystery still further. In his theory of the separation of the mental act from the idea, he raises the entire question of the self. Many of the succeeding thinkers, influenced in one form or another by this, formed various opinions concerning this theory. Kant said we know the self; Bergson, we know it intuitively; Hume and James deny such identity; Schopenhauer and Fichte denominate it will. To be sure, they were influenced in this regard by all the predecessors of Berkeley, but his thought on the subject added impetus to the development.

As to the effect of Berkeley on our own philosophy, we can briefly say that by directing a successful attack against materialism he supplied the entering wedge between it and modern objective idealism; to those who prefer such idealism as a ruling philosophy of life, his services are of inestimable value. We must conclude that the English School initiated by Bacon, developed by Locke, advanced a little further by Berkeley—which school of thought was responsible for materialism and spiritualism—logically culminated in the philosophy of David Hume, who cast doubt upon the existence of both matter and mind. This, therefore, directs our thoughts to an examination of the skepticism embodied in the creed of the logical successor to both Locke and Berkeley—David Hume.

CHAPTER IX

DAVID HUME (1711–1766)

1. *Introductory Remarks and Life.*

DAVID HUME epitomizes the age of skepticism, the period in which the leading thinkers of the day made a serious attempt to dislodge reason from its high pedestal, to mark its boundaries and check its application to realms which it obviously could not explain. The scientists, the naturalists, the exponents of materialism, were more than anyone else responsible for this apparently unwarranted extolling of the achievements of the intellect. It was a propitious time to call a halt, to scrutinize reason more closely, to examine it minutely so as to make sure that there were no gaps left unbridged. If reason can withstand such criticism it will emerge more triumphant than ever, if not, no sincere thinker should then desire to extol it, because of his inclinations so to do. It seems, therefore, a very healthy experience for one to engage in the kind of skeptical thinking so ably presented by Hume. To be sure, many of his predecessors had similarly cast doubts upon reason. Descartes pushed his doubts almost to an absurd degree, in order to lay the foundation for a new philosophy, but the very essential principle on which he built—*cogito ergo sum*—was itself so vulnerable that the whole superstructure was bound to topple over, upon a critical examination of its foundation. Then there were those who looked with suspicion upon all evidence furnished by the senses, although it would seem that experience furnishes at least one of the essential elements in our knowledge. Locke, too, was skeptical in reference to the existence of the secondary qualities, as distinguished from the primary, with the disastrous results to his doctrine so ably demonstrated by Berkeley. Hume, however, attempts, as he puts it, to introduce only moderate skepticism, purely for the sake of arriving at a more clear and more thorough understanding of the effectiveness of a rational explanation, in whatever province it admittedly applies.

David Hume was a Scotchman, born in Edinburgh, in 1711, and died in 1776. His life was uneventful; he devoted himself to literary and philosophical work. He was, as we have already pointed out, particularly influenced by Locke and Berkeley. His main attention is directed to the epistemological problem, the theory of knowledge.

2. *Theory of Knowledge. Causation.*

Up to his time we find two distinct theories about the essential constitution of the world, some holding that it consists of material substance, others, that it is identified with spirit or mind. Hume concluded that as far as we may validly know, it is neither. What then, are the constituent elements of such valid knowledge? To answer this question, Hume most logically starts from the bottom. Knowledge, he says, is based (1) upon impressions, vivid, lively perceptions, our actual experiences, and (2) upon ideas which are copies of these impressions; when we re-live our experiences in our memories, we then have only ideas of them. It follows, therefore, that there can be no idea unless there is some impression behind it. Thus a valid idea is one which faithfully represents a vivid perception or an impression. No impression, no idea of it. If you still claim to have such an idea it is fictitious, a mere word. In this last category may be classified ideas of substances, material or spiritual, ideas of abstract existence, of external existence and the like. All of these are not based upon real experiences, because no such experiences are possible.

The moment you are committed to this line of reasoning, Hume's conclusions follow most naturally. Our ideas, he says, follow three laws: resemblance, contiguity in time and

place, and causation. Resemblance means that if you experience things similar to each other, subsequently the idea
of one will recall the idea of the other. This is another way
of stating the common law of association of ideas. Contiguity
in time and place resolves itself into this fact; if you experience two events simultaneously or directly after each other,
the idea of one will at once recall the other; also if you experience two objects contiguous in space, in juxtaposition to each
other, the ideas of these will be associated together in the
mind. It is clear that if you observe a table and a chair next
to it, that the idea of the table will recall that of the chair.
Causation, too, helps the connectedness of our ideas. Since
experiences known as causes precede those called effects, the
ideas of these will pursue a similar course.

Hume's attack is especially directed against this idea of
causation. He analyzes its constituent elements and reaches
what to him is the unassailable conclusion that it cannot possess
the meaning attributed to it by his predecessors. The classic
conception of causation is that once the cause is given, the
effect must necessarily follow, provided the attendant conditions are similar to those on all previous occasions. Hume
attacks this element of necessity. Here we must revert to his
original definition of idea. The idea to be valid must have an
impression as its basis. Therefore, if the idea of causation entails necessary connection between cause and effect, it must be
based upon some experience in which such necessity is an
indispensable element. Such an experience, asserts Hume,
is impossible to find. Consider any causal impression in
the outside world, two billiard balls for example. When one
strikes the other, the other moves. We then say that the
striking is the cause, and the motion of the second ball is
the effect. But do we observe any force, any power emanat-
ing from the first into the second to cause the motion to
follow? How again do we know that the same result must
happen in the future? What is true of this causal impression
is typical of all such experiences in the world at large. The
inevitable conclusion is reached that we have no such per-

ception of events in external nature to furnish us with the basis for the idea of causation, including the element of necessity advocated by its supporters.   Let us turn then to experiences within us.   We may assert that the mind desires the body to act and the body obeys, thus furnishing causation between mind and body.   Here again, what power or energy flows from mind to body to make it absolutely necessary for the body to obey?   Furthermore, the connection between mind and body is the most baffling mystery; how can such communication between them serve as the basic impression for the element of necessity in causation?   The mind, too, very often commands the body, but due to some illness, for example, the body cannot obey, hence showing that no such necessity exists.   We also cannot move all the organs of the body with like authority; "why has the will influence over the tongue and fingers, and not over the heart or liver?"   Finally anatomy shows "that the immediate object of power in voluntary motion is not the member itself which is moved, but certain muscles, nerves and animal spirits, and perhaps something still more minute and more unknown, through which the motion is successively propagated. . . ."[1]   Can there be a more certain proof that the power by which this whole operation is performed is in the last degree, mysterious and unintelligible?   But to go one step further.   Are we conscious of a power or energy in our own minds, when our will can raise up a new idea, turn it on all sides, contemplate it, and dismiss it, or supplant it by another idea?   Shall we then assert that this furnishes the impression of necessary connection between cause and effect?   Obviously not; can we pretend to know the nature of the soul and the nature of our idea, or the aptitude of the one to produce the other?   In short, is it possible for us to know the relation here so that we may deduce therefrom the element of necessity in causation?

We are thus forced to deny the existence of any impression,

[1] "An Enquiry Concerning Human Understanding," Section VII.

either external to us or within our own make-up, which can
serve as the basis for the idea of causation, in the accepted sense
of the necessary and inevitable effect following its cause.
Since no such impression exists, by definition the classic idea
of causation does not possess any validity.   What then becomes of causation?   Causation, answers Hume, merely means
a succession of events, in which we denominate some, causes,
and others, effects.   When on innumerable occasions we observe certain experiences succeeding others, we naturally feel
that under similar circumstances in the future like events or
causes will be followed by like effects.   Briefly, Hume contends, that only custom or habit may validly be said to serve
as the foundation for this causal idea.   Although the customary succession of events of the past gives an indication
that the future most likely will follow a similar pattern, it
does not guarantee that such must be the case.   The most we
can say is that probably the same causation will prevail, since
it has for such a long period in the past.   But it may very well
be that in the future the sun may rise in the west and set in the
east, as far as the theoretical analysis of causal relationship is
concerned.   Thus we confirm the fact that experience does
not and cannot yield any more than probability; by its very
essence the element of necessity or of universal application
must be eliminated from causality.

3. *Nature of the Existence of Objects.   The Ego.*

Doubtless Hume is the chief exponent of the theory that
knowledge is exclusively limited to experience.   The moment
you depart from sensation, that moment you are treading on
very dangerous ground.   But such a conception requires
more modification of some of our other concepts, hitherto
considered beyond refutation.   Does experience furnish us
with valid knowledge of the continued existence of objects
or of the independent existence of such objects?   Here, we
must return to Berkeley's conception that all we possess consists of our own ideas, our own impressions, our own experiences, and no more.   If such is the case, how account for our

beliefs either in the continued existence or in the independent existence of objects?

Only three of our faculties can possibly be responsible for such invalid opinions, says Hume; now let us see which is the direct cause for such conceptions.   Beginning with the belief that obviously only sensations and experiences constitute our knowledge, the senses are not responsible for our ingrained conviction that objects continue to exist, for the moment the senses are through experiencing the object or event, they cease to function, hence it is impossible for them to assert that such events continue to exist even after they no longer operate. The imagination, however, is the culprit here.   Our experiences are constant; they appear to be identical, we wake up every morning with the main body of our experiences unchanged.   Moreover, they are coherent, even when some modification takes place in our sensations, it coalesces and causes no disturbing element.   The imagination, therefore, because of this constancy and coherence, regards them as continuing to exist, not as being experienced anew each time. But how is this possible?   How can an experience continue its life, since by its very nature, the moment it passes, its existence is gone, rendering survival impossible?   Reason then enters with its artificial explanation.   Reason asserts: true enough, experiences as such cannot last indefinitely, but still we must account for their being so constant and so coherent.   The only rational explanation is that we have objects existing independently of us, these objects, which are always identical in their continued existence, we experience anew each time.   Since they are the identical objects, our experiences of them must be constant and even when slight changes occur they must present a picture of coherence.   This explains both the fact that our experiences do not continue to exist, which is rational; at the same time, we are constantly confronted with the same objects, the sources of our impressions, therefore these possess constancy as well as coherence.   But Hume insists upon impressing us that this is an artificial creation of the mind, erected for the purposes of satisfying our

imagination as well as our reason; such a consideration, however, does not alter the fact that we have no valid knowledge
either of the independent or of the continued existence of
objects.

How does this theory affect our belief in the existence of
an Ego, an identical self? We have referred several times
to Hume's opinion that no such Ego exists, a theory concurred
in by William James. It now behooves us to explain his
theory as to this. By introspection, says Hume, all we ever
find is a succession of mental experiences, beliefs, ideas.
Under no circumstances can we ever fix our attention upon
one substance, a self. How then do we derive such a conception? Here as in the case of objects, reason imposes an
artificial structure. Our mental experiences, too, show constancy and coherence. The imagination glides over this succession of mental elements and considers them as continuing
to exist. Reason sees that it is impossible to attribute such
continued existence to our mental elements, since by definition an experience ceases to be, once it has done its work;
therefore it calls for an identical self, an Ego with which we
must always experience in the same manner. Such artificiality, however, cannot serve as a substitute for valid knowledge,
which must insist upon believing only that which is borne out
by experience.

4. *Liberty*.

But Hume does not stop here. He applies his theory also
to human liberty. This has always been a bone of contention not only among philosophers but among religious advocates. Hume simplifies the problem by showing that there
is no real distinction between liberty and necessity. He points
out properly that if you adopt the classical theory of causation, that the effect must necessarily follow the cause, you may
then have the right to argue that in human conduct no such
element of necessity exists, hence liberty is not synonymous
with necessity or determinism. On the other hand, if you
agree with Hume that all causation implies is the fact that

judging from the customary or habitual succession of events, bearing the causal relation, the probabilities are that in the future similar succession will take place, what then becomes of the distinction between this and so-called human liberty? Does not history teach us that human conduct in the past presages its behavior in the future? Do we not build and plan relying on such evidence? Do we not lay out sidewalks, because we feel that humans have used them in the past and therefore they will in the future? Such and similar considerations conclusively prove that human liberty is no different from our conception of causation in the mechanical realm.

5. Skepticism.

This skeptical philosophy is a result, so Hume tells us, of a study and analysis of human nature and of the human understanding, for that *is* the foundation of all branches of human endeavor. Human nature is the root of all the sciences, mathematics, natural philosophy, natural religion, logic, morality, criticism, politics. We must study this nature from observation and experience, and in morality we must view the behavior of men in all situations under all circumstances. True, such an effort results in limiting reason to matters of experience, it results in casting doubts upon many principles which have from time immemorial been so dear to humans; it even questions the possibility of valid knowledge of the existence of nature in our sense of the word. At this point we may frown upon the kind of skepticism which undermines the very groundwork of our daily life, but Hume assures us that, although theoretically we are led to the inevitable conclusion that as far as experience goes, we do not know whether objects even exist, at the same time, nature relieves this pressure. Every time reason casts clouds over such questions—Do I derive my experiences from external objects?—Do my experiences resemble such objects?—Are there any such objects altogether?—Nature herself comes to the rescue and dispels them. "Nature cures me of this philosophical melancholy and delirium, either by relaxing this bent of mind; or by some avocation, and lively impression of my senses, which obliterate all these chimeras. I dine, I play a game of backgammon, I converse, and am merry with my friends; and when after three or four hours' amusement I would return to these speculations, they appear so cold, and strained, and ridiculous, that I cannot find in my heart to enter into them any farther."[2] Thus we see that Hume does not tolerate excessive skepticism, but he admits that experience is the only way by which we can deal with matters of fact and existence, and experience can never go beyond probability.

6. Religion.

At this point, it becomes interesting to see how Hume applies this skeptical philosophy to the treatment of religious questions. With Bacon he holds as a general proposition that theological subjects are purely a matter for faith, revelation, not for philosophical speculation. Clearly this must be so, for matters of religion doubtless belong to a province beyond experience, which reason, aided by observation, cannot penetrate. But Hume does not discard this vital question with a mere gesture, he exhaustively proves that religious issues are incapable of demonstration. To do this, he borrows from Plato the dialogue method, and discusses the subject in the "Dialogues Concerning Natural Religion." The characters in these dialogues are three: Cleanthes, Demea, and Philo.

Cleanthes presents the so-called *a posteriori* argument for the existence of God. We observe that nature exists, therefore God must exist as its creator, resembling a human artificer. This is analogous to the teleological proof for God, which argues that since nature exhibits fitness and comprehends all available means to serve innumerable purposes, especially those of humans, there must exist a creator, intelligent, and resembling the human mind to explain such meaning.

[2] "The Treatise of Human Nature," Book I, Part IV, Conclusion.

Demea, on the other hand, attempts to establish the existence of God—*a priori*—basing his arguments upon the ontological and cosmological theories, with which we have been confronted in Cartesianism, and to the latter of which Locke has devoted so much effort.

Finally, Philo, representing Hume's own beliefs, refutes all of these proofs, and relegates the whole subject matter of God's existence to the realm of faith.

What, then, are Philo's or Hume's contentions against the thesis of Cleanthes?   In the first place, we know only a small part of the universe; science, too, shows how infinitesimal a portion of the world we really understand; how can such inadequate knowledge argue for a God based upon the fitness of the whole of nature?   Again, we are wholly ignorant of the origin of the world; how argue for a God, necessary for its creation?   God, too, is supposed to resemble mind, the universe is essentially material; how explain the connection between body and mind, a baffling mystery, which up to Hume's day, has not been solved?   If, adds Hume, you argue from the similarity of the effects in nature to the similarity of the cause or God, since nature resembles animal more than mind, why then not claim that generative power rather than mind is the constituent attribute of the creator?   Moreover, the world is full of evil, imperfection, misery; how account for that with a perfect God as its originator?   This is the age-old question of evil, which Hume, with his practical bent of mind, could not explain in a manner similar to that employed by the Stoics or by the Scholastics.

But does Demea fare any better in respect to his effort to demonstrate the need and existence of God?   As far as the ontological argument is concerned, namely, that the idea of God proves his existence, Hume is not much swayed by it, for, as has been seen in our discussion of Descartes, this idea does not exist universally, and even if it did, the idea cannot by itself prove God.   The cosmological argument carries us no farther. Locke said that there must be a cause for the origin of the whole chain of causation, or for the universe, otherwise it would be produced by nothing, and nothing cannot be a cause. Hume, however, denies this reasoning. To him no demonstrative proof is possible to show the need of such a cause altogether. The same criticism applies to the line of thought that everything in the universe is contingent or dependent upon everything else, therefore, we must postulate a necessary, independent being or God, outside of this contingent realm. Not at all, says Hume. Nature itself, in its entirety, may be that necessary being, embracing all the contingent elements within itself. To be sure, Hume does not even concede that we are obliged to look for any necessary being as a cause, for the contrary is equally possible, namely, that no cause at all is required. Finally, intuition cannot come to our aid in solving any of these problems, since no such intuition of God exists because of the inadequacy of our knowledge.

What, then, are Philo's own conclusions on this most important of religious issues, the existence of God? Philo says, popular religion is pernicious, oppressive, it furnishes the wrong motives for human conduct, it is superstitious, melancholy and should be discarded. In view of the fact, however, that the arguments for God are greater than those against him, our faith may sway us to believe in Him. Revelation will in the future help us to learn more about Him. We may also say that if God exists, he bears some small resemblance to human intelligence. It is very interesting here to go along with Philo in his discussion of the relation of God to morality. To him God may be either wholly good, wholly bad, both good and bad, or neither. It is preferable, he says, to place God above goodness or evil, in our sense of the terms, thus considering him as possessing neither of these qualities.

7. Conclusion.

This entire system of philosophy shows a consistent, logical skepticism, without going to such extremes as to make us intolerant of its application. Both Descartes and Hume begin with the same aim in view, namely, to clear the decks of all philosophical preconceptions for the purpose of building anew on a solid foundation; both resort to the study of the human mind to aid them in their undertaking.   But what divergent results they achieve!   Descartes, the rationalist, employing the deductive method, reduces all to that for which the mind can vouch, irrespective of experience.   In fact, experience is given only secondary consideration to confirm, not to refute, the elaborate structure evolved out of the primary principle that I am a thinking being.   Hume, on the other hand, the empiricist, approaches the subject by induction.   To him all validity in knowledge must be a result of experience.   Rationalism, or the belief that knowledge contains a non-empirical element, is anathema to him.   Descartes, with the vanity which usually accompanies the reasoning of one who delves into theoretical realms, undaunted and unassailed by doubts which are natural to the thinker who must confront and explain the multitudinous complexities of the everyday humdrum of life, is willing to doubt even the most obvious facts of existence, because he is assured that the more suspicion he casts upon the prevailing opinions, the more willing shall we be to accept his conclusions on the rebound.   But Hume cannot go so far.   He places his entire faith in experience, in the pluralistic aspect of the universe, therefore he must concede certain facts as being present, even though admittedly they cannot be demonstrated to exist.   He is much more cautious in his approach, he acts as if he himself were reluctant to face the results of his skepticism.   By that alone, his philosophy, in so far as it applies, should be considered the more cogent.

To be sure, Descartes reduces all to the container, consciousness, disregarding in a large measure the contents; while Hume stresses emphatically the contents, the facts of sensation, without giving proper regard to the container.   We may, with Kant, criticize Hume on this point of the denial of the Ego by pointing out the impossibility of having an object without a subject.   How is knowledge conceivable, when its most important element, the relation of subject, the knower, to the object, the known, is eliminated? How do we explain knowledge, when admittedly, in Hume's opinion, all we have is just the material for knowing? Both methods, deduction and induction, both the Ego and the object of consciousness, the experienced facts, must be included in any real philosophy, which attempts adequately to explain the universe, with all the factors comprehended under that term.

Nor need we hesitate to compare Hume with Spinoza. The latter is a rationalist of the first magnitude. He employs deduction to the nth degree. He attains intellectual heights which we find often impossible to ascend. At the same time experience is patently disregarded. All exists for the infinite; whatever little regard is paid to the finite minds, wills, bodies, is only for the sake of bringing to the foreground the unattainable infinite. But what about our own lives, our own trials and tribulations? To say that we all can act to harmonize with the rational universe is poor consolation indeed. Experience must always be taken into consideration, and if Hume served only the purpose of emphasizing the need of including sensation in our problem of knowledge, he has most assuredly performed a great service.

Hume, too, does not encounter the difficulties of Leibniz, the German rationalist. Leibniz admits that the finite monads are all-important; this lends some meaning to our own lives and aims. Yet in attempting to furnish an all-inclusive system of metaphysics, in attempting to explain the origin of things, he was obliged to resort to the absurd explanation of the law of Preëstablished Harmony. That is a result of the vaunted ability of these rationalists to probe the mysteries of the world, which no experience can ever explain. Hume does not undertake to explain anything else but what we observe and sense, hence he has clear sailing to a maximum degree. We must not overlook, however, the fact that empiricism, the school of thought which culminated in Hume, also has many shortcomings.

We have pointed out some of these in Bacon and Locke. In addition, by what criterion does Hume conclude that experience is the one valid basis for knowledge? If you say experience itself is its own voucher, then you are offending by permitting experience to lift itself up by its own bootstraps, an extremely irregular practice. Moreover, Hume discusses causation; experience clearly does not of itself furnish the idea of causation. There is no reason why sensation as such should be divided into causes and effects. This idea we no doubt already possess when we come to experiment and to observe. These, and similar considerations, demonstrate that empiricism by itself is just as inadequate as rationalism.

To form a proper estimate of Hume's contribution to our own philosophy of life, we may profitably travel along with William James in his discussion of the "Sentiment of Rationality." He argues that the elixir which we all seek is a feeling of peace, ease and mental satisfaction. The moment a disturbing element enters, we become at once irritable, and we feel ourselves abandoned in the midst of a confused sea of complexities. To restore our equilibrium we desire some anchor to which we may affix our apparently disjointed details of life. Such a central, fundamental principle both the rationalists and empiricists attempt to furnish. Spinoza reduces the entire universe to simplicity: nature, viewed from without, is matter; from within, mind. The infinite God permeates it throughout, and is the pivot around which all finite things revolve. Such simplicity does no doubt appeal to many minds, accustomed to theoretical speculations; they feel at rest, being assured of the rationality of the world on which they pin their hopes. Hume, the empiricist, prefers to supply us with a world, clear in detail; a pluralistic world, full of particular events and experiences, but which nevertheless can be readily understood in all its manifold elements. This, too, appeals to many who are of a practical or of a scientific bent of mind. It offers the added advantage of compelling us to face the facts of life squarely, not permitting us to divert our attention to such problems as do not affect our ordinary conduct. Still, it, too, has its drawbacks. It is confusing, it does not furnish a principle of coherence, whereby all the apparently unconnected experiences may derive the underlying unity so necessary to render the world intelligible. The obvious solution, then, is to include both of these theories in our philosophy. In fact, science does proceed along such lines. It attends to observation and experiment, whereby all details are furnished, and at the same time it formulates general laws, under which such complex·series of events are classified.

Then, too, Hume renders great service to us in his moral and religious teaching. Freedom of the will, which had been a center of controversy for many years, which, on account of the sterile discussions concerning its validity, had diverted attention from the application of such effort to the amelioration of the admittedly existing evil, he solves with the obvious explanation that it is identical with causation. That does not, however, derogate from human dignity, as the case would be, if we were to adopt the usual theories of mechanism. In fact, it adds to the high esteem in which human conduct is considered. Certainly, the human who could not be depended upon, who could vary his actions according to mere whims, would not be a proper person with whom to associate.

Finally, Hume's polemic against the superstitious, popular religion is indeed worthy of consideration. He properly and advisedly relegates religion to faith. He has a perfect right to condemn natural religion, for if there is any powerful factor that might serve to convert men into atheists, it would be that of permitting nature to be the evidence, in and by itself, for the existence of a benign, perfect, and merciful God. Nature does unquestionably exhibit many wonderful purposes, but how about the opposite picture? Natural forces that are responsible for the destruction of homes of the needy, for tornadoes, for earthquakes, that cause fathers to be snatched from families, children from the embraces of mothers, and cause all other obviously untoward occurrences, need much deeper explanation than merely to denominate them chimeras or to reduce them to dreams. In short, Hume's insistence on facing facts is not only a healthy but also an encouraging and invigorating force in our lives.

The upshot of this entire philosophy, however, is that it by no means writes finis to philosophic development. We have already pointed out many of its difficulties, particularly the fact that, in Hume's conception, our experiences have no anchor, no unifying force. How does he derive the idea of causation from experience? What remains of causation altogether, if we attribute to it only the basis of custom or habit? How are we to plan our lives in the future, if we are not absolutely certain that the same laws which prevailed in the past, will also govern in time to come? If necessary sequence is eliminated, and only probability is substituted, our plight, assuredly, is not enviable. Considerations like these led Hume's successor, Immanuel Kant, to evolve a critical philosophy, to correct the defects found here. To discover whether his attempt was successful, we must next turn our attention to the study of the thought embraced in the doctrines of Immanuel Kant.

CHAPTER X

IMMANUEL KANT (1724–1804)

1. *Life*.

IMMANUEL KANT was born in Königsberg, an old German city, in 1724, and spent his life without leaving his native province. In 1732, he entered the Collegium Fredericianum, where he remained for eight years. The religious teaching there so tortured and embittered him, that he never overcame his loathing for the institution. Later he attended the University of Königsberg, where he was so influenced by Knützen, a professor of philosophy, and an ardent disciple of the celebrated Wolff, the great propagator of Leibnizian philosophy, that he was led to abandon his earlier plans, and to turn to science and philosophy. At the age of forty-six he was appointed professor of logic and metaphysics in his Alma Mater. He published his "Critique of Pure Reason" in 1781, but being disappointed at the fact that no one seemed to grasp its real meaning, he then wrote "A Prolegomena to Every Future Metaphysic," which appeared in 1783. In this treatise, he expounded for the benefit of teachers of philosophy the central thesis of his first Critique. The "Critique of Practical Reason" appeared in 1785, and the "Critique of Judgment" in 1790. He also wrote on religion in his essay "Religion within the Limits of Bare Reason," published in 1793. He published innumerable articles on a variety of subjects. In 1804, at the age of eighty, he died in his beloved Königsberg, and was accorded final honors at his burial, both by the university and by the city.

Some of the factors in his early life doubtless were responsible for the point of view in his philosophic works. His condemnation of certain phases of the evangelical religion may readily be attributed to the torture he endured at the first school he attended as a child; weary hours were spent there in sermons and catechizing in order to search the youthful soul and to bring home to it the religious truths of the day.   The moral influence exercised by his father, who impressed upon him most vigorously the virtue of truth, accounts in part for the emphasis Kant placed on morality, regarding it as the central interest in life, more important than intellectual pursuits.   His poverty, as in the case of Spinoza, was a contributing cause to his serious outlook on life, reflected in the austere style of his philosophical works.   They lack warmth and literary charm so essential to attract students of such weighty problems as he presents.   All in all, however, Kant revolutionized philosophy, doing for it what Copernicus did for astronomy.   The effects of his doctrines are felt even to this day, and we shall find it a most profitable undertaking to return now to a careful scrutiny of his philosophy.   This philosophy is divided into three Critiques.   They represent the three-fold division which is commonly attributed to the human make-up, reason, will and feeling.   The first Critique develops a comprehensive, critical survey of the certainty and of the extent of the theoretical understanding; the second shows what an essential ingredient of life *will* is and what purposes it effects; the third, manifests, though not in so conclusive a manner as the other two, the function of feeling, of intuition, of the aesthetic sense, which Kant claims we all possess.   The first object of our study, however, is the "Critique of Pure Reason."

2. *Critique of Pure Reason.*

At the time when Kant developed this first part of his philosophy, two diametrically opposite theories had hold of the intellectual world, rationalism, or, as he calls it, dogmatism, and empiricism.   The first considered the mind as withdrawing more and more into its own inner recesses, until there was nothing left for it upon which to dwell, rendering it a useless tool for purposes of life; the other, regarded experience as a magnet, which drew everything away from the mind, leaving all to sensation, again causing mind to be a useless tool. Kant was dissatisfied with both, yet felt that each contained a kernel of truth. Why then not combine them? He therefore turned his attention to the epistemological problem, similar to the approach made by Hume. Of the two prevailing philosophies, the conclusions reached by Hume unquestionably more directly influenced Kant to attack this problem. Hume's lucid reasoning that experience yields no certainty but only probability left knowledge in a sorry plight, indeed. Of what use is knowledge, either for itself or as an instrument for life, if it contains neither necessary nor universal truth? For example, if causation is only custom or habit, if the effect need not follow the cause, if this sequence of cause and effect is not of universal application, then the concept is a mere word, an ineffectual weapon in our study of, and struggle with, nature. Furthermore, says Kant, that is not scientific knowledge. Such knowledge must possess both necessary and universal application, to make its laws valid. True enough, Kant admits with Hume that experience alone does not furnish any more than probability, for by its very nature it is only partial evidence of what occurs in front of our very eyes. No number of experiences, in the duration of our lives, can by themselves offer sufficient proof that they must always follow the same pattern; nor, considering experience all over the universe at one moment of time, may we be sure that the same sequence takes place universally, since we can only observe a most insignificant portion of the world. But need we despair on that account? Of course not. We simply must include another element in knowledge, besides experience, an invariable factor, a factor which by its very essence must have necessary and universal validity, otherwise knowledge is impossible. Such a factor is the *a priori* element furnished by the mind prior to dealing with the world-experiences. From this angle, it is logical for Kant to divide the first part of his philosophy, the Critique of

Pure Reason, into two elements—that derived from sensation, which he calls Sensibility, and that supplied by the mind, known as the Analytic.

In this Critique, then, Kant wishes to discover the answer to this question: How is scientific knowledge possible? If we recall that to him scientific knowledge must be something which will add to information we already possess, and must contain, besides, necessary and universal validity, which requires an *a priori* act of the mind in conjunction with experience, we are then not feazed by the other way he puts this same question: How are synthetic judgments *a priori* possible? Judgments may be either analytical or synthetic; they may assert something about the subject under the discussion, previously known, or they may add to the subject that which was never thought of in logical connection with it. To illustrate: Body is extended; a dog is an animal, are analytical, because the very essence of body is extension, and of a dog, its animal-like quality. Heat expands bodies, the dog chases a rabbit, these are synthetic judgments; the ideas associated here are in their nature separate. Now says Kant, if we have the latter kind of judgments, and if they apply necessarily and universally, then we have real knowledge. To discover how this is possible is our main task.

Valid knowledge, says Kant, must contain an empirical element, a factor derived from sensation; an objective element supplied by the world outside of us, through experience. But, he continues, every such sensation of any object or event must be related to space and time. You cannot experience a table, unless it has a locus in space and is connected with some moment of time. In short, it is an impossibility to abstract from sensations all consideration of space and time and still have anything left in an experience. Now, on the other hand, it is equally impossible to experience space itself or time itself, abstracted from the experienced objects or events. You may close your eyes, attempt consciously to disregard everything else, but concentrate your attention on pure space and time and your task is bound to be hopeless. That indubitably shows that these are not objects of experience, but, as he calls them, the primary intuitions of sensation, the mental elements supplied by us, the indispensable conditions under which sensation becomes possible. It is comparatively easy to show further that space and time themselves are not objects of experience by the fact that the infant, prior to any experience whatsoever, already possesses the sense of direction in space and of succession in time. Also the fact that arithmetic and geometry are based on time and space respectively shows that these are not objects of experience, but *a priori*, since such mathematical judgments are universally true. What then does sensation supply? Some objective element yielded by that which is behind phenomena, behind appearances, the thing-in-itself, the noumenon, the essential characteristics of which we find impossible to define.

Thus far Kant presents the method by which we are able to experience events in the phenomenal world. Some element is furnished by that which is behind appearances, and our intuitions of space and time remould it, converting it into a sensation suitable for us. But what about this natural realm of experience? Are these experiences disjointed, unrelated to each other, just casually connected with each other, or do they exhibit an underlying unity? Here the difference between Hume and Kant becomes acute, indeed. Hume holds that we have no right to attribute anything more to experiences than what we actually sense. Kant, on the other hand, considers this position untenable. In the first place, such a contention, if valid, renders knowledge of the world impossible and ineffectual; if nature is a jumble of unconnected events, no intelligent plan can be devised to understand or to control it. But a more vital consideration is that nature, contrary to Hume's analysis, really does present to us an orderly series of occurrences. Therefore, Kant claims, we must incorporate a second element in our knowledge to explain the fact that our sensations and experiences show this unity and order. This is treated in his Analytic.

Our understanding, he says, attacks these sensations of the

phenomenal world with its own weapons, *a priori*. These are not objects of experience themselves, similar to the innate intuitions of space and time.   In other words, the mind pours all its experiences of the world into its own moulds, into its own categories, which thus impose an intelligible character upon our observations.   These weapons of reason are the categories, quantity, quality, relation and modality.   Every phenomenon possesses quantity and quality; every phenomenon, too, is tied up with causality, and finally, every such phenomenon is possible which conforms to natural laws, and necessary if its non-existence would constitute a suspension of these laws, or a miracle.   In short, Kant simply reverses the process here.   Instead of nature furnishing us with these attributes of objects by experience, the mind imposes these upon the objects or events.   The difference in approach by Hume and Kant now becomes evident.   Hume says that the succession of events yields the only basis for the causal relation, therefore it is clear that it need not always be true.   But to Kant, causality or relation must be necessarily and universally applicable, because the mind refuses to consider any phenomenon, except through the lenses of such causal relation. The understanding starts with the *a priori* consideration that no phenomenon is possible unless it bears some relation, either as cause or as effect, to something else.   Once this Kantian position is adopted, his theory of scientific knowledge becomes self-evident.   Synthetic judgments *a priori* are possible, provided the world supplies the material for sensation and the mind the *a priori* element, which gives these judgments the necessity and universality so essential as ingredients in scientific knowledge; such *a priori* elements are the categories just discussed.

But that very solution of our original problem shows the limitation of the human mind.   To illustrate: Heat expands bodies, we say, is a scientific judgment.   It is synthetic, because we add something new to heat of which we have previously not been aware in its own definition; the fact of the causal relation between its application to a body and the resultant expansion is furnished *a priori* by the mind.   In order, however, to prove this scientific statement we must resort to experience, otherwise, even if theoretically we felt that heat would always expand bodies, if we could never prove it by observation, we would have no content for our theory. Therefore, such scientific knowledge, as Kant develops in his first Critique, must be limited only to the phenomenal world, in which sensation can contribute one of the essential elements.   The moment, however, theoretical reason attempts to go beyond experience, that moment it has overstepped its boundaries, and the result is doomed to failure. You cannot have scientific knowledge of anything beyond the world of sensations.   In short, since such objects beyond experience are the subject matter for metaphysics, metaphysics can never be a science.   How then does it occupy such a position in thought?   Why do we yearn for it?   Kant answers, that it is our natural inclination to "follow through" a concept or a thought; we therefore want to classify our experiences under still more general heads, such as God, soul, universe, absolute, thing-in-itself, and the like.   This discussion Kant carries on in the third part of his first Critique, the Dialectic.   Properly speaking it does not belong to scientific knowledge, but as we have just pointed out, he aims to show us the limitations of science.   What happens, if we step beyond the boundary of observation?   We find, answers Kant, that both sides of the question, though diametrically opposed to each other, may be equally proved, as far as theoretical reason is concerned.   These are known as antinomies, and he relates them to the categories.   In reference to quantity, we may show that the world is both limited and unlimited in space and time; qualitatively, we may prove that matter is composed of atoms and also that it is infinitely divisible; causally, that there is freedom and that the world is subject to necessity or mechanism; in modality we may with equal conviction demonstrate that there is a God, or that no such Being exists.   In connection with this last antinomy, Kant at great length shows the untenability of the prevailing proofs for God, which we found in Hume, the ontological, the cosmological, and the teleological.

The ontological proof he discards with the explanation that while the idea of God may be useful, still being only an idea, it is incapable of increasing by itself alone our knowledge with regard to the existence, or even the possibility of existence, of God.   The cosmological argument Kant puts in this fashion. If there exists anything at all, there must exist an absolutely necessary Being also.   I, at least, exist, therefore there exists such an absolutely necessary Being.   Reason now concludes that this Being is the First Cause.   Kant validly contends that in the world of phenomena, we must look for causes, but how do we make the transition from this contingent world to a Being outside of it?   How in short do we permit the fact that everything needs a cause, which is only true in experience, to lead us to a realm outside of experience, in which no causation may prevail?   But even admitting the existence of such a first cause, a necessary Being, how do we identify Him with the religious God, possessing all the properties involved in such a concept?   To do this we must consider that the idea of this necessary Being, in and of itself, proves His essence, His identity with the religious conception of God.   That really is the ontological proof, which we have already discarded. The very basis of the cosmological proof turns out to be the ontological argument.   That foundation being untenable, the second proof falls to the ground.

Let us now turn to the teleological, or as Kant calls it, the Physico-theological proof.   The principal points of this proof are the following: (1) There are everywhere in the world clear indications of an intentional arrangement carried out with great wisdom.   (2) The fitness of this arrangement is foreign to the things existing in the world, it can only be explained by the fact that it has been effected by a rational principle acting for that particular purpose.   (3) There exists, therefore, a sublime cause or sublime causes responsible for the world. (4) The unity of this cause may be inferred from the unity of the world. · The objections to this proof are similar to those against the cosmological argument. In the first place, how can you argue that there is design or purpose in nature, since what may be good for one class of beings may have the opposite effect on another? The lion may be thankful to his Creator for having endowed him with so much strength, but such a Being must certainly resemble a demon, to the poor lamb's way of thinking. Then again, even if there is purpose in this contingent realm, how bridge the gap between it and a necessary Being or a God, who admittedly exists outside of the world? To go one step further. Even if you do proceed from the consideration of design in nature to a rational, intelligent cause for such fitness, you must then employ the cosmological argument to explain causal relation, but that in turn depends upon the ontological, the untenability of which needs no further discussion. Therefore the inevitiable conclusion must be reached that no logical proof of God is possible, and the so-called arguments for such a Divine Creator, which theology strives so hard to sustain, must fail, after a careful, critical scrutiny of their implications.

Thus the Dialectic shows that all the objects of metaphysics, because by their very nature they lie beyond experience, because they are noumena, as contrasted with phenomena, cannot be the subject matter of scientific knowledge. Such knowledge is limited only to this natural realm, and the function of metaphysics is to supply to the mind these regulative principles, ideas, concepts, which may help to satisfy the unbounded intellectual curiosity, as well as mark the definite limits to the theoretical understanding.

To recapitulate: Hume is correct in his premise that if experience were the sole contributing factor to knowledge, only probability would be possible. But that is unthinkable. We must have certainty, we must have universally and necessarily true judgments; they are the *sine qua non* of scientific, or of real knowledge. We must, therefore, consider that the mind's own contributions, the *a priori* categories, are as essential as that of sensation. The two together constitute synthetic judgments *a priori*. The world in some form supplies the matter for sensation, these sensations become possible through space and time, which are *a priori;* once the wealth of sensations is accounted for, the mind then pours them into its own innate moulds or categories; but not yet satisfied, it puts them into still more general, more unified, classes, the subject matter of metaphysics.   The latter, however, can never possess scientific validity.   At this point it may be well to point out, with Kant, that we already have evidence of such synthetic judgments *a priori,* in mathematics and physics, which are based on such principles.

To return to another contrast between Hume and Kant—we refer to their respective conceptions of the Ego.   Hume consistently maintained that experience furnishes no evidence of such an identical Ego, but only successions of mental impressions.   Kant must be in accord with this; but he insists upon such a self, nevertheless.   To him the "I" must accompany every belief, idea, or impression, otherwise, we lack the subject, the knower, in knowledge, which is certainly just as indispensable as the object, or the known.   Were Hume correct in his contention, we would never know in our observation of change or causation in the world, whether it is due to the change in our own mental series, or in the succession occurring in the outside world.   In short, we would be unable to declare in any instance, whether it is a succession of apprehension in us or apprehension of succession in nature.   This would be fatal, indeed.

What conclusion may we now reach concerning Kant's Critique of Pure Reason?   It deals with the rational part of our make-up.   It attempts to criticize its functions, to show its extent, its reliability, and at the same time tries to show that it has no right to lay claim to all the unlimited power advocated for it by the rationalistic school.   Further, Kant demonstrates that this nature, this phenomenal world, is the sole subject matter for scientific study.   This world of experience dominated by science, hence, is governed by mechanical laws—laws of space, time and causality.   He does not condemn us for our natural inclination to go beyond the observed facts, as long as we do not consider all such objects, noumena, as possessing scientific validity. The moment these noumena are included in knowledge, antinomies and other fantastic conclusions must be the inevitable consequence. That, however, should not be interpreted to mean that Kant categorically denies the existence of these objects. Far from it. All he desires to impress upon us is the fact that reason cannot demonstrate their valid existence; but there is another phase of our constitution which may vouch for their existence even more than theoretical demonstration; that other element in us constitutes our Will. This, Kant develops in the Critique of Practical Reason, to which we next turn our attention.

3. Critique of Practical Reason—Morality.

Among all things, beyond the visible world or phenomenal nature, says Kant, these three beliefs are of extremely vital importance to us—freedom of the will, immortality of the soul, and God. They cannot be demonstrated to exist, the theoretical understanding offers no solution for our problems relative to them. They are not the subject matter for scientific study. Shall we then say that they therefore cannot exist? Not at all, answers Kant. They are of indispensable importance to our moral life, they are the very conditions which make morality possible; they are, in other words, the three postulates of morality. Hence, as a practical matter they exist even with more certainty than if they were mathematically proved. They are the moral axioms. But why do we consider them the *sine qua non* of the moral life?

The essence of morality, says Kant, consists in the possession of a good will which acts in accordance with duty, not inclination or desire; a will, moreover, which attends to the maxims, the principles, of conduct, rather than to the ends to be achieved. This type of will should be highly esteemed for itself, for its own principle of volition; it acts rightly without regard to achieving any particular goal. Such a will acts out of respect for the moral law, or out of respect for duty. To evoke such unqualified respect on the part of every moral will, this law must certainly be of universal dignity and application. In short, it must hold true universally and necessarily. Such a law, therefore, must contain an *a priori* element to give it this universal and necessary cogency. It is, continues Kant, the Categorical Imperative. This principle may be stated in two ways: "*Act only on that maxim whereby thou canst at the same time will that it should become a universal law.*" That version considers action from the rational point of view. It may also be stated from the social angle: "*So act as to treat humanity, whether in thine own person or in that of any other, in every case as an end withal, never as means only.*" To illustrate both of these versions: Should a man commit suicide? He is in misery and feels that for the future duration of his life he will have more unhappiness than satisfaction. Self-love, therefore, prompts him to end it all. But this principle of self-love tends in nature to improve life, how can it similarly be the maxim for the destruction of life? Therefore, it could not serve as a universal law of nature, hence it cannot justify such conduct. Socially, the same holds true. If you once agree with Kant that rational nature, man, must be considered as an end in himself and not as a means to achieve a certain result, then by committing suicide you use a man as a means to escape intolerant conditions, again demonstrating clearly that it flies in the face of the Categorical Imperative. Almost any act with moral significance attached to it can be shown to be right or wrong, applying this universal law of morality as a criterion. We call it categorical, because it applies, regardless of consequences, contrasted with hypothetical imperatives which call for an act to serve as a means to effect some result.

But how does this discussion relate to the three problems confronting us in morality? The Categorical Imperative commands you to act in one way rather than another. That, by very definition, must imply that you have an alternative, that you may conduct yourself in a wrong as well as in a right manner; what is that but the admission of freedom of the will?

The very life, the very intelligibility of the moral principle involves, in and of itself, the existence of freedom of the will, otherwise, the moral criterion is meaningless. Therefore, Kant concludes, the first postulate of morality is that freedom of the will prevails, although as we have previously seen, the antinomy of relation proves beyond a doubt that it is impossible to demonstrate rationally the existence either of necessity or of freedom.

We are, however, faced with another difficulty at this point. True, we should act in accordance with duty, not desire. But do the facts bear this out? Is it not evident that duty runs counter to inclinations? Is it also not true that happiness for us in this life consists in satisfying desires, whereas duty is rigorous and often renders us unhappy? How resolve this conflict between what we ought to do and what actually yields happiness and satisfaction? This is where immortality comes to the fore. Morality would indeed be an empty concept if it did not resolve this conflict; it must hold out as an ideal in the future, as the goal which we may definitely hope to achieve, the fact that at some time to come, duty and happiness will be harmonized. At present, the will is tempted by all kinds of phenomena in this realm of nature, it has not reached the stage where it always and spontaneously acts morally, hence this opposition. But given time for indefinite development, the will must reach such a state where that which is in accordance with duty will likewise be identified with happiness. This second requirement of morality, the ideal in which all conflicts will be resolved into a unity and harmony, is supplied by immortality of the soul. Here, too, such immortality is the indispensable condition, the postulate of morality.

But, say you, it may be mere fantasy to promise such a future realization; there seems to be no assurance of its ultimate accomplishment. Why, then, exercise self-hypnosis to assuage our intellectual pain? Kant answers this by furnishing us with a God. God guarantees that this ultimate harmony will become an accomplished fact. God, therefore, must also be considered as the third and last requisite of morality to complete the moral world, hence He, too, is the postulate of the law of duty.

⌐To sum up then, Kant shows in the Critique of Practical Reason that morality, based on will, is far more important to us, than mere intellectual research.   It is a greater force in our lives, and therefore entitled to greater consideration. The moral will must be guided by a universal and necessary principle of conduct, the Categorical Imperative, which contains an *a priori* element.   That criterion commands certain acts, which would be meaningless unless alternative possibilities of conduct were equally existent.   This implies freedom of the will.   This conduct in accordance with duty conflicts with our present conception of happiness, which is based on desire.   Such a state of affairs is intolerable, but still it seems to be an existing fact.   Therefore, immortality becomes necessary to give the will an opportunity at some indefinite time to develop in such a way that a conflict will no longer disturb it.   In order to guarantee such a unity, God must be postulated.   He assures us now that this far-off harmony will be achieved, hence we can have peace of mind. To be sure, these beliefs are incapable of demonstration, but since they are the very bases of morality, and since morality is the very basis of our lives, much more so than is theoretical study, the practical proof of their truth is more forceful than the theoretical, even if the latter were possible.

Kant's conclusions in the second Critique leave us with an almost insurmountable gap between two worlds, so-called. On the one hand, he furnishes us with nature, mechanically governed, to be studied by experience, putting limits to our understanding of it, amply demonstrating that our theoretical mind cannot penetrate the region behind it.   On the other hand, he presents us with a world of human souls, human wills, in which freedom of the will governs, in which the only criterion is the Categorical Imperative, at the head of which stands God, as a guarantor that the ideals morality so eagerly desires will be attained.   Is there any connecting link between them? How bridge this chasm? The answer to this question Kant supplies in some fashion in his third Critique.

4. *Critique of Judgment—Aesthetics.*

Here, as in the other Critiques, Kant begins with the individual. Each of us, he says, possesses an aesthetic sense, a sense of the beautiful. This faculty causes us to appreciate beauty in the world not with relation to any purpose it may serve for us, but disinterestedly, for its own sake. It is unique. A work of art delights us, because it harmonizes our imagination and reason. Viewing a raging sea our reason informs us of its constituent elements, the natural laws it obeys. Reason follows all these factors to their infinite possibilities, the tidal forces, and the like. At the same time our imagination disturbs our equilibrium. The imagination cannot follow reason into its depths of infinity. But the aesthetic sense extends the limits of the imagination and limits the extent of reason. That produces such harmony between them that we can peacefully contemplate the ocean for its beauty. That produces aesthetic pleasure. Our artistic sense moreover is subjective, a result of our own make-up, similar to space and time, which are intuitions of sensations supplied by the mind. To have any real validity, it must also be universally applicable, hence it must possess an *a priori* element, not yielded by the world of phenomena.

How, then, does it serve to bridge the gap between the natural world and the ideal realm of moral beings? The first, reason claims, is governed mechanically, the scientist certainly must exclude all consideration of purposes, ends, in his subject matter, otherwise he is not true to his guiding principles. That causal explanation, however, becomes most inadequate when we observe living organisms. Here the concept of purpose is paramount. Here, too, teleology must push mechanism out of the way as far as possible, for the living organism is self-building, self-recuperating, a phenomenon no mechanical principles have as yet been able to explain adequately. Reason and will, therefore, seem to be diametrically opposed to each other. Ordinarily, when reason finds itself unable to solve a certain difficulty, and will is likewise powerless to effect a solution, we appeal to intuition. That is really what Kant does. He says that with our aesthetic sense we may penetrate behind it all and find in reality that in which both mechanism and purposiveness inhere. In other words, let us regard mechanical and teleological explanations not as constituting the actual essences of reality, of the noumenon, but only as instruments for understanding and for observing the natural and the ideal worlds. In that case, if we abstract from reality the cloak imposed upon it by either theoretical reason or by practical reason, and penetrate within, we may find that the cause, effect, and the end or purpose are really one and the same thing. What lends color to this conclusion is the fact that causal relation is one in time, that an end or purpose also requires the temporal element to make it intelligible. But time, as we have previously seen, does not inhere even in the phenomena, it is a product of the theoretical reason. Therefore, time may be eliminated, and the *real* will then in its timeless aspect represent the union between reason and will, treated in the first two Critiques.

We must be cautioned, however, not to conclude that Kant means to assert that the aesthetic sense defines the nature of reality; that to him is impossible. It may approach it, however, by a different method from the one employed by the other two faculties; it may speculate on the possibility that the real is above mechanistic or teleological explanations, or that it includes both, contrasted as they may appear in the present, inadequate state of our knowledge. Such speculation is the more necessary in view of the fact that neither of the two explanations is adequate, either by itself or in conjunction with the other, to explain all existence. The living organism appears to be self-caused, not produced by a creator or designer, in the orthodox, theological sense of the meaning of God; it continually creates itself, as shown by its growth and recuperative powers. Nature, on the other hand, cannot be wholly explained by mechanism, in view of the fact that it includes living organisms. Nature also cannot be teleologically explained, resembling a living organism, because we are not sufficiently well acquainted with all its parts, and the relations they bear toward each other. In short, we do not at this time know its organic unity.

5. Conclusion.

Such is the brief résumé of Kantian philosophy. It will be recalled that Kant worked out his doctrine to correct the defects in Hume's conclusions. Has he succeeded? In the first Critique he most convincingly points out the barrenness of rationalism, the school founded by Descartes, culminating in Leibniz, whose disciple at first influenced Kant. Wolff lost sight of the really worth-while phase of his master's doctrine, the conception of force, but emphasized only the rational element, not quite so important. Kant likewise caused us to eschew intellectually the empirical conception of probability in all events, by its contention that experience is the sole judge in knowledge. Doubtless, Hume could not explain how we have the idea of causation altogether, because experience, by no stretch of the imagination, could supply it. What solution does Kant offer? He combines some of the elements of the two theses. Nevertheless he is not a mere eclectic, as was Empedocles. He adds new elements, original conceptions. Unfortunately, he overreaches himself, he ascends such heights in his speculative, theoretical philosophy that we lose sight of the foundation. After all, when we consider that the mind furnishes space and time, without which experience is impossible, that the mind supplies the categories, the conditions indispensable to knowledge, the *a priori* elements, which cause our experiences of objects and events to have universal validity; what remains for the outside world, the so-called thing-in-itself, to offer? What, in short, does sensation mean but, in the Berkeleyan sense, our impressions and our perceptions, without any external element to support them?

Does not this really make Kant a subjective idealist? Kant would strenuously object to such a line of thought. To him there surely exists an objective something without us. To him the reason why change in the world has meaning is because it is set off against a background of changelessness, permanence, connected with the thing-in-itself. To him, moreover, our knowledge contains an objective element supplied by nature, because we cannot change the course of nature, which we certainly could do if all things were products of our own minds. In nature, heavy bodies fall downward, no matter how hard we would strive to have it otherwise. Still, the fact remains that the thing-in-itself is so mysterious, so unfathomable, fulfills such an unnecessary function in knowledge, that we may deny its existence altogether. Berkeley argued similarly in reference to the existence of a material substance; if it can be perceived, then it is an idea like the rest of our beliefs, if not, of what use is it? We may just as well and just as profitably deny its existence altogether. Why does not the same reasoning apply here? If this noumenon is the subject matter of sensation, then it must be allocated in space and have reference to time, both of which are *a priori*, hence nothing tangible is really left to it; on the other hand, if it cannot be sensed, as Kant argues, why bother with it? What purpose does it serve?

In fact, the conclusion to dispense with the thing-in-itself in the Kantian sense was actually reached by his disciples, Fichte, Schelling, Hegel and Schopenhauer, and was incorporated as a part of their respective philosophies. But what does this show? It proves that just as Hume, by his skepticism, although he was an exponent of empiricism, really ended by denying in fact empiricism altogether, so Kant, in his eagerness to restore knowledge to its rightful dignity, contrary to Hume, really disregards the value of experience, reducing everything to the mind. Hume insisted upon observation and sensation as being the only vehicles through which knowledge can be obtained, but in following out his conclusions probability only was rendered possible. That left reason an empty shell, even from the empirical point of view. Kant, too, wants to have knowledge so universally and so necessarily true, that he must have recourse to the only possible source for such universality, the mind. He must, therefore, attribute less and less significance to experience until we need but remove the thin boundary line existing between the phenomenon and the noumenon, and thus dispense altogether with their contribution to knowledge. Thus we may conclude that, although Kant succeeded in his polemic against Hume's probability, he gave us too much certainty, universality. But at what great sacrifice!

This theoretical philosophy, furthermore, bristles with numerous other difficulties. Kant rightly identifies the subject matter of philosophy and science. The world of nature serves as the hunting ground for both, it offers innumerable opportunities for investigation. To be sure, he distinguishes between the methods employed by each. Science, in the popular sense, uses the *a posteriori* type of approach, it begins with observation and experiment, and then works up to general laws; philosophy on the other hand, employs the *a priori* approach, as we have seen. Kant never intended that philosophy, because of its *a priori* element, should look down upon the empirical sciences, for he insists that the innate categories would be devoid of all content, if they did not include experience; they would thus be rendered useless. At the same time, however, because of the distinction in the methods of study, which he so clearly indicates, it lends color to the theory, subsequently so ably developed by his disciples, that philosophy uses a speculative method, solely appropriate to its purpose. Once such speculation is attributed to philosophy, there is no end to what heights it can lead us. Why bother with sensation, with empirical facts? Why not deduce everything from the mind itself?

Hegel is the chief exponent of such a theory. Philosophy, to him, deduces entire reality from reason; nay, it identifies reality and reason. It makes the categories the very essence of being, of existence. Such assumptions could not long endure; therefore, after reigning supreme for a while, they fell into disrepute. True, Kant himself was not the chief offender in this respect, yet his philosophy contained the germ which could be developed into this type of thought, hence it must reflect upon his doctrine. To our way of thinking, a philosophy which brings about any situation whereby it dissociates itself from the sciences, disregarding their contribution, is indeed worthy of condemnation. Science and philosophy should go hand in hand. In ancient Greece, philosophy, typified by that of Plato and Aristotle, was considered the source of the individual sciences, showing their interrelation; it was unified scientific knowledge; that conception contains the most fundamental truth, the significance of which is felt to this day. The conception of the Kantian definition of philosophy, or perhaps we ought to say the misconception, simply dispelled this meaning of the term for a short while, until the Hegelian influence waned.

Besides, another element in his theoretical philosophy requires some comment. Kant emphasizes again and again the fact that the understanding applies only to the world of experience. All speculations beyond it are purely metaphysical, hence they are only natural inclinations without scientific validity. Why the distinction between these metaphysical subjects, such as God, thing-in-itself and universe, and the categories, which, he admits, constitute the very fabric of valid knowledge? They, too, are products solely of the mind; why not call them mere inclinations? Why not admit with Hume that all we have is sensation, probability, but the mind, because of its natural inclination, not pleased with such probability, proposes the categories to feel more at ease, because of the harmony they introduce into the world? Why, in short, do we concede more validity to these categories, which constitute the first story, so to speak, of the mind, and deny equal certainty to the classifications treated by the Dialectic, because they are one story higher? Then again, the categories embrace experiences, supplied by sensation; the higher, more general, classifications such as God, universe, embrace such sensations plus the stamp placed upon them by the categories.   Neither class is devoid of content.   Why the distinction?   Perhaps with some ingenuity, it may be just as possible to point out antinomies with relation to the categories themselves, in their application to experience, similar to those referring to the metaphysical subjects.   Hume finds it quite simple to show that the world of experience needs no causal relation at all, although Kant feels it to be axiomatic that it must be bound by a causal chain.

To go one step further.   Kant relies, in his denial that knowledge can reach beyond experience, upon the fact that we can prove both sides of the question.   What of it?   The mere fact that we can demonstrate the existence or non-existence of God, for example, shows that reason may have it as its object of study and investigation.   But, he asks, which is correct?   That is no argument for denying the application of the term knowledge to it.   Many questions, obviously concerning the objects of knowledge, may be argued differently, with diametrically opposite answers, yet that simply means that we must look for an additional, extraneous element, to support one side rather than the other.   Kant may be right in contending that since each side of the argument for God may be carried to its logical consequences, the pragmatic attitude, supplied by will, may help us to adopt one in preference to the other, but still it would be reason that has demonstrated the existence or the non-existence of God.   To find support for his contention that God cannot be the subject of the theoretical or logical proof by criticizing the three classic arguments for His existence, weakens Kant's position.   We know that these proofs are antiquated, showing God to be anthropomorphic; therefore, they should not even be considered the proper object of attack for a philosopher of Kant's eminence.   Also, why may we not assert that the mind refuses to regard the world unless it is embraced in a universe, that the mind refuses to regard nature unless it is under the guidance of a God, the position Kant takes with regard to the categories?   Finally, even when Kant proves his three beliefs by the moral arguments, does he not here count on theoretical understanding?   What determines that the categorical imperative implies an alternative of action, or of freedom of the will?   The theoretical understanding, for will has no thought attached to it, simply action.   In fact, all his moral philosophy in reference to its postulates cannot dispense with intellect for evolving what the will requires.   Is that the method of showing the limitations of reason?   Assuredly not.   The farther Kant develops his philosophy, the more he convinces us, though against his will, of the supremacy of reason, in its logical conceptual aspect.

Let us turn now to Kant's Critique of Practical Reason. Let us consider for a moment the three postulates of morality —freedom of the will, immortality of the soul, and God. Does Kant persuade us of the validity of his arguments? After all, is he not arguing in a circle?   He dogmatically asserts that the only good will is one which acts out of respect for the law of duty, the Categorical Imperative.   That imperative commands a certain line of action in preference to any other, implying, therefore, that the will is free to adopt either alternative.   This situation in turn causes a conflict between duty and desire, hence an indefinite period of time is again required by implication to achieve harmony between them; immortality thus becomes a salient factor in our morality. Lastly, God guarantees that such harmony will be attained. The three implications of morality are thus seen to hang on the fact that the will is autonomous, is its own master, is independent, and acts in obedience to universal laws.   Remove that consideration, and what have you?   The whole superstructure falls.   Suppose the will does not act because of duty, but it must necessarily follow mechanical laws, similar to all other natural phenomena, then can any consideration be given to the factors implied in the imperative?   True enough, if Kant simply emphasized the pragmatic aspect of the postulates, if, in other words, he wanted to impress on us that our lives would be richer, fuller, more significant and more energetic, if we "carry on" under the belief that there is freedom, immortality, and a God, we would most assuredly not quarrel with him. Our objection is to his insistence that there is necessity in these beliefs, not choice. In effect, he is saying, I refuse to consider my moral action unless I regard it as the result of an autonomous will, acting under the guidance of a Categorical Imperative, with freedom, immortality and God as indispensable conditions. But that is no proof that the facts are actually so. That is subject to the same type of criticism as we leveled against Berkeley's philosophy. There, the "ego-centric predicament" fatally undermined Berkeley's principle that perception and existence are identical, by pointing out that it is quite possible that there are other types of existence not essentially perceivable.

Here, too, Kant has no right to identify morality with acting according to duty and the implication of freedom, when it is quite possible that there is no such freedom. In fact, the objection here is even stronger than the attack against Berkeleyanism. In the case of Berkeley we simply say that there *may* be existence without its being perceived, but we do not possess real examples of such existences. In Kant's case, however, materialists and scientists show time and again that so-called human freedom is a myth, that much of man's activity may be identified with his nervous system, reducing it all to mechanical principles. To be sure, theirs, too, are not the last words on the subject, their theories are subject to attack, but at least the whole investigation shows that Kant cannot by mere words assert a principle, and thus give it universal validity. Dogmatism, which he condemns in rationalism, seems to be the keynote of this Critique of Practical Reason.

Then again, the human being is doubtless a part of this mechanical world of nature. How then does Kant attribute freedom to him? Kant here adduces the conception of the two realms, one, the mechanical, the other composed of human souls, the free. But is that a sufficient explanation? Kant brilliantly argues that man is essentially free, that he voluntarily imposes upon himself the mechanical laws which appear in nature, therefore, necessity shows no limitations to his complete freedom. In other words, the ideal world is free, the phenomenal world is subject to necessity, but it is only the appearance of the world behind it.   Similarly the human, in his soul and will, represents the noumenon, which expresses itself through the body, the phenomenon.   The latter only is mechanically governed, but even that is a result of the free soul's own doing.   Just as we freely acquire habits, which later become so strong that they appear to govern us, though in fact they are a product of our own violition, so phenomenal nature presents the habits developed by the ideal world.   This is an extremely ingenious theory, but it approaches very closely the type of explanation which Spinoza calls an "asylum of ignorance."

In the same manner Kant stresses the autonomy of will by his insistence that the Categorical Imperative, which commands a definite line of action, is our own imposition, otherwise, here, too, we should be subject to an external factor, thus robbing the will of its perfect freedom.   Moreover, God, who, as the head of the kingdom of ends, of souls, of the moral world, appears at first to compel us to obey the law of duty, represented by the Imperative, is introduced by Kant merely to sanction this universal principle, not to force it upon us.   Because of God's approval of this principle, Kant desires to persuade us of its essential validity, of its appropriateness to serve as our guide.   Regardless, however, of this explanation, the actual fact remains that the moral law is a divine command, that we must respect it accordingly.   The deistic conception of God offered by Kant is crude, and far inferior to that of Spinoza.   The latter, at least, conceives of God as the whole of reality, permeating it, including our own lives. Kant conceives of Him as set apart from us, whose presence is required for explaining and for validating certain facts on which he has set his heart.   Then again, would it not be a more exalted thought to consider morality as a result of our own character, our own intelligence, rather than bring to bear upon it the stamp of approval of any external being?   The former type of morality would certainly exert greater influence and possess a stronger appeal.

In spite of these objections, Kant's philosophy has great merit.   In fact, it would not occupy its admitted position of importance in the history of thought, were it not full of brilliant suggestions both for scientific study and for moral behavior.   Kant solves to a large extent one of the most troublesome questions of all time—the conflict between science and religion.   Religion had always been very sensitive about any attack made upon what she considered her impregnable position.   The thought uppermost in the minds of intellectuals had always been that these two methods of studying the world were mutually exclusive—the mechanical, scientific view of phenomena must eliminate any possibility of purposive or theistic theories, even about that which lies behind appearances.   On the other hand, religion always struggles to exclude natural explanations, even of phenomena.   This apparently irreconcilable conflict led to many unjust punishments visited upon leading thinkers by the religious zealots, who happened to wield the then existing power.   Socrates was condemned to die for the denial of the gods.   Anaxagoras was banished, because of the fear, engendered by his natural explanations, that the pedestal of the gods would be undermined.   In comparatively modern times, Bruno was burned at the stake; Descartes, as we have seen, made many concessions to the Church in his philosophy; Spinoza was excommunicated by his own people.   Leibniz, on the other hand, making the most extraordinary claims for religion, was extolled and showered with honors.

This kind of a conflict, however, need not exist altogether. Let science control its province, and religion that which belongs exclusively to its domain.   The moment one does not attempt to usurp the domain of the other, such opposition comes to an end. Spencer, for example, attempted to reconcile the two in this way: Science is unable to explain the ultimate elements of the universe; no matter how far you may carry your explanation, there is always a residue left which does not lend itself to analysis, that constitutes the "Unknowable."   Religion, too, he says, finds itself unable to offer an adequate and satisfactory theory for creation of the world, for example. Therefore, it, too, results in an "Unknowable." The two, science and religion, have this unknown in common, which furnishes the background for their harmony. This, apparently, is not very satisfactory. Nothing positive is offered here. It simply removes us to an unknown realm, which is tantamount to saying that the harmony between the two is unknown.

Kant, on the other hand, does supply some way of harmonizing the two. After all what is religion, but faith that the phenomenon, that which appears before us, does not tell the whole story? But Kant shows that very thing. In his first Critique, he pushes theoretical inquiry as far as possible. He demonstrates in a most able manner that nature is the subject matter for science. He argues, as effectively as any professed scientist would argue, that no other but a rational, mechanical explanation must enter into our inquiry of this visible world. His polemic against the admission of God's creation or of the presence of design or purpose in the natural realm, should satisfy the most rabid scientist. This, therefore, marks the domain of science. Then, he proceeds to the kingdom lorded over by faith, by morality and religion. Behind these phenomena, he says, we have the noumena, which by their very nature cannot be the subject of scientific investigation. We must have faith, we must postulate the three requisites for making human conduct intelligible, we have no choice in our beliefs of freedom, immortality and God, but we must necessarily consider them as valid and as actually existing. If it were a question of choosing to believe or disbelieve in them, we would be making or unmaking our own God. Then God would no longer be the Being to whom we are to look for guidance and comfort. Of what use would He then be to us? Once such faith is exercised, our lives are properly anchored and admit of infinite possibilities for realization. Our souls are then not limited to phenomena, but, endowed with freedom, they may realize themselves in an infinite time under the direction of an infinite God. This

theory of the co-existence of science and religion, of reason
and faith is of tremendous, vital force in our practical lives.
It does not attempt artificially a twofold doctrine of truth,
as do the Scholastics.   It does not demand that when you
study a phenomenon scientifically, you must rule out of your
mind the presence of free will or of a deity, but it urges
you to feel such presence at the very time you observe the
sequence of nature, considering it as the expression of the much
more important, necessary noumena behind it.   To be sure,
the scientist may frown upon this type of belief, but he cannot
claim that it derogates from the dignity of science to entertain it.

Then again, Kant, like no other modern philosopher, attempts to solve our individual problems.   In each of his three
Critiques, he starts from our own experience.   In the first,
he calls attention to an individual bit of perception.   What
are its constituent elements?   It consists of some material
element furnished from without through space and time, on
which the mind has impressed its four categories.   In other
words, this particular sensation which has become mine by
means of my spatial and temporal contribution must possess
quantity, quality, causation and modality; it must be tied up
to the universal chain of causality, and must conform to the
natural laws of temporal existence.   What, again, does my
moral act signify?   It means that I act freely, in accordance
with duty, and with the firm conviction that it meets with
God's sanction.   My own appreciation of beauty also indicates that my aesthetic sense beholds in the object that which
neither reason nor will can supply; it penetrates within and
proves that the real world may satisfy my artistic demands.
It, too, is of universal validity.   We thus notice that although
Kant's philosophy results in the application of universal,
rational laws to nature, of universal, moral laws to the will,
and of universal laws of beauty to judgment, it begins with our
individual experiences; the whole superstructure has only one
purpose—to explain to us what their import is.   This may
enable us to lead our lives, rationally, morally, and aestheti-

cally, more in conformity with what the world requires, a world which can be, and therefore should be, viewed from these three different aspects.

To return, then, to the position Kant occupies in the development of philosophic thought. His predecessors grappled with the problems confronting them with the sincere desire to understand the world. Cartesianism, doubting all prevailing opinions, ended in rationalism. Hume, likewise, casting suspicion upon beliefs firmly entrenched, ended in Empiricism. Kant combined the two, and added to it his remarkably cogent reasoning. Plato's division of reality finds a surprising parallel in Kant's line of demarcation between the phenomenal and the noumenal realms. Our philosopher does not argue with Spinoza that nature as we behold it is necessarily, mechanically governed, but he objects most strenuously to the Spinozistic conception that phenomenal nature is all there is. To him, the thing-in-itself is more important than appearances. Freedom is superior to mechanism, a thought clearly foreign to Spinozistic teaching. The personal God, in Kant, his predecessor would have rejected as unsuited to the scheme of things. In this conception of a personal God, Descartes, Leibniz, Locke and Berkeley are in perfect accord with Kant.

Nevertheless, Kant is more important for the subsequent development of thought, for which he is responsible. We have already referred to the necessary implications in his Critique of Pure Reason. We have seen that since we alone are responsible for space and time in sensation, and for the categories in our scientific knowledge, there is practically nothing left for the world without to contribute. What is this thing-in-itself, which is responsible for the external element in our knowledge? Kant cannot explain it. It was, therefore, relatively easy for Kant's successors to dispense with it altogether, or to attribute to it some positive characteristics. This could be done by making everything dependent upon our own minds, leaving no room for any objective, external element; it could also be explained by identifying the thing-in-itself with Reason, one of the essential elements of our make-up, or by calling it Will, another equally important component of our being.   The first was developéd by Fichte, whose conclusions inevitably led to the adoption of either of the other two alternatives—one by Hegel, and the other by Schopenhauer.

Let us, therefore, now turn to the study of that philosophy which adopted Reason as the objective element in the world, the philosophy which was a necessary result of Kantianism, but to which Fichte's thought also contributed—the philosophy of Georg Wilhelm Friedrich Hegel.

CHAPTER XI

Georg Wilhelm Friedrich Hegel (1770–1831)

1. *Relation to Fichte and Schelling.*

Georg Wilhelm Friedrich Hegel was born in Stuttgart, August 27, 1770, and died in Berlin, in 1831. While he was not a brilliant pupil, he was always sure and steady. He attended the gymnasium in his native town, and later the university in Tübingen. In 1801 he was appointed lecturer. There, in collaboration with Schelling, he edited the *Journal für Philosophie*. He was appointed professor of philosophy at Jena in 1805, and, ten years later, he was offered the same appointment at Heidelberg. Later, at the University of Berlin, he became a leader of one of the most powerful schools of philosophy of modern times.

Needless to state, Hegel's philosophy is not an isolated system. It not only exerted great influence upon subsequent thought, but it is vitally connected with many philosophic theories that preceded it, particularly with Kantian philosophy. The transition from Kant to Hegel, however, is not abrupt. The gap is bridged by the contributions of Fichte and Schelling.

Johann Gottlieb Fichte (1762–1814), the founder of German Idealism, was very much impressed with Kant's primacy of Practical Reason. To develop this thought further, to bring to the foreground the prime importance of morality, of the Will, Fichte devoted all his energies. He cultivates a system of intellectual reasoning to serve purely as an aid to moral development. To him, Kant's assertion of the thing-in-itself, without definite description as to its qualities and characteristics, is meaningless. Why not, then, identify that mysterious element with the Self, the Ego? Why not call it a creation of the thinking subject? Fichte considers this logically conceivable and morally necessary. Logically, he continues, the Ego thinks, but about what? About some object, which, in thought, must appear foreign to the subject. There is nothing, however, to indicate that this object is not a creation of the Ego itself. In other words, to think, to exercise its essential characteristic, the Ego simply sets up for itself an objective, foreign element, but that is all. In the last stage of such thinking, the Ego and its object, or the non-Ego, reciprocally limit each other. Each sets boundaries to the other, so that they may enter into a relation, which we denominate knowledge. To be sure, Fichte admits that by no power of thought may we remove this non-Ego, this world of experience; it must exist, because of the logical necessity implied in the subject's thought. That, however, does not argue for its objectivity, either in the sense of empiricism, which calls the phenomenal world the one important element in knowledge, or even in the Kantian sense, which considers it as furnishing a partial factor in knowledge. The world, the non-Ego, is purely a creation of the Self; the fact that it cannot be obliterated shows our limitation, our finitude. In this analysis, Fichte employs the dialectic method which Hegel later uses with a vengeance. This method proceeds along these lines: Thesis: The Ego creates itself; it affirms itself as a subject. Antithesis: In affirming itself it must produce or set up the non-Ego, the so-called objective world, here it negates itself. Synthesis: The Ego and non-Ego enter into the relation of knower and known, completing the act of knowledge, of thought. The conclusion, however, is that if you suppress the Ego, you suppress the whole world.

But the question remains, why this elaborate structure? Why should the Ego require this objective, natural realm? Here, the moral consideration assumes paramount significance. The real motive in life is the development of the will, moral self-realization.   This can only be achieved by struggle, by overcoming obstacles and temptations.   Therefore, the Self, from the moral point of view, sets up its opposite, its own limitation, so as to overcome it and thus realize its own freedom.   Such freedom can be attained only by overcoming phenomena which are merely appearances of the true reality behind them.   That reality is the Moral Will, which uses theoretical reason for its development.   The understanding supplies the world of sensations in time and space, but the will regards them as successive stages through which it must gradually pass, to emerge triumphant at the end, a free, moral soul.

This subjectivism was critically examined by Friedrich Wilhelm Joseph Schelling (1775–1854).   Schelling proceeds, in his critical analysis of Fichte, in a manner similar to the method that may be employed by a layman.   If Fichte assumes, he says, that the Ego's activities would be meaningless without the object, why give precedence to the Ego? Does he not necessarily imply in his own theory that the Ego and the non-Ego are of equal importance?   No subject without an object, no object without a subject.   This is assuredly true.   The Ego and the non-Ego occupy equal positions of importance in knowledge, hence Fichte's solution cannot be tolerated.   We must look for their synthesis in a higher principle, one that includes them both.   This higher principle, Schelling calls the Absolute.   This Absolute is identified with neither the Ego, nor with the non-Ego, nor with both. It is the source whence they emanate; they are its expressions. An analogy to this conception, though by no means exact, is Spinoza's God.   There, too, the infinite may be viewed from two aspects, thought and body.   Schelling's Absolute is somewhat similar, the Self and the world are ways of studying Him. It cannot be too strongly emphasized, however, that he differs radically from Spinoza, in that he identifies this Absolute with Will.   He argues that intuition can grasp the true nature of the whole of reality.   It returns us to the Absolute, the source whence we came.   He concludes that feeling, the artistic sense, is superior to philosophy, it penetrates to the very heart of the real, the true, the beautiful, in the Universe. "Philosophy conceives God; Art is God."

Thus it is readily seen that Schelling, like Fichte, employs the dialectic method to reach a certain result. The three elements in his philosophy are: Thesis, the Ego; Antithesis: the non-Ego; Synthesis: the Absolute. This philosophy, however, leaves us with a sense of dissatisfaction. It considers the relation between the Absolute and its two constituent elements as external. The Absolute is superimposed upon the Ego and the non-Ego, it towers over them, so to speak, but it does not identify itself with them. Hegel turns his attention to the correction of this proposition. Let us therefore consider the Hegelian philosophy, somewhat in detail.

2. *The Absolute. The Dialectic Method.*

Hegel's Absolute is synonymous with Reason; not your reason and mine, but the World Reason, Universal Consciousness. It is not dependent upon my Ego, but I, myself, am dependent upon it. It is not external to our individual selves, but permeates them; the texture, the stuff of both consists of the same element. To illustrate the difference in meaning between Schelling and Hegel: To Schelling, the relation between the Absolute and both the Ego and the non-Ego may resemble that existing between a parent and child. To Hegel, the closest resemblance would be to the relation existing between the figures in the Trinity. We find the spiritual identity there impossible to sever. To Hegel, too, the relation between the Absolute and the Ego and the non-Ego is similar to that between whiteness and milk. You cannot dissociate one from the other.

The important question then is: How are we to learn the true nature of this Absolute? How are we to study its essential characteristics, with a view to applying the results of our efforts to the world in which we live and in which we develop? Once we adopt the principle that Reason, Reality and Absolute are synonymous, we must apply the same principles in studying them as we would employ in the analysis of any other rational element, or rational act.   Such principles are furnished by logic, and the method is "the dialectic."   Its essential characteristic is the principle of contradiction.   Hegel by no means invented this method.   Socrates was a master in the use of it. By his irony he led his adversaries to make clear their position on the subject under discussion, but ended by reaching the opposite conclusion.   Plato, adopting the Socratic method, employed this manner of opposing one theory with another in order to develop a subject comprehensively.   Kant in his antinomies showed how one belief theoretically leads to its opposite.   Fichte and Schelling, we have just seen, apply it to their philosophies.   Hegel, however, really subjects all existence, including nature, art, morality, religion, politics, to its scrutiny and thereby evolves a comprehensive system of thought.   You may deride it, you may consider it worthless, you may frown upon it as a web spun by a mind which was not feazed by concrete facts, but you must admire it, nevertheless.

To return then to the Hegelian Absolute or World Reason. This conception that Reason is the stuff of the world must be *a priori*.   No number of experiences, in and by themselves, can possibly lead us to such a conclusion.   Nevertheless, the world of experience, if we apply the dialectic method to it, must inevitably lead us to understand the working, the development, and the essential characteristics of the Absolute. To illustrate: "being" is the most general concept we have. It means existence in general.   That constitutes our thesis. But its very generality robs it of any distinguishing marks, it, therefore, renders it impossible for us to mark it off from nonbeing or non-existence.   That is the antithesis.   We must then harmonize both of these into "becoming or change." That is the synthesis.

In becoming we have both what is and then again that into which it changes, or what it is not, thus negating its previous status.   This characterizes the method he applies everywhere. We must analyze everything into what it now is, then analysis

will show that it contains its opposite, which in turn will have
to be harmonized into something that includes them both.
But the resultant synthesis will itself be subject again to a
negative element, this then, will be resolved into a still more
comprehensive synthesis, which will be subjected once more
to the principle of contradiction.   The final solution, the ultimate harmony, the last synthesis, the step when it will no
longer be necessary to go higher, will constitute the Absolute.
The Universe as a whole harmonizes all contradictions, it is
the perfect whole, it is the synthesis which we are seeking as
our final solution.   It, therefore, constitutes the true, the
rational, the goal of the dialectic method.   The conclusion is
that only the whole of reality is rational, because that furnishes
a complete view of all things; it is the Absolute, the World
Reason, God.

[This world of experience in its separateness, in its detail,
is irrational; each experience is a partial view, it contains a
contradiction, it obliges us to seek for further solutions for
the contradictions it presents.] That very thing constitutes
irrationality.   Does not this theory find a real place for our
world?   Does it not fix our attention upon the fact that the
Absolute is not far removed, that it is not an abstract principle,
a brilliant creation of a brilliant mind?   Does it not induce us
to learn from the humdrum of life the essential quality of that
which underlies it?   Does it not, in short, compel us to seek
unity, wholeness, as a result of the incompleteness which our
own experiences indubitably show?   Consider your experience
of the table before your eyes.   The table given as a fact is the
thesis, but this very experience carries with it the opposite, the
destructibility of the object, or the antithesis.   This has to be
resolved into a synthesis, or the dust to which the table will
ultimately be reduced.   Such dust will contain both the table
that was and what it was not; that in turn is subject to destruction, or its antithesis, which will oblige us to harmonize further
and further until we get to the Absolute, the harmonizer of
all contradictions.   Thus the inadequacy, the impermanence
of our ordinary experiences must lead us to the Universal

Reason.   Shall we condemn this phenomenal realm on that account?   Far from it.   It is because of the inadequacy of phenomena, it is because of the irrationality apparent in detailed experience, that we can view the rational, the wholeness, behind it.   Hegel goes even further.   He says that the Absolute develops by means of these contradictions.   Evil, suffering, partial developments and all the other elements found in nature constitute the material upon which the Absolute draws.   In short, Hegel glories in things as they appear, for this yields the Rational Whole.

Such a theory results in optimism.   Why be concerned with the trivial elements in the world which, although they oppress us, really do not count materially, when we are certain that it all resolves itself into an absolute harmony in which our Egos find great significance?   Such a theory affords us a great deal of pleasure.   We may first of all be amused at the insistence of the untutored and uncultured upon the disproportionate importance they attribute to their beliefs.   The empiricist believes that he has found a haven to shelter him from intellectual strife.   Nothing else matters but the object experienced at this very minute.   Is that really true?   He must define this object with reference to time and space, which Kant showed are not objects of experience themselves; they are, moreover, of universal application, and therefore not experienced right now.   Then again, this particular object must be related to other objects in the world, otherwise it does not enter into the context of our consciousness, we do not understand it in isolation.   Therefore, empiricism, which prides itself on the particular (thesis), necessarily implies the opposite, universality, the non-experienced (antithesis).   To Descartes, too, the Hegelian philosopher makes answer. How can you, he asks, found your philosophy on skepticism, on doubting everything and still consider yourself existing? If you doubt your own existence, which must include your existence even as a thinking being, then how can you build a philosophy altogether?   If you do not doubt your existence as a thinking being, then your premise of doubting everything is insupportable.   In either case, it bristles with contradictions.   In the same tenor, we may discard the consideration of any other factor in our observation of nature.   Suppose someone points out a great evil in the world, war, for example. He bewails the suffering entailed as a result of it, the havoc wrought upon nations and individuals by its instrumentality; the Hegelian disciple asks, What of it?   War is the thesis, it must carry with it its opposite, the antithesis, peace.   Therefore, all is well with the universe as a whole.   War simply shows the temporary nature of so-called stable society, but it must pass.   Not only is war inevitable, but it is also a factor of great importance in the development of the Absolute which rises to a higher stage, whose Ideals are expressed by the victorious state.   We thus approach nearer to the goal, we have access to the realized whole, to Reason, to the Absolute.   The moment we conclude that the details of the world, that the individual experiences, that the phenomena, are merely stepping stones to the ultimate goal of our efforts, that moment we are free, we are no longer enslaved to their oppressive demands.   We can then caricature everything.   We analyze it, we show what disproportionate claim it makes, what importance it assigns to itself in order to survive.   Then we deny existence to it, we point out that it carries by implication its own opposite, its antithesis.   Not only should this amuse us in the process of denuding the experience or the theory of its unwarranted assumptions, but it is the self-same process which is so vital in attaining the goal of our conceptual thinking—the Absolute, God.

To sum up then: Hegel conceives *a priori* that the underlying substance of the world is Reason.   The phenomenal world is its external expression.   To study this Reason we must apply logical thinking; the method employed is the dialectic, which is based on the principle of contradiction.   Abstractly, the thesis, antithesis, and synthesis lead up to the Absolute as the ultimate harmony of all contradictions.   The world of concrete experience furnishes us the means by which this dialectic method may be applied to reach this goal.   Every bit of experience carries with it its antithesis, which finally yields the Rational Whole. The very fact that every factor in the world is not the whole, shows its irrationality, and inevitably leads to the conclusion with which we started, that Reason is the permeating principle, the essence of the world.

3. *Nature. Mind.*

To apply then this dialectical method to two of the most important aspects of life, Nature and Mind. We referred several times to the fact that Hegel considers his theory to possess universal application. Necessarily it must be so. It is a metaphysical philosophy, all-inclusive; it covers not only every phase of human endeavor, but it delves even into the mysterious realm of the invisible. Obviously, from that aspect, we see the validity of its application; because of the inexorable logic, the conclusions are inevitable. In short, from concrete experience we are led step by step to the most abstract concepts, and we infer that behind the phenomena, the dialectic applies with equal force. From this we are led to study the application of the Hegelian principle of contradiction, first to nature and then to mind, which is an important part of nature.

Nature is divided into: Thesis—Inorganic Matter. It possesses no distinguishing characteristics, it is formless throughout. Antithesis: Chemical reactions by which this matter is particularized, by which it assumes individuality and differentiation. Synthesis: The living organism—here both undifferentiated matter and individuality are harmonized to produce the living things, resulting finally in the *human* being, who stands at the apex of the organic world. At this point we pass to a higher, more vital, feature of the universe—the world of mind. What about the principle of contradiction here? It works equally well in mind. We have: Thesis—the Ego, or the individual mind; it is particular, subjective, egoistic. Antithesis—Society. Here we find the so-called objective mind, the collective mind of one's fellow men, which limits the individual's Ego. The personal will is here suppressed and chastened by the impersonal will of society. The problem is to make this objective mind become the individual's own. That leads to the Synthesis—the Absolute Mind. Here, all the barriers between my Ego and the will of society are removed. They are both seen as being subject to the rational law, to Reason, to Truth, to Perfection, which can only be achieved by the whole. Hence all humans realize that their salvation lies in getting away from partial or prejudiced points of view, in removing mind from the inadequate pictures presented by phenomena, and thus reaching the whole, the universal mind, the common ground for the harmony between all apparent contradictions existing among the individual minds. For are they not all striving after the same goal? Are not all wills after freedom? Are not all minds after complete, perfect Reason?

4. *Dialectics of History.*

Thus far we have observed the general manner in which the Hegelian logic applies. But he goes further. He shows that the dialectic applies to every feature of these general conclusions. Consider Society or the Objective mind, for example. This part of his philosophy is known as the Dialectics of History. Here the Absolute Reason has the whole world for its stage, and empires for its actors. It unfolds itself successively until it gradually will emerge in its pure, unadulterated form. In the midst of the confusion created by war, by rebellions, by natural as well as unpredictable political developments, the underlying principle always consists of the universal Reason, striving to realize itself by means of the principle of contradiction.

The State, he says, is the realized ethical ideal of spirit. It is the Will which manifests itself. The individual's duty is to be a member of the State, because in that way alone can he have an ethical status. Therefore, all those who advocate the contract theory of the State—Hobbes, Rousseau, Spinoza, Locke—are wrong, for then one could choose to be or not to be a member, which is unthinkable. The State is the actualization of freedom, it is the march of God in the world; through it, Reason has the power to realize itself, as Will. For such realization, we are again confronted with the Hegelian method. We have Thesis—Reason as actualized in a particular State. Antithesis—this Reason as it appears in a State or States external to the first political unit. Synthesis —Universal Reason as it emerges in World History, in which one State is vanquished by another, and the victor is in turn conquered, until there constantly appears the political organization which portrays the Ideal more and more perfectly.

This Hegelian reasoning explains adequately many of the political phenomena which are usually lamented as evil. The very fact that the Absolute must pass through successive stages in order to develop progressively, inherently shows that the particular State is doomed to destruction. If it were otherwise, we should be bound to argue that any individual government has already attained the most perfect ideal, which is absurd. Once you admit that its existence is purely temporary, then war is no longer an absolute evil. It becomes a weapon used by Reason to pass on to the next stage. It is also necessary to expose the contingent nature of the finitude of the State, including life and property in it. By war, he says, people escape the corruption that results from everlasting peace. This particularity involved in the State necessarily also implies that it should have external relations with other States. That furnishes the basis for international law. But if they cannot agree, war is the inevitable result. "The destinies and deeds of States in their connection with one another are the visible dialectic of the finite nature of their spirits?" [1] Out of this dialectic, the sublimated spirit emerges. It exercises its rights of a judge upon the lower spirits in World History. The World History is not a Court of Judgment whose principle is force; it is self-caused, self-realized Reason. States, peoples and individuals are unconscious tools of the World Spirit. It passes through different stages. A nation

[1] "Philosophy of Right," by S. W. Dyde, page 341.

is assigned the accomplishment of one of these stages, it flourishes for a while and then gives way to another. It then disappears and another, superior State emerges. At the summit of all of these actions on the world stage stand individuals. Each leader is a living embodiment of the deeds of the World Spirit, but even he himself is unconscious of this. Most assuredly he is rarely appreciated by others. It is the right of heroes to found States.

To complete the discussion of this World History, Hegel surveys four world-historic kingdoms: (1) The Oriental Empire, the absolute monarchy. Its chief characteristic consists in the utter suppression of individuality. The State so dominates the individual that it almost annihilates him. (2) The Greek Empire. The monarchy is replaced by republics. The individual here comes into his own, and the State becomes aware of the importance of its component members, through whose coöperation it triumphs. (3) The Roman Empire. The individual, who ran riot in the Greek Empire, is now reduced to obedience. All diverse nations are thrown into a confused heap. Here the World Spirit retreats into itself. (4) The Germanic Empire. Here the individual and State are harmonized. The equilibrium is restored between these apparently conflicting interests. The modern monarchy is to Hegel the synthesis of political development. To be sure, in comparison with what is to come, with the Ideal State, it, too, seems barbaric, but at least it contains the best evidence of the Spirit's progress.

The upshot of this entire dialectic of history is that the World Reason must progress through contradictions. The State in its finitude and limitations, while it lasts, actualizes the Spirit. Its self-aggrandizement, its desire for survival, conflicts, as may be expected, with another State, whose sole ambition is similar to that of the first. War ensues out of this conflict, war, to be sure now more humanely conducted than heretofore, but a deadly struggle, nevertheless. As a result, a new State emerges, in which the Ideal State is more nearly typified.   The process is then repeated; thus step by step we approach a closer realization of the Ideal.   Since a political unit must act through the wills of individuals, the hero represents the Spirit in its march through history, no matter how unconscious he may be of his mission, or how unappreciated his deeds are by his fellow men.   This clearly shows that the logical principle of contradiction, whether we apply it to the clashing of individual minds, or to the conflict between States, finally leads us to the Absolute, Universal Reason, World Spirit.   True enough, the political unit does not yield absolute satisfaction to the mind in its search for the true nature of the Absolute, for it falls short of the Ideal.   Art penetrates the phenomenal world and finds that the Infinite Reason behind it all and our self-consciousness are identical.   Religion identifies this Universal Reason with God.   Philosophy or science employs reason, instead of feeling, the organ of art, or imagination and faith, the weapons of religion, to demonstrate the same result, to show that our finite minds and the Absolute are composed of the same stuff.   Here Reason comes into its own and proclaims that which the other two had already anticipated.   Science further shows that nature, the State, and the Ideal World are manifestations of the Absolute Spirit.

Hegel carries his dialectic method into every branch of each of these phases of human activity.   An illustration of the religious development by means of the principle of contradiction will suffice to prove the aptitude of such an application.   The Oriental Religion pays attention exclusively to God, the Infinite, the Creator.   He is everything, man is nothing. Greek Religion, on the other hand, takes the opposite view. Man is extolled, even the Gods are personified.   The finite is preferred to the conception of the infinite.   The Christian creed combines the two; finite man and infinite God are harmonized.   God is conceived both as far removed from us, and also as walking in our midst.   The same logic applies to art, and to philosophy.   In fact, it even applies to the different stages in art, furnishing the dialectic of its development, culminating in its present, modern aspect.

5. Conclusion.

This Hegelian philosophy is a most comprehensive system of thought. No matter how we individually may react towards the method employed, and towards the conclusions reached by Hegel, we must admire the ingenuity displayed by him in weaving this theoretical doctrine so that it covers, with some degree of plausibility, not only every phase of human activity, but also those unseen elements which have always tried the human mind in its unceasing effort to understand and explain them. This philosophy, too, is an integral part of the development of thought. With his predecessor, Kant, Hegel agrees that the three compartments of the human make-up contribute materially to a wholesome understanding of our Universe. As in Kantianism, faith or the will plays an important rôle, intuition in art penetrates the inner constitution of the universe, showing that there is a Universal Spirit or a God. But now they come to a parting of the ways. Kant assigns to theoretical reason or logic the comparatively inferior task of studying only the visible world, leaving the explanation of some of the noumena to faith. Hegel, on the other hand, extols, and rightly, too, the function of reason. Reason is the stuff of which the world is composed; consequently, it must be capable of explaining all. In fact, our self-consciousness, being reason in a finite sense, is so akin the Universal Reason, that it must assuredly know it logically or scientifically, for does not like assimilate like? Furthermore, Kant's denial of the science of metaphysics leaves even his morality hanging in the air. To be sure we may have moral development without relation to metaphysical theories. The naturalists, for example, who deny that there is anything supernatural, anything above nature, base morality upon environmental influences and upon character development. At the same time a metaphysics extends the horizon of moral progress; James contends that even pragmatically life possesses great zest, if it is chained to a belief that the world is at bottom, moral, that God sanctions moral standards. Hegel's metaphysics, developed dialectically, therefore supplies the factor so essential as an anchor to human conduct. In Kant, the negative attitude he adopts towards metaphysics is even more objectionable, because, unlike the naturalists, he makes his entire Practical Reason depend upon metaphysical beliefs—God, immortality, and freedom. Yet he in no way supplies a rational basis for their existence. To say that the Will needs them for its development, and simultaneously to assert that they exist, because the Will postulates them, means no more than what the mere words imply. Then again, why should he attribute more importance to the Will than to Reason? Is not Reason the vehicle for expressing conceptually what the Will does practically? How could a system of ethics be developed and be transmitted from one people to another, unless rational or logical arguments are used for purposes of persuasion?

But the real distinction between Kant and Hegel is this regard lies in this: Kant considers Reason as an instrument for studying the world; the mind, therefore, uses the categories as its weapons with which to analyze nature. To Hegel, on the other hand, Reason *is* the world, the categories are not weapons of the mind, they are the very essence, the inner stages, of that Reason, of that Universal Mind, through which it progressively develops. In short, in Kantianism, Reason is an external beholder of the process that goes on before our very eyes; in Hegelianism, it is the process itself.

In connection with this, we may also say that even the ancients regarded reason as primary. Plato considered a moral life, one in which reason dominated and in which will under the guidance of reason controlled the emotions. Aristotle clearly gave reason the chief position in the soul. The Stoics urged us to study the world rationally, and by means of the divine reason, of which we partake, to lead a perfect life. The Epicureans, too, although they desired pleasure as the end of life, wanted rational knowledge to be used as the means for the selection of one kind of pleasure in preference to another. It is needless to dwell at great length on the supremacy of reason, developed by most of the modern philosophers, except to point out that the rationalists evolved the entire universe out of the mind, and the empiricists employed reason to show the inconsistencies in other theories.

With Kant, Hegel also agrees that intuition or feeling is the key to the innermost nature of the universe. Kant threw out a hint to that effect; Schelling considered art as the "organon of philosophy"; Hegel used it as a contributing element to science or logic, to demonstrate by means of both that God, Reason, Spirit, Absolute, Reality—all synonymous terms— are akin to our self-consciousness, and therefore, we may be hopeful that we can understand that which lies behind the phenomena. We may point out here that subsequent idealistic philosophers might have had their attention fixed upon intuition as a most effective instrument for studying the universe, instead of on reason, if the theory of Schelling had held sway, instead of Schopenhauer's method of will. From this we conclude that Fichte regarded reason as the instrument of will, whereas Hegel assigned to will the function of anticipating the conclusions reached by reason in its dialectic. Doubtless, Fichte's conclusion is untenable. He effectively points out the objection to Kant's thing-in-itself, as we have already seen, but his affirmative contribution has little merit. At most it is subjective idealism. His own theory regarding God is fatal to his philosophy, but even if that were not the case, the objections to Berkeley's idealism are just as applicable and fatal to the doctrines of Fichte. Schelling's negative influence, too, serves the function of forcing the props from under Fichte. At the same time his conclusion of an Absolute, standing over and above the Ego and the non-Ego, cannot hold water. It is an "asylum of ignorance," it does not explain the Ego and the non-Ego in which we are most interested; it simply removes the needed explanation to a more remote source, the Absolute. Therefore, it is perfectly proper for the idealist to identify all with either Reason or Will: Hegel chose the former, just as logically as Schopenhauer, the latter. Both do not regard the world as a product of the individual Ego, in the Berkeleyan sense, they consider it as objectively existing, independent of us, but composed of the same mental stuff.   In short, both are objective idealists.

Surely, Hegel devised a system which demonstrates how gigantic a task a thinking mind can accomplish.   That, however, does not tell the whole story.   The *a priori* element plays almost the exclusive rôle in this philosophy.   True enough, it calls upon concrete experience in nature, in politics, in religion, in art, in science, to bear out its preconceived conclusions, but we always feel that this is simply for the purpose of filling in gaps, not for any independent contributions.   The moment a theory finds no snags anywhere, that moment we must call a halt, and examine it most carefully.   We have already referred to the fact that the distinction Hegel makes between the method used by the concrete sciences and the one employed by philosophy—*a posteriori* versus *a priori* —played a great part in discrediting philosophy in subsequent thought.   This *a priori* device inherently possesses the characteristic of attempting to get farther and farther away from life.   Just by that alone it is rendered useless as an instrument for life.   Hegel offends seriously in this way.   He attributes too much to Reason.   He extols it to a point where it means almost the complete annihilation of experience.   He finds the mind possessed of the infinite capacity for theorizing, and he stretches it as far as it will go.   By means of this he explains all things along the same tenor.   Evil is bad, but he exhorts us not to take it too much to heart, because it is only temporary, relative, it must be replaced by the good, its opposite.   War is bad, you say; why worry about it?   The Absolute needs it for development.   It is the most effective weapon in World-History, it is the means by which one civilization passes into another.   It is also essential to show the finitude and impermanence of the particular State.   We may rest assured, however, that it will be replaced by peace.

To all this we answer that it offers no consolation to us, poor mortals, who happen to be affected by the evil, or who have lost our dear ones in war.   Then again, the age-old question confronts us.   Why could not the Absolute Spirit, God, work otherwise than by the dialectic?   Surely he is not limited in his power to do so.   This clearly shows the defect of preconceived theories as a means to showing how things should be reasoned out, and the fallacy of these laborious attempts to fit the facts into the theory.   They often result in absurdities and contradictions.   We may, in conclusion, point out perhaps the most fatal defect in Hegel's philosophy.   He continually emphasizes the fact that only the whole is rational and true; that all other things, being relative, have their own implied contradictions, but that the whole, the final synthesis, can no longer be opposed by anything else, hence it is the last word of Reason.   From this angle he criticizes the various philosophies of his predecessors; we referred especially a short while ago to empiricism and skepticism.   But is not this objection equally true of his own philosophy?   Surely, Hegel, the finite man, cannot expect us to believe that his theory, the product of a finite mind, is more than relative; he must realize that his own system, too, must be subject to an opposing doctrine, and from the conflict, a new, superior philosophy will emerge.   If such should be the case, and we are forced to admit this possibility by applying Hegel's own reasoning, then what becomes of his analysis that the universe is Reason, the nature of which is to be understood by means of the "dialectic"?

Nevertheless, this system of thought must be given credit for many features useful for our practical lives.   By showing the infinite possibilities of the Self, enabling it to realize itself in every branch of human striving, he lends the importance to each of us, so necessary to encourage us in our combat with forces which often tend to discourage us to the point of despair.   The identify of the Self with the substance of the world makes us feel at home here.   This in turn enriches our experiences, and renders our lives more fruitful.   William James says that if we believe there is a God in the world, who is really interested in our welfare, it humanizes nature; the environment then offers more stimuli for action.   This pragmatic aspect applies with equal force to Hegel's conception.   It offers the solace and comfort of religion, with the added consideration that God's nature is so akin to ours that we need not fear the lack of our capacity to understand him.

Psychologically, Hegel's analysis of the soul into reason, will and feeling is in accord with the theory advanced by many other thinkers.   Politically, his assertion that the State is the product of our own will, through which the will of the Universal Spirit is manifested, calls for patriotism, and for devotion to the task of making the State an adequate expression of our inner nature.   It is no longer an artificial creation to be nursed along by politicians for their own profit.   It is a vital necessity in our lives, and calls for constant, patient duty to the State.   His expression of faith that the hero is the embodiment of the World Spirit, lends impetus to the development of such heroic stuff, so essential to the culture and progress of the race.   The fact that the hero is unconscious of this mission, and the additional consideration that he is not appreciated, should not deter him from fulfilling his function, appropriate to his inherent natural aptitudes. From the artistic point of view, Hegel certainly encourages genius in art, for such a genius will see the beauty that resides in the Universe, which is not recognized by the naked eye.

Finally, he tells us to be rational, to face things calmly and in spite of the overwhelming evil, war, and suffering so apparent in nature, we may rest assured that the Absolute Spirit will emerge, vindicated, more free than ever before.   He furnishes us with liberty, he emphasizes the individual Ego in each of us, he does not belittle, but rather elevates, the human spirit.   He tells us that we are not puny little beings in this vast universe, that we are so much greater and superior to all phenomena, because our self-consciousness can understand them, whereas they doubtless cannot understand us.   Even if we do not logically agree with this conclusion, from the pragmatic point of view, his philosophy contains many elements which cause us proudly to extend the horizon of our activities, to lead an energetic, moral life, with the boldness and assurance that betoken a Self—free, infinite in its power, and akin to the very texture of this Universe.   Such a glorification of the human spirit has never been equalled.

This Hegelian influence exerted great force on many of the subsequent systems of thought, but in many cases the doctrine was so altered as to be unrecognizable.   In America, its chief exponent, although with real modification, is Josiah Royce, whose philosophy we shall discuss shortly.   In the meantime, let us turn our attention to the second line of philosophic development, which also was a direct result of the Kantian thing-in-itself.   This philosophy is embodied in the doctrines of Arthur Schopenhauer.

CHAPTER XII

ARTHUR SCHOPENHAUER (1788–1860)

1. *Life.*

ARTHUR SCHOPENHAUER was born in Danzig in 1788. His father was a merchant, and his mother an author. Both families were proud and aristocratic, and to that Schopenhauer attributed his own independent spirit. His father was eager to have the boy continue the business which he had founded, and to that end educated and prepared him. He even promised him a trip on the Continent, as an added inducement. The father's efforts were rewarded and Arthur began his business career. He was extremely unhappy in his occupation, and soon after his father's death, he procured the assent of his mother to give it up. With his father's comfortable fortune he was enabled to retire from economic life and to devote his attention to his heart's desire—the study of philosophy. He attended the gymnasium at Gotha, specializing in the study of Latin. Later, he also devoted a great deal of time to Greek. He attended the University of Göttingen, and under the guidance of Professor Schulze he read a great deal of Plato and Kant. He also made the acquaintance of Fichte during his studies at Berlin University. During the war for independence from Napoleonic rule, he retired into seclusion and wrote his first book. Before the age of thirty, he published his major work, "The World as Will and Idea."

His philosophy at first attracted very little attention. There were too many outstanding thinkers of the day, who held the attention of the literary world. Then again, the others, like Fichte and Hegel, held chairs of philosophy in universities, whereas he was a private scholar.   This neglect of his doctrine embittered him; he spent many years in recriminations, in denouncing teachers of philosophy.   But during the last ten years of his life, his philosophy did attract a great deal of attention not only among the lay intellectuals, but also among professors.   Praise was heaped upon him.   He reveled in it, and drank it all in like wine.   He died very happily and peacefully in Frankfurt in 1860.

Schopenhauer lacked the capacity for real love.   He despised women, yet he had many affairs with them, some of them quite sordid.   He was very morose and an inveterate pessimist.   His pessimism so affected his mother's social guests, who would disperse after his lengthy discourse on the uselessness of everything, that she finally forbade him her home.   He parted from her, never to see her again.   He was a great student of Buddhism, to which we may attribute his pessimism to a large extent, and the doctrine of the negation of the will.   Other causes may be that he inherited from his father a psychopathic disposition, and also his unpleasant home life.   His antipathy towards his mother is a known fact, a fact which did not add cheer to his bleak outlook on life.   He was never married, perhaps mainly because of the fear that it would cost him his independence.   He was a brilliant conversationalist; his audience, consisting of a small circle of friends, would often listen to him until midnight.   He never seemed to tire of talking, even during his last days.

2. *Relation to Kant, Fichte, Schelling and Hegel.*

Schopenhauer, like Hegel, is a disciple of Kant, but his philosophy branched off in a different direction.   Both were dissatisfied with Kant's analysis of the world behind the phenomena.   The Kantian thing-in-itself seemed so unnecessary, in view of the utter inability of reason to comprehend it, that the most logical thing was to identify it with some element whose nature might be known to us.   Hegel called it Reason; Schopenhauer, Will.   To be sure, Kant, too, attached a great deal of importance to Will, making it superior even to reason in its successful attempt to postulate the existence of freedom, Immortality and God, which the intellect cannot establish.   Fichte went one step farther, making will the instrument by which the non-Ego is imposed by the self for its moral development; Schelling finally called the Absolute, Will.   But these theories only were the starting point of Schopenhauer's conception.   To them, Will is intelligent, rational, working for a goal, the good, the moral, the true, the beautiful.   To Schopenhauer, it is irrational, blind effort, stormily and with gigantic strides sweeping majestically through the world.   In fact, intellect is by far secondary to this Will.   It is a later development.   It serves as a sort of a light to the Will, but it adds no essential contribution. The main purpose of the Will is not to attain a goal, but simply to go on willing, to go on striving, ceaselessly and aimlessly to continue on its way.   We readily see that this conception is radically different from the Kantian root, from which it sprang.

3. *The World as Idea and as Will.*

How, then, does Schopenhauer show that the noumenon behind appearances is Will?   One of the simple ways, perhaps, by which we can develop this view is to take ourselves as an example, and then strike an analogy between us and the world.   Each of us possesses a body and a will.   The body is the phenomenon, the external object by which we communicate our desires and wishes to others.   This phenomenal body, however, is but the external manifestation of the will within. The will is unitary; it is a single force clamoring for expression.   The body serves this purpose in multitudinous ways. The body has teeth, for example, to express the will's desire for biting, chewing; feet, because of the urge for locomotion; eyes, because of the want to see.   In spite of the variety of ways by which the body expresses our will, the latter nevertheless is a single, willing force.

Let us now extend this analysis to nature or to the world

as a whole. It is legitimate for us to do this, for are we not a part of this nature? Here, we may recall that Spinoza, too, felt that since we possess body and mind, nature certainly should be considered as possessing these two attributes. Therefore, we may conclude that the natural phenomena composed of all the objects and beings before our eyes, are simply expressions in manifold forms of the unitary, single, Universal Will behind them. Our intuition serves us well here. It enables us to penetrate within the obvious, and thus observe the reality behind it. Once this initial step in Schopenhauer's philosophy is postulated, the rest follows most logically. The phenomenal world, he maintained, is only my idea of it. In the Berkeleyan sense, if my mind were otherwise constituted, this world of appearance would seem different; hence, it is really a creature of my own mind. This realm of nature, too, is, as Kant said, governed by mechanical laws. Schopenhauer reduces the Kantian complex categorical tabulation to only three such laws, causality, space and time. He further denominates these the principle of Sufficient Reason. These laws and all the phenomena exemplifying them must first be known immediately by the understanding, must be apprehended through perception, before they can pass into abstract consciousness or reason. Every one of the great discoveries, such as Newton's laws of gravity, is an operation of the understanding, an immediate intuition, a flash of insight. Deficiency of understanding is stupidity. The understanding, therefore, being the weapon of perception, brutes possess it as well as humans. Reason, on the other hand, which uses abstract concepts, only humans possess. This division also explains this fact. That which is correctly known by the understanding is reality, that which is correctly known by reason is truth. Error, a deception of reason, is opposed to truth; illusion, a deception of the understanding, is opposed to reality. Because reason and reflection are the sole and exclusive endowments of humans, they have deliberate actions, conducting themselves by maxims, as against brutes, who act instinctively. Humans also use language to enable reason to perform its functions, "communication of truth, . . . thoughts and poems, dogmas and superstitions.   The brute first knows death when it dies, but man draws consciously nearer to it every hour that he lives. . . . Principally on this account man has philosophies and religions."[1]   Schopenhauer concludes this part of his philosophy by showing that our individual bodies are the immediate objects of our consciousness, they are the objects on which the understanding dwells most intimately.   Through them we perceive the application of the principle of Sufficient Reason to nature, and the relation of them to the other material objects in the world.

The study of the natural realm, from the aspect of the phenomena, however, only scratches the surface of Schopenhauer's doctrine.   It is obvious, he says, that Berkeley is correct in his analysis of the world of appearances, by which he demonstrates that it is composed of our own ideas, impressions, sensations.   But Berkeley stopped too soon.   He offers no substitute in place of matter as an objective element, external to us and independent of our minds.   Hence his philosophy is subject to fatal attacks.   It is subjective idealism, and it does not explain the relations among humans, either rational or social.   Schopenhauer, on the other hand, furnishes such an objective independent order, the Kantian thing-in-itself, which he identifies with Will.   That this is the essential characteristic of the world behind the appearances, as we have already shown, we learn by analogy to ourselves, aided also by a flash of intuition.   Such intuitive insight shows the unity and the working of the Universal Will.

What picture, then, does Schopenhauer present of the world as it really is, the objective realm, the region which we by experience cannot penetrate, the Will?   It is blind effort, capriciously wending its way through the world.   It is timeless, for time is applicable to phenomena only.   The principle of Sufficient Reason does not apply to it.   It creates nothing new, everything has been here right from the very beginning, our limited capacity for understanding uncovers

[1] "The World as Will and Idea," First Book, Section 6.

from time to time that which has always existed. The Will has no rational purpose, it has no aim or goal, it simply strives. In the course of its majestic sweep over the universe, it passes through universal phases of development, analogous to the Platonic Ideas. These universals must be typified by particular existences. They are represented by all the individual instances before us in this world of phenomena. Universal Man, for example, is typified by all the individuals of the genus, man. The same is true of all other universals. These universals, moreover, are the same in every instance that manifests them, at all times and in all places. This unity in all phenomena, this unchangeable constancy in the appearances of these particular examples is called a law of nature. If such a law is once learned, then we may forecast accurately the phenomena of the specific universal force of nature under discussion.

Thus our wills, as we have already learned, objectify themselves in our bodies. By means of the body it expresses its insatiable desires; that gives to the body its teleological character. "Teeth, throat and bowels are objectified hunger; the organs of generation are objectified sexual desire; the grasping hand, the hurrying feet correspond to the more indirect desires of the will which they express." [2]   Nature as a whole, too, is the objectification of the World Will. Since it is the nature of the Will to strive, we, therefore, find in all grades of existence, the inorganic, the vital, the human, a constant struggle going on. In the lower grades, each wants to appropriate matter of the others for itself. The magnet that attracts a piece of iron carries on a perpetual conflict with gravitation, which has a prior right to it. In the human stage, a constant battle is waged against the many physical and chemical forces. The burden of physical life, the necessity of sleep, and of death show how the forces of nature win back from the organism the matter it took from them. In the animal kingdom, the universal conflict is most evident. Here they prey upon the vegetable kingdom, and upon each other. The will to

[2] *Ibid.,* Second Book, Section 18.

live everywhere preys upon itself, and is its own nourishment.

Thus far, Schopenhauer illustrates, somewhat concretely, the struggle and strife that goes on everywhere, demonstrating clearly the essential, striving characteristic of the World Will.   Now he adds another consideration to show that Kant's thing-in-itself is Will—the fact that empirical science supports this contention.   He refers to the statement by Sir John Herschel, who, in his "Treatise on Astronomy," reached the conclusion that gravity shows that bodies are urged downward by some force or effort, or that there is a Will existing somewhere directing the action.   Herschel, however, attributes consciousness to this Will, which Schopenhauer denies. Schopenhauer urges us to recognize volition in every effort which proceeds from the nature of a material body.   The lowest, most universal manifestation of will is gravity, which on that account is considered a primary characteristic of matter. Contrary to the customary view that bodily motion has two different origins, from the inside, or will, and from the outside, or causation, Schopenhauer insists that only will is motion.   In inorganic nature, the *a priori* principle of causality is more evident, whereas in the higher realms of existence, especially in man, we view things empirically, *a posteriori;* cause and effect loses most of its bearing, and *will* assumes a prominent position.   It just happens that when one of these is more comprehensible, the other is least evident, therefore we suppose there is a conflict between cause and will, but in reality, will permeates all of nature, animate as well as the inorganic.   Reason is responsible for this dissection of nature into two conflicting principles, but by intuition, by a flash of genius, we get back the unity of the will, the insoluble x.

We have had occasion to refer to Schopenhauer's insistence that there is nothing new under the sun; the Will has existed, in all its glory, from the beginning.   The development we see taking place in time is the visible element, the uncovering by our consciousness of that which has always been present in the world. From this angle he disagrees with Lamarck. Lamarck argues that the living organism strives to attain a certain goal; hence, in successive moments of time, it develops the organs suitable for achieving that goal. To Schopenhauer, the end, and the will striving towards that end, both are really there at first in nature. We simply have pulled them apart, but then we intuitively see the original unity again. Furthermore, he argues, if Lamarck were right in his contention that the animal intelligently prepares its weapons in succession of time, it would destroy the species. It would take too long to acquire the organs needed for self-preservation; in the long interim, the entire species could not maintain itself in the severe struggle we witness in the world. In short, he asserts that animals manifest the will to employ organs which they do not yet possess. The ox butts before it has horns, the wild boar attacks before he has tusks. That conclusively shows that the inner will to exist, to be, is the principal factor in development. In man, to be sure, the will has supplied itself with the highest weapon, the intellect. He cautions us, however, that this intellect is only a servant of the will, not its master.

4. *Morality.*

Thus far we find that the world may be considered from two aspects: (1) as my idea, the phenomenal realm, governed by the principle of Sufficient Reason; (2) as will, the noumenal world, free, neither hampered, nor guided, by the intellect, subject to no laws. This is analogous to Kant's two worlds, one mechanical, the other, free, subject only to the Categorical Imperative. But now this question remains: How does this apply to practical life, to morality? At this point, Schopenhauer departs radically from the prevailing views on this subject. Kant and his successors supplied us with a moral order, intelligible, working towards an ideal goal, offering innumerable opportunities for self-realization. They hold out the hope of salvation, they force upon us the conviction that all is well with the world. Schopenhauer supplies the opposite picture. He strenuously objects to the Leibnizian theory that this is the "best of all possible worlds." On the contrary, it is the worst. The Will never ends its striving; its insatiable, indefatigable force manifests itself in the struggles of all its phenomena. All possible atrocities we find in nature are evidences of its ceaseless strife. Evil, pain, suffering, all else that we humans condemn, predominate. Just as the Universal Will is never satiated, so our own will, which partakes of this World Force, is never satisfied. No sooner do we attain the goal that we set out to reach, than we at once desire something still farther away. Complete satisfaction is always beyond our reach, like a constantly vanishing goal.

How then can we obtain relief from this continuous, never-ending, painful process? In two ways, Schopenhauer suggests. In the first place, through art. A genuine work of art represents not the particular object, but the universal type, the Platonic Idea. In portraying man, the artist may begin with a particular man as his model, but to constitute a genuine piece of art, the genius must represent the universal characteristics of man. Art views things independently of the principle of Sufficient Reason. When we contemplate such a work of art, we lose contact with the turbulent stream of detailed existence around us. We identify ourselves with the universal Idea; that clearly offers relief from the painful, evil and continuous strife in the midst of which we are so firmly entrenched. Nevertheless, this affords only temporary relief. No one can continue indefinitely to contemplate works of art. Therefore, the only permanent relief possible is by the denial of the will to live, by the eradication of our desires, of our instincts, by the renunciation of all we consider worth while in practical life. This furnishes the evidence that Schopenhauer's moral philosophy offers no positive pleasure; the very characteristic of our will is to give pain, never happiness. The most, therefore, for which we can hope, is a sort of negative pleasure, a way of living in which the struggle will affect us least. That can be achieved only by doing away with the principle of self-perpetuation, the desire to exist; in short, by leading a kind of "living death." He insists that committing suicide will not help to assuage one's suffering, for all that death accomplishes is the destruction of the phenomenon, leaving the will to continue striving. We cannot escape from ourselves.

At the same time, he emphasizes pity or sympathy as the cardinal virtue. In sympathizing with others, we immerse ourselves in their troubles, and we lose sight of our own pain. The whole contention here is that while we have to go on living, let us do so under the least painful conditions; never hoping, unless stupidly, for the world to offer a balm for our wounds, never entertaining the least thought that nature will straighten matters out; in short, to say that "there is a silver lining to every cloud" is only self-hypnosis. Happiness is a Utopian Ideal that we must not entertain even in our dreams.

5. *Estimate of the Philosophy.*

This résumé of Schopenhauer's philosophy creates a certain amount of antagonism in us. A metaphysic based on constantly unceasing strife, supporting an ethic which yields nothing but despair, offers little solace and satisfaction to anyone. To be sure, we can readily explain his pessimistic attitude towards the world and towards life. Plato describes the democratic man as the son of the oligarch who enjoys wealth and who, besides, allows his passions rather than reason to govern him. He develops such a temperament that he cannot endure any obstacles whatsoever. This rôle Schopenhauer appears to fill to some extent. His father, wealthy and devoted to the boy, promised him many things and fulfilled his pledges to a large extent. He gave him, for example, a trip to the Continent for two years as one of the inducements for him to enter a commercial life. But that type of life irked Schopenhauer. That readily explains one of the causes of his irritability. Then again, the breach with his mother explains not only his sour outlook on life, but his distrust and contempt for women. Entering upon an academic life somewhat later than the ordinary person, he examined the various philosophies which he studied with a more mature mind, and might readily have concluded that some changes would be salutary.   Because of these considerations, the Buddhistic doctrine was just suited to him.   The fact that his work was not recognized for a long time embittered him.   Instead of calmly and rationally attempting to convince his adversaries, he raved and ranted against them, showing the type of temperament he had either developed, or possessed from birth.   This, surely, portrays the democratic man of Plato's conception.

Whatever causes, however, contributed to Schopenhauer's pessimistic outlook, the fact remains that he developed a cogent philosophy to support it.   His idea of Will as the most fundamental force in the world is by no means a novel doctrine.   Bruno, vaguely, and Leibniz, much more exhaustively, had already conceived of force as the central thread in the universe.   Science, too, conceives of energy as one of the ultimate elements, if not the sole element, in the composition of the world.   Kant, Fichte, Schelling and Hegel have touched upon will as one of the real entities in nature.   Idealistically inclined, Schopenhauer cannot but accept a mental factor as the substratum of the world.   What better element to choose than Will?   It explains energy as emphasized by those scientifically inclined, and at the same time it lends dignity to the human mind in selecting one of its essential, component parts as the fundamental substance of the Universe.

Ordinarily, when the world is conceived as mental in character, we feel at home in it.   It is akin to what we ourselves essentially are, and therefore we ought to be able to understand its moods and possibilities.   That should render us optimistic.   But Schopenhauer gives it a different twist, to suit his personal nature, hence pessimism is the consequence.   Here is a Will, blind, impulsive, majestically sweeping through the world, not caring a whit whether it destroys or builds as it wends its way, unconcerned with time or with the other laws included under the principle of Sufficient Reason.   Theoretically, it is indifferent to progressive development, it has no aims, no goal to reach.   Its main motive is to continue striving, to continue living, so to speak.   Somehow or other, however, it does bring progress in its wake.   True enough, a great deal of destruction is left behind, but it appears that the new level that emerges is superior to the old.   The Will furnishes us with the inorganic, the vital, and mind, resembling the levels of matter, life and mind so ably presented by Lloyd Morgan, a modern scientist.   These new emergences cannot be anticipated, the lower level cannot by any definite law cause us to anticipate the subsequent step, but they all happen to spring up.   That is exactly Morgan's conception of development, or, as he terms it, Emergent Evolution.   This Will, furthermore, permeates everything, it is in all and yet above all.   This resembles the *élan vital* of Bergson's thought.   It needs aids in its progress, it cunningly selects them; it employs bodies to express its insatiable impulses.   In the lower realms of existence, matter displays the motion or energy so characteristic of the Will; in the higher kingdoms of animals, the bodies of such living organisms with their instincts and sensations reveal to the onlooker what the Will within desires. When we reach the human or mental level, the brain with its delicate construction becomes of tremendous service in carrying out the Will's manifold demands.   Doubtless, continues Schopenhauer, the presence of the Will is not always apparent.   In the inorganic regions of nature, we must stretch our imagination a bit to see evidence of the Will in our understanding of the world, for causation, in the mechanical sense, predominates.   But intuition shows us that the inner essence of nature resembles our own.   Then it becomes comparatively simple to see how this Will operates through the principle of Sufficient Reason.   This forces again to our attention the effectiveness of intuition, and its superiority to reason.   Kant, too, in his Critique of Judgment, suggests that perhaps feeling may uncover more of reality than the intellect or the will. Schelling calls art, dependent on feeling, the "organon of philosophy," the revealer of all mysteries in the universe. Hegel, too, gives intuition some significant place in his philosophy, and now Schopenhauer considers it as the one appropriate instrument to bring back to us the unity of the world, which reason, with its analysis, constantly loses for us. Bergson, whom we shall discuss shortly, comprehensively develops a whole theory of knowledge based on intuition alone.

The upshot of this philosophy is that the Universal Will can never be satisfied. To fulfill its desires would constitute killing it entirely, because it would remove its most essential characteristic, or its attribute, in the Spinozistic sense. Therefore, we, too, can never be happy or contented. But that is the very belief to which we object. How go on living, without hope? James says that to give us peace of mind, a moral philosophy must define the future as congruous with our most cherished powers. We must not have a world in which either the inexorable laws of mechanism, or the principle of predestination, govern; in short, a world in which we have no say, no possibility of changing to suit the principles of development, so necessary to render human life tolerable. This opinion is not adduced here for its cogency of demonstration, but because it is a very sane and wise comment. Schopenhauer clearly offends in this respect. In the first place, he takes away free will altogether from the human actors. He says that the World Will is capricious, wholly free, but since all things have existed from the very beginning, our actions, too, have always been there. We cannot change them, we are simply conscious of them, therefore, we think we conduct ourselves freely. This is false, he says. We, in conjunction with other animals, must behave in a particular way, only they are not conscious of their conduct, and we are; hence, we believe that we possess free will. That this is erroneous is clearly demonstrated, if we have a clear conception of the Universal Will.

Then again, Schopenhauer's Moral Philosophy is repellent to any thinking being. We admit, the Leibnizian theory that this is the best of all possible worlds is even inferior to pessimism. It is non-invigorating, whereas Schopenhauer supplies the force to make us hard-living individuals, to put us on our guard against the incessant strife that is waged around us. It is much more refreshing than the former theory. But granting all that, what does it offer, besides? To tell us that we are waging a losing battle is discouraging. To urge us constantly to fight the Universal Will, as well as our own, to undo, in short, what the Will has wrought, causes despair, indeed. The Will is much more powerful than we are; what chances of success have we for ultimate victory? The kind of asceticism he suggests, the denial of the will to live, which results only in negative pleasure, is an empty shell. The most we can say for Schopenhauer's moral doctrine is that it contributes to our own practical life negatively. It shows us why pessimism should be avoided. It demonstrates the emptiness of despair, the uselessness of dwelling upon the evil in the world to the exclusion of everything else. Assuredly, it contributes very little of positive value to life. It is perfectly proper to argue for pity or sympathy as a cardinal virtue, but not for the purpose he suggests. To argue that one should pity his fellow men, because that will effect a certain line of conduct, such as charity, benevolence, is indeed worthy of much praise. To urge it, however, in order to help ourselves out of our dilemma, to assuage our own pain, is to be condemned. True enough, pain and suffering are the badges of humanity, but that is due to the fact that we are highly sensitized organisms, with reflection and reason, which distinguish us from brutes, but the same reflection should convince us that such pain is not the sole consideration in life. Why not use it as a means of betterment, of improving our present status? Why, in short, not be thankful for the fact that because of pain, we are forced to pause in the midst of our affairs to take stock of what we have already accomplished, with a view to change the future? Buddhism, presenting the same solution as Schopenhauer offers, may be a fit philosophy for its adherents, because of the environment in which they live, and the type of life, in general, to which they are accustomed, but certainly it is not suited to our civilization.

Then again, what particular function does Schopenhauer assign to the Will? It simply goes on, aimlessly striving, but whither? Is it not preferable to attribute to it some task, some function to perform, more nearly in accord with our dispositions? Hegel emphasizes the striving of the Will for the Good, for an ideal goal. That clearly is the preferable theory. Even Nietzsche's theory, attributing to the Will the motive of developing the superman, possesses more content. The whole German idealistic school, with the exception of Schopenhauer, views Will as an instrument for moral development, enabling the ethical life to progress indefinitely. To that we may subscribe without derogating from our own dignity as human souls, whose infinite potentialities may find a place in this rational world to develop and to effect such changes as will harmonize with what we seek, the good, moral life.

6. *On Women.*

Schopenhauer's morbid outlook on life is reflected in his discussion of women. He considers them far inferior to men, both physically and mentally. Woman is not meant to do great labor; her life should be more gentle and peaceful than that of man. "They are directly fitted for acting as the nurses and teachers of our early childhood by the fact that they are themselves childish, frivolous and short-sighted; in a word, they are big children all their life long." [3] Nature has endowed woman with certain weapons, beauty and charm, in order to conquer man; but being economical, nature does not allow this to last. After giving birth to one or two children, a woman generally loses her beauty, just as the female ant loses her wings, after fecundation. He then continues in the same vein: "The nobler and more perfect a thing is, the later and slower it is in arriving at maturity. A man reaches the maturity of his reasoning powers and mental faculties hardly before the age of twenty-eight, a woman, at eighteen. And then, too, in the case of woman, it is only reason of a sort —very niggard in its dimensions. . . . The weakness of their reasoning faculty also explains why it is that women show

[3] "Essay on Women."

more sympathy for the unfortunate than men do . . . and why it is that, on the contrary, they are inferior to men in point of justice, and less honorable and conscientious." [4]

The fundamental fault with women is that they have *no sense of justice*. They are the weaker sex, they depend upon craft, rather than strength. Their cunning is the cause for their tendency to say what is not true. The art of dissimulation with which nature endowed them is their most powerful weapon. Then again, they exist solely for the propagation of the species. That renders them more thoughtful towards the species than towards the individual, which gives their life a certain levity so fundamentally different from that of man that it is the greatest cause of marital discord. "It is only the man whose intellect is clouded by his sexual impulses that could give the name of the *fair sex* to that undersized, narrow-shouldered, broad-hipped and short-legged race. . . . Instead of calling them beautiful, there would be more warrant for describing women as the unaesthetic. . . . Women have, in general, no love of any art; they have no proper knowledge of any; and they have no genius." [5] They are inferior to men in every respect, we should treat their infirmities with consideration, but it is ridiculous for us to revere them, in fact, such reverence lowers us in their eyes. In the Western World, where we treat woman with great honor and veneration, where we call her *lady*, we put her in a false position; it makes her arrogant and overbearing. We must put a stop to this lady-nuisance; we must relegate her to her true position, accord to her the status she holds in the East, and which she occupied in ancient Greece and Rome. The European marriage laws consider women as the equal of men, that is a wrong as well as an unnatural premise. Women do not, as a rule, and should not, inherit property. Man has labored for its accumulation, and it is unjust to permit her to squander it foolishly. Most of the inheritance laws of ancient, as well as modern states, have provided that only male descendants

[4] *Ibid.*
[5] *Ibid.*

shall inherit.   The female becomes heir only if no males survive.   That is just and proper.   Finally it is evident that
woman naturally is meant to obey, for no sooner does she have
complete independence, than she attaches herself to some man.
This is so, because she needs "a lord and a master."

This brief summary of Schopenhauer's discussion on women
shows what a warped mentality can effect, even with reference to the obvious.   It is quite possible that the rift between him and his mother caused his contemptuous regard for
women, but that alone is not quite sufficient to account for it.
To attribute to woman no sense of justice, no valid reasoning
faculties, no sense of the aesthetic, is utterly absurd.   To go
even further and say that she has never achieved anything is
flying in the face of facts.   Why should not woman be considered man's equal?   She may reach her conclusions more
directly than man, by means of a short-cut, as Schopenhauer
admits, but that appears to endow her with a superior quality,
rather than the opposite.   To judge from the position accorded to her by the ancients or by the Orientals, what treatment she ought to receive now in the Western World is
absurd and unfair.   She has been emancipated, she has developed tremendously in a very short period of time.   She is
responsible for many achievements in almost every phase
of life.   Her age-old position of submission was due more to
the fact that the laws were man-made, than to any other cause.
Now when she has acquired the right of suffrage, her progress
will be tremendously swift, for she surely possesses great mental faculties.   In short, here as in the other parts of his philosophy, Schopenhauer's contribution to our practical view
of life is negative, demonstrating what we should avoid,
rather than any positive element on which we may lay hold
to our advantage.

7. *Conclusion.*

In conclusion we may say that Schopenhauer develops a
philosophy which here and there shows traces of genius, which
appeals to the imagination, which has influenced many of his

successors, notably the voluntaristic school. His doctrine reconciles the *a priori* and *a posteriori* methods, assigning proper functions to each. This, too, shows that science and philosophy are not diametrically opposed to each other, but employ similar ways of reaching conclusions. To study the essential nature of the Will, we must observe *a priori* causation, and *a posteriori* organic life; then by intuitive insight we must observe the unity of the Will throughout the universe. We may, *a posteriori*, see that even in inorganic nature, motion and energy constitute the essential characteristics of the Will. Clearly life indicates its presence. This theory, unlike Hegelianism, does not require us to overlook the facts before us. To assert with Hegel that reason is the constituent element may induce us to be skeptical as to what reason is shown in inorganic nature, for example. Will, on the other hand, is more easily explained, as we have just seen. At the same time, to agree with Schopenhauer that will is irrational, blind, and impulsive again confronts us with the difficulty that the world actually appears rational, orderly; if we disbelieve that, then this world becomes an impossible scene for our activities. Schopenhauer, therefore, does not have the last word on philosophic development; we must proceed to seek new and more adequate explanations for the universe.

The German School of Idealism, of which the last philosophy forms an integral part, had a most logical development in the history of thought. The ancient Greeks extolled reason; to them the intellect was a mighty weapon for probing the mysteries of the universe. It was an aid not only to theoretical investigation, but also to the practical, moral life. Socrates identified virtue with knowledge. Plato attributed to the rational life the highest standing, befitting the dignity of the human. Aristotle, too, contended that reason should govern, so that it may point out the "means" or "virtues" to the human being in his search for the guide of life. Both felt that by means of reason, metaphysical speculations may be firmly entrenched. Plato's World of Ideas, the so-called noumena, are clearly a result of dialectic, of logic, by which the philosopher can attain an understanding of both their existence and their function.   Aristotle solved this dualism by a monism, by one realm of existence, in which nevertheless the Idea finds a place, in which the Form unites with matter to express what lies before us.   The highest function of God is to lead a life of contemplation, a life of thought.   The Stoics clearly indicated that Divine reason permeates the world, and we must use this Divine spark in us to fathom nature.   This reason also is our guide in practical conduct.   Even the Epicureans, in spite of their insistence on pleasure as the aim of life, emphasize knowledge as the best means to select the proper kinds of pleasures.   Thus it is readily seen that the Greek period placed no, or very little, emphasis on faith and on dogmatism, as an aid to study or to action.

But this picture changes completely in the Middle Ages. Then, the Church, firmly entrenched on its throne from which it was most reluctant to be displaced, insisted that faith be the cardinal principle, and in fact used force to retain it.   Blind dogmatism became the leading guide of the times.   To be sure, at the end of the Medieval period, reason began to exert a more powerful influence, but the period as a whole is still characterized by the supremacy of faith.   This state of affairs could not last long; the Renaissance was the result. Then, the Medieval influences were discarded as rapidly as possible, and new criteria were established.   Most of the new standards harked back to the Greeks.   Philosophy, too, felt these influences.   The leading thinkers began to search for new foundations on which to build.   Descartes was the product of this age.

Cartesianism resulted in rationalism; Spinoza and Leibniz developed it further.   But their product was barren, empty of the type of content which would appeal to serious thinkers. Hence empiricism was the reaction.   It attempted to refute most of the conclusions reached by the rationalistic school, and to substitute experience as the new criterion of philosophy, before whose altar we must bow.   But this, too, overreached itself, finally resulting in the theory, so ably demonstrated by Hume, that nothing is certain.   Such a conclusion could not, by its very nature, be satisfactory.   Therefore, Kant and his disciples attempted to strike a middle ground between the two prevailing schools of thought.   This brings us to the school of objective idealism; one phase represented by Hegel, who claims for the external world objective validity, by identifying it with Reason; the other phase, developed by Schopenhauer, who asserts that Will is the central thread of the world. Neither, as we have seen, has the last word on the subject. Each has his disciples, who modify, enlarge, or make some other changes in the doctrines of their masters.   Thus thought progresses, thus thinking men develop theories which are always attempting to get closer to our needs, nearer to what they conceive as constituting the truth of the world, of life.

We may, however, approach idealism from a different angle.   We may demonstrate that it is not only a result of a chronological development in the history of thought, but also a metaphysical philosophy attempting to set itself up against the only other comprehensive metaphysical explanation, whose defects it desires to remedy—we refer to materialism or naturalism.   To study this angle of approach, we must now turn our attention to a discussion of Materialism versus Idealism.

BOOK III

FIVE DOCTRINES OF PHILOSOPHY

CHAPTER I

MATERIALISM [1]

1. *The Development of the Theory.*

THE thesis of materialism is that reality is composed of matter and motion; that this natural realm before us is all there is, that it is governed by mechanical or scientific laws. Obviously, it excludes the possible existence of anything above nature; it excludes freedom of the will, immortality and God; it eliminates all such subjects which Bacon relegated to the realm of theology. At first glance this theory is refreshing, invigorating. It enables the understanding to rest on its own proper ground, in the field of all possible experience, the laws of which may be investigated and serve to enlarge knowledge without end. This theory does not tolerate the consideration that the cause of anything should be sought outside of nature, God, for example, because we know nothing else but nature, which alone can offer us objects and instruct us as to their laws. Likewise, it does not concede that a faculty such as freedom be presupposed to act independently of the laws of nature, for this would limit the operation of the understanding in investigating, according to necessary principles, the phenomena in this world. These considerations show why materialism appeals to hard-headed, practical men, who pride themselves upon the possession of an overwhelming wealth of common sense. Why be concerned with mysterious, supernatural factors, when we have a ready-made explanation of reality which relies only on experience? Then, too, such a

---

[1] In the treatment of the doctrines of philosophy in Book III, the author acknowledges the material aid he received from "Types of Philosophy," by William Ernest Hocking.

metaphysic is more in accord with science than any other theory. To be sure, science does not attempt to explain all of reality, but at any rate it travels in the same direction as the philosophy which limits its investigations only to the phenomenal world, which, furthermore, derives a great deal of its validity from empirical observation.

That this type of philosophy is not mere dilettantism, but a sincere attempt on the part of serious, thinking men to explain what reality means, is demonstrated by its development through the history of thought.   Throughout the ages, philosophers attempted to explain the unseen by the visible, by the obvious.   In the Milesian School, we find such explanations offered of reality, as water, air and earth.   Heracleitus, a most brilliant thinker, reduced all reality to fire. Besides, he felt that change and motion in the phenomenal world are the most essential characteristics of the real world. The moment Parmenides attempts to oppose him by his theory of permanence as the ultimate essence, in spite of appearances, we get the dawn of the idea of epiphenomenalism or the conception that the phenomenon is neither the true, nor the whole, picture, but that there is a reality behind it.   The real contribution, however, to materialism is first made by Democritus, who regards reality as composed of atoms, regulated by mechanical laws.   Here again, we find the conflict between mechanism and free will in the theory later propounded by Epicurus that the atoms move by chance, not by mechanical necessity.   Needless to add, Plato is a materialist in so far as this temporal, visible world is concerned.   It is the realm of the Heracleitan Flux.   Aristotle shows the germ of materialism in his doctrine that form is never dissociated from matter, and that motion is the efficient cause of all things. True, both of these Greek thinkers go far beyond the claims of materialism.   Their emphasis on the existence of a God, their emphasis on the teleological character of the world, are elements foreign to the philosophy under discussion.   Epicurus, as well as his disciple Lucretius, is clearly a naturalist. Life after death, the existence of gods as necessary explanations for natural phenomena, and all other similar, theological beliefs are anathema to him.

To go one step further.   The Scholastics, being dualistic because of the demands of religion, cannot be regarded as materialistic, in the true sense of the word.   Nevertheless, when we study Descartes' doctrine, we find that his dualism did not prevent the germ of materialism from taking root. God, true enough, created the world, but then it fashioned itself by means of matter and motion.   Spinoza was more of a materialist, because he insists upon natural laws exclusively governing the entire domain of reality.   It would appear at first that Leibniz, the last of the triumvirate of these rationalists, should not be classed among materialists, but his reduction of everything to force certainly is no less vigorous a statement of such a philosophy than that of Herbert Spencer, for example.   Many leading materialists contend that force is the ultimate element out of which reality is composed.   This is sometimes known as energism.   When we turn next to the English School, we find that the chief exponent of such a metaphysics is Thomas Hobbes.   He reduces even thought to the motion of the physical brain.   Locke insists that mechanical laws govern the universe, and so does Hume, although the latter is skeptical as to the necessity implied in the laws of causation.   But the period in which materialism flourished was the 19th century, in which we find Darwin, Huxley, Spencer, Comte, and other illustrious thinkers.   Before discussing this period, let us first consider some other phases of this cosmic theory, its logic, its ethics and its religion.

2. *Logic.*

We have previously stated that materialism emphasizes the fact that nothing exists beyond the phenomenal realm.   It, therefore, finds confirmation and support for its thesis in any contention which denies the possibility of proving any supernatural existence.   It appears almost paradoxical that the man who was most influential in the development of the German School of Idealism should be the very person responsible for supplying materialism with this powerful argument —we refer to Immanuel Kant.   He demonstrates by means of-the antinomies that the intellect finds itself powerless and in the grip of logical contradictions when it attempts to reach out into regions beyond the world of experience.   He is especially useful in his polemic against the ontological, cosmological, and teleological proofs for the existence of God.   That amply shows the consistency in the naturalistic argument that this world is all we need for satisfying our intellectual curiosity, as well as the requirements of practical life.   Herbert Spencer, too, demonstrates that we cannot prove that God created the world, for the question will be, Who created God? Therefore, we conclude that, although from the nature of the theory it is impossible to show affirmatively that it is true, for it is not feasible to demonstrate the entire content of a cosmic explanation, yet negatively it is supported by the inability of the intellect to go beyond nature.

3. *Ethics and Religion.*

Friedrich Wilhelm Nietzsche (1844–1900).   Then again, naturalism offers an ethics more or less suitable for us, humans. To be sure, it derogates from human dignity by showing so little regard for the human mind, and by extolling so highly the body.   After all, we do pride ourselves upon the distinction between brutes and ourselves in our possession of reflection and Reason.   Materialism, however, considers reflection and Reason to be a matter of evolution, and that fundamentally the physical is the important consideration.   Nevertheless, such a metaphysic does not render an ethics impossible.   It is not absolutely essential for morality to go hand in hand with a metaphysical philosophy which allows room for God, immortality, freedom.   It is really a matter of training, of character, of environmental conditions.   If these are propitious, we may become very ethical personalities.   In fact, we have examples of naturalistic ethics, which has served its purpose quite well.   Epicurus recommended a life of pleasure, but even he emphasized mental pleasures, because they are more durable, and accompanied by less pain than the fleeting, sensuous, physical joys. Passing from him, through thousands of years, to Friedrich Nietzsche, we are met with an entirely different system of ethics, but one which still may be entertained by humans, as contrasted with brutes. Nietzsche follows Schopenhauer in the theory that the will always strives to live. Schopenhauer resigns himself to the evil in the world as a result of the incessant strife of the World Will. Nietzsche attributes dignity to this evil. He gloats over its existence, because by means of its presence are we able to develop into supermen. He decries the fact that Christian Ethics has borrowed from the Jews the idea of servility, humility, sympathy, as the central thread in morality. To him strength should occupy this position. Be ruthless even to yourself, he advocates. Forget God, forget the weakening influences of the existing system of ethics; cultivate your will to power, your innate desire to mould nature to your own purposes, so that you may build yourself up in order to assume the proper place due the strong character. He continues: In the past, morality was a result of fear, it was meant to make men gregarious, but that renders people puny and of no account. We want leaders with the will to power. We admit that the existing morality was useful previously, but that is no reason for allowing it to debilitate us at present. Our virtues also were based upon fear, but we insist that our virtues should make us leaders, even though they cause us to suffer. In this way, we shall become beneficial to humanity. We feel that it is suffering which enables the virtues to flourish. We want more suffering, always more suffering, so that we may develop supermen. Such men are beyond good and evil in the accepted sense of the term. They make their own world, their own codes of ethics; they furnish their own guides for their conduct. They are free men, and their ethics are the ethics of "self-expression." We respect the saint, he says, because we admire the will to power he possesses and for which he suffers. These supermen, too, are the result of natural evolution. Nature, in the course of its progress towards her ideals, destroys the unfit, the weak, the feeble.   Out of this human wreckage, emerges the superman, strong, proud of his prowess to conquer, free, master of his own destiny.   It is even a virtue for us to yield to our superiors, if we are less worthy.   In this manner will society benefit in the future.   In conclusion, we may point out that such an ethics lacks any appealing element.   To admit the existence of evil and suffering is a valid assumption; to urge its amelioration or extermination is indeed a worthy aim. But to revel and glory in it smacks of such barbarism that were it not for its uniqueness it would not be entitled to much consideration.   Nevertheless, it does apply to humans; in fact, the development of such supermen is the entire aim of nature, Nietzsche argues.   All of which shows that we may have a materialistic ethics without recourse to God or to some other supernatural source.

Let us turn now to other advocates of naturalistic ethics.

Herbert Spencer (1820–1903).   According to Spencer, a true theory of right living is based upon an equilibrium between our inner constitution and the external environment. When we adjust ourselves to nature, we derive the greatest amount of pleasure, which type of life represents the ethical ideal.   This resembles the theory of utilitarianism so ably presented by J. S. Mill, but with this exception—to Mill, only by trial and error do we discover that actions are conducive to the greatest amount of pleasure or pain, whereas Spencer insists that by studying the principles of nature and the adjustments of our inner desires to external conditions we may substitute a definite rule for this speculative, unsatisfactory method of Mill.   One of the principles of nature is to preserve and increase life.   Therefore, we should enhance our own physical and mental capacity for living.   This entails not only striving after health and mental development, but also cultivating the type of social environment which will not rob us of the opportunities for such development.   In a military society, egoism is predominant, the conflict that is always raging is destructive of life, and places the emphasis upon subjection to the military head.   This takes away the freedom necessary for developing our minds, and negates happiness or pleasure.   On the other hand, when this is replaced by an industrial state, destruction of life is eliminated; free and equal opportunities are extended to all members to flourish physically and mentally.   Egoism then is gradually merged with altruism, more free communication takes place, men get to know each other better; lack of ignorance of our fellow men removes hate, and the pleasures of others then become identified with our own.   In such a Utopia, there is no distinction between egoism and altruism, for then we derive as much gratification from the happiness of others as from our own joys.   Spencer concludes that natural evolution is constantly tending in this direction.

John Stuart Mill (1806–1873).   We have just said that Spencer's theory of ethics is utilitarian.   Let us now briefly survey the philosophy of John Stuart Mill, who is the chief exponent of this type of ethics.   He says that of the two types of moral theories, the intuitional represented by Kant, and the evolutionary or inductive advocated by him, the latter is preferable.   It judges moral acts by the results they achieve, and properly so, for are not such acts primarily directed toward achieving some ends or some purposes?   "Utility, or the Greatest Happiness Principle," he continues, "holds that actions are right in proportion as they tend to promote happiness, wrong as they tend to produce the reverse of happiness.   By happiness is intended pleasure, and the absence of pain; by unhappiness pain, and the privation of pleasure." [2]   To the objections offered against such a theory, Mill has ready answers.   Some contend that it is based on expediency, on what the moral actor prefers for himself, as opposed to right.   Mill answers that the act must promote the happiness of the greatest number of people, not the actor's own.   That explains the high esteem in which we hold the saint who sacrifices life itself in his fight for a principle, by which entire humanity may

[2] "Utilitarianism, Liberty and Representative Government," Chapter II, Page 6.

be benefited.   Similarly, he shows it to be true that we cannot stop to weigh the consequences each time we act, but the
same objection may be made against any moral theory.   But
how about the sanctions for such a theory?   Does it have
the same support as the established and accepted systems
of ethics?   Surely, says Mill.   If the sanction for morality
is external to us, such as reward and punishment by our fellow
men for right or wrong conduct, clearly to promote the happiness of others will be highly rewarded, and the opposite line
of conduct punished.   Suppose, however, such sanction is
internal, by conscience, for example.   If this conscience is
innate, implanted in us by a Divine Being, is there any reason
why it may not be based on utility?   On the other hand, if,
as Mill believes, conscience is acquired from our observation
of the reactions of our fellow men towards our conduct,
then surely utility, which always looks towards the promotion
of the happiness of others, must serve as the best basis for the
development of conscience as our guide.   Further, Mill has
no difficulty in finding proof for his theory.   He founds his
demonstration on empiricism.   We know, he points out, that
happiness is desired as one of the aims of our actions.   But
is it the sole end?   The answer is obvious.   Whatever
goal we have in mind, whether it be honor, riches, social ambition, they are simply a means to happiness or pleasure,
which really resolves itself into pleasure as the ultimate end
of life.   Justice, too, he concludes, is based on utility.   Justice applies, among other things, to treating people equally;
we are not to break faith, not to deprive anyone of his legal or
equitable rights.   Although in the narrow sense of the term,
justice means a duty one has to perform, because there is a corresponding right in some *specific* person or persons, our sympathy and intellect have broadened this concept to include
the rights of all mankind.   The real basis of justice is utility,
the consideration of the happiness of others.

   Thomas Henry Huxley (1825–1895).   Another leading
exponent of a naturalistic ethics is Huxley.   His main contention is that our ethical development is a constant struggle

against the evolutionary principle prevailing in nature; in other words, ethics is not a result of the law of evolution propounded by Darwin. He says that in a "state of nature" the Darwinian principle of natural selection, in the midst of the universal struggle for existence, with its accompanying features, dominates. Contrasted with this we have a "state of art," exemplified by the horticulturist, who voluntarily desires to cultivate certain plants. Here the principle of direct selection prevails. The horticulturist must check the natural forces from destroying his work, he must arrest the struggle for existence by restraining undue modification and also by creating artificial conditions of life better adapted to the cultivated plants than the conditions in a state of nature. Huxley then concludes that neither of these principles is applicable to human society. If human beings were permitted to multiply without limit, and if, therefore, the struggle for existence were allowed to operate unchecked, then the social unit could not develop. In short, we must rule out as far as possible the struggle for existence and make all component parts in this social unit coöperate, to afford society the opportunity to flourish. This coöperation, by which humans can successfully defend themselves against natural forces, he calls the ethical principle. It is based primarily upon the development of sympathy on the part of the individual. Such sympathy is the cementing force prevailing in human society. Thus far Huxley has eliminated the principle of the "state of nature" from ethical development. He also rules out the second principle of direct selection. It is impossible, he says, to get such a wise administrator of the social unit that he will always know how to select the proper units, as the horticulturist does in the case of plants. Moreover, even if such a wise guardian could be found, and if such direct, conscious selection were practiced, it would undermine sympathy, upon which the very existence of the State depends. In short, if wholesale destruction of the unfit and the undesirable were practiced in society, similar to the elimination of weeds in the garden, then clearly sympathy or the ethical principle would be completely nulli-

fied.   The final word on the matter is that ethical development is only possible if the evolutionary principle in nature is
suppressed in the social organization.   The various systems of
ethics, he continues, bear out this contention.   Every such
moral theory emphasizes either suppression of all desire to
live and to be happy, exemplified by the Indian philosophies,
by the Stoics, or it calls upon every individual to love his fellow
man, to help him, to coöperate with him—clearly not the type
of theory that can apply to nature, in which the vicious qualities, selfishness and aggressiveness are the only forces that
enable the organism to survive.

We may briefly point out that perhaps Huxley over-
emphasizes the contrast between the struggle for existence in
nature and the coöperation among humans.   True enough
such a struggle is necessary to furnish the foundation for the
"survival of the fittest," out of which man emerges.   This
struggle, in itself, sharpened the wits of human beings as contrasted with lower animals, it developed their intelligence, it
developed sympathy, it resulted in the emergence of social
qualities among humans, in short, it is responsible for man
and all his tendencies.   To be sure, because of his intellectual
and social qualities, man fights the so-called natural forces
with effective weapons; he imposes artificial restraints upon
the principles that flourish in a wild state of nature.   Regardless of these considerations, however, we have no reason to
suppose that the law of evolution does not encompass all the
principles of development, including struggle for existence,
direct selection and sympathetic coöperation.

The upshot of these various statements of naturalistic ethics
is that although we have no metaphysics allowing for the
existence of God, immortality, or freedom, we may still formulate a system of conduct which will adequately guide us in our
own behavior, as well as in our actions towards others.   Such
an ethics, which exhorts us to live and behave with decorum,
unsupported by supernatural sanction, appeals to us as intelligent humans.   Obviously, materialism deprives morality of
a great deal of its sanction.   If our will is not free, and our

soul shares the same fate as matter, moral ideas lose a great deal of their force.   Under such conditions our moral outlook is narrow, limited, and we are incapable of adopting the point of view which idealistic ethics furnishes, with its emphasis on the infinite potentialities of the soul, capable of ultimate ethical realization.   Nevertheless, we cannot charge materialism with depriving us of a system of ethics altogether.

Religion.   When we turn to religion, we are confronted with the following naturalistic explanation.   Religion has been an important force in the development of the race. While the human was in a primitive state of development, while he was uncivilized, it was necessary to supply some guiding force, some supernatural threat, to inspire him with fear of the consequences of the violation of the spiritual laws.   But since our civilization is now far advanced, we may easily dispense with the artificial stimuli offered by religion.   We can now stand on our own feet.   In short, "religion is simply so much dead weed in our stage of progress."   One of the chief exponents of such a theory is *Auguste Comte (1798–1857)*.

Comte is the exponent of positivism, that form of naturalism which insists that all that is real must be the subject matter of some one of the positive sciences.   Positive philosophy is not distinct, either as to method or as to subject matter, from any of the other positive sciences.   It employs the *a posteriori* method, experience; it is unified scientific knowledge. It systematically coördinates human knowledge.   It has as its object the whole world of phenomena.   The human mind, however, does not reach the positive or scientific stage all at once.   It passes through three successive phases—the theological, the metaphysical, the positive.   In the first stage, we have polytheism or theism, either many gods are in control, or only one Divine Being is.   This is necessary in a primitive state of society, because the mind is infantile, it cannot grasp abstractions, it must strike an analogy between itself and the outside world, in order to feel at home in the world. Next, we have the metaphysical stage, in which objects are considered as controlled by certain entities within them, not by external wills, but by certain forces, principles. Heat, for example, is a result of a certain essence mysterious and indefinable. The last step, the one which Comte advocates, is the positive, in which phenomena are explained by scientific, positive laws. The mind was not able to leap across the chasm which separates the theological from the positive, all at once. It had to be prepared for such a diametrically opposite view of the universe. Metaphysics fulfilled this function very well, indeed. It removed from thought the necessity of divine beings, it supplied more abstract forces as the explanations for natural events; therefore, it paved the way for the mind to understand science, which explains nature by universal, mechanical laws. Comte concludes that philosophy is emerging from the metaphysical, and is entering into the realm of the positive stage. The so-called positive sciences similarly passed through such three stages. These sciences, which he classifies in accordance with their increasing complexity, consisting of the science of number, astronomy, physics, chemistry, biology, sociology, are all positive, with the exception of the last. Sociology, on account of its comprehensiveness, is the last to be raised to the rank of a positive science.

This brief survey of Comte's philosophy shows why he cannot advocate religion, in the accepted sense. Philosophy is limited to the study of phenomena, clearly excluding the supernatural. Then, too, theology has been replaced by positivism, hence all subjects properly theological in character must be banned from this system of thought. He does not deny religion altogether, however. For traditional religion he substitutes "Religion of Humanity." According to its tenets, the external world has no intrinsic value. We must have something that affects us morally. The individual is the creature as well as the organ of the race to which he belongs. The tissue of life is woven for him by the collective activity of humanity. This humanity is the Providence which mediates between him and external nature. Why then is it not a proper object of worship, since it is the source of our very life? Since it is not omnipotent, we do not expect the impossible of it, as we would in the case of a religious God. It is a finite Absolute contrasted with the Infinite. It is an object of worship which has content, which possesses concrete qualities that we can understand—all of which does not hold true of the Creator religion so zealously imposes upon us. We must study nature scientifically for the purpose of the development of humanity. Aside from that, knowledge is really useless. Comte goes even further and substitutes his Trinity for the existing belief. To him, World Space is the Great Medium; Earth, the Great Fetish; Humanity, the Great Being, whom we must worship. Briefly, we may comment on this Religion by asking Comte what is the connection between Humanity and Nature. True, we are a part of Humanity, but it in turn must derive its essence from the cosmic world. How then can we stop there? To profess ignorance of such a relation yields nothing profitable. Agnosticism has never been an adequate answer to any query. Furthermore, his religion is subjective, leaving the universe out of account. This entire theory is a result of a dualistic conception of the relation of man to his environment, but if we consider the organic unity between them, such a religion cannot hold. Then it is necessary for us to go deeper than he does, to seek for a religious meaning which can explain it. Such a conception idealism supplies, which, however, is not our purpose to discuss at this point.

4. *Objections.*

Thus far we have indicated the position of materialism with reference to the cosmos. It is a metaphysical explanation of all it conceives as existing. It is a monistic philosophy, reducing all being to matter. Contrasted with the dualism of Plato and Descartes, it is more in line with the tendency of modern thought, which is monistic. Materialism has no patience with the Platonic conception of the cosmic opposition between matter and Idea or Spirit, nor with the opposition supposed by him, and by Descartes, to exist between body and mind. It points to the unity of the world, manifested by universal space, time and law, which reign uniformly. It emphasizes the unity expressed by the cosmic organization, the organization of the universe into planets, these into other subdivisions, and so on down the line. It focuses our attention upon the fact that all theories of the formation of the world, including the nebular hypothesis, show that matter existed originally, that mind was a later development, hence, bearing out the fact that the physical is the all-important consideration.

Unity. In spite of these factors, however, the materialistic philosophy is open to grave criticism. We must begin with the premise that to occupy the important position of a meta-physics, materialism should explain every element in the universe, including mind and life. It attempts to do this by every weapon at its command, but as we shall shortly see, its efforts are doomed to failure. According to its thesis, stated in the most common form, everything, including mind, is reducible to atoms in motion, governed by mechanical laws. In the first place, the obvious objection here is the epistemo-logical. How can you have an object, matter, without a sub-ject, mind? The fact that out of matter mind develops does not answer this question; for we must give mind as in-dependent a position in the universe as we attribute to matter, in order to make knowledge intelligible. This is analogous to the query put by Schelling to Fichte, when he inquired, Why attribute more importance to the Ego when obviously the non-Ego is equally necessary? Then again, we are confronted with this common-sense consideration—How do these in-numerable atoms constitute such a unity as is exhibited in the world? What is the reason for the diverse, ultimate elements arranging themselves in such a symphony of harmony? When we are referred to the fact that universal, mechanical laws controlling the universe explain this unity, we fare no better. Does not Hume's criticism most persuasively swing our minds away from the claims materialism makes for such laws? Hume convincingly explains that the most definite scientific law, that of causation, is nothing else but a customary or habitual sequence of events. If that is true of causation, how much more force can we apply to other scientific laws? How little they really explain of that which is in the noumenal world? No one decries the need or the practical effectiveness of these formulae for furnishing aid to our everyday life, but a metaphysic is required in order to take us farther. It must not only explain phenomena, but interpret the meaning, the significance, the so-called purpose behind it all.

Mind. But the most insuperable obstacle to the materialistic conception of the cosmos is the evident lack of an adequate explanation for mind and life. Let us first consider mind. Everyone admits that mind is not, on the surface at least, identical with matter. The mind has memory; it is intangible; it does not occupy space. None of these are essentially characteristic of body. This contrast indubitably shows that phenomenally the two do not resemble each other. Many explanations are offered by materialists for the existence of this mental phenomenon. Some, like Hobbes, declare that the brain is set in motion by objects around us through the nervous system, this motion is thought. The obvious difficulty with this theory is the fact that by the same reasoning the motion of a table should likewise be thought, since in the materialistic conception one physical object is no different essentially from any other. The latter result is absurd, hence Hobbes' conclusion is equally unthinkable. Another theory, and the one which materialists are most anxious to adopt, is that of interaction. According to this, the mind and the body bear a causal relation towards each other. The physical is the cause of the mental. Unfortunately, this position is untenable. In the first place, such a theory should be borne out by experience, for materialism prides itself on the fact of its scientific basis. But experience clearly is silent on this point. Nowhere in the world do we find evidence of such interaction. Furthermore, if this were true, it would violate one of the most fundamental conceptions of science, the law of conservation of energy. If physical energy can be transformed into mental, then the physical is thereby destroyed, which is contrary to the above-mentioned scientific law.   Realizing this inconsistency, materialists have finally been led to adopt the theory of psycho-physical parallelism, the position held by Spinoza.   This suggests that the whole universe can be explained from the physical angle only by deterministic, scientific laws.   We need refer to no mental phase of life at this point.   On the other hand, we find the mind present in the world.   This, too, runs throughout the universe, parallel to that of body.   It, too, is to be explained through mental laws, alone.   There is no interaction, no point of contact between them.   For every body we have a mind, for every idea we have a parellel physical act.   What does such an explanation offer?   Less than nothing.   In the first place, it is not factually true that the mind is entirely dissociated from the body in real life.   Such a mind would be devoid of all content, would furnish no *raison-d'être* for its existence.   No different is the picture of body in our actual world.   It too is not, and cannot be, dissociated from mind.   It has no significance apart from its unity with the mind.   Besides the consideration of the falsity of such a position, we are also led to make this observation: If materialism can explain only body and must hedge, in so far as mind is concerned; if, in addition to this, it also derogates from the dignity of human beings by paying no attention to our mind, which after all does differentiate us from brutes; if, on the other hand, idealism, the opposing metaphysics, can explain body, matter, and thought, and at the same time attribute to mind its proper significance, why not adopt the latter?   That consideration alone, apart from all other added elements, should give the idealistic conception of the universe the preference over the materialistic.   Some of the other reasons for preferring idealism we shall discuss later.

Life.   The result is that materialism finds itself unable to explain adequately mind and thought.   It fares no better with reference to life.   Here, too, we all recognize that the living organism consists of something which cannot be reduced to the same stuff from which the inanimate derives its source.   No one seriously contends that life can be explained mechanically.

It is self-building, self-regenerating, wholly unlike the machine to which mechanism must reduce it in order to subject it to laws of causation. Recognizing this marked difference existing between the living and the lifeless, the older vitalists introduce an external force into the organism to explain life. But this does not show the purposive, the selective, adaptation of the organism, nor explain the fact that all the parts coöperate for the welfare of the whole. If a part is injured it heals itself. The neo-vitalists, whose outstanding representative is Driesch, criticized the materialistic attempt to reduce life to mechanical processes, but they, too, lapse into the categories and terms of the older vitalists. They explain life by an entelechy, similar to the internal force in the metaphysical stage, in Comte's analysis; this does not explain the essential characteristic of the organism. Bergson has the right idea of life, as we shall see later. Modern biology liberates us from this earlier attempt to explain the living principle by means of deterministic laws. It recognizes its peculiar constitution, and its distinction from the mechanical automaton or machine.

Materialism, however, does not yield its position so readily. It argues that as our knowledge progresses, we shall learn more about life, and the time may come when we shall readily explain it mechanically. Our contention, however, is that our most exhaustive studies show that life is of such a nature that it does not lend itself to mechanistic explanation. But materialism goes further. It calls upon the evolutionary theories to aid it in its attempt to bring mind and life within the mechanical categories. We must, therefore, now turn to an examination of the theories of evolution propounded especially by Charles Darwin, Herbert Spencer, and C. Lloyd Morgan.

5. *Theories of Evolution. Darwin, Spencer, Lloyd Morgan.*

CHARLES ROBERT DARWIN (1809–1882)

In his "Origin of Species," Darwin sets out to establish his theory by first pointing out what occurs in the cultivation of domestic animals and plants.   Changed conditions of life are of the highest importance in causing variability.   They act both directly on the organism and indirectly by affecting the reproductive system.   Variations among plants and animals are an important factor in domestic cultivation.   Inheritance and reversion to type determine whether these variations shall endure.   Such variations are governed by many factors: the conditions of life, the use or disuse of certain parts, the intercrossing of originally distinct species, food and climate. In spite of the fact, however, that variations do exist and are aided or hindered by these causes of change, the real power behind it all, in domestic animals and plants, is man's cumulative selection.   Nature gives successive variations, man adds them up in certain directions useful to him.   Thus he makes for himself very desirable forms of life.   The principle of selection is "that which enables the agriculturist, not only to modify the character of his flock, but to change it altogether. It is the magician's wand by means of which he may summon into life whatever form and mould he pleases." [8]

Proceeding logically from conscious selection by man, Darwin points out how much more powerful Natural Selection is.   Nature possesses so much more material upon which to act, its domain is much more extensive; the variations on which it can fasten its attention are so much more numerous, that it is not difficult to be convinced that the explanation of all the various living forms that have existed in the universe lies in the natural selection of such living creatures as can survive in the universal struggle for existence so vigorously waged in this realm.   He shows that it is the most flourishing, the most dominant, species which on an average yield the greatest number of varieties.   This is most natural.   Their numbers are larger, their descendants are more numerous; therefore, the factors which help variations in domestic selection have a better opportunity to work here, producing more and greater varieties.   The result is that the larger species tend to become larger, and throughout nature the forms of life which are

[8] "Origin of Species," Chapter I.

now dominant will become even more dominant by leaving many modified descendants.

Throughout nature a severe struggle for existence goes on among living creatures. There is no doubt that living beings multiply at so high a rate, that, if some were not destroyed, the earth would soon be covered by the progeny of a single pair. Malthus makes a similar observation concerning the human race. According to him, if unchecked, the race would double itself every twenty-five years. The world cannot possibly supply the sustenance for so many creatures, if they were allowed to multiply inordinately. The human, to be sure, can control his numbers by the preventive check, by the conscious control of procreation. But even in the case of humans, in uncivilized countries only the positive check keeps numbers down —death, starvation, disease. A high birth rate is accompanied by a high death rate. Among the lower animals, conscious control of numbers is out of the question. Therefore, they must be destroyed by other forces. The keenest struggle is present among such creatures as are accustomed to the same food and conditions of life. Therefore, it is most severe between individuals and varieties of the same species. Since sustenance is inadequate for all, nature must select only such as are able to survive. Only such as possess favorable characteristics for survival can be thus selected. These favorable characteristics or variations consist in the qualities which render the animal more skillful in adaptation, or more powerful so that it may overcome its enemies, or which render it invisible to the eye of an attacker; for example, an animal with a dark fur may blend with the environment, and thus escape the hunter more readily. The same may be said about fleet-footedness, about the possession of alert senses. The lion, too, is not concerned about attacks as much as the little lamb; the eagle, not as much as the canary bird. To be sure, Darwin adds that sexual selection helps in survival. The victorious male leaves progeny, hence more varieties, whereas his unsuccessful rival remains alone to wage his battle for survival. Obviously, he is far less favored than the former.

Darwin concludes that the development of life progresses in this manner.   Living organisms possess certain variations or characteristics favorable or unfavorable to their adaptation to life.   These variations are due to a number of considerations, most of which we have already pointed out in domestic selection.   These organisms tend to increase out of proportion to the means of sustenance.   A struggle for existence is thus constantly waged among them.   Nature selects for survival only those which possess the favorable characteristics. The last is known as Survival of the Fittest.   Lastly, he represents evolution in the form of a tree, conceiving of all living organisms as descending from a common root or from a common progenitor.

"The green and budding twigs may represent existing species; and those produced during former years may represent the long succession of extinct species.   At each period of growth all the growing twigs have tried to branch out on all sides, and to overtop and kill the surrounding twigs and branches, in the same manner as species and groups have at all times overmastered other species in the great battle for life. The limbs divided into great branches, and these into lesser and lesser branches, were themselves once, when the tree was young, budding twigs; and this connection of the former and present buds by ramifying branches may well represent the classification of all extinct and living species in groups subordinate to groups.   Of the many twigs which flourished when the tree was a mere bush, only two or three, now grown into great branches, yet survive and bear the other branches; so with the species which lived during long-past geological periods, very few have left living and modified descendants. From the first growth of the tree, many a limb and branch has decayed and dropped off; and these fallen branches of various sizes may represent those whole orders, families and genera which have now no living representatives, and which are known to us only in a fossil state.   As we here and there see a thin straggling branch from a fork low down in a tree, and which by some chance has been favoured and is still alive on its summit, so we occasionally see an animal like the Ornithorhynchus or Lepidosiren, which in some small degree connects by its affinities two large branches of life, and which has apparently been saved from fatal competition by having inhabited a protected station.   As buds give rise by growth to fresh buds, and these, if vigorous, branch out and overtop on all sides many a feebler branch, so by generation I believe it has been with the great Tree of Life, which fills with its dead and broken branches the crust of the earth, and covers the surface with its ever-branching and beautiful ramifications." [4]

Proceeding to the human being, Darwin shows that there is a great deal of evidence for the Descent of Man from some Lower Form.   (1) The Bodily Structure of Man.   Man is constructed on the same general type as other animals, the bones in his skeleton, nerves, blood-vessels, internal viscera, brain.   Man can receive from, and communicate to, lower animals, disease such as cholera, hydrophobia.   Monkeys are subject to catarrh.   Man is also similar in reproduction, from courting to birth and nurturing of the young.   (2) Embry-onic development.   Man comes from an ovule the same as other animals.   The development of the embryo is likewise similar.   (3) Rudiments.   Similarities in the rudimentary organs exist: sense of smell, although modified in man, hair growth, spinal cord.   Males of the human species and of other mammals possess rudimentary mammae.   Darwin further adduces evidence to demonstrate that man developed along the same lines as the lower forms.   Among humans we find variations due to the operation of laws similar to those at work among lower creatures.   Environmental conditions make a difference.   The stature of man is affected by his environment.   Use and disuse influence parts of the human organism; muscle development, eyesight, attest to that fact.   Correlated variation exists here also, evidenced by the fact that two parts are affected in the same way, muscles of the arm and of the leg, for example.   Struggle for existence and the checks to natural increase exist among humans, as pointed

[4] *Ibid.,* Chapter IV.

out by Malthus.   Darwin concludes that man is the most
dominant of animals.   He owes this dominance to his intellectual and social faculties as well as to his corporeal
structure.   Man owes his present structure to natural selection.   This structure differs from that of lower animals; he is
a biped, which gives him free use of his hands.   He lost his
canine teeth, because he developed weapons with which to
fight, rendering teeth useless for that purpose.   He possesses
a more powerful spinal column to support a larger head; this
he has because of his higher intellect, which is dependent on
the size of the skull.   Man may be defenceless now physically,
but his social and intellectual qualities aid him tremendously.
If man were too powerful physically, he could not be a social
creature.

This brief discussion of Darwin's evolution illustrates the
natural development of life in the universe, without the intervention of a Deity or of any other non-scientific factor.
The materialists, therefore, felt that this conception aided
their cause.   But has it done so?   Does Darwin explain the
origin of life?   Does he show why such and no other characteristics are possible?   In short, all Darwin achieves is a
description of what actually takes place before us.   He is at
a loss to solve the riddle of life in its essential characteristics.
He merely adopts certain premises, such as varieties, struggle
for existence, natural selection and survival of the fittest,
fits them together and produces a theory most persuasive in its
conclusions.   Even if we admit, however, that all he says is
true, it does not carry us very far.   Even if life, after it
appears, does develop along Darwinian lines, what is its
origin?   How do the varieties occur?   Why do they develop
along certain lines?   Why do they exist altogether?   Lamarck's theory is really superior to Darwin's in this respect.
His contention is that the will to survive within the animal
causes it to develop certain characteristics for survival.   It is
the giraffe's desire to live that forces him to stretch his neck to
reach food on trees, which finally results in his possessing a
long neck.   This in turn enables him to acquire food more

easily, hence to survive. But the moment we talk about the will of the living organism as being responsible for its development, we stray far afield from materialism and enter into the realm of idealism, to which we shall shortly turn our attention. In the meantime let us discuss the theories of Herbert Spencer.

HERBERT SPENCER (1820–1903)

The Unknowable. We have previously made brief references to Spencer's ethical and social theories. It now becomes necessary to develop his thesis on evolution as described in the "First Principles." This law applies to the known realm of nature, as contrasted with what he terms the "Unknowable." This law explains the phenomena in nature, the phenomena which lend themselves to analysis and observation. Perhaps, for a better understanding of the application of evolution to the "Knowable," we should say a word about his treatment of the mysterious Absolute, the region beyond our knowledge, the phase of the universe to which agnosticism most forcefully applies—the "Unknowable." As we have already mentioned, Spencer is sincerely interested in reconciling religion and science. He asserts that neither religion nor science can fill the whole realm of thought. There is always left an insoluble x, which knowledge cannot penetrate. All our knowledge is relative, it must not lay claim to understand all there is. But that does not signify that an element, though unknown to us, does not exist. The very fact that our knowledge is relative argues for that which is not relative, which is absolute, otherwise there is no meaning in attributing relativity to our intellectual powers. What then is this "Unknowable"? Both religion and science admit that it exists, and this is the point at which they meet. Starting with the premise that every religious creed must contain some vital element, some kernel of truth, he examines various religious beliefs to discover what is their common denominator, which in turn will be identified with this unassailable truth. His conclusion is that "religions diametrically opposed in their overt dogmas, are yet perfectly at one in the tacit conviction that the existence of the world with all it contains and all which surrounds it, is a mystery ever pressing for interpretation. On this point, if on no other, there is entire unanimity." [5]   To be more explicit, all religions agree that the power which the universe manifests to us is utterly inscrutable. One illustration will perhaps clarify this conclusion. All dogmas attempt to solve the question of the origin of the world. We have several hypotheses. "It is self-existent, it is self-created, or created by an external agency, God. But all of these are meaningless. Self-existence is unthinkable, self-creation really means that it existed before it actually existed, otherwise how did it create itself?" As to the third alternative, the question is pushed further back— How did this external agent come into being? The same alternatives then arise, with equally insoluble results.

When we turn to science we fare no better. Here, too, science assumes certain ultimate elements, space, time, motion, matter and force. It is impossible, however, for any scientist to define the essential characteristics of any of these. Space and time can neither be classified as subjective conditions, nor as objective realities. Then again, we cannot intelligently comprehend either the infinite divisibility of matter or its opposite. In the same way, we actually know nothing about the essential nature of motion and force. Therefore, ultimate scientific ideas, like ultimate religious ideas, are all representations of realities that cannot be comprehended. Thus Spencer clearly indicates that the real reconciliation between science and religion lies in this fact. Science teaches us that there is a power in the world which is utterly inscrutable, incomprehensible, unlimited; religion voices the same opinion. In fact, anyone who wants to define this mysterious power in the universe is an heretic. The scientist who recognizes that the governing power in the universe is unfathomable is by far more religious than the fanatic who attributes the most detailed, definite characteristics to God. The agnostic is superior to him who renders God anthropomorphic. Religious

[5] "First Principles," Part I, Chapter II, Section 13.

faith, which recognizes the mystery of the Creator, is aided indeed by science, which confirms and strengthens such a belief.

The Knowable. In this manner does Spencer dispose of that phase of the world with which our knowledge cannot deal. He now turns his attention to the realm which is the subject matter of scientific investigation, and to which the law of evolution applies; we refer to the "Knowable." Spencer now considers the phenomenal world, which is characterized, to his way of thinking, by development, growth, progress, evolution. Let us adopt as a premise, he says, that the ultimate scientific ideas consist of space, time, matter, motion, and force. Let us further add these truths, the indestructibility of matter, the continuity of motion, the persistence of force, and the law of evolution has clear sailing. "Evolution is an integration of matter and concomitant dissipation of motion; during which the matter passes from an indefinite incoherent homogeneity to a definite coherent heterogeneity; and during which the retained motion undergoes a parallel transformation." [6] The meaning of this law of development is very clear and is borne out by all existences in the universe. To illustrate: Let us consider the nebular hypothesis of the formation of the world. Originally, the nebular mass was indefinite, incoherent and homogeneous; it was a uniform mass of matter without well-defined boundaries, or distinction of parts. As the universe began to develop, however, this nebula assumed different shapes in its respective parts; it formed mountains, valleys, oceans and numerous other things existent in this world. This rendered it coherent and heterogeneous. We are now able to distinguish between its various parts, we can define it most clearly, we observe harmony and coherence in its component elements. Thus far, the first part of the evolutionary law is indicated. But we know that matter must always co-exist with motion. It is comparatively easy to observe what transformation took place in motion. Originally, when the nebula was homogeneous, not integrated,

[6] *Ibid.*, Part II, Chapter XVII, Section 145.

the motion assumed a similar pattern.   As soon as the matter became integrated, became more and more compact, which is the natural result in the formation of objects in the universe, some of the original motion was squeezed out, was dissipated. At the same time, the motion which was retained throughout the evolution of the nebula from its original state to the developed stage, necessarily underwent the same changes as those to which the matter was subject.   We can thus clearly see that however complicated the statement of the law is, its application is simple.

This law not only holds true of cosmic development, continues Spencer, but of every other situation which confronts us.   Consider the State, for example.   In primitive society, there was no division of functions, the chief of the tribe was the political as well as the religious leader.   He administered judicial, executive, and legislative offices.   There was a great deal of waste of effort; in short, it typifies the incoherent, indefinite homogeneity of the Spencerian law.   In modern society, we have exactly the opposite situation, division of labor, of functions; the judicial, legislative and executive branches are clearly defined.   We now find that society has passed from the indefinite, incoherent, homogeneity to a definite, coherent heterogeneity.   Also a great deal of the effort or motion exerted in primitive society is wanting in the modern political unit, and the remaining effort, utilized in the fulfillment of all its functions, has also become more definite and coherent.   These illustrations serve to indicate how comprehensive, how general, how all-inclusive, this law of evolution is.   It penetrates every phase of the universe, and is borne out by our empirical observations.

Spencer, however, is not satisfied with this inductive proof for his law.   He brings to bear upon it also deductive considerations, the fact that it must necessarily, as a logical matter, be true.   We must accept the self-evident truth of the persistence of force—and to him nothing is more axiomatic; we also find that the homogeneous is unstable.   Nothing in the world can remain in a state of equilibrium.   Every object is exposed to force, and its various parts are affected differently by the forces to which they are exposed. Hence, it must change constantly. The homogeneous object then must become heterogeneous, must undergo transformations. But each of these new forms in turn is exposed to different forces, thus each again undergoes modifications, becoming even more heterogeneous. This he expounds under his theory of multiplication of effects. The resulting changes are much more numerous than the causes exerted by the pertinent forces. The final result is that the formula of evolution, which describes the passing of matter from the homogeneous to the heterogeneous, with all the other necessary implications, is thus proved to be true as a matter of deduction, which adds its voice to the inductive, empirical demonstration, with which Spencer initiates his doctrine.

How does such a theory aid materialism in its hitherto fruitless effort to reduce mind and life to mechanical processes? We said previously that Darwin did not explain the origin of life; he did, however, break down the barriers between the lower and higher organisms, tracing their continuous development, without teleological or theistic considerations. Spencer attempts by his comprehensive law to trace life from the lifeless, and the mental from the non-mental. "It could easily appear to Spencer that the difference between the living and the non-living had already become a matter of the degree of complexity of the molecule of protoplasm, and of the high instability of compounds of nitrogen." [7] Consciousness he considers as an accompaniment of changes in the brain, but he does not identify it with brain motion. Without going into any lengthy explanations, we can readily see that the problem is by no means solved. To say, for example, that consciousness is associated with changes in the brain, causes us to inquire, Why is it present? What is its nature?

As a matter of fact, the entire evolutionary theory of Spencer is subject to grave criticism. It is a brilliant generalization,

[7] "Types of Philosophy," by William Ernest Hocking, Page 55.

to be sure, but how much more does it offer?   Darwin's theory is scientific, it is of definite and limited scope, based on evidence of particular facts.   It is also not prejudicial to other scientific theories.   Spencer's evolution does not meet these requirements.   We do not call a theory definite or limited which attempts to explain how the whole world came into being.   It cannot be confirmed or refuted by specific facts.   It is also of little value as a metaphysic, because it does not tell us anything.   It is too vague, too general.   Philosophy makes use of evolution, but it cannot be based on evolution, because evolution is based on the distinction between that which evolves and the environment, which is stable.   Evolution, therefore, treats of only part of the real, in contrast with the other phase which does not evolve, hence to consider Spencer's evolution as a complete philosophy is a contradiction in terms.   Any formula of evolution must begin with subjects which already have some definite character.   Spencer does not comply with this condition.   He attempts to derive evolution from a perfect homogeneity, which yields no contrast, no definite phase of reality.   The conclusion thus reached is that his theory is neither scientific nor metaphysical.   His agnosticism certainly does not recommend itself to us.   His conclusions concerning the reconciliation of science and religion are not persuasive.   The scientist, as well as the religious devotee, must recognize that a mysterious power exists, before whom we should stand in awe, he contends.   This is a very *tenuous doctrine* and one which does not satisfy us to any extent.   Lastly, it does not materially contribute to the materialistic quest for an adequate explanation of life and mind.

Do we fare any better with the idea of emergent evolution propounded by Conwy Lloyd Morgan?

CONWY LLOYD MORGAN (1852–   )

Emergent evolution declares that certain combinations yield something new, not only a result which is a summation of the component parts, but also a new thing.   In short, Morgan says that evolution produces in its different steps of

progressive development a new thing which could not have
been anticipated before it actually emerged. He goes on
to explain that there are three levels in the universe. At the
bottom we have the matter level. Then we have life, and
finally we have mind, in the sense of the highly developed
mind. In each of these levels, there is a certain effective
agency directing it to go one way rather than another. He
shows that in each of these levels there are combinations which
give rise to new relations; for example, a certain combination
of atoms in the matter level gives rise to molecule, or as he
calls it, molecular relation. Then certain combination in the
matter level finally cause the emergence of life. In the same
way, certain combinations in the life level cause the emergence
of mind, the highest stage of which we see illustrated in the
mind of civilized man. But Morgan goes still further. He
attempts to discuss the meaning of God in the universe. In
one sense of the word, God may mean the most highly developed mind that evolution can bring forth. If such should
be the meaning of God, even science will have to support it,
because science does say that each individual is different from
every other in the world and, therefore, it is necessarily true
that God in the sense of a unique personality may develop or
exist. This conception of God means, of course, that development takes place only on the line of mental evolution.
Morgan, however, does not yield to this conception. To
him God means the universal, immanent, effective principle
of development in the universe, causing the whole cosmic
evolution to follow the direction we have found it to pursue.

In order to support his theory of Emergent Evolution,
Morgan goes into more detail, in the development of mind,
especially. He agrees with Spinoza that throughout the
universe mind and body exist in correlation with each other.
He means by that, that even at the lowest level, namely,
matter, we already have the tendencies, the elements, the possibilities, for the emergence of mind at the later stage, if certain
combinations occur. He then goes on to show that at a low
stage of mental development, memory works in the following

manner: When an actual sensation or experience occurs, that recalls a similar experience which had occurred to the same observer at some previous time.   In short, at a low stage of mental development, an actual sensation is necessary to bring to the consciousness of the mind some image of the past, but at the highest stage of mental development, you no longer need an actual experience in order to evoke a past experience by memory, but even a line of poetry that you hear will recall to your mind the poem in which it occurred, the circumstances under which you read the poem, the circumstances of the writing of the poem, if you knew them in the past.   In short, in the highest stage of mental development, the mind by itself can evoke a train of thoughts of images similar to the one on which it is actively engaged for the moment.   In this and in similar ways, Morgan shows that certain combinations at a lower level or at a lower stage do result in something new at a future time.

Morgan, however, is not satisfied as yet with his theory. He goes one step further.   He says that although we cannot prove or demonstrate the existence of the outside world independently of the mind, yet we acknowledge its existence. This independent world furnishes us with the skeleton which we clothe with our own experiences.   This process by which we color the skeleton with our own points of view, he calls projicience.   Then the process by which we go from, "I want x," to "You want x," he calls ejicience, which supplements projicience.   Then to top it all, he acknowledges, as we have mentioned before, the existence of a Deity as the immanent principle of universal development.

Mr. Morgan also anticipates the objection that may be leveled against his theory, namely, that it is in conflict with the conception of science.   He says that the old conception of causation, which means that the cause must precede the effect, is no longer necessary for science, because the time element in causation can be dropped.   All that scientific laws mean to-day is that they are laws of the universe, under which things occur.   Therefore, Emergent Evolution itself is also under a universal law, which says that certain combinations will yield

something new.   The reason why we cannot anticipate the
something new is because we do not know what combinations
are necessary to produce that new emergent.   In short, Morgan shows that without the conception of God, altogether,
Emergent Evolution is as scientific as any other concrete,
definite, scientific theory, because it can work under a universal
law.   But he does not like to stop there.   He says that by
acknowledging the Deity we make Emergent Evolution more
complete, more satisfying, and yet not in conflict with science,
but supplementing scientific theory.   In short, we can say
that science works under causation, meaning under universal
laws of nature, but at the same time, behind this working of
laws, behind the appearances of things, behind this world of
nature, there is a meaning, a purpose, exemplifying the Deity
as a universal, immanent, progressive and effective principle
of causality.

This is a brief outline of the theory of Emergent Evolution
as expounded by Morgan.   Now what can be said with reference to it?   In the first place, this theory, which attempts to
show that the world, including evolution of living beings, expresses an all-pervasive purpose, is contrary to the theory of
Charles Darwin.   Mr. Darwin absolutely ignored any conception of purpose as underlying evolution.   Still Darwin was
unable to explain the origin of life, the reason for the existence
of variations, the reason for the presence of the kinds of variations which were useful for the development of the organism.
Under Morgan's theory all of these questions can readily be
answered by referring to them as the expressions of the
hidden, universal purpose or meaning.

In the second place, this theory of Emergent Evolution
does not harmonize readily with the theory of Herbert
Spencer.   Spencer attempted to explain cosmic development
by natural laws, and as far as he went he accomplished his
purpose rather well.   Spencer, however, encountered many
difficulties which he could not answer.   Spencer, himself,
reached the conclusion that both science and religion termi-
nate in an Unknown.   He takes pride in showing that his
conclusion is by far more religious than that of many Theists,

because the very fact that we cannot explain the nature of God shows how superior God is to us.   That shows a great deal more reverence for God than the theistic idea, which attempts to explain His nature, His attributes, His qualities.   Here again, we must say that the admission of a universal purpose in the world satisfies the mind more than does Spencer's philosophy, for all naturalistic theories abound in insoluble puzzles.

Without going into detail, it is easy to show that Huxley and Morgan differ.   Huxley is a naturalist, whereas Morgan is a teleologist.   Huxley has great difficulty in explaining how the law of the struggle for existence, which is the most fundamental principle of evolution, must be almost eliminated before the human being can acquire those faculties which are so necessary for his social and moral development.   Morgan would have no trouble on that score.   To him, the differences in the principles, even if such differences were admitted, which, Huxley claims, prevail in the inanimate kingdom and in the animate kingdom, are simply the methods by which the universal purpose manifests itself.

In conclusion, we must say that although Morgan's theory bristles with difficulties for the strict scientist, yet he does furnish a satisfying explanation.   Morgan is almost pantheistic in his theory, which might offend Theists.   However, his acknowledgment of the type of God who pervades the universe and is not an occasional visitor coming into the world at intervals, is by far a more sound proposition than the Theistic dualism of God and the world.   In short, while this Emergent Evolution does not meet every difficulty, does not solve every riddle, does not answer every question, in view of the enormous subject matter with which it is obliged to deal, we believe, nevertheless, that it is more attractive than the other theories.   It detracts nothing from science, but in fact emphasizes the need of scientific laws for the world of nature; it can be explained, as Morgan points out, under a universal law; but even with the conception of a Deity as a part of the theory of Emergent Evolution, in order to complete it and make it more adequate for our needs, the whole theory supplements science, satisfies our subjective craving for harmony and is therefore very commendable.

However, in so far as Emergent Evolution applies to the explanation of life and mind so eagerly sought by materialism, we must say that it offers very little encouragement. In the first place, it does not reduce either or both to mechanistic processes. Far from it. It leaves them as mysterious as ever, merely describing how they happen to occur. Moreover, he really concludes that life or consciousness cannot be reduced to matter and motion in the naturalistic sense. His conclusions regarding an immanent purpose, as shown by his second conception of the Deity, most assuredly places him more in the ranks of the idealists than in those of the naturalists. Consequently, materialism is still faced with this problem, which it is unable to solve satisfactorily.

6. *Conclusion.*

What, then, must we conclude in reference to this first metaphysical theory, materialism? Doubtless, it is appealing; it tallies with many of our everyday conceptions of the phenomena before us; it leans towards the scientific; it explains much, but yet not enough. True, it does not obviate ethics, yet it narrows the limits of moral development. It derogates from that human faculty which the leading thinkers of the past, as well as of the present, have always considered as the mark by which we are distinguished from brutes—mind. It really affords no place for religion, and yet in the words of Spencer, there must be something vital in religion, which caused it to survive throughout the ages. Particularly, however, it explains neither life nor consciousness by its method. This clearly is sufficient for us to militate against it as an adequate philosophy with which to explain the universe. It, therefore, behooves us to direct our attention next to the opposite metaphysic, to learn whether its thesis meets all our necessary demands—Idealism.

CHAPTER II

IDEALISM

1. *The Thesis of Idealism.   Contrast with Materialism.*

THE principal thesis of idealism is that the stuff of the universe is mental in character, that the apparent materialistic aspect of the world is illusory that although reality is composed of the same mental texture as is the fabric of our own minds, nevertheless, it is not dependent on the Ego of the subject or perceiver, in the Berkeleyan sense.   In short, the external world possesses objective validity, a claim also made by materialism, but idealism identifies its essential characteristics with mind instead of matter, energy or force.   Thus far, we have clearly seen the inadequacy of naturalism to explain consciousness.   We have observed that the final conclusion reached by its advocates in the solution of this problem is psycho-physical parallelism, which really explains nothing. Objective idealism, however, asserts that if we identify reality with mind, it not only affords a reason for the existence of consciousness but it offers an equally logical theory for the existence of body.   To illustrate this point of view we need but refer to Schopenhauer, for example.   We have seen that by analogy to ourselves, we may discover the essence of the universe.   Our wills, if accepted as fundamental, must express themselves through our bodies, our physical actions are manifestations of the will behind them.   The *world,* too, may be considered as embodying a Universal Will which expresses itself through the manifold phenomena in the world.   In short, the material is a requisite for the understanding of the spiritual.   Besides this voluntaristic theory of Schopenhauer, objective idealism may take the direction of the Hegelian

World Reason as the essence of the Universe. This does not make any difference in our interpretation. Here, too, the reason behind phenomena requires necessarily such external expressions for its communication and for its understanding. Even assuming that we had no other considerations but these to persuade us of the cogency of the idealistic philosophy, we ought to lean more favorably towards it than towards naturalism. Given two hypotheses, each laying equal claim to being a comprehensive explanation of all existence, of all reality, each also impossible of being positively demonstrated, because of its universal character—if one cannot properly explain mind, of which we are so proud, and the other not only takes care of the mental but also of the physical, why should it not by that fact alone be preferred as a metaphysical philosophy?

But we may approach this objective idealism from another angle. Materialism began with the central theme that the external world is composed of matter and motion. No one philosopher did more to disabuse our minds of such a belief than Berkeley. We have seen how he most emphatically and forcefully shows that each of us only experiences his own ideas, his own impressions of this natural realm. His *esse est percipi* principle is also adopted by Schopenhauer, in his treatment of "The World as My Idea." This is indeed true. We really know only what our mental conception of an event, object, person or occurrence is. This disposes of an independent, material order. Unfortunately for Berkeleyan philosophy, it is subject to such grave criticism that we cannot possibly accept its affirmative thesis. Some of these objections we have already pointed out previously, the "Ego-centric" predicament, "fallacy of definition by initial predication," solipsism. It also presents a false picture of what actually takes place in our world of social relations. Our conclusion, therefore, is that Berkeley is far more important for the negative phase of his philosophy than for any positive contribution he makes. He irrefutably annihilates the naturalistic conception of an independent world of matter, but he does not offer a substitute for the objectivity of the world,

which he eliminates from materialism.   If such objectivity
is denied, solipsism reigns supreme; *that* we cannot tolerate.
Therefore, objective idealism is the ideal solution.   It does
recognize the materialistic insistence on the objective ex-
ternality of the world, but since this cannot be identified with
matter, as Berkeley amply demonstrated, it must be mind.
Thus we are inclined to favor idealism, as a synthesis of the
best elements both in naturalism and in Berkeleyanism.

Once we are persuaded to look with favor upon the idealistic
metaphysic, we may find many features in it to satisfy our
demands.   It explains the connection between mind and body,
a problem which has puzzled philosophers for many ages.
Since in this relation, mind is the all-important consideration,
even if death does destroy the body, we have no reason to suppose that our mental life ceases likewise.   No doubt, this
allows room for a belief in immortality.   Moreover, it pro-
fesses, and rightly, the reign of freedom in this animated,
mental realm.   It is the essential characteristic of mind to
be free, to impose its own laws upon its behavior, to formulate
its own standards.   With this in view, natural laws may be
explained as acting mechanically, without being prejudicial to
the idealistic conception.   Just as we individually are the
cause of our own habits, which later become so hardened as to
render us slaves to them, in the same manner, the World-
Mind has imposed these natural laws upon itself—they are
immutable, uniform, even more than our habits, because of the
character and magnitude of their author.   This attitude
towards phenomenal nature, of regarding it as an expression
of the noumenal reality within, allows for a teleological interpretation of nature, far superior to the theistic argument from
design, advanced with such gusto by the frocked gentlemen of
the Church.   Not only can the latter not withstand the fatal
criticism of Kant, but we may also dispose of it from this angle.
The theologian argues that this world is the result of God's
creation; the Divine Author brought it into being for a purpose.   The usual meaning attributed to such purpose is that nature exists for the welfare of human beings.   But this concep-

tion is most assuredly very vulnerable. Does not nature teem with forces inimical to humans? How about earthquakes, disease, plagues, tornadoes, and the innumerable other forces of nature? Can anyone sanely argue, that the goal sought by an omnipotent, omniscient God should be placed so far afield? If the welfare of man were intended, surely all of nature should be conducive towards his happiness, but as an actual fact, this is far from true. Moreover, does a God of the character attributed to Him by religion use such inadequate means to produce the desired result? Why is nature so wasteful, so destructive in its production of life? Millions of fresh eggs are destroyed before one actually develops into a living thing. Such blundering certainly does not betoken a God as the author of the universe. Besides, the anthropomorphic attributes of such a *deus ex machina* are offensive to those who really venerate and revere the Highest Being. On the idealistic hypothesis, all these defects and objections disappear. We have, it postulates, unity in the world. Even materialism admits that. While materialism, however, is unable, as we have seen, to explain such unity, idealism says that the World Mind or the World Will being unitary clearly indicates the unity of the world. At the same time it expresses itself most adequately only through the multiplicity of phenomena in nature. Laws are the instruments through which it operates. This possesses the added advantage that it is not prejudicial to science, in fact, it calls upon the aid of scientific development to show how the world purpose can be studied by means of the weapons it employs, by means of the laws of space, time, motion, force, causality. Without proper scientific data, we may know that there is a world purpose, but our knowledge of its external character would be limited indeed.

One of the most important questions any metaphysic is obliged to answer, Why does nature exist? To be sure, materialism is not concerned vitally with this problem, because nature is its entire and exclusive subject matter. Idealism, however, which emphasizes the mental feature, and which relegates the phenomenal world to second place, must make its position more clear.   This is a question similar to that asked in our discussion of the Platonic Worlds—of Ideas and of Sense.   There, too, we legitimately ask, If the World of Ideas is the essential reality, why bother with the temporary, sensory realm of experience?   The answer is clearly indicated that the Idea of the Good, or God, being constituted of love and of goodness, must express itself, and the phenomenal world offers such an opportunity.   Similarly, in idealism, we concede that the noumenal reality is mental, but at the same time we must not lose sight of the fact that we must have means of developing the mind, means of communicating with other minds, in order to lead a social existence.   We need bridges, whereby we may cross from one phase of reality to another. What is a more effective instrument for this purpose than our own bodies working in conjunction with the corporeal nature of the world?   Generally speaking, therefore, Nature exists to afford the means of communication.   It also is necessary to supply our minds, our wills, with material for development. We need content to supplement the container, mind.   The two together constitute a whole which is intelligible, and which becomes a potent instrument for the effective realization of our potentialities.

2. *Ethics.*

This consideration of the world leads us most logically to a discussion of Idealistic ethics.   Generally speaking, we require a world as the scene of our activities in order to develop morally.   We need obstacles to overcome, to improve our ethical realization.   No one could be considered a saint, if he were never obliged to overcome temptations.   But further than that, the will must have material with which to work, to bring to the foreground its possibilities.   Such considerations swayed Kant and his disciples in their respective theories of morality.   In our historical sketch of Kantian philosophy, we showed that he postulates freedom of the will, immortality of the soul, and the existence of God, as the indispensable conditions of morality.   The Categorical Imperative, too, ful-

filled the function of supplying the proper criterion for our
actions, as free souls and free wills.   These postulates are the
very principles propounded by the metaphysics of objective
idealism.   The defect in Kantianism lies in its furnishing no
metaphysics to support its ethics. The moral system is left
hanging in the air, so to speak.   His contention is that conceptually we cannot penetrate the realm beyond the phenomenal world, but practical reason must assume the existence
of these three noumena, otherwise, moral development becomes an impossibility.   While pragmatically, this argument
may be persuasive, yet it is far from being as convincing and
as cogent as if, besides such practical considerations, we also
find that the very fabric of the world can be shown by our
conceptual thinking to consist of such mental stuff, in which
these principles must be constituent elements.   That is pre-
cisely what objective idealism supplies.   It argues for mind as
the essence of the world; it contends that we have freedom,
immortality and a Supreme Spirit in this world.   Once we
adopt an ethics, either wholly Kantian in nature, or something
similar to it, how different an aspect it presents from the
naturalistic ethics!   To be sure, even materialism, as we have
seen, does not leave morality out in the cold, but what does
it really offer?   An evolutionary, teleological system of behavior, in which the consequences are the sole guide.   While
this is quite refreshing to many practical men, does it possess
the breadth, the force, the desirable features, of a system
which considers each man as an end in himself, which regards
the soul of everyone as possessing infinite possibilities for
development, which, furthermore, views each will as inhering
in a World Spirit akin to it, with an indefinite time for realization?   Moreover, even in Kantian philosophy, consequences
are not disregarded.   We cannot obey the Categorical Imperative, without achieving certain effects in our environment;
these results demonstrate whether we did treat the human
being as an end in himself or as a means to an end, or what
will ensue if our action became universalized.   Furthermore,
objective idealism regards the universe as essentially moral.

That causes us to live strenuously, as James puts it. In the evolutionary ethics, which considers the universe as unmoral, our conduct is bound to assume an artificial character, we become "soft-livers," more or less carefree, more along the lines laid down by Epicurus, although with some modification. Then, too, Idealism furnishes the type of world in which we feel at home, if we consider it composed of the same mental stuff as our own make-up. That alone removes the coldness, the hardness, the aloof and indifferent character, of nature. This in turn helps to encourage us in our conduct, to make us trust in the successful outcome of a moral venture that we assume in our premise to be ethically correct.

From this point of view, Fichte, as we have seen, considering the will as *the* all-important part of us, allows the Ego to impose restrictions upon itself in the form of an opposing non-Ego. By overcoming the obstacles in nature, the will emerges more triumphant, morally. Hegel, too, by his characteristic method traces moral development in this way. At first the individual will isolates itself, holds itself aloof from any common enterprise with other wills. Then it asserts itself in opposition to, or in disregard of, the objective will of society; finally it attains the ethical ideal of freedom by active participation and coöperation with other selves in institutions and common ventures. At this point, the will attaches itself to the universal elements in the world.

To be sure, this type of morality may be spurned by those who lean toward the materialistic code, by those who feel that it is a sign of weakness to be swayed by considerations other than by those empirically observed; still we are presenting the theory for such as may not be so inclined. This ethics has the further advantage, that besides offering us the dignity to which we are entitled in the scheme of things, it does not run counter to science, if we limit, as we should, scientific laws to the phenomenal world only. In that event, freedom, for example, in no way interferes with the natural, deterministic laws reigning in the world of matter, as we have previously pointed out.

Many of the above factors in the idealistic philosophy have previously been covered in more detail in the historical sketch of the German School of Idealism, initiated by Kant. We have seen that the theory proceeded along two main branches of development—on the one hand, the Hegelian line of reasoning, which identified Reason with Reality; on the other hand, Schopenhauer's voluntarism. Both of these were developed further by the followers of these respective schools. Let us, therefore, now turn to a discussion of the philosophies of two thinkers—Josiah Royce, the disciple of Hegel, and Friedrich Paulsen, of Schopenhauer.

3. *Josiah Royce.* *(1855–1916)*

Royce approaches the problem of metaphysics in the usual manner of the objective idealist. He first analyzes the world as we perceive it. In this he agrees with Berkeley that this is such stuff as ideas are made of. It is a world for us to know, it is presented to us as ideas. If, then, it is a world of mind we can know it; if not it is a bare x. If it is a bare x, then science can have no objective validity, for science is concerned only with ideas. To be sure, we feel that the world is composed of stubborn material, but ideas are also stubborn, they cannot always be overcome. Once our analysis of the universe yields the conclusion that the world is mental, it is easy, says Royce, to show that it is One Absolute Self. This is reached by the method known as Synthetic Idealism. To escape from our own skepticism, we must assert that the world is essentially one world. Any object about which we think stands in the relation of object to our thoughts. We must *mean* it; we must *recognize* it, when we see or when we recollect it. This relation is made possible because our larger self has both our present state of mind and the object before it. Because our larger Self already possesses the object, we can *mean* it when we see it. Therefore, in the world, there is such a Supreme Self to whom all things are present and known, a Self who knows all truth. It is certain that such a Self exists, otherwise nothing could have meaning, which is the relation of ourselves to an object beyond us for the moment.   This ultimate Self must be One, otherwise, such selves would have relations towards each other, which would have to be synthesized again into a larger Self.

Royce, therefore, concludes that the world is mental. Thought possesses all things.   The world, however, is very real.   It extends beyond our private consciousness, because it is a world of a universal mind.   The only thing certain about this world is that it is intelligent, rational, orderly, essentially comprehensible; that all its problems are somewhere solved; that all its mysteries are known to the Universal Spiritual Self.   This Self includes us; hence it is at the very least a person.   It is not remote from us.   There is no thought that does not contain and embody something of this "Divine Logos."

Thus far for Royce's metaphysics.   But his philosophy has taken more of an ethical turn, embodied in his doctrine of "Loyalty to Loyalty."   In accordance with the Hegelian point of view, Royce recognizes that to develop morally we must emerge out of our own shell, we must coöperate in social matters; in short, we must, as he calls it, enlist in the service of worthy social causes, we must be loyal to such causes.   In loyalty, he continues, is the fulfillment of the whole moral law.   In order to understand this last statement we must define our principle.   It means that we must have a cause to which to be loyal, then to devote ourselves willingly and thoroughly to it, and finally to express such devotion in a sustained and practical manner.   "The devotion of a patriot to his country, when his devotion leads him actually to live and perhaps to die for his country; the devotion of a martyr to his religion. . . ." [1] exemplify Royce's meaning.   The cause, too, must be one which we personally value, it must be objective; we do not attribute value to it because of our personal pleasure, but because it has objective value, we love it. Lastly, loyalty is social, the cause concerns others besides ourselves.   We need such loyalty, because our duty is to act in

[1] "The Philosophy of Loyalty," Lecture I, Section III.

accordance with our station and dignity in life; in short, we must be clearly conscious of our will to learn what is good and proper for us to do. This cannot be done by brooding over natural desires, or by acting capriciously. I can never define my duty simply in terms of pleasure or pain. Therefore, to furnish for ourselves a proper plan of life, we must resort to something beyond us as a guide. We first learn to have a will of our own by imitating others. Then, such social training teaches us that our will is in contrast with others, which drives us back into our own shells for guidance. Thus we are in a vicious circle morally. We are seeking for a plan, we do not get it from within; we look for help from without, in social life, but here, we simply find a sharp contrast between our own will and that of society, then we lose confidence in social guidance. How then shall we solve this problem? How unite this inner self with the social world? This is where loyalty enters. Suppose our country is in danger, says Royce. The patriot then develops the war spirit. This spirit harmonizes the patriot's self-will and his conformity to society. ˙ It gives him a plan of conduct which on the one hand is through and through social, and on the other, an exaltation of the inner self. All conflict here disappears, the patriot turns into a hero. Loyalty to a cause, then, is the way by which we develop a plan of conduct which is satisfactory to our demands. The causes may be domestic, religious, commercial, professional, and they may have many other forms.

To those of us who are loyal to a cause or causes which possess the characteristics of resolving this conflict, and of intensifying both the inner and outer feelings, the cause takes the place of conscience, it is the guide of our lives. One difficulty, however, remains. All cannot serve the same causes. Very often loyalties of different individuals conflict. It would indeed be a disparagement of a type of morality, if the loyalty of one group in society would be destructive to the loyalties of another contingent. Such a principle of duty would result in conflict and would not be conducive to a universal standard of conduct. But Royce explains that the highest principle is, "Be loyal to loyalty."   No matter how the loyalties of others differ from ours, we should respect their loyalties also.   Each opponent must respect the loyalty of the other. In this manner, our ethical principle will promote and encourage loyalty.

The conclusion is clear.   This principle of loyalty is not something hanging in the air.   It is based upon the fundamental reality behind the phenomena.   This realm of reality is conscious, is united, is self-possessed, and is perfected through the very wealth of the ideal sacrifices and of the loyal devotion which unite to constitute its fullness of being.   "Loyalty," now can be defined, "as the will to manifest, so far as is possible, the Eternal, that is the conscious and superhuman unity of life, in the form of the acts of an individual self." [2]   Royce continues "Loyalty is the Will to Believe in something eternal, and to express that belief in the practical life of a human being." [3]

Let us now turn to a brief discussion of Friedrich Paulsen.

4. *Friedrich Paulsen.*   *(1846–1908)*

Paulsen approached metaphysics from two angles.   To begin with, metaphysics answers the inquiry as to what constitutes reality, or the underlying substance of the world. Then again, it also explains the cause for the unity so clearly displayed in this world.   As to the first query, the dualists attempt to show that the common-sense view that body and mind, distinct from each other, constitute reality, applies. But the later trend, as we have seen, is away from dualism, towards monism.   Here we approach the problem we have been discussing all along—Materialism versus Idealism. Showing the insufficiency of materialism, along lines similar to those we have previously mentioned, Paulsen concludes that idealism is the only tenable hypothesis.   The world consists of mental stuff, but the primary element is will, in Schopenhauer's sense of the word.   It is comparatively

[2] *Ibid.*, Chapter VIII, Section 1.
[3] *Ibid.*

simple, says Paulsen, to strike an analogy between our own
wills and our bodies as their external expressions, to a World
Will manifesting itself through physical nature. The conclusion, then, is that all of nature is alive, the expression of a
soul. Why, then, do we find it so difficult to adopt this
idealistic hypothesis, when it would appear that it is superior
to the naturalistic attitude? Because, answers Paulsen, of
two erroneous notions we entertain concerning the phenomeno-
logical content of soul life and the metaphysical constitution
of the soul. If we erroneously adopt the intellectualistic
psychology, that the soul is primarily reason, intellect, we
find it difficult to ascribe such characteristics to lower animals,
to the vegetable kingdom, and especially to inanimate nature.
Since Idealism, being a theory of metaphysics, must explain
the whole universe by its hypothesis of mind or soul, if any
phase of it remains unexplained, Idealism must collapse.
Paulsen, however, urges us to adopt the voluntaristic psychology—the soul is essentially will. From that angle, even
so-called inorganic nature can be conceived as living, as displaying the characteristics of will, consisting of energy, motion, effort, striving. The whole of nature at the very least,
possesses motion and energy. This alone demonstrates the
presence of will in its less apparent characteristics, in the
lower stages. In its more obvious manifestations, the will
appears in the higher natural realms, especially among humans.

The second erroneous popular conception concerns the
metaphysical constitution of the soul and its seat in the body.
Plato considered the soul a substance, simple, indivisible and
therefore indestructible or immortal. Descartes, too, considered it a substance situated exclusively in the brain.
Naturally, if the soul requires a brain for its existence we cannot attribute soul-life to the whole of nature. Such a highly
centralized nervous system, which is associated with a brain,
is lacking among lower animals, the plant kingdom, and that
part of nature denominated inorganic. This, however, is false.
"The soul," he says, "is a plurality of psychical experiences

comprehended into a unity of consciousness in a manner not further definable. We know nothing whatever of a substance outside of, behind, or under the ideas and feelings." [4] The soul is not a substance, we have no soul atom, as some argue. Psychology is no more interested in the soul atom than is science in the atoms constituting matter. Both employ the terms for analysis, but do not consider the atoms as constituting reality. In short, science employs atoms in the same way as arithmetic makes use of certain units in calculation. Arithmetic does not question whether these units are ultimate or indivisible. They serve the purpose regardless of that consideration. Thus we see that science and psychology may employ the conception of atoms, without considering them as the ultimate, indivisible, rigid constituents of reality.

Not only is this theory of the identity of the soul with a simple substance untenable, but the same fate is shared by the Cartesian conception that the brain is the seat of the soul. In Paulsen's view, the whole body is such a locus, the body possesses sensation at every point. Physiology is more inclined to the belief that the concomitant phenomena of psychical processes extend over a large territory. That the brain is not the seat of the soul is attested by these facts: (1) The thoroughgoing unity of corporeal life suggests it. This shows that the whole body is the expression of the soul-life. (2) Biological and evolutionary facts lead us to the same conclusion. We attribute psychical life to the lowest form of animals, although they have no nervous system. "Every infinitely small piece of protoplasm is the seat of psychical processes." (3) Although in the lowest forms of animal life, the entire body is sensitive to stimuli, in the higher organisms, some of the reactions are not conscious, otherwise, they could not preserve themselves in their complex environment. Therefore, even in humans, psychical life is not necessarily conscious. A great deal of it is subconscious, beneath the surface stream of conscious life. From this angle, we have no reason to suppose that the whole world may not possess the

[4] "Introduction to Philosophy," Book I, Chapter I, Section 7.

kind of psychical life which never reaches the level of humans. Thus, once we eliminate the errors just mentioned, no obstacle stands in the way of adopting the idealistic or spiritualistic theory.

We referred above to the fact that metaphysics also supplies the cause for the unity prevailing in the universe. We need not discuss the theistic argument that God is directly responsible for this harmony. We disposed of that effectively in our previous discussion. The atomistic doctrine also does not persuade us of its cogency. We are confronted with this dilemma. How can the multiplicity of the atoms account for such unity? Therefore, we are led to the conclusion that the world is pantheistic, that there is a World Soul, which manifests itself through the material world; that this Soul accounts for the singleness and unity in nature. Finally, nature, being alive, is teleological in character, it possesses a purpose which is effectively expressed through laws of science, of which causality is one of the most important. Such teleology is distinct from the religious theory; besides, it is not only non-prejudicial to science, but it actually calls upon science for aid and support. From these premises, the usual idealistic ethics and religion follow most naturally in Paulsen's philosophy.

To conclude this theory of Idealism we are led to consider the contribution made by William Ernest Hocking

5. *William Ernest Hocking.* (1873–)

Professor Hocking subscribes to the principal tenets of objective idealism. The world is essentially mental. Body, matter, is the expression of mind. Natural laws are the means through which the purpose within the world, behind appearances, works. Freedom of the will reigns supreme in this realm of mind. Immortality and God are existing realities. How do we know that this nature, this universe, is a Supreme Self? Aside from all other considerations with which objective idealism reënforces this conclusion, Professor Hocking adduces this fact to demonstrate that this Self directly reveals itself to us through nature.   We deal in this world, he says, with our own selves, with so-called physical objects, and with other minds.   We intuitively know our own existence, as Bergson aptly demonstrates.   No dissension seems to prevail among thinkers as to the fact that we know physical objects in nature.   But how are we aware of the existence of other minds?   Professor Hocking cuts across the theories of other idealists on this point, and reaches the conclusion that we do know other minds, because the objects dealt with by us already possess a social quality, that is, we know them to be experienced by others in common with us.   The irreducible minimum of such sociability in objects is space.   The infant has his first experience in space, by which he gradually becomes aware that such space is also enjoyed by other minds similar to his.   Therefore, it is obvious that the purpose of nature, of which space is an integral part, is to enable us to lead a social existence.   Thus nature itself is shown to be social.   From this, it is readily seen that there must be a Supreme Self, speaking to us through social nature, supplying us with the conditions and with the indispensable factors necessary for our having communication with other *selves.* This means that it is not through other minds that we know this Self or God, but it is through God that we know other minds.   Nature as a whole is a social field of experience, and through this immediate experience we know God as the Other Mind, which in creating nature creates us.   The fact that we can work with nature shows that it is an Absolute Order.   God furnishes us with a persistent sense of reality.   This shows that we may employ the ontological argument for the existence of God, but not in the old form.   Hocking's statement of the argument is: "I have an idea of God, therefore I have an experience of God."

In short, the other arguments for God which we have discussed, proceeded from the world to God.   They reason that because the world is, God is.   That is effectively criticized by Kant and shown to be illogical.   But Hocking's argument is that "Because the world is not, God is."   It is because we

are dissatisfied with the world as it appears, because it does
not meet our demands, that we lift our eyes to a God, a Self,
whom we can address with the assurance that we may fulfill
our proper functions and duties in life.

Such a theory has an effect upon our standards of morality.
True enough, our individual Selves are a part of the natural
realm, but they are more than mere objects.   They have infinite possibilities for development, they are creative; by
their association with the Supreme Self, they are capable of
finding their proper realization in this social nature.   Therefore, in morality, Hocking urges, "Universalize thyself."
We must consider ourselves as unique beings, rendering our
private attitude towards the world universal.   We must
create and re-create, effect changes in the world which should
last permanently.   In all our actions we must lay down certain truths which may have general acceptance, because our
worth and essential characteristics are of universal character.
In our practical life, continues Hocking, we have ethical and
aesthetic standards of conduct.   We have also the standard
of honor, a very high criterion for our behavior.   While a
code of ethics need not depend upon a metaphysic, such
standards are, nevertheless, not alien to reality.   If, then,
we agree with the idealistic conclusion that reality is a mind,
a Self, it certainly "cannot be a matter of cosmic indifference
whether we observe them. . . .   This metaphysic carries
with it a further presumption that the good will, as being in
accord with the ultimate power of the world, is *ipso facto*
succeeding in its unknown cosmic business. . . .   For the
objective order of the world is not a mechanical but a moral
order." [5]

6. Conclusion.

What then can we say about Idealism as a metaphysical
theory?   Doubtless, materialism explains many phases of the
universe, it appeals to our practical, common-sense view of
things.   It is in line with modern scientific progress.   It has

[5] "Types of Philosophy," Page 321.

answers for the historical development of religion, as well as explanations for its apparent uselessness at present, in the light of our current enlightenment.   Then, too, it deals with matter, forces, energy—phenomena with which we are well conversant, and which do not possess the occult, unseen qualities attributed to them by Idealism, in the sense of ascribing mentality to them.   It is an imposing theory, indeed.   It supplies us with a code of ethics which for all practical purposes—and ethics is essentially practical—serves well the purpose of the individual as well as the social unit.   Nevertheless, in spite of this vaunted superiority, materialism fails completely in some of the most important branches of existence; it is utterly at a loss to explain adequately life and mind.   In view of the fact that we are vitally concerned with these, we must turn to Idealism as a more adequate and a more comprehensive theory for satisfying our craving for an intelligent understanding of the universe.

Idealism, indeed, does not fall into the pitfalls of the subjective branch of its theory as propounded by Berkeley. Since it bases its tenets upon the fact that mind is the most essential element of the world, the social intercourse between minds assumes paramount importance.   This, in turn, must exclude solipsism.   Then again, Idealism is a synthesis, combining the essentially true and persuasive elements of naturalism and of subjectivism.   It furnishes a more reliable background for ethics, it widens the scope of our moral activities, it demonstrates as far as a metaphysical theory can, that we are essentially a part of the underlying reality, or mind.   It, therefore, urges us to assume our proper dignity in this respect and to express our moral action in a manner that may become universal.   This is our duty, our happiness, our function.   It does not derogate from religion, but establishes the fact that religion is creative; by giving us a God, a Supreme Spirit, it encourages us in our social relations with men, it enables us to build further, to plan and arrange our lives with the firm conviction that the cosmos is friendly to us.

To be sure, some hard-headed practical men may denominate this type of ethics and religion self-hypnosis, as too sentimental, but, unfortunately, they propose no adequate substitute. To scoff at something which possesses the beauty of poetry, the grandeur of genuine art, the truth of real, dialectical reason, requires a great deal of temerity, unless we are able to substitute a superior explanation, which may satisfy the human yearning for companionship, for solace and for comfort in times of distress. Spinoza may argue that to regret is weakness, but the fact of the matter remains that we do regret; therefore, we ought to have a way out of our regret, our despair. Idealism does supply this, materialism fails in this respect.

In spite of these commendatory remarks, Idealism is not the last word in philosophy. True enough, it has many followers, its influence is great. Nevertheless, it is subject to criticism. The pluralist, viewing the world disinterestedly, and beholding the multiplicity in it, may severely criticize the insistence of the Idealist upon perfect unity. The intuitive knowledge of the existence of the Self may be subjected to severe scrutiny. Hume and James feel that introspection yields only a series of mental impressions, ideas, images. If such should be the case, what becomes of all the idealistic conclusions based upon the creative activity of the Self? Its dialectic method, by which it reaches the conclusions that mentality reigns in the world, the scientific analyst may contemptuously discard, because of his familiarity with the method of induction, because of his constant handling of objects phenomenally appearing to us. We may perhaps interpolate the remark here that we see no reason why deduction is not as important a method as induction, since the mind is certainly an important factor in all knowledge. Then again, Idealism may be accused of vanity, in its conclusion that mind is the creator of all things; that the Supreme Spirit is all-inclusive. Finally, a theory which attempts to find an explanation for everything is subject to suspicion. It reduces all existence to too much simplicity, when as a matter of fact, the world is quite complex. These and similar objections are included in a new theory of philosophy, to which many of the contemporary thinkers subscribe—we refer to Neo-Realism.   We shall defer a discussion of this doctrine, until we have first briefly examined Pragmatism and Intuitionism.

CHAPTER III

1. *John Dewey. (1859–   )*

PRAGMATISM is a movement in philosophy with which
William James and John Dewey are primarily associated.
Both urge that we turn away from the established, traditional
systems of thought, especially from rationalism and abso-
lutism, and direct our attention to the practical consequences
that may ensue from our actions. John Dewey says, a true
philosophy becomes an outlook upon future possibilities, attempting to attain the better and to avert the worse. The
old tradition that philosophy deals with reality must be abandoned. In its stead philosophy must take its stand with
science. Science maintains that the difference between true
and false is only in the mode of treatment, not in fixity of
existence. Similarly, a pragmatic philosophy makes the Self
not something that views objects and events as fixed existences
from the outside, but as part and parcel of the course of events.
Knowing thus comes to mean anticipating. Pragmatism is
a philosophy that affords guidance to our actions. Under
this theory, to know means the act, aided by our foresight of
the possible consequences, of securing or averting such results. Intelligence here means a creative intelligence, a mind
whose function it is to free experience from caprice, to tie up
our past experiences with the new and the novel. From this
point of view, the pragmatic intelligence considers that idea
true just in so far as it helps to perform a marriage function
between our existing experience represented by the idea and
other parts of our experiences. This is the instrumental view

of truth, that an idea is true if it works, if it produces the desired result, if it does link up experiences satisfactorily.

This instrumental view is taught by Dewey in conjunction with Schiller, although Schiller's particular brand is known as "Humanism," meaning that the true idea must serve human interests only. According to this view, even the most ancient truths were once plastic, they became true in so far as they tied together still earlier experiences and what in those days were considered novel. Truth, therefore, means to bring about such practical consequences as will be beneficial. To argue with the traditional philosophers that truth is independent, static, absolute, is not only meaningless, but the query also is, What function does the idea then perform? John Dewey has developed this theory of Pragmatism quite extensively in modern times, and at present it has become a social pragmatism, signifying that that belief is true which works for the great majority of people. Only social experiment can verify such an idea or belief. From this angle, tenets of religion, ethics, and of other phases of human life, "are to be judged true or false according to what social experience teaches as to their beneficial effect upon mankind."

Let us now turn to a more detailed consideration of the philosophy of William James.

2. *William James. (1842–1910.)*

William James states that Pragmatism is derived from a Greek word, meaning action, from which our word practical comes. Mr. Charles Peirce introduced it first into philosophy by his article entitled "How to make Our Ideas Clear," published in 1878. He points out that our beliefs and ideas are rules for action, meaning to effect certain practical consequences. James borrows this conception and develops what we shall now discuss as his theory of Pragmatism.

Pragmatism, James asserts, is a method of study as well as a theory of truth. As a method it signifies "the attitude of looking away from first things, principles, categories, supposed necessities; and of looking towards last things, fruits, consequences, facts." [1]   James continues, Pragmatism "means the open air and possibilities of nature, as against dogma, artificiality, and the pretense of finality in truth." This type of philosophy, in his opinion, is best suited for our temperaments, for philosophy is a question of temperament, no matter how much we try to disguise it. We have had, he says, the tender-minded and the tough-minded in our schools of philosophy. Under the first we may classify those who are rationalistic, intellectualistic, optimistic, idealistic, religious, indeterministic, monistic, dogmatical. Under the latter category we have those who are empirical, sensationalistic, materialistic, pessimistic, irreligious, fatalistic, pluralistic and skeptical. Each disdains the other, but Pragmatism furnishes a middle ground between them.

With these preliminary remarks concerning the method, let us now develop the pragmatic theory of truth. This theory holds that an idea is true if it works, if it effects the practical results it aims to produce. Suppose we stand at a fork of two roads, and we desire to reach a certain inn, the true road is the one which leads us to our goal. Similarly, a belief, to be true, must work. The difference between the true and false consists in this: the true achieves the desired results, the false misleads us. That, James says, is the *cash-value* of the idea. It must be verified by experience in a practical manner. "Those thoughts are true which guide us to beneficial interaction with sensible particulars as they occur, whether they copy these in advance or not. . . . All the sanctions of a law of truth lie in the very texture of experience. Absolute or no absolute, the concrete truth for us will always be that way of thinking in which our various experiences most profitably combine." [2]   Nevertheless, even if an idea or belief possesses cash-value, it may still not be considered true if it clashes with our main body of beliefs. The new idea must conform to the stock in trade our mind already has. But these two tests are still insufficient. The new idea must also

---

[1] "Selected Papers on Philosophy," Chapter X, Page 204.
[2] *Ibid.*, Chapter XI, Page 229.

conform to our ethical, religious, and similar ideals.   But
once it fulfills these three requirements, we may then unhesi-
tatingly label it as pragmatically true.

To supplement this discourse we must consider what influence the pragmatic attitude towards truth exerts upon ethical
and religious beliefs especially.   Pragmatism has no *a priori*
prejudices against theology.   "If theological ideas prove to
have a value for concrete life, they will be true for pragmatism, in the sense of being good for so much.   For how much
more they are true will depend entirely on their relations to
the other truths that also have to be acknowledged." [8]   But
how do we arrive at our ideas of religion or morality?   James
agrees that agnosticism is correct in its assertion that such conceptions are beyond the power of the intellect to discover.
Shall we despair, then, of ever achieving such knowledge?
No; the *will* can aid the intellect in this respect.   William
James develops this idea further.   In situations with which
we are confronted in our daily life, he says, we have the option of adopting or rejecting certain lines of conduct, ideas
and beliefs.   Some of these options (alternative lines of conduct or of thought) are living, forced, and momentous.   In
other words, suppose we are asked whether we believe in
Christianity.   We have the option of affirming or denying
such a dogma.   The question is of living interest to us, in no
way similar to the query whether Buddhism is valid.   That
may be of living interest to the inhabitants of India, but not to
those of the Western world.   Besides, this question is of
momentous import, it concerns us vitally.   Lastly, we are
forced, we are compelled, to choose at once.   We cannot be
indifferent to it.   Therefore, since we must take sides, and
since, because of its very nature, the intellect really cannot
decide this question for us, only one other phase of our
make-up can move us—the will.   "Our passional nature not
only lawfully may, but must, decide an option between propositions, whenever it is a genuine option that cannot by its nature be decided on intellectual grounds; for to say, under

[8] *Ibid.,* Page 213.

such circumstances, 'Do not decide, but leave the question open,' is itself a passional decision—just like deciding yes or no—and is attended with the same risk of losing the truth." [4] Thus, James concludes that genuine options are found in religious and moral beliefs, which cannot be handled by the intellect; this forces us to call upon the "will to believe" or to doubt them.   The most powerful incentive for believing or for doubting is the difference it makes in our concrete life. If believing in God will cause our lives to be richer, fuller and permeated with more confidence, trust and faith, then we should accept such a Being.   The same is true of the belief in free will.   The only consideration then is, What concrete difference does it make to us in our daily life?   James himself is inclined to adopt the affirmative side of both of these doctrines, existence of free will and of God.

That freedom reigns in the universe should be our conviction, because the opposite theory of determinism places us in a dilemma.   Determinism is defined to mean that the parts already laid down in the universe determine those to come. The course of the future is laid out by the past, mechanically; we have no choice in shaping our destiny.   This type of belief results either in pessimism, fatalism, or in romanticism, the feeling that all occurrences are to be judged purely by the subjective emotions we experience as a result.   Neither is healthy, nor truly effective.   To illustrate: Suppose an atrocious crime is committed by one of our fellow humans.   We feel a keen sense of regret at such an occurrence.   If we are determinists, we are faced with this dilemma.   On the one hand, we know that this crime was bound to happen; we have no free play, no choice in our conduct.   On the other hand, our feeling of regret indicates that we desire to avert such a situation. What is the meaning of such a judgment of regret, if we are helpless in the matter?   The escape from this dilemma is, as we have said, either to consider fatalism as the dominant factor in life, which should cause us to shut our eyes to such events, or to assert that even though we can effect no change

[4] "The Will To Believe," Page 11.

in our environment, still all happenings are sources of satisfaction or pain to us subjectively, in our own minds. It becomes immaterial then whether we can, or whether we are unable to, alter conditions. It is doubtless true that either one of these avenues of escape renders us weak, incapable of applying ourselves with the proper zeal and vigor to nature, life. But if we believe in indeterminism, in the fact that there are potentialities in the future which our own efforts may help to actualize, that our coöperation is a potent factor in changing the environment and the life around us; how much more effectual we then become! What zest is added to our conduct if we consider that it is of material importance in the cosmic development around us?

In addition to this belief in free will, James argues for God in a similar manner. Does it matter to us in concrete life whether God does or does not exist? The fact that there is a God does not necessarily prejudice our belief in free will, as some advocates of predestination may argue. True enough, God may know the ultimate outcome of our fate, but in the meantime, we have freedom in our acts and movements. James illustrates this point by citing an example of two chess players. One is an expert and is bound to win; the other is a novice. But even the expert does not know in advance all the moves the novice will make during the game. The application of this to God is obvious.

Such a God, too, would supply the "casuistic" standard for morality. In moral actions we are vitally concerned with the question as to which is the preferable duty to perform. All of our duties are based upon corresponding rights and claims of others. The one valid test to apply, therefore, is to satisfy as many demands of others and to destroy as few as possible. If we admit a God who encourages such a standard, we live more strenuously, we then have an anchor for our morality. To be sure, we need not believe in God, but then we become easy-going in our practical life, we feel that morality is purely a matter of our own creation. The same considerations apply to our belief of whether the world is moral or unmoral at bottom.   The first renders us more firm in our moral life, we feel that our conduct is tied up with reality; the other leaves things hanging in the air, and we may become soft, as we have just mentioned.

This belief in God yields even greater practical consequences.   All our reflex action, continues James, consists of sense impressions, reflection and action.   In short, the sensory impression exists for the sake of awakening the central processes of reflection, and these processes in turn call forth the final act.   Thus perception and thought exist only for the sake of our behavior in the external world.   That theory supports Theism.   In order that the universe may appeal to us so that we may react to it effectively and thus obtain the richest results, it must be rational.   We must feel at home in it.   Rationality, as we have seen previously, means peace of mind, and a feeling of security.   Therefore, anything short of God is irrational, because we do not feel at home.   Anything beyond God is impossible, because it means that God is not a power outside of us, but a part of us, or a fusion.   Under such a conception, our religious energy is not released, it does not aid us in our practical life.   We must, therefore, conclude that the theistic idea of a God as the deepest power in the universe, with the characteristics of a mental personality, does make a difference to us in life and in our actions in this world.

Such a theistic belief aids greatly in making "life worth living."   We need not concern ourselves with the optimist, who looks upon life cheerfully and hopefully.   We must address ourselves to the pessimist.   We must relieve his despair by discarding natural religion and by appealing to his fighting and hating instincts.   Natural religion, which conceives of God as manifesting Himself exclusively through nature, renders us pessimistic, indeed.   Does not nature raise havoc on numerous occasions?   Does it not cause suffering to the innocent, and often give pleasure to the guilty?   Nature as such is unmoral.   We must postulate a supernatural world, in which the suffering endured in this existence will

have the proper significance.   Science, insisting that this natural realm is the only one existent, has not the final word.
We have a right to let loose our religious instincts by the
former hypothesis.   Religious faith is just as legitimate a
belief as any scientific theory.   Then again, we must appeal
to the pessimist's own fighting proclivities.   We must say to
him: Fight your own battle, eliminate all the evil with which
you personally are confronted; let the rest of the world take
care of itself.   In this manner, life is made worth living,
indeed.

3. Conclusion.

To conclude: Pragmatism is a type of philosophy which is
not concerned with metaphysical issues, regarded as barren,
but with the way of knowing concrete truth.   Truth is plastic,
fluid.   It is concerned vitally with the practical consequences
which will ensue as a result of adopting one or the other of
two beliefs.   The mind becomes an organ, an instrument for
living, not merely for contemplating passively the panorama
of events.   We feel that some of the objections leveled
against this theory of truth are untenable.   One such criticism is made by Professor Hocking.   He says: "Suppose two
men receive at the bank in exactly similar bags the same
number of new coins; and, suppose that, without knowing it
each takes the other's bag.   Pragmatically, there is nothing
to shake the belief that each has the bag given him.   Are these
beliefs then true?" [5]   We answer, Why is the pragmatic conclusion not true?   What difference does it really make who
gets which bag, if by our premise, there is such perfect identity, that they may be interchanged.   The same consideration
may be applied to many of the other polemics directed against
James.   But in certain instances, Pragmatism is subject to
severe criticism.   If we agree with James, that we have the
choice to believe in, or to deny, the existence of God, even if
we adopt such a belief, it is still a God of our own creation.
Hence, what kind of God does Pragmatism yield?   The

[5] "Types of Philosophy," by William Ernest Hocking, Chapter X, Page 162.

same is true of any ethical ideal, which our will formulates. Again we subscribe to a creature of our own making; what is that but self-hypnosis?   Clearly, a most unattractive, as well as unsatisfying, hypothesis.

In spite of these comments, Pragmatism is a refreshing doctrine.   It attributes to the intellect a creative function; it urges that mind be the moulder of experience.   It runs counter to rationalism, which makes the intelligence a passive spectator, a mere container of experience, not the heroic shaper of the destiny of our lives.   Furthermore, while it agrees with agnosticism as to the inability of the intellect to ascertain certain truths, nevertheless, it urges that the will aid the intellect to attain such understanding.   Whether or not we believe in the intellect's lack of power to achieve this, alone and unaided, depends on our own philosophic temperaments.   Idealists clearly deny such agnostic assertions.

In conjunction with this pragmatic assertion that we must invoke the help of will in the discovery of truth, we next turn to a discussion of another philosophy, likewise interested in finding a method of discovering truth, which the intellect is reputed to be powerless to achieve—we refer to Intuitionism, expounded by Henri Bergson.

CHAPTER IV

HENRI BERGSON (1859–   )

INTUITIONISM

1. *Intuitionism versus Science.*

THROUGHOUT the history of thought, philosophers have invoked the aid of intuition to help them attain truth otherwise supposedly inaccessible by the ordinary channels of conceptual knowledge.   They felt that intuitive conclusions have more certainty and are far more reliable than mere logical thinking.   Intuition, or an immediate or direct perception, carries with it, in their opinion, such indubitable, incontrovertible conviction, that demonstrative support becomes not only useless, but must actually be relegated to an inferior position.   Plato introduces it to enable the philosopher kings to grasp the World of Ideas, and especially the Idea of the Good, directly, without the intervention of mathematical demonstration.

Plotinus, the mystic, clearly relies on intuition to visualize the spiritual unity in the world.   The Scholastics emphasize faith or feeling as a most important organ of understanding.   In modern philosophy, it is far from neglected.   Descartes employs it to reach the knowledge of the Self—a most essential intuition for Idealism.   Spinoza says that by means of this intuitive knowledge, we grasp the essence of the whole of nature.   It yields the "Intellectual Love of God," so famous in his philosophy.   Locke, too, arrives at the nature of the Self by means of intuition.   When we consider Kant and the German School of Idealism, we find it in the foreground, indeed.   Kant develops the Critique of Judgment exhaustively to show what feeling achieves in the way of arriving at the union between the mechanical and the teleological realms of the universe. Schelling calls it the "organon of philosophy"; Schopenhauer develops his entire thought of the "World as Will," based not upon the intellectual analysis of nature, which appears to us as our own ideas and impressions of it, but upon intuition, which penetrates within the phenomenal region, furnishing us with the clew to its essential characteristic—Will.

Bergson, therefore, does not undertake a novel task when he attempts to found a system of thought upon this faculty of feeling, of intuition. At the same time, he does succeed in developing it more exhaustively than his predecessors, and his contrast of it with scientific analysis deserves great consideration. Bergson says that there are two ways of knowing a thing: We may move around the object or we may enter into it. The first depends upon the point of view at which we are placed, and upon the symbols we use to express our meaning. The second is a unique process, dependent on neither of these. The first yields relative knowledge, the second, absolute. The first is science, the second, intuition. Intuition is the "sympathetic intelligence" by which we enter into the object, by which we identify ourselves with it, by which we feel its pulse, by which we view it from within, by which, in short, we reach what he terms, the absolute, the unique characteristics of the object. On the other hand, science, by analysis, views the object from without, represents the parts by symbols, employs concepts to convey its meaning, must fix its attention upon various aspects of the object from different points of view. The difference in the mode of treatment is evident. The first, which is metaphysics, yields knowledge of the object in its wholeness, in its uniqueness; it yields the real duration of the object, the real motion, the real element of time with which the object is concerned, the real change that occurs in it. The scientific method is relative, abstract, partial, external. Science cannot give a true picture of motion or of duration. We remember how Zeno, the disciple of

Parmenides, attempted to prove that no combination of a series of points of rest, as evidenced by the flight of the arrow, could yield real motion.   He concluded, therefore, that our sensations are illusory.   Bergson employs a similar argument to show that real motion must be grasped only by intuition. Physics must use concepts, which are static; such concepts, if they should change constantly, would then be rendered useless for scientific purposes.   No concept of motion yields real movement.   All that we may represent by way of symbols, in the motion of a horse, for example, is simply the different positions of rest it occupies at different points; the kinematograph fuses these points, giving us the illusion of continuous motion.   But the only real method of arriving at this is by viewing the horse's movements from within, grasping the continuous movement first, and later dividing it into discontinuous parts, for purposes of analysis.   At this point, we must not be misled as to the intentions of Bergson. He does not deny that science has a legitimate reason for using symbols, concepts for its analysis; that is the only method by which it can develop and become serviceable to us in practical life.   All he contends is that metaphysics is the only way by which to grasp the real, the unique.   Up to this time, he claims, we have attempted to reconstruct an object from its parts; this is the function of science.   Now we must reverse the process, and derive the parts after we have grasped the unity of the object.   The latter is not only more effective, but also the only true procedure.   To illustrate: If after we have visited Paris, we examine certain sketches taken of its various parts, we find it easy to reconstruct the city as we viewed it, but no number of sketches, even of the most minute details, can give us a picture of the true city, if we have never been there.   No amount of all the qualities that an author contributes to his hero can ever be equivalent to the simple feeling, which we experience, if we identify ourselves with the hero, himself.   As it is, all the traits belonging to him are only symbols and points of view, they place us outside of him, they point out things he has in common with others. "Coincidence with the person himself would alone give us the unique, the absolute, in him."

2. *The Self.*

But do we find any confirmation of such intuitive knowledge? Bergson answers in our knowledge of the Self. Our Self, which endures, is at least one reality which we seize from within, without symbols. In our contemplation of our own Self, we first sense all the perceptions it possesses of the material world. Then we find the memories which serve to interpret the perceptions. Finally, we perceive the tendencies and motor habits, virtual actions. These form the "frozen surface," but beneath it, we find the most unique continuous flux; in the succession of mental states, no one of them begins or ends, they all merge into one another. No matter, continues Bergson, what ingenious imagery we may employ to represent this inner life, we shall always omit something; in short, we must conclude that it is beyond symbolic description. We are no more successful in describing it by concepts, by abstract ideas. Concepts may be employed only as tools of intuition, but never as a substitute. Our Self is both a multiplicity and a unity, yet it is not merely a combination; intuition yields its uniqueness, transcending any conceptual representation. From this angle, we see how such intuitive knowledge of the Self removes the dispute between empiricism and rationalism. The empiricist seeking the Ego between the gaps of the psychological states, fills them with more mental states, and the Ego approaches zero, yielding the conception held by Hume; the rationalists, seeking for the Ego in the mental states, abstractly ascribe unity to it, without clothing it with the concrete coloring it deserves. This type of unity is the same as a table or any other object may be said to possess. Intuition, however, identifies the Ego with neither, nor with the union of both; yet it does recognize both. Under such a view, the argument between these schools becomes meaningless.

The method of intuition with reference to the Self shows

how it applies to everything else in the world.   All objects or things which endure, which possess motion, which undergo changes, possess unique characteristics which can be grasped only by "sympathetic intelligence," although they may also be subject to scientific analysis.   Bergson concludes that all of nature is alive, that behind the frozen material surface, there is a continuous pulse of life, of motion, and that we may seize it from within, intuitively.   This pulse, this *élan vital*, continually goes on creating.   This is somewhat similar, as we have already seen, to Schopenhauer's will, but with this exception.   Schopenhauer contends that there is no creation, for all has existed from the very beginning, but it is uncovered before us gradually.   Bergson's vital impulse does create, as it courses through nature.   Such a conception of life clearly argues for freedom.   Science may divide time into successive stages, hence the preceding cause is followed by a succeeding effect, but in Bergson's view, real time cannot be so divided; life, of which time and motion are indispensable qualities, has no line of demarcation between past, present and future, they all merge into one another; therefore, causation is inapplicable, freedom becomes the dominant factor.

No doubt there is a great deal of merit in Bergson's emphasis upon the fact that intuition is the one effective method by which we may grasp the uniqueness of the Self.   To be sure, empiricists like Hume, and advocates of other systems of thought, among whom we may number William James, assert that no amount of introspection yields any more than a plurality of mental states.   Most of us are inclined, however, to believe that the Ego must consist of more than that, it must enter into a relation with its manifold experiences of objects, therefore, it must possess some characteristics over and above them.   While some philosophers argue that we reach this knowledge by means other than intuition, Bergson's method is as good as, if not superior to, their suggestions.   The fact, however, that the Self is thus known does not of itself give Bergson the right to assume that nature throughout is alive.   True enough, the letters and words used in a poem are expressions of the living author. We may, then, perhaps by analogy show that behind the material objects in the universe, there is a flux of life. Still, this is by no means as convincing an argument, as in the case of the Self. The Idealist, too, strikes analogies between himself and what must necessarily be the essence of the external world. Thus far, then, Bergson is initiating nothing new. Of course, he contends that we can grasp such a vital impulse at the core of nature, intuitively, but even he admits that it is an extremely difficult task. The upshot of the whole matter, then, is that he now dethrones intuition and seeks the aid of conceptual, logical knowledge, in order to arrive, in Schopenhauer's manner, at the underlying pulse of the cosmos.

3. *Conclusion.*

Thus far Idealism and Intuitionism agree; both feel that the Self is an entity, both contend that the world is alive, both also assert that freedom prevails, which in turn expresses itself externally through mechanical laws, conceived as habits of the cosmic life, similar to the habitual modes of conduct we develop in our lives. But now they come to a parting of the ways. Bergson relegates the intellect, with its conceptual and symbolic representations, to a place of secondary importance. Intuition employs these, but they are only its servants. To support this view Bergson dwells on the impossibility of building a continuity out of the discontinuous divisions, which is so vital to intellectual processes. The idealist, however, presses this point. The mere fact that Bergson holds the discontinuous to differ from the continuous shows that he already has a concept of what continuous means. In our opinion, this is not a persuasive argument. We all observe that finite objects exist in the world. We denominate them finite in contrast to the infinite, yet no one seriously contends that we have a definite concept of infinity. Still the contrast is legitimately made. Moreover, Bergson may begin with the intuitive perception of continuity, which gives him the uniqueness of motion, change, duration; then, he legitimately may demonstrate that the discontinuous points of motion do not yield what his intuition already furnished.   In that event, he need have no concept of continuity, he merely uses the expression to denote what he means negatively.   Bergson admits that we must use concepts to communicate our thoughts and ideas, but so do we use letters of the alphabet.   No one seriously contends that the letters *per se* are constituent elements of the thought of the poem, or of the hero described therein.   No more are the concepts employed in a description of nature characteristic of the life that flows throughout nature.

To conclude: The last two theories discussed, Pragmatism and Intuitionism, are really not exhaustively metaphysical in their nature.   They are ways of knowing, of reaching truth, which the intellect, in the agnostic sense, is unable faithfully to represent.   Pragmatism calls upon the will, and Intuitionism, upon the faculty of feeling, to offer their help.   It would appear that it is rather artificial to draw a line of demarcation between the three compartments of the human make-up —reason, will and feeling.   After all, by what process can we put our finger on the boundary beyond which each of these cannot go?   After all, do they not coalesce, do they not merge into one another?   Our conclusion is that the rational part of our constitution is the master, that it is the faculty of understanding, the organ of research employed in metaphysical investigation.   It must necessarily invoke the aid of all the weapons at its disposal, nevertheless it is still in control and should not be deposed from its citadel.

We have just mentioned that Bergson is of great help to Idealism.   This theory, as we have seen, is a comprehensive metaphysics, explaining mind and its external manifestation, body.   It is conducive to a better kind of ethics, to a better comprehension of the cosmos, to a more rational understanding of our relation to the underlying reality.   It adds dignity to us as humans, it extols the mind, by which we are differentiated from brutes, it does not clash with science to any extent, on that account.   It offers unlimited opportunities for the realization of the infinite possibilities of the human soul. It puts us on our mettle to effect such changes in the world as may have universal significance, for it impresses us with the fact that we are capable of such action. In spite of these laudable qualities, Idealism has in recent years been subjected to criticism by a new school of philosophy, Neo-Realism, to a consideration of which we shall now turn our attention.

CHAPTER V

Neo-Realism

1. *Relation to Naïve Realism, Dualism and Subjectivism.*

REALISM is a doctrine of philosophy to which many of the leading contemporary British and American thinkers subscribe. While we recognize that it is neither the best, nor the most profitable, procedure to group philosophers under one school of thought, in view of the divergent opinions they represent, yet we must realize that it is not within the scope of a book of this kind to treat in detail each man's individual views. It is therefore with reluctance and with the realization of the inadequacy of the statement that we point out that among the advocates of realism, the following may be mentioned as contributing to a greater or lesser degree:—Edwin B. Holt, William P. Montague, Ralph Barton Perry, George Santayana, Bertrand Russell, A. N. Whitehead, and many others.

The new realism is historically related to naïve realism, dualism and subjectivism. Naïve realism, or what may be termed the common-sense view of the world, considers objects as directly presented to the mind. Appearances constitute reality, noumena have no room for existence. Unfortunately, we find error, illusion, in this realm which this theory is unable to explain adequately. Dualism, therefore, comes to the rescue, and by dividing the world into mind and matter, conceives of the mind as the seat of all illusions, fancies, dreams and similar fantasies. It is further considered as a potent factor in the creation of mental images. From that, the transition is easily made to subjective idealism or the Berkeleyan type of philosophy. The mind now constitutes the originator of all things; once we admit its existence, the rest of nature is unfolded with great ease. But this assumes that we possess a unitary, spiritual Ego; when a question is raised about the composition of self-consciousness, whether it is an identical substance or made up of a plurality of mental experiences, subjectivism falls to the ground. This, of course, is aside from the argument of solipsism which, as we have shown, is a most fatal objection to such a theory. Neo-Realism, therefore, again attempts to formulate a philosophy which harks back to naïve realism; at the same time it strives to correct the defects which the primitive theory had been unable to remedy.

2. *Its Aims.*

Neo-Realism thus undertakes to perform two functions— to attack the traditional philosophic conceptions, and then to furnish a doctrine of its own by which the world can be explained and thoroughly understood. As to the first, it directs its polemic primarily against subjectivism, because it is the final step logically proceeding from naïve realism, as we have just seen. Yet we must not lose sight of the fact that this new realism must clear the ground of all other features which it considers objectionable. Therefore, besides criticisms like "ego-centric predicament" and "fallacy of definition by initial predication," leveled against subjectivism, which we have already discussed under the philosophy of Berkeley, we shall now turn to a consideration of some of the other aims it desires to accomplish.

Neo-Realism asserts that traditional philosophy may be charged with "pseudo-simplicity." The moment something can be reduced to a simple datum, philosophy assumes that it must be valid. Under this fallacy, we find conceptions of will, soul, life, in idealism, and matter, in naturalism. Then again, systems of thought assume that certain terms belong exclusively to them. Materialism insists that bodily events are its particular province, but we know that such events have no meaning unless they are connected with other things which are not physical in nature, such as time, place, number. Moreover, philosophies assume that there is an all-pervading principle, which explains the universe and its contents, that there is unity; but this assumption is unwarranted, for we must first discover whether such a principle exists altogether. This untenable hypothesis, known as the "Speculative Dogma," runs through many of the leading systems of thought. Many of the prominent philosophers also assert that because something is self-evident, it is, therefore, of great importance. Idealism offends most in this respect. It assumes that each of us is intuitively aware of our self-existence, hence, it bases an entire system upon this axiomatic principle. But there really is no logical basis for such an assumption, for two of us may differ as to what an object really is, although each one may be absolutely certain that his identification is correct.

Because of such prejudices and unfounded dogmatic assertions, traditional philosophy has erred greatly. It behooves us, therefore, contends the Neo-Realist, to formulate a new program. We must use words most scrupulously, we must define our expressions; we must especially employ analysis to discover reality. We must reduce complexities into the most simple constituents, in order to acquire proper knowledge. We should, as philosophers, call upon logic to aid us in our search for truth, and we may certainly find it easier to reach the proper conclusions, by dividing every question into its various branches. Let us attack one thing at a time and confusion will be put to rout. Moreover, we must not identify philosophical study with the history of philosophy. The latter is important and significant, but the real task is to study each philosophical problem itself, untrammeled by what some great thinker said about it.

3. *Its Program.*

Neo-Realism thus clears the mind of all prepossessions, of all rationalistic methods of thinking, of all Baconian "Idols." It then proceeds to map out a program of its own, allied closely both with common sense and with Greek philosophy, especially as outlined by Plato and Aristotle. With naïve realism it pleads with us to consider the world as we find it. Nature consists of innumerable objects and events. Let us not read any occult meaning into these. Let us not deem it essential to unify this multiplicity, or to consider it as an external manifestation of some noumenon behind the appearances. Among these phenomena we also find consciousness, mind. The latter possesses no more dignity than any other natural event. To be sure, objects are presented to consciousness in the relation of knowledge, but knowledge is simply another event in this real world. From this angle, all factual items in the universe are "neutral entities"; they may belong both to the mental world and to the facts in nature, or, if anything at all, they belong more to nature and not at all to the mind. When the mind sheds its rays, so to speak, upon any portion of experience, the "neutral entities" are then temporarily assimilated in the mind, which enables us to know and to understand them. That, however, does not change their essential character, they still do not depend upon the mind for their existence. This point of view, besides representing the theory of naïve realism, is in accord with the Aristotelian doctrines. Aristotle, too, wants the world to speak for itself. All phenomena are there for what they are worth, they are dependent in their fundamental nature upon nothing else, but upon themselves. God, also, is one object among many, he is not a unifying, all-comprehensive substance or Being, in the theological sense. No Realist objects to any spiritual principle being recognized as existing, provided it does not remove the autonomy of the individual objects in the world.

The upshot of this brief survey is that to Realism objects have an independent existence; they do not require mind to account for their being. In so far as this signifies that we can dispense with the Berkeleyan type of philosophy, whose contention is that the subjective Ego is responsible for all reality, we have no serious quarrel with this theory. Clearly, the external world possesses an independent quality, otherwise, as we have said previously, no social existence is possible. Such a contingency is ruinous and unthinkable. But even as to this, realism finds itself in an extremely embarrassing position. In order to keep to its main thesis, it must not only recognize the "neutrality" of objects in nature, but also of such things as secondary qualities, dreams, images, mirages, hallucinations, general and abstract ideas. In this respect it agrees with Platonic realism, under which Ideas exist in an intelligible realm of their own, not in the mind which conceives them. This too marks a line of demarcation between Neo-Realism and common sense, for the latter would find it difficult indeed to subscribe to such a thought. Still, we present the argument for what it is worth.

But how do we reach such a conception of reality? Not by metaphysical speculation in the traditional manner, not by eliciting all from mind, not by mystical experiences, which are ineffable, but which are nevertheless in the opinion of the mystics the most convincing road to truth, not by any non-scientific ladder, but by logical analysis, by the aid of scientific instrumentalities. Such analysis will lead us as far as possible to the innermost region of reality. Such analysis at present convinces us that the world is pluralistic rather than monistic. It demonstrates that as we progress in the perfection of analytical methods, we shall discover the "facts" of nature; even now we see that no underlying unity is responsible for this universe with its myriad experiences. Besides, if we grant for the sake of argument, that monism is the valid interpretation of what we see before us, it is meaningless. What significance has mind if it occupies the world stage exclusively? If matter or the physical also exists, then by contrast mind denotes something, has meaning, otherwise, not. By way of passing, we may answer the last objection very readily. If the Neo-Realist means that mind evokes no image in our thoughts because mind is solely responsible for the physical (the idealistic thesis) then it is purely tautological. For even Idealism admits that mind expresses itself through the physical, therefore, there is certainly sufficient contrast to render mind full of meaning. Even if we concede, however, that mind reigns supreme in the world, it still is significant, for does it not, in the spiritualistic philosophy, contain all we find in the universe? That is more than sufficient to render mind full of content, hence most pregnant with meaning.

In so far as its emphasis on analysis as the only road to reach reality is concerned, Professor Hocking points out that such analysis has succeeded in reducing the physical realm to its ultimates—atoms, electrons. It has not yet succeeded in reducing thought to such elements. If, therefore, mind is a fact equal to the other facts in the world, why this failure? How account for the utter inability of realism to approach the essential composition of the mind? If we admit, and we are forced to such a conclusion, that it is not the same as matter, then we may even be so bold as to argue that it may be superior to the body, hence we may also suggest that perhaps it is the support of the physical.

4. Conclusion.

Neo-Realism, as we have said, is very subtle, and its supporters are quite ingenious in expounding its theories. They are by no means feazed by the problems which may prove embarrassing to the ordinary thinker. They, therefore, do not evade difficult tasks, but attack problems with great vim. This philosophy is primarily a polemic against traditional thinking. It vigorously attacks subjectivism, but that seems to be wasted effort for the theory has been discredited even by the school of Idealism, which makes use of some of its valid principles. It represents, at first, that it will return to the common-sense view of things, but as we have seen, it ends by making the most exorbitant claims. By insisting upon the independent existence of mirages, hallucinations, errors of judgment, and of similar mental facts, it reverts to Plato, whose World of Ideas must certainly be discarded by practical men, to say nothing of serious thinkers. To say that the content of consciousness, of the type just described, is a fact like time, space and number requires an almost impossible

leap of the imagination.   Its polemic against objective idealism, in denying mind as the substratum of reality, has some
merit, but it has by no means made out a very strong or appealing case.   To argue that all things do not depend upon
mind, because the mind is shown to reach out beyond itself
in knowledge, does not hit the mark.   Objective idealism
admits, that my mind is not the basis of reality; it concedes
the objective existence of the world, hence this view that
knowledge extends beyond the subject's own mind is quite
accurate.

Realism defeats itself by its own argument.   It insists
upon analysis as the method of learning the truth, but it
fails to diagnose mind into the same constituents as body.
To argue here that perhaps in the future we shall succeed in
this attempt avails us nothing, for the fact now remains that
mind and body are not similar in character.   The contention, moreover, that monism is not a true picture of the
world is in the first place nothing remarkably new, nor seriously fatal.   It is comparatively easy to argue for the obvious,
but we have shown that such a pluralistic view leaves many
things unexplained.   It especially does not satisfy us as to the
reason for the harmony that prevails in nature.   Hume, the
pluralist, was forced to reach conclusions about causality, which
led Kant to revise philosophy so that it would furnish us a solid
foundation for planning our life, with some certainty that
the cosmos favors stability and soundness in the future.   In
connection with this pluralism, we raise no question here about
the Realist's view of evil, because it creates no more novel
consideration of the problem than what has already been
discussed under the various philosophies.   To be sure, pluralism accounts for evil as one of the facts in the universe to be
recognized and remedied, if possible; but a monistic philosophy need not despair on that account.   It, too, can explain evil as an element necessary to attain the good, as a
stepping stone by which we can ascend to a more pure and
higher realm.   Our final word must, therefore, be that Realism performs a proper function in pointing out the facts of

the world, in awakening in us that scientific spirit, which it urges us to employ in philosophic research, in again emphasizing the futility of subjective idealism; in short, it does stir us to study nature anew, clearing our minds of all prejudicial tendencies, which may blind us to the unadulterated truth.   At the same time, we submit, that Neo-Realism is far from being a philosophy satisfactory to meet our intellectual demands.

CONCLUSION

THE history of philosophy just presented is an imposing array of thought. The leading figures contributed to it materially—some by developing original ideas; others by eclectic methods, but resulting, nevertheless, in the addition of a clearer exposition; still others, by furnishing a new point of view for existing theories and hypotheses. The Pre-Socratic philosophy clearly indicates the close alliance between it and mathematics. It also demonstrates that the insatiable curiosity of the human mind leads to a keen desire to search for ultimate truth, for the absolute, for the underlying reality. Even at such an early stage of philosophic thought—the dawn of philosophy—a line of demarcation is already established between the two schools which dominate modern thought—those who believe that the phenomenal world is all there is, and those who have faith in a realm of noumena. Heracleitus and Parmenides may be roughly considered as representing such theories. To be sure, metaphysical speculations are in their infancy during this period, but in addition to the exponents of the two leading hypotheses, we also encounter the atomic theory by Democritus, explaining nature by mechanical laws, and the teleological principles expounded by Heracleitus in the Logos, and by Anaxagoras in the Nous. Materialism versus Idealism, mechanism versus teleology, thus confront us at the very origin of the history of philosophic thought.

The Humanists, Socrates and the Sophists, turn away from what they consider idle speculation concerning the composition of nature, and direct their attention to problems affecting human relations. Ethics thus becomes their cardinal doctrine. There is very little to choose between the Protagorean doctrine of "Man is the measure of all things" and the Socratic teaching "Virtue is knowledge." In the one case, the Sophist frankly states an individualistic doctrine, whereas in the other, Socrates, the foe of sophistry, furnishes a common, universal standard for all to follow. At the same time, we must admit that it is each man's own knowledge which is to guide him in his ethical conduct, and since each one's knowledge differs from that of any other individual, each really is the measure of his own conduct. Socrates, however, attempts, theoretically at least, to formulate a universal code of ethics, which is his important contribution. A system of behavior which is individualistic cannot serve society in its collective sense. Philosophy, in its ethical aspect, must recognize that the social interest is, if not paramount, at least equal, to the individual's. Socrates wants to harmonize the two, and while we find it inadequate for our complex system of life, the germ is there. All it needs to flourish is proper nourishment, which was supplied by subsequent thinkers.

The most important Greek contribution to the development of thought, however, is made by Plato and Aristotle. Plato's Realism represented by the World of Ideas influences even one of our contemporary philosophies—Neo-Realism. His conception of two realms of existence is the most comprehensive attempt to harmonize the phenomenal and the noumenal worlds, the mechanical and teleological spheres. His doctrine of Ideas is so impressive that even a thinker of Schopenhauer's type borrows from it. His insistence that the Idea is even more really existing than the visible object exerts the greatest influence upon the Scholastics, all of whom, with but few exceptions, follow this teaching. To them, the Idea of the Church possesses more essential reality than the individual churches, which we see before us. To be sure, his doctrine is eclectic to some degree, but, as a whole, it teems with originality. His theory of creation as an expression of Love and Goodness is as noble a thought as has been devised by the most zealous protagonists of theological beliefs. His idea that number is the essence of the phenomenal world, a conception

originally entertained by Pythagoras, is an indication of the
thought cultivated by philosophers, such as Descartes and
Spinoza, that the mathematical method is the most convincing
approach to the key of the universe.   Plato's arguments for
immortality of the soul are as imposing an array of logical
proofs as has been devised by any other thinker.   His contention that the soul is a simple substance does not meet
with the approval of modern psychology, yet it is a thought
developed later by Descartes.   We find nowhere else finer
expressions of the equality of men and women in all walks of
life, nobler portrayals of communistic life along Utopian lines,
than in Plato.   His theory of the philosopher-king is most
ingenious, and we have no doubt that it would operate to the
great advantage of both the community and its members, if
our political figures were selected from such a class of un-
selfish men and women devoted to the common weal.   In
short, Plato's thoughts along all lines, theoretical and practical, are worthy of great consideration.   While we may discard many of his beliefs as unsuited to our own practical lives,
yet his philosophy stirs our imagination and helps in rousing
us to progress intellectually.

Plato's successor, Aristotle, has his feet more firmly planted
on the ground.   He, too, is a Realist, but of a different type.
His realism is more akin to that of common sense.   We have
only what we see before us, he says.   The particular object
contains form and matter, but no other world exists to help
us in solving puzzles that confront us in nature.   His God,
the Unmoved Mover, is a sort of *deus ex machina*, and is very
helpful to theological thought.   God, away from the world,
is more helpful to the church than Plato's doctrine that the
Idea of the Good permeates the world, which may be crudely
described as pantheism.   Aristotle's insistence upon experiment and observation indicates a line of thought later followed
by Bacon.   His practical bent of mind, displayed especially
in his politics and his ethics, is of greater benefit to us than
that of Plato.   Both, however, do add a great deal to philosophic development.   They are teleological, they insist that

the world is ruled by a principle other than matter, they emphasize that the human, after all, is differentiated from lower brutes by his reason; hence, that must be the ruling faculty. Their influence on subsequent theories has already been discussed on various occasions, and we may conclude that intellectual progress has been immeasurably aided by their contributions.

The Stoics and Epicureans are of chief concern to us because they represent two extremes in moral development. The Stoic considers the human a rational machine, with the ability to eliminate all emotions and instincts; the Epicurean conceives him as a purely physical animal, guided only by the amount of pleasure he can derive from life. Neither is tenable as a working hypothesis. At the same time, these two theories have exerted, and still are exerting, great influence. Stoicism is the cardinal principle of Christian morality, with this exception: Christianity considers emotions of love and pity as interwoven with the virtues, whereas the Stoic relegates virtue to pure reason. As to Epicureanism, what is it but a veiled Utilitarianism? John Stuart Mill believes that the pleasure of others, not the agent's own, is the controlling factor; thus far he is an Epicurean heretic, but the underlying idea that pleasure is the sole motive of conduct is present even in Mill's theory.

Plotinus, the mystic, influenced by Plato, initiates in a comprehensive manner, a movement in philosophy that is still dominant—we refer to mysticism. William James seriously contends that the mystical experience leads us to a vision of the truth, to the Ineffable One, who has no substitute. This type of philosophy has prevailed for many ages and is even at present dominant among some who believe that through the mystical experience they behold unity where there appears only multiplicity, both to the naked eye and to the theoretical understanding.

This brief discussion amply demonstrates that Greek philosophy gives impetus to many of the movements subsequently developed in the history of thought. We discover in it the germs of idealism, materialism, realism, mechanism, teleology; we find in it the various doctrines of ethical realization, the line of demarcation between phenomenon and noumenon, arguments for immortality, and certain conceptions of God's relation to the world.   But when we reach the Medieval Era, we must admit that the results are barren, indeed.   It is more noteworthy for its negative than for its positive results. By placing faith on a pedestal, by dogmatically asserting that its beliefs must be accepted without argument, it inevitably leads the mind to turn from it with dissatisfaction and to direct its attention to finding a logical foundation for the acceptance, or for the rejection, of tenets it is inclined to consider.   Thus the Renaissance comes into being.   "Reason must displace faith" is the battle cry now.   This leads to the period of modern philosophy.

We are now confronted with the controversy between Rationalism and Empiricism.   The Rationalists, Descartes, Spinoza and Leibniz, emphasize the crying need for eliciting all from the mind.   The Empiricists, Bacon, Locke, and Hume, have the mind fix its attention upon experience.   The first yields a container without a content; the second, a content without a container.   Kant then appears on the horizon.   He desires to pacify both of these contestants.   He, therefore, calls upon mind and upon experience to share in knowledge. But he builds better than he plans.   His doctrine, although it theoretically allows some room for the existence of the phenomenal world, the thing-in-itself, yet practically, reduces the sensible world to nothing.   Hence German Idealism is the final result.

Throughout this development of philosophy we encounter certain waves of thought.   At first, the human, proud of his mental faculties, is eager to study logically reality, truth, ethical necessity, with the exclusive aid of the theoretical understanding.   But this leads to the vain assumption by the mind that it is the final arbiter in all matters.   It attributes to the understanding too much power.   A revulsion then sets in, and the human turns to another source of inspiration.   It may consist of faith, or mysticism. That, in turn, after being entrenched for some length of time, assumes too much for itself, becomes too dogmatic, and reason is again substituted. The understanding now comes to the fore and this is the result: Skeptics point out the impossibility of attaining certain knowledge by mind alone, hence empiricism looks for aid from the observation of events in the world. Later, idealism attempts to reconcile conflicting interests, but the scientifically inclined minds prefer to treat of the world as material. This leads us once more to naturalism. This theory points out that certain regions of reality the intellect cannot penetrate. What is the result but agnosticism? This does not please many who feel that agnosticism is no explanation whatever. They, therefore, seek for some other element that may aid in the search for truth. Thus we call upon the will or upon intuition to lend us encouragement. We may also retrace our steps to show that logic can still be effective to offset the objectional features of Idealism, even though it has not succeeded as yet in penetrating all regions of reality. That is the theory of Neo-Realism, whereas the former beliefs are represented by Pragmatism and by Bergson's Intuitionism. The final word has by no means been written to philosophic development. In this lies the salvation of human thought and of human cultural development.

In the midst of this profusion of thought, in the midst of this wealth of philosophic material, is it surprising that many of us are unable to determine what course to pursue? Is it any wonder that we find it extremely difficult to decide upon a philosophy to which we may anchor our apparently disjointed daily acts, which, however, must be bound up in some form to make them the constituents of a rational life? We may approach the selection and adoption of a philosophy in two ways: We may do so with hostility, determined in advance to reject all philosophy, relegating it to the realm of the purely theoretical, the fantastic product of still more fanciful dreamers, bearing no relation to life. We may, then, with an air of sophistication reject philosophic guidance entirely, and in support of this attitude point out many inconsistencies, irrelevancies and contradictions in the various systems under consideration.   Such weaknesses may readily be encountered in any theory which deals with such comprehensive subjects as the universe, life, ethics, politics.   To attack a foe at his weakest point may appear unsportsmanlike, but it is fine strategy. This may be applied to the attack against a philosophic formulation of an adequate explanation of reality.   But such rejection is "easier said than done."   It may appear relatively easy to abandon philosophy, but as a matter of fact, it is the most difficult of tasks.   The most important thing about any individual is his philosophy, his plan of life, the central theme of his prosaic and of his ideal existence.   Philosophy tickles us; it is big, it is important, it is life.   Our temperaments are vital factors in our choice of a philosophy, but aside from that, we do want *some* philosophic guidance.   If, in spite of these considerations, some are still disinclined to dwell upon such an important phase in our intellectual development, then we do not meet on common ground.   In that event, we cannot address ourselves to such individuals on this subject at all.

On the other hand, we may approach philosophy with a spirit of friendliness, with a spirit of coöperation, with a sincere and ardent wish to be enlightened.   We feel that an aimless life is worthless, that unless we have a goal sufficiently momentous to accord with our human ability and aspirations, we are no better than the lower brutes.   We then are eager to examine the various philosophic theories to discover what is best suited for us, besides learning which is nearer to the truth, so far as such truth can be verified.   With this spirit, we become convinced that even metaphysics, to say nothing of the other divisions of philosophy, instead of consisting of webs spun by fanatical theorists, is a most essential and indispensable element in life.   Under these circumstances we have not only the right but the duty to address ourselves to this class, and to suggest perhaps some help by which they may find it easier to reach a decision.   The first question now is, What metaphysics should we prefer?   We have already shown that Naturalism and Idealism are the only two real, metaphysical theories—the other systems being essentially and primarily interested in discovering methods of reaching truth. We have further seen the bases for each, the logic of each, and how adequately each explains all the problems confronting us.   With this in mind we may ask each member of the class of those who desire to be disciples of a philosophic school: Which do you prefer?   Do you want a world of unity, in which multiplicity, nevertheless, has a proper place, or are you looking for a pluralistic realm with no unity?   Do you want mind to be the basis of the universe, or matter to be more fundamental?   Will you feel more human if your actions are freely determined if your actions are the product of a will which inheres in a universal Will, or do you prefer to be considered as a mere cog in this material world, swayed by forces not under your control, possessing no more freedom than the lowest animal, or the atom of inanimate nature?   Admittedly, if there were a demonstrative proof to show which of these hypotheses is the only true explanation, such a pragmatic attitude would be utterly misplaced, but since the subject matter is not of the scientific type, and, because of its universality and comprehensiveness, does not lend itself to mathematical proof, we must adopt that metaphysic which will aid us to fashion our entire career more rationally than if we adopted some other scheme.

We may here offer the suggestion that even judging by this criterion, the idealistic metaphysics appears to be the more desirable hypothesis.   It explains body as the expression of mind, it adds to our dignity as humans by endowing our souls with infinite potentialities for realization, it has something to say about God, more in accordance with our fervent hopes, and yet lacking the anthropomorphic characteristics of religious theories, it offers an explanation for immortality, it attributes to us free will, it adds significance to us as rational souls in a rational world.   In spite of all these advantages, it does not fly in the face of science, it yields to science that which belongs to it; it does not represent God as a creator, in the deistic sense, it argues for the newer teleology, in which the purpose within is manifested by mechanism without; in short, it offers many benefits with few disadvantages.   Idealism, too, broadens the horizon for ethical development; it limits the religious influence, but yet it does not outrage its principal tenets.   Some of us may argue that idealism is untenable, that the external facts in nature do not permit such an interpretation, that it is preferable to live in a world of reality rather than in a world of illusion.   True enough, if we sincerely feel that way about it; but, one of the salient considerations here is, How do we know that the facts do not warrant an idealistic interpretation?   Of two possible alternatives, if they are equally undemonstrable, why not select that one which may go far afield for an explanation, but which yet satisfies us more adequately?   If the scientific thinker feels that idealism would make him relegate explanations to an "asylum of ignorance," which will materially interfere with his work; or if a layman thinks that naturalism is the only theory which will render him self-reliant, by all means, let him adopt naturalism.   We are addressing ourselves to those who are vacillating and who are eager to acquire an hypothesis which will tend to help and encourage them more than any other.   To these we say that the idealistic metaphysics seems, even by the pragmatic test, to be the more desirable, to possess more utility.   The mere fact that intellectually it satisfies our craving for mental peace and satisfaction, because of its synthetic conclusions, because it makes less of a mystery of mind and life, because it allows room for the possibility of a future life, in itself bolsters up these practical considerations.   We must not, however, be charged with applying a shallow test to the adoption of one or of the other of these theories; we admit that we must sincerely apply ourselves to learn the truth embodied in each by considerations other than mere utilitarian applications.   We simply urge each and every one to be favorably disposed to a metaphysics, because it makes a concrete difference in life. We also urge that although agnosticism may be a legitimate result of a certain type of reasoning, it is not on that account either profitable or helpful.　Let us get away from the Spencerian type of philosophy; the Unknowable may be a term with some connotation, but it does not add much to knowledge or to conduct.　Let us also regard metaphysics as a real factor in our lives; let us consider an explanation of the cosmos as something vital, as a central thread, which may appreciably help us to mould our careers.　Let us, in short, desire a philosophy, and let us select that one which not only intellectually but also practically yields the greatest benefit.

BIBLIOGRAPHY

R. B. Perry. *The Approach to Philosophy.*
R. B. Perry. *Defence of Philosophy.*
R. B. Perry. *Modern Philosophical Tendencies.*
A. K. Rogers. *Student's History of Philosophy.*
A. Weber and R. B. Perry. *History of Philosophy.*
F. Thilly. *History of Philosophy.*
Alfred William Benn. *Early Greek Philosophy.*
C. M. Bakewell. *Source Book in Ancient Philosophy.*
B. A. G. Fuller. *History of Greek Philosophy, Thales to De-mocritus.*
B. A. G. Fuller. *Sophists, Socrates, Plato.*
B. A. G. Fuller. *Aristotle.*
A. E. Taylor. *Plato.*
A. E. Taylor. *Aristotle.*
G. L. Dickinson. *The Greek View of Life.*
Plato. *The Republic,* trans. by H. Spens.
Plato. *Dialogues,* trans. by Jowett.
Plato. *Selections, Modern Student's Library* (Scribner's) by Raphael Demos.
Aristotle. *Nicomachean Ethics,* trans. by D. P. Chase.
J. L. Stocks. *Aristotelianism.*
W. D. Ross. *Aristotle.*
Aristotle. *Selections, Modern Student's Library* (Scribner's) by W. D. Ross.
Epictetus. *Moral Discourses.*
Marcus Aurelius. *Meditations.*
Lucretius. *On the Nature of Things.*   (De Rerum Natura.)
R. D. Hicks. *Stoic and Epicurean.*
W. D. Hyde. *Five Great Philosophies of Life.*
Henry Thomas Buckle. *History of Civilization in England.*
M. De Wulf. *Mediaeval Philosophy.*
Joseph Rickaby. *Scholasticism.*
Descartes. *Discourse upon Method.*
Descartes. *Meditations.*
Descartes. *Selections, Modern Student's Library* (Scribner's) by Ralph M. Eaton.

SPINOZA. *Ethics.*

SPINOZA. *Selections, Modern Student's Library* (Scribner's) by John Wild.

JOSEPH RATNER. *The Philosophy of Spinoza.*

LEIBNIZ. *Monadology,* trans. by Robert Latta.

HOBBES. *The Leviathan.*

BACON. *Novum Organum.*

LOCKE. *An Essay Concerning Human Understanding.*

LOCKE. *Two Treatises of Government.*

BERKELEY. *A Treatise Concerning the Principles of Human Knowledge.*

BERKELEY. *Theory of Vision and Other Writings.*

HUME. *The Treatise of Human Nature.*

HUME. *An Enquiry Concerning Human Understanding.*

HUME. *The Dialogues Concerning Natural Religion.*

HUME. *Selections, Modern Student's Library* (Scribner's) by Chas. W. Hendel, Jr.

THOMAS HUXLEY. *Ethics and Evolution.*

FRIEDRICH PAULSEN. *Introduction to Philosophy.*

BERTRAND RUSSELL. *Scientific Method in Philosophy.*

BERTRAND RUSSELL. *The Problems of Philosophy.*

JOSIAH ROYCE. *Spirit of Modern Philosophy.*

JOSIAH ROYCE. *Philosophy of Loyalty.*

WILLIAM E. HOCKING. *Man and the State.*

WILLIAM E. HOCKING. *The Meaning of God in Human Experience.*

WILLIAM E. HOCKING. *Types of Philosophy.*

WILLIAM JAMES. *The Will to Believe and Other Essays.*

WILLIAM JAMES. *Selected Papers on Philosophy.*

WILLIAM JAMES. *Pragmatism.*

WILLIAM JAMES. *Some Problems of Philosophy.*

HENRI BERGSON. *Time and Free Will.*

HENRI BERGSON. *An Introduction to Metaphysics.*

HENRI BERGSON. *Creative Evolution.*

R. F. A. HOERNLE. *Idealism as a Philosophy.*

AUGUSTE COMTE. *Positive Philosophy.*

JOHN STUART MILL. *Utilitarianism, Liberty and Representative Government.*

JOHN DEWEY. *Reconstruction in Philosophy. Need for a Recovery in Philosophy* (Essay).

JOHN DEWEY and JAMES H. TUFTS. *Ethics.*

F. C. S. SCHILLER. *Humanism.*

KANT. *Critique of Pure Reason.*

KANT. *Critique of Practical Reason.*
KANT. *Critique of Judgment.*
KANT. *Selections, Modern Student's Library* (Scribner's) by T. M. Greene.
KANT. *Metaphysic of Morality,* trans. by John Watson
KANT. *Prolegomena,* trans. by Paul Carus.
A. D. LINDSAY. *The Philosophy of Kant.*
HEGEL. *The Logic of Hegel,* by W. Wallace.
HEGEL. *Philosophy of Right,* trans. by S. W. Dyde.
HEGEL. *Philosophy of History,* trans. by J. Sibree.
HEGEL. *Selections, Modern Student's Library* (Scribner's) by J. Loewenberg.
SCHOPENHAUER. *The World as Will and as Idea.*
SCHOPENHAUER. *Selections, Modern Student's Library* (Scribner's) by DeWitt H. Parker.
RAND. *Modern Classical Philosophers.*
ERNST HAECKEL. *The Riddle of the Universe.*
HERBERT SPENCER. *First Principles.*
HERBERT SPENCER. *Data of Ethics.*
FRIEDRICK NIETZSCHE. *Beyond Good and Evil.*
GEORGE SANTAYANA. *Skepticism and Animal Faith.*
E. B. HOLT and others. *The New Realism.*
CHARLES DARWIN. *Origin of Species.*
CHARLES DARWIN. *On Descent of Man.*
LLOYD MORGAN. *Emergent Evolution.*

INDEX

F

I